God in Public

GOD IN PUBLIC

Four Ways American Christianity and Public Life Relate

Mark G. Toulouse

Westminster John Knox Press
LOUISVILLE • LONDON

© 2006 Mark G. Toulouse
Foreword © 2006 Westminster John Knox Press

Book design by Sharon Adams
Cover design by Eric Walljasper, Minneapolis, MN
Cover art: Billy Graham Preaching to Crowd © *Bettmann/CORBIS;* International Church Leaders Protest Potential War with Iraq © *Mark Wilson/Getty Images News*

First edition
Published by Westminster John Knox Press
Louisville, Kentucky

This book is printed on acid-free paper that meets the American National Standards Institute Z39.48 standard. ∞

PRINTED IN THE UNITED STATES OF AMERICA

06 07 08 09 10 11 12 13 14 15 — 10 9 8 7 6 5 4 3 2 1

Library of Congress Cataloging-in-Publication Data

Toulouse, Mark G.
    God in public : four ways American Christianity and public life relate / Mark G. Toulouse. — 1st ed.
        p. cm.
    Includes bibliographical references and index.
    ISBN-13: 978-0-664-22913-9 (alk. paper)
    ISBN-10: 0-664-22913-1 (alk. paper)
    1. Christianity and politics—United States. 2. Church and state—United States. I. Title.

    BR516.T68 2006
    261.70973—dc22

                                                                        2006042187

This book is dedicated to the members and ministers
(past, present, and future)
of South Hills Christian Church in Fort Worth, Texas,
with appreciation for all who gather there
to share a faith that is genuinely public

Contents

Foreword

The first pages of this book, during which Mark Toulouse takes us back with a metaphoric "time machine" to the 1950s, might lead a reader to think that the point of arrival there is to find a "time capsule" from which images of a half century ago are being unearthed and then left for display. No, this is not a book about 1956 and 2006 but rather a valuable and careful chronicling and dissection of themes, events, and arguments at many chronological stops along the way. Historians are more at ease with the eighteenth and the nineteenth centuries, or any century before those, than with the twentieth, which often gets viewed as "contemporary history." Meanwhile, journalists are more at ease with today and yesterday, the literal and not metaphoric yesterday. Yet to make sense of either "then" or "now" it is necessary to see how the two connect, what people in church and public life have retained. This book makes those kinds of connections. Toulouse is interested in continuities as much as in disruptions—where leaders in church and public life innovated, or where external circumstances impinged on them and they had to adapt.

There are good reasons to hope that leaders and other readers in the Christian community will let this book reach them. What Toulouse finds in his reading of major Christian magazines through a half-century should serve to dull the edge of raw ideologies (left and right) without letting believers off the hook and keeping them away from public concerns and interventions. If it is chilling to read how liberal and conservative Protestants in 1956 depicted the threat of the Roman Catholic Church to American public life, it is also informative to trace with Toulouse the shifts in allegiances and alliances as Catholicism, "mainline Protestantism," and evangelicalisms found reason to make new assessments and alliances along their way.

Whatever Toulouse's intentions might have been with respect to reaching mostly a Christian audience with *God in Public*, the outcome of his endeavor is or should be quite different. The book is as relevant for the academy as it is for the church. As one can deduce from many pages of the book, there is a lot of "Christian church" in the academy and other agencies of public life, and there are many of the academy who are also of the church. But there is more to my point than these recognitions might imply. As I read page after page, I kept thinking of people in the academy, public affairs, politics, and culture-in-general to whom I would like to direct his narratives, explanations, and arguments. Many of these people, and almost all who depend on the mass media for communication about God-in-Public or God-and-Public, are deprived of the historical context one needs to make informed judgments about urgent issues and directions. Toulouse provides one.

One is less likely to take the word of Protestant partisans who are committed to "public-life" thinking when they claim to have found absolute, enduring, and all-purpose groundings in theology for their stands when one sees how those stands have shifted through five decades. I consider that change all to the good, because in a dynamic, pluralist culture, those who want to be faithful to the Christian message have to be alert for changes around them and for reasons that they might have to change. If Toulouse were eager to plump for a rigid party line or a fresh revelation, the reader might have reason to worry, for he would make himself a candidate for the ash heap when the next cultural change came along, and the reader would be left on a barren landscape.

Instead, without stopping to set up billboards or rent megaphones, Toulouse does plant guideposts and utter verities that can help the reader along. His range is impressive. Though I have read the periodicals, judicial decisions, presidential inaugural addresses, and other documents that provide grist for *God in Public*, I still found Toulouse's book a figurative refresher course in history, a book of discoveries, a clarifier, and a subtle appeal for Christian church involvement on fresh or at least more informed terms. His range is astonishing, and his balance is a wonder to behold. Of course, he is neither a fire-breathing right-winger nor a predictable left-winger, providing ammunition for the "culture wars" that he handles with so much care. But he is also not a writer who lacks opinions and a choice of usually implicit counsels.

His fair-mindedness is most evident when he deals with theologians, publicists, and public theologians who vehemently disagree. He steps in, as it were, and bids antagonists to lay down their rhetorical arms long enough to listen to one another. He does this, I think, not only because he has an irenic temperament and a love for dialogue in the republic, but because of his fundamental vision of American public life. Whether he is talking about the "establishment" or "free exercise" clauses of the United States Constitution, the numberless United States Supreme Court decisions that have exegeted and applied them, the changing scholarly "takes" on those decisions, the turns and twists of public theology, the lines and "walls of separation between church and state," or matters of race relations, that fundamental vision comes through.

He comes close to spelling it out when he does a bit of archaeology among his own earlier diggings, as when he spoke of "the muddled middle" that exists between and sometimes overlaps with cultural, political, and theological radicals left and right. He does it when he lets words like "muddy" seep into his paragraphs. He shows us that the complex history of American public life, the diversities among religious interests, and the concerns of citizens who tend to favor mutually exclusive readings of historic, especially judicial, documents can never be neatly drawn with "walls" or with clearly distinct and permanent lines and definitions. Wouldn't it be nice, many ask today, if one or another of these final, all-purpose, defining contentions could win? No, it wouldn't be nice, I read Toulouse saying. When the "muddle," the "middle," the "muddy," and the "messy" get defined or scoured away, legitimate interests of citizens as individuals or in groups will be overlooked or spurned. The U.S. body politic and church would be quieter entities; but, then, so are people when they are in a coma or in institutions after their decline and well into their fall.

As I point out the complexity of American institutions and celebrate Toulouse's recognition that they are hard to define and grasp, I do not mean that he despairs of providing any useful guidance to address them. Readers will find helpful definitions of "civil" and "public" religion, of "public theology," and "the public church" that could be put to work effectively. They will also have occasion to ponder the force and content of basic documents in American history.

Toulouse's narrative speaks freely of the "we" and the "us" who are part of the Christian communion. He does so without speaking over the heads or behind the backs of academics who have not been part of the church. This book is a discussion that easily includes them and speaks in relation to their work. Those in academe who have slighted religion will find new ways to locate it in the American past, and those who have treated it glibly will be brought up short and can henceforth treat the subject with the attention it deserves. The issues to which Toulouse points and that he clarifies are far too important to be left to the mere three-fifths of the people who identify with religious groups, most of them Christian. Let the other two-fifths in on what is going on here, and we'll all benefit.

Martin E. Marty
Fairfax M. Cone Distinguished Service Professor Emeritus
The University of Chicago

Introduction

If you could get into a time machine, set the date back to somewhere around November 1956, turn the dial for a traveling destination to any city in America, and push the start button, when the machine stopped and the door opened, you would find yourself in a very strange place indeed. Dwight D. Eisenhower would have just won his second term as president. You might pick up a newspaper and read editorials about the Soviet crushing of Hungarian freedom fighters the month before, or about the year-long Montgomery bus boycott led by twenty-eight-year-old Martin Luther King Jr. If you landed in Los Angeles, you might want to visit two-year-old Disneyland, where you could plunk down $2.72 for admission and rides, and another eighteen cents for souvenirs—things like Disneyland pennants and maps, and Donald Duck caps.

Time-machine travel would reveal the state of Christianity to be, from all immediate appearances, very good in 1956. The 1950s "revival" was one of the dominating features of domestic America at the time. Church membership rose steadily (five percentage points) during the early part of the decade. Two years before your time machine landed, Congress added the words "under God" to the Pledge of Allegiance. The words "In God We Trust" were officially adopted as the

national motto in 1956. Corporations and civic organizations decided that providing outlets for prayer made good business sense. Church building boomed.
Religious book sales soared. Television, the propaganda potential of which people were only beginning to realize, spread religious images far and wide. Billy
Graham's urban crusades were packed with people, and he became America's
most well-known religious figure for the next several decades. By the end of the
1950s, nearly 69 percent of Americans were church members (5 percent more
than the decade before). The trend was very good for the church, and it looked
like the whole population would be attending church by the 1970s.

But did these things indicate a vital Protestantism, or did they indicate something else at work? Leonard Sweet would later accurately describe the 1950s as
the "triumphant decade for the definition of church membership as going to
church rather than being the church."[1] At the time, Martin E. Marty described
the revival as one that revived "religion-in-general" (more on this below) rather
than historic Christianity.[2] These developments helped constitute the first mass
marketing, more show than depth, of American Christianity; they represent perhaps the beginnings of the modern version of the "material Christianity" that has
become so much a part of our religious context today.[3]

Since the mid-1950s, Protestantism has gone from cultural monopoly to displacement and fragmentation.[4] Pluralism has exploded in this country, not only
as the expression of a variety of religions within American culture but also as
diversity within Christianity as well. As Marty is fond of pointing out, all we have
to do to get a picture of how diverse Christians are when they address the public
sphere is to mention the names of four of the better-known Baptists in America:
Jesse Jackson, Jesse Helms, Jerry Falwell, and Harvey Cox.[5] But pluralism in
America is vastly more expansive than the diversities present within Christianity.

Diana Eck's *A New Religious America*, published in 2001, examines, as its sub-
title makes clear, "how a 'Christian Country' has become the world's most religiously diverse nation."[6] This diversity is a reality despite the fact America's
population is still dominated by a Christian majority. The deepest reason for our
religious diversity is America's fundamental commitment to religious freedom,
but the more immediate reason is the 1965 Immigration and Naturalization Act.
This act changed American immigration policy, opening the door to immigration from many parts of the world for the first time since the 1920s. The civil
rights movement of the 1950s and 1960s brought new attention to issues of discrimination found in America's immigration policy. The 1965 law eliminated
quotas and provided a "relative opening" of the door for immigration. This context has provided Americans with the opportunity to understand America as a
nation based not on race, ethnicity, or religion, but on a common commitment
to the democratic, and essentially secular, ideals of the Constitution.[7]

As the work of Bill Hutchison has shown, American attempts to understand
the depth and richness associated with pluralism have resulted in a slow but "per-
sistent process of redefinition." He points to three stages along the way: pluralism as toleration, pluralism as inclusion, and pluralism as participation. Though

Americans have made some strides in understanding that pluralism requires new appreciation for toleration and inclusion, they have generally struggled with the concept that the Americans who represent this new pluralism, like all Americans, deserve full participation in shaping the public life of the nation.[8]

Instead, Christians have focused on their own troubles, particularly their internal battles and on the loss of their previously formidable cultural power. The fragmentation of Christianity in this country has gotten considerable press these days. James Davison Hunter's book on the issue is well known.[9] He defines the nature of cultural war today to be a "political and social hostility rooted in different systems of moral understanding." The "orthodox impulse" in American Christianity is at war with the "progressive impulse." In Hunter's view, liberals and conservatives are at war.

Few would doubt the wisdom of Hunter's analysis that competing moral visions exist in today's society. And few would question the passion, even militancy, with which certain elements of our culture act out those visions. Robert Wuthnow, another sociologist of religion, supported Hunter's culture-wars thesis in his book *The Restructuring of American Religion*, which argues that the issues of American public life, especially those emerging since the 1970s, have produced a deep chasm between liberal and conservative Christians, a chasm deeper even than the one that existed during the cultural arguments over civil rights and Vietnam. Though he does not use the term "culture war" to describe this chasm, it is clear that he describes an American Christianity at war with itself, characterized by a clear division between liberal and conservative Christians.[10]

Are these images appropriate: "Culture Wars" and "An American Christianity at War with Itself"? In my opinion, they are not. I have spent the past ten years reading independent Protestant and Catholic magazines dating from the mid-1950s to the present. My own research points to a somewhat murkier picture than the one presented by either Hunter or Wuthnow. Instead of affirming the existence of a chasm between liberals and conservatives, my work points to the development of what, for lack of a better term, I have come to describe, in work published elsewhere, as "the muddled middle." This muddled middle is neither well defined nor well organized, and it cannot properly be fully characterized as either liberal or conservative. As debates over controversial issues have intensified, divisions among Christians have most certainly occurred, but more along lines tending to divide liberals from liberals and conservatives from conservatives, than along lines distinctly dividing liberals from conservatives. Further, precisely differentiating conservatives and liberals is difficult when individual Christians are seemingly "conservative" in their thinking on one issue and "liberal" in their thoughts about a different issue. The majority of Christians are not purebreds one way or the other. The divisions among the Left and among the Right on any given issue have left a rather wide-ranging group of Christians who have drifted toward, but not solidified around, a somewhat undefined and muddled center.[11]

I do not intend for the term "muddled middle" to carry with it a necessarily negative connotation. Some confusion is always a good thing in that it prevents individuals and groups from taking a hardened perspective on controversial issues. The muddle of the middle represents, as well, the diversity that exists within subgroups of Christians, some of whom possess a fair degree of clarity in their thinking but without what might be described as consensus. Further, part of the muddle of the middle may arise from two conflicting points: on the one hand, there is a broad consensus on values (caring, response to human needs, importance of relationships, etc.) whereas, on the other hand, there is no consensus concerning "values" kinds of questions (issues like homosexuality, abortion, etc.). Finally, I am using the term "muddle" in somewhat the colloquial sense of "muddling through" by encouraging continued discussion and debate in order to advance public understanding.

Even though I do not think "culture wars" is the most appropriate image for American culture today, there has been a struggle present within American Christianity to orient itself to changing cultural circumstances. This struggle is evidenced through developments on several fronts since World War II. Included, of course, are such things as the declining significance of denominationalism, the explosion of technology and media, the mobilization of the new Religious Right, and the growth of special interest groups in American religion. I have been most interested in the question of how the displacement of Protestantism and the arrival of a more "fully realized pluralism"[12] naturally helped to bring changes in the relationship between Christian faith and American public life since about the 1950s. In 1951, the *Christian Century* published an editorial titled "Pluralism—National Menace," demonstrating the fear associated with emerging pluralism, even among more liberal Christians. Christians after the 1950s, of whatever theological stripe, can no longer take American public life for granted.

Why mark the late 1950s as a turning point for American Christianity? Part of the answer is found in the new and exciting leaders who emerged in both political and religious realms, including John F. Kennedy and Pope John XXIII. Their respective roles symbolically marked the outlines of a new environment. Catholicism's rise to prominence as a major player in the shaping of culture, as exhibited in these two figures, had a rather disquieting effect on all forms of Protestantism in America during the 1950s. But it really should not have been all that surprising to Protestants. Though Protestants had maintained dominance in a number of areas of American culture, particularly in the federal government, corporations, and other large-scale institutions, Catholic strength elsewhere in the culture had been revealed decades before through local politics and a strong private-school network, and in other ways. The strength of non-Protestant immigration showed itself in various ways, well before the last half of the twentieth century.[13]

Today, it is not easy to remember a time when Catholicism seemed monolithic and rigidly intolerant of other Christian expressions. With some measure of legitimate rationale, pre-Vatican II Protestantism worried about what a politicized American Catholicism might try to accomplish in the name of the Vatican. For example, contributors to *Christianity Today* hypothesized in 1958 about what might happen if a Catholic became president or if the United States became 51 percent Catholic. The "worship of Protestants would probably not be banned," they speculated, but "Protestant church signs would be prohibited."[14] In 1957, an article in *Christianity Today* warned, "The Catholic church can [outbreed] and is through its opposition to birth control outbreeding Protestants."[15] W. A. Criswell, speaking from the pulpit of First Baptist Dallas on July 3, 1960, warned that a Kennedy presidency would "spell the death of a free church in a free state."[16] Most Protestants feared not only the possibility of a powerful Roman Catholic politician but also the growing American Catholic population. These fears did not reside among conservatives alone but among mainline Protestants as well. All Protestants were fearful of being displaced in American culture.

Throughout Kennedy's presidential campaign, the *Christian Century* openly questioned Kennedy's fitness for high office based largely on his family's religious background, though it sought to avoid religious bigotry as it did so.[17] The very fact that editors had to ask themselves whether it was possible for a Catholic to be president is evidence of how powerful the Protestant hold on the culture had been over the years. As the final days of the campaign wound down, and after the televised debates, editorials at the *Century* revealed less concern about religion as an issue, especially after Kennedy's famous speech to Houston ministers. Winthrop S. Hudson pointed out what editors at the *Century* probably should have realized sooner when he wrote that Kennedy's "religious faith" had "been shaped more by the contemporary cultural climate than by the church."[18] Kennedy's election broke the exclusive hold on the presidency maintained by Protestants. In doing so, it helped to indicate the cultural trends toward Protestant displacement. Even the most liberal among Protestants did not know quite what to think about that.

By the 1950s, values in American life that most Protestants had always taken for granted had been substantially displaced. Further, principles associated with religious pluralism began to reach new levels of importance in America. In most cases, the acceptance of religious pluralism at the time did not extend much beyond a new appreciation for Catholicism and Judaism. The term "Judeo-Christian" suddenly became prominent during the 1950s. Three books published around the same time, one each from a Jew, a Protestant, and a Catholic, point to this shift in American religion.

First among them was Will Herberg's *Protestant-Catholic-Jew* (1955). Herberg pointed out that Catholicism and Judaism had joined the ranks of Protestantism as equal components of America's normative faith expressions. His book criticized the "American way of life" cultural religion, something he also called "civic religion," and argued that Catholicism, Protestantism, and Judaism represent the "three great branches or divisions of 'American religion.' " For Herberg, only these three ways of seeing the world were acceptable. Protestantism, Catholicism, and Judaism were "three diverse representations of the same 'spiritual values,' the 'spiritual values' American democracy is presumed to stand for." Each of these three religious expressions, argued Herberg, "is equally and authentically American."

The "American way of life religion" dangerously competed for the souls of adherents from among each of the three traditional faiths.[19]

Martin E. Marty's *The New Shape of American Religion* (1959) raised an argument against the way much of Protestantism in America had been enculturated and syncretized into a "blurry, generalizing religion," which Marty referred to as "religion in general."[20] The 1950s, Marty argued, had brought a revival of "religion in general" rather than a revival of historic Christianity. He affirmed the pluralism of the post-Protestant age but warned against the power of generalized religion: "There are four major partners in the religious situation of today's America," he wrote.

> Three of them—Protestants, Catholics, and Jews—go about their business in relatively peaceful coexistence. The fourth partner, however, is gaining, and at the expense of the other three, for he draws his recruits from among their members. What is more, the "convert" to the fourth partner may retain his membership in his original community of faith. The national religion thrives on "plural belonging." It makes fewer demands on potential converts and operates with an inner logic that defies massive refutation. . . . In most respects Protestantism has suffered more than the other conspirators. Its prior and larger investment made it more vulnerable. . . . Protestantism accepted without enthusiasm and sometimes with distaste the Roman Catholic and Jewish minorities as co-informers of the culture, but all along it coexisted with the nascent secular national religion that now is flowering.[21]

Marty suggested by the end of the 1950s that this revival, rather than benefit Protestantism, actually served as the agent to usher in the "post-Protestant" years of American life. Rather than reviving Christianity, the revival actually took its place. It fostered "an attitude toward religion" that Marty claimed became "a religion itself." Whereas the "old shape" of American religion had been "basically Protestant," the "new shape" became something else. Protestantism's power "as virtual monopolist in penetrating and molding the religious aspect of national culture" had "disappeared." Protestantism's power in culture was displaced by what Marty called "religion-in-general." For the most part, the cultural revival presented a God who was "understandable and manageable, . . . an American jolly good fellow."[22]

This "religion-in-general" received aid and support from many religious leaders throughout these years. The Gallup poll of 1958 revealed that the people chose Billy Graham, Fulton Sheen, Norman Vincent Peale, and Oral Roberts as four of the five "most admired" religious leaders (the fifth being Pope John XXIII).[23] Even though Graham could occasionally wax eloquent about what he considered to be the sins of America (usually associated with welfare spending, foreign aid, and communist influence in high places) and Sheen could occasionally criticize the excesses of American capitalism, they and others were well-known for their confidence in America's standing before God in comparison to all other nations. Rather than think of God as the one who through Jesus Christ communicates the desire to save all humanity, including the communists, Americans tended to think of God as an American, just like them. And this led many American Christians to confuse the trappings of their culture with God's will. For a good number of these Christians, women belonged in the kitchen, blacks belonged in menial jobs, and God certainly never intended for blacks and whites to live in the same neighborhoods. For Protestants, culture reflected what they perceived to be their values.

Prior to the mid-twentieth century, Protestant Christianity held a virtual monopoly in American public life. But change was brewing in the land. By 1958, the gain in church membership fell off drastically compared to the general population growth. The voices of the "cultured despisers" of religion once again rose to rather vital expression. And Protestantism was beginning to discover the true meaning of religious pluralism. By the mid-1960s, other religious expressions became both more common and more visible in America. Rapid urbanization, technology, mobility, an emerging drug culture, a rebellious generation of youth, a civil rights movement, a fledgling feminist movement, the beginnings of an Asian war—all these things contributed to an atmosphere where traditional Protestant values in America were seriously challenged. The bridge between Protestantism and culture began to break down. Marty chronicled this change with another book (*Second Chance for American Protestants*, 1963). In it, he argued that this new "post-Protestant America" might give Protestants a "second chance" to take a more prophetic stance toward American culture, one grounded in the gospel rather than in "religion-in-general."[24] Marty offered America's Protestants a challenge to relate their faith meaningfully to the public life in the United States, one where the principles of faith, rather than cultural principles, were to define the relationship. With these early books, Marty began to analyze how Christians engaged what he later described as "public theology."[25]

The last person representing this trilogy of Jewish, Protestant, and Catholic authors who marked the shift in American religious life is John Courtney Murray (*We Hold These Truths*, 1960). Murray also stressed four components of the pluralist society, "a pattern of interacting conspiracies" that he described as "Protestant, Catholic, Jewish, and secularist." "Perhaps then our problem today," wrote Murray, "is somehow to make the four great conspiracies among us conspire into one conspiracy that will be American society—civil, just, free, peaceful, one." Where secularism would push religion into irrelevancy, or into "religion-in-general, whatever that is," the three great religious traditions were best suited to impart the fundamental human meaning present in American politics from the beginning: "the sovereignty of God over nations as well as over individual men."[26] The pluralism of American society made Murray nervous, but he believed Protestant, Catholic, and Jew could find common ground in the "natural law tradition" and fend off the negative influences of secularism in American public life.

These books, from Herberg, Marty, and Murray, all expressed concern about a national religion that seemed to compete with the three historic religious expressions known as Protestantism, Catholicism, and Judaism. This national religion, "civic religion" or "American way of life religion" (Herberg), "religion-in-general" (Marty), or "secularism" (Murray), co-opted many of the symbols of the three traditional faiths and provided them with new meaning. The power of its attraction, argued these three scholars, confused members of the three faith traditions and led them to abandon the prophetic and publicly relevant aspects of their faith in favor of the generic religious expression found in the public life of the nation. Since the famous essay published in 1967 by sociologist of religion Robert Bellah, the merits and demerits of this generic religious expression have been argued under the rubric "civil religion."[27]

Civil religion is not a unilateral expression of religion. Sociological and theological study of it has revealed its complexity. Civil religion can be nationalistic, in which everything America represents is assumed to be representative of God's will. Or it can be, as both Robert Bellah and Sidney Mead at various times believed it could be, more representative of an attitude of reverence for a transcendent reference that judges all nations equally. In this sense, civil religion becomes prophetic and calls Americans to represent global rather than merely national values. Advocates of prophetic civil religion in America always point to Abraham Lincoln as its supreme example. In that crucial second inaugural address, during the Civil War, Lincoln warned Americans, both North and South, who liked to think that God had taken their side in the conflict, that "the Almighty has his own purposes."[28] The very fact that Lincoln is always the example used to represent it indicates how rare this prophetic form of civil religion actually is in American expression.

But this book is not primarily about civil religion. Rather than rehearse the history of civil religion, and the debates among scholars about it, I am primarily interested in talking about how Christian faith and public life in America interact in a pluralistic world. As both a professor and a minister, I hope that something I say here may be of help to Christians and their clergy as they think about how Christian faith and the life we all share in the public beyond the church relate to one another.

The transition since the 1950s from an America that usually reflected Protestant values to a thoroughly pluralistic nation today has had a profound effect on Christian groups and their struggles to think about the nature of their relationship to public life. To help set the context for this discussion, the first section of this book provides an examination of the First Amendment by looking at the two aspects of the *religion clauses:* establishment (chap. 1) and free exercise (chap. 2). In this context, I also take a look at the development of public life in America and the nature of Christian responses to it.

In chapters 3 and 4, I take a closer look at how *public life* in America occasionally exercises a controlling influence on the way Christians read their Bibles and even form their personal faith. At key points throughout American history, Christians have confused public life and faith and have offered biblical and theological rationales for assumptions important to narrow views defined by culture, but not to broader conceptions defined by faith. Christians have also tried to grab hold of public life to define it according to exclusive and absolutist categories. In all these activities, both Christians and public life have exhibited characteristics associated with what might be described as either "iconic faith"[29] (chap. 3) or "priestly faith" (chap. 4).

On the other hand, there are clear instances in American life when broader perspectives provided by Christian faith—those resulting from a Christian commitment to justice, for example—have sought to create possibilities for wider participation in public life for all Americans. In this analysis, it is essential that theological beliefs be carefully considered. They do not tell the whole story, yet, to a substantial degree, they help to establish the general ethos of a group's approach to public life, particularly as the faith of the group seeks expression on particular social issues of importance. In most cases, theological reflection provides the self-identified boundaries for the acceptable levels of Christian participation in the formation of the nation's public life. In this section of the book, therefore, chapter 5, "Public Christian," and chapter 6, "Public Church,"[30] examine the way that *faith* relates to the public life of the nation.

In a sense, the four chapters contained in sections 2 and 3 discuss four styles of interaction between Christian faith and public life. Though I prefer the language of "styles of interaction" to that of "types," the reader will no doubt consider these styles as typological. The categories used here, as is true of all typologies, are not hard and fast. Christians do move in and out, among and between, these styles; occasionally, they occupy two of them simultaneously, when one considers views held on different issues contemporaneously. Some Christians, like the Amish, for example, do not fit well in any of these particular styles, since they avoid any association with public life as a part of their faith. When one understands typologies to be literally and absolutely true, as definitive categories rather than as suggestive and symbolic categories, one hardens them beyond all usefulness. Instead, I intend for these styles to be understood as interpretive tools that help to make sense of the usually convoluted relationship between Christian faith and public life. They do not fully explain it, but they might help us to see it with a bit more clarity. I hope they will assist Christians who want to understand the difference between relating to public life through either cultural symbols or a fear of pluralism and relating to it through the meaning represented in the fullness of Christian theology, grounded in a profound sense of human finitude and history.

H. Richard Niebuhr has offered a classic typology of the relationship between Christ and culture. He spoke of Christians who saw Christ "against" culture, "of" culture, "above" culture, "transforming" culture, and in "paradoxical" relation to culture.[31] Obviously, Niebuhr's types are all relevant in the consideration of the relationship between faith and public life. *Christ & Culture* is as important today as the day it was written. In some ways, my questions obviously relate to those explored by Niebuhr. In other ways, I'm taking a different kind of look because I am concentrating on the present, attempting to map the terrain that marks the ways faith and public life currently interact in America.

Several of Niebuhr's categories work within and across both the types I'm calling the public Christian and the public church, because Christians and churches in both these categories represent varieties of Niebuhr's typology, some living in sustained tension with culture, some living in peace with culture, some attempting to create a synthesis between their faith and culture, and some trying to transform culture. I do, however, want to be clear. I do not mention Niebuhr's book because I consider myself doing anything to replace it. I don't see this as that kind of book at all. In fact, I don't think that kind of book could be written. I mention it because some readers might attribute motives to me related to Niebuhr's book that do not exist.

The final section contains one chapter, "Faith and Public Life in a Postmodern Context" (chap. 7). This chapter explores the contemporary context for understanding the relationship between Christian faith and public life. This context takes seriously both pluralism and insights associated with postmodernism. The postmodern approach to reason and its rejection of universals (foundationalism) can actually place the contribution of theology and Christian faith (or any other religious faith), in our day and context, on an equal footing with contributions offered by those who solely depend on secular reason when it comes to the public debate about public life. I illustrate this point by comparing the approach of two kinds of theological perspectives that take seriously the postmodern context of contemporary theology: the postliberal perspective (Stanley Hauerwas, a contemporary "public Christian") and the revisionist and pragmatic historicist perspectives (David Tracy, James Gustafson, and Linell Cady—theologians who articulate a public theology in ways that continue to call for activities of a "public church").

With the completion of this book, I want to express my appreciation to the Association of Theological Seminaries (ATS) and their program supporting sabbatical leaves. In 1997–1998, the ATS named me a Luce Fellow and helped to fund a year's research leave by providing half a year's salary and benefits. This book, not the original project funded by ATS, has grown naturally out of the project funded by the ATS Luce program. The funded project concentrates instead on the relationship between faith and public life during the past forty years by analyzing Christian responses to the issues themselves (i.e., abortion, feminism, sexuality, homosexuality, civil rights, Vietnam). Though that research has resulted in numerous articles on these topics, the book project related to it has been shelved while I have worked on this project for Westminster John Knox Press.[32] Both projects have also benefited from the support of a small grant from the Lilly Endowment and several summer research grants from Brite Divinity School. For all these venues of support, I am extremely grateful.

A few readers may recognize hints of things they have heard from me in various lectures and presentations over the years. I am thankful for the opportunities presented by those occasions, and by those who attended, to work on these themes. Though I can't mention all these by name, I hope sponsors and some of those in attendance might recognize something here and claim a piece of it. I'm especially appreciative of those who asked me to share some of this work in church settings. Because it is my prerogative to do so, I provide a special word of appreciation for my own congregation, South Hills Christian Church in Fort Worth, and dedicate this book to its members and ministers (past, present, and future). During the twenty years our family has been associated with this congregation, it has nurtured the meaning of public faith for its members.

I am grateful for the work of student assistants over the years. Most of these helped gather periodical materials for the first project. Thanks to Michelle Johnson, Holly Stovall, Mark Young, Renée Hoke, Jennie Huff, Tom Graca, Perryn Rice, Tom McCracken, Adrian Brown, Shawn Wallace, and Owen Chandler for all those trips to the library and time spent at copy machines. My current student assistant, Dyan Dietz, has provided invaluable assistance in getting this book project in on time. She possesses a dedicated work ethic, combined with both intelligence and critical insight, and a commitment to the calling of both the ministerial vocation and theological scholarship. Over this past year, she has gathered and worked on resources relating to this project. Though I cannot mention all of them by name, I'm also appreciative of my colleagues and friends at Brite, particularly Dr. Stacey Floyd-Thomas, who took the time to read and respond to portions of this manuscript. Thanks are due as well to Don McKim, who embraced this project enthusiastically when I spoke with him about it, and who encouraged me to pursue it with all deliberate speed when he offered me a contract with Westminster John Knox Press.

Without the loving companionship of my spouse, Jeffica, and her emotional and intellectual support, this book could not have been finished. Together, across three decades, we have worked to understand and appreciate the relationship between our faith and the world we share. I hope the younger generation of Christians finds something in this book that is useful to them as they struggle to relate faith to public life in the years ahead: in our family, that generation is represented by our son, Joshua, and our daughters Marcie and Cara, and their husbands Kevin Hunt and William Wallace. They, along with the variety of students attending Brite's classrooms and the young persons in the pews of our congregations, give me hope that the question of faith and public life in the future will be in good hands.

Mark G. Toulouse
February 1, 2006

PART I
THE FIRST AMENDMENT

Chapter 1

The Establishment Clause

"Congress shall make no law respecting an establishment of religion . . ."

On March 2, 2005, the Supreme Court heard oral arguments in two cases involving the public display of the Ten Commandments on government property in Texas and Kentucky. Justice Scalia interrupted the argument being presented by Erwin Chemerinsky, an attorney arguing against the display's legitimacy, to offer commentary rather than a question:

> It [the Ten Commandments] is a profound religious message, but it's a profound religious message believed in by the vast majority of the American people, just as belief in monotheism is shared by a vast majority of the American people. And our traditions show that there is nothing wrong with government reflecting that. I mean, we're a tolerant society religiously, but just as the majority has to be tolerant of minority views in matters of religion, it seems to me the minority has to be tolerant of the majority's ability to express its belief that government comes from God, which is what this is about.[1]

Many American Christians would readily agree with Justice Scalia's little speech. Christians in America, many argue, are giving up too much public ground to satisfy minority discontent concerning public Christian expressions. Government, under the guise of the separation of church and state, has become increasingly

3

secular. In the process, so goes the argument, it has become hostile both to Christianity and to religion in general.[2] In order to gain a handle on whether this claim is true, it is important to take a closer look at the history of the relationship between church and state in America.

One of the first points to recognize in this discussion is the inadequacy of the terms *church* and *state*. There never has been just one "church" or even just one "state." The term *church* contains a Christian bias, even when it is recognized that there never has been one "church" in America. In today's pluralistic religious context, *church* does not work particularly well as a description of mosque, synagogue, temple, gudwara, or other gathering places for the religious faithful. Neither does the term *state* describe well other forms of civil authority, including government agencies, cities, zoning commissions, and so forth. As long as we understand that the popular terms *church* and *state* are far from precise, both historically and in the present, then, with conscious recognition of these qualifications, we can continue to use them.

CHURCH AND STATE IN COLONIAL AMERICA

The question of the relationship between church and state is contested today in ways never envisioned by those who wrote and those who voted to ratify the Constitution and the Bill of Rights. The truth is, not everyone agreed about how church and state were related in the late 1700s either. From the beginning of American history, as colonies began to emerge, many different patterns developed. Virginia's first charter (1606) contained laws protecting uniformity of belief and provided financial support for the Anglican Church. Several other colonies established Anglicanism from the beginning, at least nominally, including Georgia, North Carolina, and South Carolina. Maryland, originally founded by Catholics, welcomed all Protestants. The Catholics were soon overwhelmed by them, and the colony became yet another nominal Anglican establishment (1703).

Some Dutch Reformed interests in New Netherlands tried to keep Lutherans, Catholics, and Quakers at bay, but early practical economic interests led to toleration and freedom of conscience. When English authority took over from the Dutch (1664), Anglicans tolerated the Dutch but were none too friendly to the motley mix of Presbyterians, Congregationalists, Quakers, Lutherans, Anabaptists, Catholics, and Jews. By the end of the century, the Dutch Reformed faced difficulties as well, but a kind of local establishment prevailed in New York after 1664. Cities chose their own Protestant church to support with their tax dollars, but others were legally tolerated.[3] Even in the midst of legal establishments, most of these dissenting groups maintained effective presence in New York. In the late seventeenth century, Dutch families outnumbered the Anglicans by at least 17 to 1. Dissenting families outnumbered Anglicans by about 14 to 1.[4] Parishes were too large, good leadership too sparse, and meaningful church authority too far away for Anglicans to put much oomph behind their establishments in the colonies.

Delaware's Swedish Lutheran population was quickly overrun with Dutch Reformed families, while New Jersey had always contained a significant number of them. Both colonies adopted fairly liberal religious policies to attract settlers and economic development. Congregationalists established their churches in Massachusetts, New Hampshire, and Connecticut. The history of persecution in Massachusetts is particularly well known by most Americans, including the execution of Quaker women, the infamous banishment of people like Anne Hutchinson and Roger Williams, and the Salem witch trials. Rhode Island and Pennsylvania established policies of religious toleration from the start. By the end of the eighteenth century, religious liberty and toleration generally controlled the day across the colonies, with the exception of the Congregationalist strongholds in New England. Any genuine establishment powers associated with the Anglican Church had pretty much disappeared as a result of the Revolutionary War.

Nine of the original thirteen colonies had establishments of religion. After the war, many of those moved in nonestablishment directions. New York, in 1777, adopted a state constitution barring establishments. Six other states made quick compromises by moving to "multiple establishments." Leonard Levy argues that these six states prove that "an establishment of religion was not restricted in meaning to a state church or to a system of public support of one sect alone; instead, an establishment of religion meant public support of several or all churches, with preference to none."[5] Massachusetts was one of these states, but it became the only state that did not extend greater protection to religious liberty at the same time. By the time the states ratified the Bill of Rights, only three of them continued establishments of any kind (Massachusetts until 1833, New Hampshire until 1819, and Connecticut until 1818).

In other words, the religious picture by the time of the American Revolution had grown rather complex. The Anglican Church, largely established in the South, found itself surrounded by all manner of dissenting groups. It is worth noting that Congregationalism, largely established in New England, found itself among dissenters in the South. In New England, the Congregationalist Church found itself surrounded by the same group of dissenters. Anglicanism found itself among the dissenters in New England. These dissenters—the Baptists, Methodists, Presbyterians, Quakers, Unitarians, Lutherans, deists, and others—continued to fight for their right to practice their faith openly and without coercive influences exerted by established churches. The different stripes of Christianity found in America nearly guaranteed that religious liberty would emerge. Sidney Mead drew the following conclusion:

> Hence the true picture is not that of the "triumph" in America of right-wing or left-wing, of churches or sects, but rather a mingling through frustration, controversy, confusion, and compromise of all the diverse ecclesiastical patterns transplanted from Europe . . . the result was a complex pattern of religious thought and institutional life that was peculiarly "American," and is probably best described as "denominationalism."[6]

Native American spirituality and religion added to the diversity of religion found in America but were not too highly regarded or respected by most Christian Americans, whether among dissenters or establishment. Native American religion was extraordinarily multifaceted and diverse and radically pluralistic. Ironically, though Christianity found diverse expression in the colonies, this transplanted European Christian presence, with its proclivity to destroy Native American life and culture, actually ended up reducing religious pluralism more than expanding it.

Within this Christian and religious mix, one must also remember the presence of African American religious understanding and expression. Blacks lived nearly everywhere in the country, with significant populations in New York, Maryland, and Delaware. They maintained majority populations in eastern Virginia and along much of the coastlines of Georgia and South Carolina. By the 1790s, black Baptists alone numbered more than twenty thousand. In addition, African Americans took leadership in creating separate black Methodist churches that prospered, numbering about 15,000 members around 1800, and grew exponentially from that time forward. But the religion practiced by African Americans cannot be so easily categorized. Native African characteristics merged creatively with both Muslim and Christian practices. Religious practice may have been abundant among African Americans, but it is worth noting that, in 1800, less than five percent of the black population (roughly 50,000 out of 1,000,000) was associated with any Christian church.[7]

White Americans attended church more frequently but perhaps not as frequently as many might assume. Estimates place church membership at between one in ten and one in fifteen Americans in 1800. It would climb much higher and nearly double by the end of the Second Great Awakening (1830). Generally, in 1800, perhaps just over 30 percent of the population might attend church on any given Sunday, even though considerably fewer were actually members.[8] White Christians certainly had power, but Christians faced serious challenges in controlling directions within the culture itself, including even whether self-identified Christians would show up for church on Sunday. Once they were disestablished, Christian churches knew their power in the culture depended on their ability to persuade others to join them voluntarily. The Second Great Awakening (1800–1830s), with the growth of voluntary societies like the American Bible Society (1816), the American Sunday School Union (1824), and the American Tract Society (1825), provides in large measure testimony to their ability to succeed in that area. Christians found renewed strength in this voluntary, rather than coerced, context for religious activity.

RELIGION IN THE CONSTITUTION
AND THE BILL OF RIGHTS

At the time Americans ratified the Constitution, at least seven states prohibited clergy by law from serving in particular (and, in some cases, all) political offices.

Eleven of the thirteen states imposed religious tests for all public offices. The only mention of religion in the Constitution, in clause 3 of article 6, states, "No religious test shall ever be required as a qualification to any office or public trust under the United States." This meant that clergy were free to stand for election to any public office in the federal government even though forbidden to do so in at least seven of the states. The Constitution actually opened the door for ministers to serve publicly and to be involved politically in ways that many states prohibited.

Meanwhile, religious tests in the various states, of course, also communicated to non-Christians, or at least the nonreligious, that they need not apply. These tests required a profession of Christianity, or an affirmation of belief in God, to run for office. Throughout the next century, most states removed these restrictions against the clergy and the nonreligious, with the exception of Maryland and Tennessee. Those two states continued their religious tests in some form or another until the 1970s.[9]

The religious test clause of the Constitution created a considerable debate during the ratification process. The Philadelphia Constitutional Convention accepted the language fairly quickly and by a vast majority of the delegates. But when the Constitution hit the streets, popular opinion quickly voiced protest against the fact that "papists," Jews, deists, Quakers, "Mohomatans" [sic], and atheists could potentially be elected to public office in the new government. Even worse, the Constitution, as sent to the states, had absolutely no mention of God. It was (and is) a completely secular document. This led to an immediate campaign to defeat the Constitution's ratification unless recognition of God was added to it. Those who led the charge, and those who fended it off, took one another on through most of 1787 and 1788. Those defending the secular nature of the Constitution won. And the adoption of this secular Constitution belies the idea that a majority of Founders supported the notion of a formally Christian nation.

Considerable significance attaches to the fact that a secular Constitution prevailed in this country, in spite of strong opposition. Its adoption shows just how strongly the Founders and leaders in most of the states were committed to the idea that the federal government must not be Christian, nor even explicitly religious.[10] Unquestioned Protestant predominance in the eighteenth century makes it all the more noteworthy that strong critics of article 6 of the Constitution (the one specifying "no religious test") were defeated during arguments in 1787 and 1788. Protestants had it within their power to make the Constitution an explicitly Christian document, or, at the very least, one that barred non-Christians from holding public office. In fact, the new constitutions in five of the states (South Carolina, Georgia, New Hampshire, New Jersey, and Massachusetts) required office holders to be Protestant. In addition, Delaware and Maryland specified that only Christians could run for public office, while Pennsylvania's new constitution required that those who sought public office could not be atheist and must believe in "a future state of rewards and punishments."[11]

But a secular Constitution guaranteed that no particular form of religion holds any kind of peculiar advantage in the public life of the nation. Members of all religions and citizens who affirm no religion stand on level ground. This constitutional posture has proven the wisdom of the Founders, most of whom possessed religious commitments. Citizens in the United States tend to take religion much more seriously than is the case in nations where religion is established or officially endorsed in state constitutions. Though many Christians believed that the Constitution, with no mention of God and no provision that leaders even affirm God in order to stand for office, would undermine Christian faith in this country, many other Christians emphasized that faith did not need government endorsement to thrive. Significant numbers of Christian dissenters had experienced persecution at the hands of governments entrusted with religious powers. Others noted how religious tests only encouraged hypocrisies and false confessions of faith in those running for public office. As Edwin Gaustad points out, "Precedent and tradition may have pointed to a 'Christian nation,'" but "principle, on the other hand, pointed to a land that would be (to cite Madison again) 'an Asylum to the persecuted and oppressed of every Nation and Religion.'"[12]

The "godless Constitution" survived many other attempts to bring God into the document. For example, Horace Bushnell, during the Civil War, condemned the "godless theorizing" behind the Constitution and urged Congress to recognize God in the document. Many others joined the call, linking the calamity of the Civil War to this neglect of God. Together, they created the National Association for the Amendment to the Constitution. Using this organization, and others to come, groups of Americans began campaigns to include God within the Constitution in 1863, 1894, 1910, 1947, and 1954. All were unsuccessful.[13]

The Constitution remains intentionally secular in spite of repeated and serious efforts to change it. The American people have somehow been able to maintain the sensibility that religious freedom meant something more than just the ability of Christians of various stripes to practice their faith unhindered by government's influence. It also meant that the rights associated with all religious expressions and no religious expression had to be respected and tolerated if this country meant to live up to its ideals. Many Americans, like Madison and Jefferson before them, have long believed that protection of the religious conscience demands a secular Constitution. A secular Constitution does not intend to guarantee a secular public square. Rather, by being secular, the Constitution guarantees the opposite, that religion is free to speak in public ways, according to the dictates of the religious conscience. Some wanted to guarantee this right explicitly through enacting a constitutional bill of rights.

By the time the Constitution appeared, eight states had already enacted bills of rights of their own. The silence of the Constitution on this question aroused significant opposition. In response, James Madison emphasized that the Constitution was a limited document. Any power not explicitly given to the federal government within the document remained with the states. Where the government did not assume power, Madison reasoned, no bill of rights to protect citizens seemed necessary. He and others had the practical task of creating a union of the thirteen states "—a government 'national' enough to satisfy folk like [Alexander] Hamilton and to get the job done and 'federal' [with very limited and widely distributed powers] enough to pacify enough states' rights people to get it ratified."[14]

Madison and other architects of the government felt the pressure of walking a political tightrope between those who wanted a strong national government and those who wanted a loose affiliation that allowed for strong and powerful states. Thomas Jefferson, as minister to France, was out of the country at the time of the Constitutional Convention. Enjoying the luxury of some distance from the political fray, he wrote Madison to stress his opinion that the document needed explicitly to guarantee the freedom of the press and the freedom of religious conscience. The document, he concluded, must contain a bill of rights.[15]

Antifederalists made the same argument because they were concerned that a federal government might overpower the autonomy of both the states and individuals. In most cases, antifederalists hoped to send deliberations back to their starting point by defeating ratification. Most preferred this option above supporting an easily revised Constitution, with new language about rights. Many called for a second constitutional convention to resolve the issue before ratifying the Constitution. Serious arguments in favor of a bill of rights also arose in those areas of the country where religious dissenters (particularly Baptists, Methodists, Quakers, and deists) possessed some strength. They supported the idea of a second convention because of their commitments to religious freedom and the separation of church and state.[16]

Madison feared that a second convention would dissolve into chaos, making ratification even more difficult. The first objective had to be ratification of the Constitution. To that end, Madison met with John Leland, the Baptist leader from Virginia who persuasively argued against ratification primarily because the Constitution contained no guarantee of religious freedom. In exchange for a promise to support the creation of a bill of rights as a first act of government, Madison received Leland's support for ratification. And Leland also helped Madison and others defend the secular nature of the Constitution. Virginia, by a mere margin of ten votes, and after strong rhetorical efforts by Patrick Henry failed to defeat it, ratified the Constitution on June 25. Four days earlier, New Hampshire had become the ninth state to ratify the Constitution, making ratification official across America.

This is not the place to tell the interesting story behind Madison's election to the new House of Representatives. His election succeeded in spite of the efforts of Patrick Henry to structure Madison's home district in Virginia ("a Henry-mandered district") to include strong antifederalist sentiment and opposition.[17] As Lance Banning has shown, Madison found himself uniquely situated in the House of Representatives in terms of influence and authority when it first met on April 1, 1789.

> Without exception, all of those whose national reputations rivaled or exceeded his had been elected to the Senate or anticipated appointments in the other branches of the reconstructed system. In addition Madison was Washington's most influential confidant at the beginning of the new administration, a principal adviser on appointments, presidential protocol, and the interpretation of the Constitution. In this unexampled situation, . . . he would draft the president's inaugural address, the House of Representatives' response, the president's reply to that response, and even Washington's reply to the initial message from the Senate.[18]

From this position of prominence, Madison presented his version of a bill of rights on June 8. As a well-known Federalist, and the most renowned advocate for freedom of conscience in Virginia and beyond, Madison had credibility on both sides of the aisle, so to speak. While remaining committed to Federalist interests, he marshaled the best arguments of both the religious dissenters and the antifederalists that stood behind the call for a bill of rights. He added Jefferson's contention that explicit rights in the Constitution would provide federal judges with the power to check any tendencies of the executive or legislative branches of government to usurp those rights inappropriately. One of the abiding beliefs of the Federalists, and of those who stood behind the Constitution, was the affirmation that "most people everywhere, in their deepest nature, are selfish and corruptible and that the desire for domination is so overwhelming that no one should be trusted with unqualified authority." The virtue of a system of checks and balances could, on the other hand, bring out the higher qualities contained within the human nature.[19]

After a summer filled with rather intense arguments and political wrangling, Congress adopted the Bill of Rights on September 25, 1789. The substantive content of the amendments can be traced to Madison's original proposal presented on June 8. Some minor deletions and alterations of language had occurred, but most of the substance originated with Madison. His original language for what became the First Amendment had read, "The civil rights of none shall be abridged on account of religious belief or worship, nor shall any national religion be established, nor shall the full and equal rights of conscience be in any manner or on any pretext infringed." The final language adopted by Congress seemed a bit more general and less defined: "Congress shall make no law respecting an establishment of religion, or prohibiting the free exercise thereof."[20] Surely, no sixteen words of the English language contained in any sentence in history have generated more debate about meaning.

Even Madison knew that meaning would not always be clear. Near the end of his life, James Madison received a letter from a Reverend Jasper Adams, president of Charleston College in South Carolina. The letter provoked him to offer some comments on the separation between church and state, set in place only some forty years earlier. Madison believed the experience of the last four decades proved the wisdom of the American experiment. "Religion," he wrote, "does not need the support of Government and it will scarcely be contended that Government has suffered by the exemption of Religion from its cognizance, or its pecuniary aid." Yet Madison also knew the relationship between religion and government had its ambiguous dimensions. "It may not be easy, in every possible case," he wrote Rev. Adams, "to trace the line of separation between the rights of religion and the Civil authority with such distinctness as to avoid collisions & doubts on unessential points."[21]

In these brief comments, Madison gave expression to at least two different aspects of the American relationship between religion and civil authority. First, he emphasized that experience proved the value of the institutional separation of church and state. Religion and government are both better off when neither controls the affairs of the other. Second, he recognized that the "line of separation" had its ambiguous dimensions as well. The Supreme Court has repeatedly demonstrated the wisdom of this early insight. In response to particular cases, the court has drawn the line first one way and then another. The line of separation has proven to be a very squiggly and unstable one, illustrated more accurately, perhaps, by the type of line walked by a drunk driver during a sobriety test than by the one drawn on paper by a straight-edged ruler.

INTERPRETING THE ESTABLISHMENT CLAUSE

Since the middle of the twentieth century, cases requiring application of the First Amendment have flooded the Supreme Court. Prior to this period in American history, public understandings of pluralism in America did not stretch much beyond various forms of Protestantism. By 1800, somewhere around 50,000 Catholics and fewer than 15,000 Jews lived in the United States. The vast majority of Americans saw themselves as making up a fairly heterogeneous community, affirming some form of Protestant Christianity. Even though Catholics reached a population of two million by 1850 and would continue to grow rapidly from there, Protestant domination of American culture continued through World War II. In this kind of context, only severe infringements of the First Amendment gained public notice, and only the most courageous of individuals dared to complain.

"Congress shall make no law respecting an establishment of religion." Emerging religious pluralism has brought with it an increasing number of cases asking the Supreme Court to clarify the meaning of these ten words. When a vast majority of Americans believed the same kinds of things, most took the relationship between the public and religion in stride. Since the 1950s, this has been increasingly difficult to do. Additionally, up until the twentieth century the Supreme Court generally refused to hear cases that challenged state laws affecting religion on the grounds that the Bill of Rights applied only to the federal government.

The first of the significant modern cases dealing with the establishment clause came in 1947 with *Everson v. Board of Education*. This case originated in Ewing Township, New Jersey. Children in both the public and the Catholic private schools rode public buses to school. Parents were able to receive reimbursement from public funds for these expenses. A citizen filed suit claiming that tax funds were being used to support religion. The Court ruled in favor of the township, claiming that safety for the children and not religious benefit was the issue in the city's decision. Yet the case proved far more important in establishing precedents for modern establishment clause interpretation than the decision handed down by the Court could possibly have indicated.

One of the more important things to note about this case is that it incorporated the establishment clause section of the First Amendment into the broad protections provided by the Fourteenth Amendment. On this point, the justices were relying on the precedent set just seven years earlier in *Cantwell v. Connecticut* (1940).[22] Even though that particular case dealt exclusively with free exercise questions, Justice Owen Roberts, in applying the Fourteenth Amendment to the case, made his reasoning quite clear:

> The First Amendment declares that Congress shall make no law respecting an establishment of religion or prohibiting the free exercise thereof. The Fourteenth Amendment has rendered the legislatures of the states as incompetent as Congress to enact such laws.[23]

The Fourteenth Amendment (ratified in 1868) was passed after the Civil War to guarantee that freed slaves received full civil rights. It contains the so-called due process clause, which reads, ". . . nor shall any State deprive any person of life, liberty, or property, without due process of law." This clause stated, in essence, that human beings possessed rights that superseded, in most cases, the ability of states to violate them without clear and broadly defensible reasons. In *Cantwell*, the Court concluded that the right to the free exercise of religion is necessarily included in these rights. In this way, the Court "incorporated" the rights of the First Amendment into the rights protected by the Fourteenth Amendment. For this reason, the Supreme Court's decision relating to the First and Fourteenth Amendments has been described as "incorporation."

Scholarship analyzing the Constitutional Convention has shown how James Madison originally hoped that the states as well as the federal government would be bound by the Bill of Rights. His original phrasing included the following sentence: "No state shall violate the equal rights of conscience, or the freedom of the press, or the trial by jury in criminal cases." The House of Representatives passed this version in 1789, but the Senate defeated it.[24] Therefore, the Bill of Rights applied only explicitly to the federal government until the twentieth century. Through incorporation, as defined by the Supreme Court in the middle of the century, these amendments now apply equally to states.

In the majority opinion in *Everson*, Justice Hugo Black relied on the precedent set by *Cantwell* and merely assumed that incorporation applied equally to the establishment clause. In a clear exposition of the meaning of those ten words, Justice Black stated,

The "establishment of religion" clause of the First Amendment means at least this: Neither a state nor the Federal Government can set up a church. Neither can pass laws which aid one religion, aid all religions, or prefer one religion over another. Neither can force nor influence a person to go to or to remain away from church against his will or force him to profess a belief or disbelief in any religion. . . . Neither a state nor the Federal Government can, openly or secretly, participate in the affairs of any religious organizations or groups and *vice versa*. In the words of Jefferson, the clause against establishment of religion by law was intended to erect "a wall of separation between church and state." . . . The First Amendment has erected a wall between church and state. That wall must be kept high and impregnable. We could not approve the slightest breach.[25]

Justice Rutledge, in his dissenting opinion, while disagreeing with the outcome of the case, echoed the majority understanding of separation:

The Amendment's purpose was not to strike merely at the official establishment of a single sect, creed or religion . . . the object was broader than separating church and state in this narrow sense. It was to create a complete and permanent separation of the spheres of religious activity and civil authority by comprehensively forbidding every form of public aid or support for religion.[26]

These two justices, on opposite sides of this case, accomplished three things with their written opinions. From this time on, the First Amendment clearly applied to state governments. Second, both Black and Rutledge chose to make Madison and Jefferson the authorities in interpreting the First Amendment. Rutledge included an appendix containing the complete text to Madison's "Memorial and Remonstrance" that acted as an exclamation point. Third, Black and Rutledge set the Court on a strict separationist path in its application of the establishment clause to modern cases. All three of these accomplishments have recently been called into question. I'll return to this point momentarily, but, first, a word about the origins of the phrase "wall of separation" is in order.

Thomas Jefferson used the phrase in 1802. Its use emerged from a context of experience that led Jefferson to place a heavy emphasis on the *separation* between church and state. First, the Baptists who wrote to Jefferson to express their support had been at work to try to move Congregationalists in Connecticut to end their establishment. Even though Baptists could direct their taxes to their own Baptist churches once they filed proper exemptions (not always easy to obtain), they hoped to end such practices. Ultimately, they succeeded in this effort when the establishment ended in that state. Jefferson wholeheartedly supported the Baptist position favoring disestablishment in Connecticut.

Second, beginning as early as Jefferson's run for the presidency in 1796 against John Adams, clergy in Massachusetts and Connecticut as well as Federalist opposition to his Democratic-Republican candidacy in those establishment strongholds issued warnings about Jefferson's infidelity. Timothy Dwight, Congregationalist minister, grandson to Jonathan Edwards, and president of Yale College, warned that Jefferson's election might result in "the Bible cast into a bonfire, the vessels of the sacramental supper borne by an ass in public procession, and our children . . . chanting mockeries against God."[27]

By the 1800 election, questions about Jefferson's religious commitments grew rapidly. Samuel Stanhope Smith, Presbyterian leader and president of Princeton University, joined Dwight and other Christian leaders who strongly and openly opposed his candidacy. Jefferson preferred reason to revelation and appeared to some clergy altogether to dismiss profound Christian commitment in the name of a radical freedom of conscience. Many Christians were offended by this statement of 1782, contained in his *Notes on the State of Virginia*: "It does me no injury for my neighbor to say there are twenty gods, or no God. It neither picks my pocket nor breaks my leg." Such statements did not sit too well with those who practiced a warm and evangelical Christian piety.[28]

When, in the fall of 1801, the Danbury Baptist Association wrote Jefferson a letter congratulating him on his recent election, clerical criticism of his character most likely still rang in his ears. These Baptists, mostly from Connecticut, represented a small pocket of support for Jefferson in a heavily hostile climate of establishment clergy. They celebrated his commitment to religious liberty and expressed their hope that his presidency would bring greater success to the cause. Jefferson responded with his "wall" metaphor.

> Believing with you that religion is a matter which lies solely between Man & his God, that he owes account to none other for his faith or his worship, that the legitimate powers of government reach actions only, & not opinions, I contemplate with sovereign reverence that act of the whole American people . . . thus building a wall of separation between Church & State.[29]

After 1947, and until fairly recently, a strict idea of separation, often using this "wall" metaphor, has marked much of the Court's approach to establishment. Following *Everson*, the court heard a case in 1948 in which it ruled unconstitutional the "released time" cooperation between a school district in Illinois and religious groups in the city of Champaign. Four years later, in 1952, they ruled "released time" to be constitutional so long as the religion classes were conducted off school campuses. This constitutional splitting of hairs has continued through the cases involving school prayer and Bible reading. The cases have generally followed a line disallowing explicit religious practice in the public school world, or explicitly providing aid for religious instruction, while trying to recognize the importance of religion as a contributor to American life.[30]

This kind of dance has been present in most of the Court's establishment decisions, right down to the 2005 decisions regarding the display of the Ten Commandments on public property in Texas and Kentucky. The Court ruled (5–4, with Kennedy, Rehnquist, Scalia, Thomas, and Breyer in the majority) that the Texas display was constitutional while it ruled (5–4, with Souter, Breyer, Ginsburg, O'Connor, and Stevens in the majority) that the Kentucky display was unconstitutional. The difference rested with the surrounding context in Texas being more historical and cultural, and inclusive of a variety of other historical monuments, and the fact that the monument had been on the grounds for forty years without objection. Concerning Texas, the Court wrote, "The public visiting the capitol grounds is more likely to have considered the religious aspect of the tablets' message as part of what is a broader moral and historical message reflective of a cultural heritage." In spite of efforts made by Kentucky, in the midst of litigation (what the majority on the Court described as "new statements of purpose . . . presented only as a litigating position"), to alter the display to be acceptable, the Court found the context and intent in Kentucky had been more clearly sectarian and an endorsement of religion in its orientation.[31] Reflected in these two decisions, with Breyer providing the swing vote in both, is a developing and significant difference of judicial philosophy regarding modern interpretation of the Establishment Clause.

I do not have the space here to analyze in detail and depth the many decisions of the Supreme Court pertaining to the establishment clause. The history of the Court in this area is so varied and so convoluted it is difficult to summarize briefly. John Witte, Professor of Law at Emory University, has recently produced a book-length analysis that includes careful consideration of nearly all these cases. His summary illustrates the difficulty:

> Few areas of law today are so riven with wild generalizations and hair-splitting distinctions, so given to grand statements of principle and petty applications of precept, so rife with selective readings of history and inventive renderings of precedent. Few areas of law hold such a massive jumble of juxtaposed doctrines and rules. Even a sympathetic reader of the Court's modern disestablishment decisions is tempted to apply to it the definition that Oliver Wendell Holmes Jr. once applied to the common law: "chaos with an index."[32]

Response to the establishment clause of the Constitution, whether of the judicial or the scholarly variety, falls into two general categories, neither of which is simply defined. These responses are considered either to be from a separationist or an accommodationist point of view. A separationist emphasizes the "wall" between church and state, between religion and civil spheres, while the accommodationist allows for a greater degree of commerce between the two institutions. Each of these positions is more complex than might first appear. For that reason, we need to give each category a broader consideration.

As indicated in the *Everson* opinions, separationists argue that civil authority should not do anything that aids religion. Further, they stress the Founders' concern to limit religion's ability to exert direct or controlling influence on government. In this view, the establishment clause means neither government nor religion should count on the other. They are two completely separate institutions and are best kept that way. Even though many separationists are themselves Christian or people of faith in other religions, they often understand religion to be a private matter. This limits the influence of religion to individuals, to the family, and perhaps to a few private institutions in society. Religion, when it goes public, some argue, naturally creates problems. Ted Jelen, a political scientist who holds the separationist position, explains why:

> First, religion makes "ultimate" demands on its adherents, which are not typically amenable to compromise. Religion deals with questions about the nature of the universe, as well as meaning and purpose of life, which are difficult to negotiate. Second, religious beliefs are difficult to verify empirically, and so may be difficult to alter through discussion and competition.[33]

Jelen defends a strict separationist understanding. Not all separationists approach the First Amendment in exactly the same way. Jelen lists two types, those who minimalize the public role of religion (the "religious minimalists," among whom Jelen counts himself) and those who "are quite solicitous of the prerogatives of religious minorities" (the "religious free marketeers"), but who, nonetheless, believe government should not be in the business of promoting or discouraging religious belief.

Carl Esbeck, a law professor at the University of Missouri and the architect of charitable choice legislation for the Bush administration, describes three kinds of separationists.[34] The strict separationists are akin to Jelen's religious minimalist.[35] Religion is a private affair. Churches have no rights against government intrusion except for those individual rights their members possess. The freewill separationists place their emphasis on the voluntary nature of the church, and the neutral position of the government. Attainment of any kind of institutionalized political power would only corrupt the church. Government should not aid particular religion, or "favor religion in general over nonreligion." But people of religious faith can address public issues, so long as they do not use the power of an organized church to do so, or try "to employ the offices of government to achieve ends reflective of a comprehensive world and life view."[36]

A third type, the institutional separationists, understands both church and state to be of divine origin, but each maintain a distinct existence. God transcends all things. Though government is accountable to God, thus preserving a "transcendent point" that preserves human rights, the nature of the God it serves "is purposely left ambiguous." But the nation must recognize that it serves a purpose beyond itself; otherwise it can become a "tyranny of the majority." People of faith cannot dictate to the government what it must believe but these separationists do affirm that "a church separated from the state need not, indeed, must not be a silent church." This is true because "religion speaks to the totality of life."[37] When one defends strict separation, where religion is completely privatized and publicly quiet, one is defending a civil order that favors secularity over religion. Strict separation between religion and the civil sphere is not merely a neutral policy.

In the last few decades, a spate of scholars have appeared to stress that Jefferson's "wall of separation" metaphor pictures too radical a division to be accurate in describing exactly what the First Amendment actually did. Even the Danbury Baptists, according to one argument, were so uncomfortable with the metaphor that they did not publicize receiving the response from President Jefferson. During the nineteenth century, the separation metaphor picked up steam as Protestants connected it to strong anti-Catholic sentiments to keep Catholics from intruding in American public life.[38] Even Sidney Mead, an institutional separationist in Esbeck's typology, preferred James Madison's "line of separation" and believed it more appropriate to the context of early nineteenth-century America than the more hardened tone represented in Jefferson's "wall" metaphor.[39] Madison's phrase allows for a much stronger sense of the ambiguity contained in the relationship between religion and government. Thomas Jefferson's "wall of separation" metaphor, more familiar to most of us, makes the separation appear much more definite than it actually is or can be. Religion has always played an important role in forming public life in America, not excluding even the Founders. This is, after all, the country that Sidney Mead could describe as "the nation with the soul of a church."[40]

Daniel Dreisbach, a noted scholarly opponent of the *Everson* point of view, has recently argued that those who have portrayed Jefferson as a strict separationist have chosen his materials selectively to support their position. Jefferson's broader body of political work regarding religion demonstrates "that Jefferson's ultimate objective was less an absolute separation of church and state than the fullest possible expression of religious belief and opinion."[41] Occasionally, this might mean some level of cooperation between religion and civil authorities. Dreisbach supports limiting government's influence on religion more than religion's influence on government. These new arguments against the separationist stance of the Court are known under the general rubric of accommodationism, but, like separationism, accommodationism also takes different forms. Esbeck lists three.[42]

The "structural pluralists," a group with whom Esbeck himself identifies, believe the government should support all institutions equally, without regard to whether they are "religious" or "secular." Thus, the state, through pay vouchers or some similar manner, should protect the right of parents to choose where their children will go to school without suffering a financial penalty. The "structural pluralist" also favors faith-based initiatives. This view "would require the state to respect and to equally nurture society's differentiated nongovernmental structures, as each institution goes about pursuing its own purposes as it understands them." This view, argues Esbeck, is primarily represented in the work of Dutch Calvinism. He gives special attention to the foundational work of Abraham Kuyper in this regard.[43] The structural pluralists see themselves advocating true neutrality in church-state relations, a neutrality that is willing to aid religion in the same ways it aids nonreligion.

Ronald Thiemann has shown just how muddy the term "neutrality" has become in judicial interpretations over the past few decades. Some justices in the Supreme Court have argued for "strict neutrality." This position keeps government from providing any aid whatsoever to religion. These justices are separationists who would negate the "structural pluralists" because the latter want to allow governmental aid to religion. Other justices have occasionally represented a softer form of neutrality that Thiemann describes as "nondiscriminatory." This position argues government cannot aid religion whenever sectarian practices are involved. Yet, government can aid religion so long as the practices of religious groups at issue serve a secular purpose or are generally cultural in nature. Justices who defend nondiscriminatory neutrality would also oppose the kind of neutrality advocated by the structural pluralists, because the latter want government aid that would ultimately support sectarian religious practices, such as religious instruction in private schools.

Thiemann's analysis reveals a third form of neutrality, "benevolent neutrality," which is much more accommodating. As suggested by the adjective "benevolent," justices who advocate it support a greater accommodation in religion. To give no aid to religion is interpreted as hostility toward religion and favoritism toward nonreligion. Therefore, these justices favor an approach to religion that is benevolent so long as it neither establishes nor interferes with the practice of religion. Government aid to religion becomes a norm. Thiemann makes a good case that, given American pluralism in religious matters today, benevolent neutrality does not define the issue of fairness between religions with respect to government aid.[44] More government aid naturally lands in the hands of those who represent a majority religious expression. Though all members of the Court generally agree that neutrality should represent the government's position with respect to religion, their various definitions of it make it clear that neutrality has become a rather muddy concept.

Benevolent neutrality is also essentially compatible with the form of accommodationism known as "nonpreferentialism." This view is quite popular today. Nonpreferentialists assert that so long as the civil authorities do not prefer one religious expression to another, they may aid all religions equally, or they can cooperate with religion and religious institutions in accomplishing societal goals without violating the First Amendment. Where nonpreferentialists might go further than some advocates of benevolent neutrality is at the point that they believe it is constitutionally acceptable for civil authorities to prefer religion to nonreligion, aiding religions in ways that might cause hardship for those who profess no faith.

Supreme Court Associate Justice William H. Rehnquist, the year before he was promoted to Chief Justice, argued in his dissenting opinion to *Wallace v. Jaffree* (1985), a case dealing with school prayer in Alabama, that the "Establishment Clause did not require government neutrality between religion and irreligion nor did it prohibit the federal government from providing nondiscriminatory aid to religion." Rehnquist's opinion is a classic expression of the nonpreferential view. "The 'wall of separation between church and State,' is a metaphor based on bad history," Rehnquist concluded, and "should be frankly and explicitly abandoned."[45]

The popularity of this view has expanded rather broadly over the past few decades. Besides former Chief Justice Rehnquist, the nonpreferential form of accommodationism found strong advocates in the Reagan administration, including President Reagan, William J. Bennett, and the Attorney General, Edwin Meese III. Speaking before the Christian Legal Society in the fall of 1985, Meese stated that the Bill of Rights only "forbad the establishment of a particular religion or a particular church." But the First Amendment "did not . . . preclude federal aid to religious groups so long as that assistance furthered a public purpose and so long as it did not discriminate in favor of one religious group against another."[46]

As Leonard W. Levy, an advocate of separationism, points out, "Nonpreferentialists do not trifle to state what part of the Constitution empowers the government to aid religion nonpreferentially." A "fundamental defect" in the reasoning of the nonpreferentialists is exposed when one remembers that this interpretation "results in the unhistorical contention that the First Amendment augmented a non-existent congressional power to legislate in the field of religion." The problem here is "that the First Amendment, no matter how parsed or logically analyzed, was framed to deny power, not to vest it."[47]

Robert H. Bork, nominated to the Supreme Court by Ronald Reagan in 1987 but unable to secure Senate approval, also supports the nonpreferentialist view. Known, along with current Justice Antonin Scalia and former Chief Justice Rehnquist, for his belief that the Constitution should be interpreted according to the original intent of the Founders, Bork consistently applies the notion to his understanding of the First Amendment when he argues, "It was not intended to ban government recognition of and assistance to religion; nor was it understood to require government neutrality between religion and irreligion." Nonpreferentialists conclude that the original intent of the Founders favors government assistance to religion. To make the case most strongly, they occasionally have to discredit the views of both Thomas Jefferson and James Madison, who were, in Bork's view, "idiosyncratic among the Founders."[48]

References to original intent by some nonpreferentialists occasionally include the assertion that America was a Christian nation, or at least a nation solidly founded in Christian principles and the Bible. Those who advocate this view often slide into the third type of accommodationists described by Carl Esbeck. He calls them the "restorationists." Restorationists desire a theocratic state. They argue for the restoration of a Christian nation. In the past two decades, this movement has grown into a formidable force among staunch conservatives by urging that America return to its former status as a Christian nation. In a more sophisticated version of restorationism, the Rutherford Institute, founded in 1982, works to promote this understanding in the courts. The Institute has had connections, through founder John W. Whitehead, with the Christian reconstruction movement begun by R. J. Rushdoony. Rushdoony openly advocated a theocracy that would include such things as the death penalty for practicing homosexuals.[49]

Whitehead has distanced himself from these views in recent years. But Whitehead's argument, connected to the long-held views of Rushdoony, that a government-established secular humanism has replaced a Christian worldview in

America remains a centerpiece of the Institute's approach to these questions.[50] Another significant figure who represented this "restorationist" view in his thought and written work during his lifetime is Francis Schaeffer.[51] His work is carried on through the work of his son, Franky, who is a cofounder of the Rutherford Institute, and the work of other members of the contemporary Religious Right. This approach always turns into "priestly faith," a posture defined and treated in chapter 4. An additional feature of both the restorationist and non-preferentialist approaches is the desire to return authority in these matters back to the states, to untangle the connections made by the courts between the First Amendment and the Fourteenth.[52]

Did the Founders intend something akin to the nonpreferentialist understanding of the relationship between church and state? First, one should note that the nonpreferentialist approach did exist during their time period. And an honest review of history reveals clearly that there are many ways, in the late-eighteenth century, that civil authorities aided religion in some respect or another. Many of the nascent government's most important documents, including the Declaration of Independence, contained references to God. Some members of the Continental Congress viewed America as a Christian nation. Government declared national prayer and thanksgiving days, employed chaplains in both the military and the Congress, and even paid for missionaries for Indians, included in provisions of treaties approved by Thomas Jefferson. Of course, in Jefferson's mind, the Indians were not American citizens but rather members of foreign nations. Jefferson refused to issue religious proclamations setting aside public days of thanksgiving while he was president. As governor in Virginia, however, he did proclaim such days.

How are these different actions to be reconciled? Most likely Jefferson believed the First Amendment prohibited the federal government from taking these kinds of actions but allowed the state to take them.[53] In general, James Madison opposed tax relief for religion, congressional and military chaplaincies, and religious proclamations made by government officials.[54] But others among the Founders supported all these things. There is no singular "intent" but rather many and conflicting "intents" that existed among leaders in the founding generation. Compromises on wording, and certainly political negotiations leading toward the overall goal of accomplishing ratification, were regularly made. The principal intent was to form a government that would endure, one that would avoid the mistakes of past governments, if possible. The genius of parts of the Constitution, like the First Amendment, lies in their brevity, allowing for broad principles to be applied and for flexibility in interpretation when needed to apply them appropriately.

In responding to the original intent argument, Douglas Laycock lifts up this kind of ambiguity and concludes that the intent "behind the religion clauses is more complex than either side wants to admit." Yet he also argues that Founders rejected nonpreferentialism as it existed in the eighteenth century. In Virginia, for example, the general assessment bill of 1784 attempted to support teachers of the Christian religion, without regard to denomination, but also made provisions for others. Madison's attempt to defeat this bill included the writing and distribution of his well-known "Memorial and Remonstrance." The assessment bill eventually went down in defeat and Jefferson's Bill Establishing Religious Freedom passed instead. In Virginia, in other words, the voters decided against the nonpreferential option. Laycock makes the important point that, despite the similarities among religious options in Virginia—among Christians ranging from Anglicans to Baptists, with a few Quakers and Mennonites thrown in— the nonpreferential option seemed unworkable. "The bill," he concludes, "would have violated the consciences of the Baptists and upset the polity of the Presbyterians."

Nonpreferentialism failed to thrive in any of the other southern colonies as well. Some form of nonpreferentialism did prevail in New England, particularly in Massachusetts and Connecticut. Laycock also rehearsed the legislative history of the First Congress with respect to the wording of the First Amendment. The Senate rejected every draft that represented nonpreferentialism.

> Occasionally the founders' intent is clear and applicable, as in their conclusion that nonpreferential establishments were still establishments and still objectionable. More often, their intent is unclear, or not responsive to the questions asked in our time. . . . We cannot escape the responsibility of self-government; we must decide for ourselves how to apply the Constitution in our own time.[55]

This being said, it is also clear, once again, that government during the 1800s supported a kind of "generic Protestantism." As Laycock put it, "no one complained" because no one, in that context, seriously had a problem with it. The establishment clause was not applied to those things because the Founders, along with most others in America, took those things for granted. Does this fact mean they intended for the establishment clause to forever excuse them? Some would argue that present-day Americans are "bound by the consensus that caused them not to think about it."[56] Others, Laycock among them, argue the broader principle by stating that "the principles the Founders developed in the context of division between Anglicans and Baptists" must now be applied "to today's divisions between Christians, Jews, Muslims, Buddhists, agnostics, and atheists," even though intent among the Founders does not make this clear.[57] Remember, the Founders and Americans of that time also exhibited strong opinions (and intent) about Blacks, Indians, Catholics, and women that they took for granted. Americans today are certainly not bound by the consensus that enabled early Americans to discriminate so dramatically and easily in these cases.

Those who argue against the original intent approach to the Constitution also emphasize that interpretation affecting society today must consider the social, political, and contextual realities of contemporary America. America today contains both a much more complex government, necessarily so, and a vastly more diverse cultural setting than existed in the 1790s. John Wilson makes this point well:

> In recognizing the new fabric that sustains contemporary American society in our era, it is clear that if these clauses are to have significance today they must express the current fundamental operating principles of the society. Now they must speak to the essential pluralism of our culture, which exists in tension with a powerful modern state. So their burden must be to support the rights of conscience, and to limit the scope of governmental power over collective and individual religious actions. Are these related to an original consensus they may have rested on? Of course. But their roles today are very different indeed, for they were originally cast to preserve the authority of the states over religion and to limit the reach of the new government. Now the authority of the federal state shields religion (collective and individual, behavior and belief) from intrusions of state and local regimes as well as of the federal government.[58]

Ultimately, one has to question, in light of these kinds of recognitions where cultural developments have delivered new insights, why the intent of the Founders, even if it could be uncovered or if it could be determined to be singular in nature, should hold sway in today's complex American society. Both separationists and accommodationists agree that the principle of religious liberty is indeed the most important principle to uphold in these discussions. It could very well be that, even if it was not within the original intent of the Founders, extensive religious pluralism requires increasing attention to separation in order to protect the rights of all American citizens today. In short, the protection of the free exercise of religion in an incredibly complex culture with an array of competing religious and nonreligious understandings of reality may require more, rather than less, careful attention to protecting separation between civil authorities and religious institutions and beliefs.[59]

While some Americans greatly fear the development of a theocracy within our government today, it will not happen (though, admittedly, historians should not become prognosticators). Though the cultural presence and power of the non-preferentialist argument today is irrefutable and most recent appointments to the Supreme Court likely hold this view, the effective power of religious pluralism in America will keep theocracy well at bay. According to Lance Banning, one lesson Madison learned in Virginia that gave him great hope was the fact that, even in the relatively homogeneous confines of that particular colony, "the multiplicity of jealous, disagreeing sects had done what no appeal to revolutionary principles and public good could have accomplished by itself." The larger the republic, Madison surmised, the more pluralistic it would become. That would ensure that no "partial interest" could ever completely control affairs of state, and "that majorities would seldom have a common interest in pursuing policies inimical to private rights or long-term public needs."[60] In today's America, as rich in religious pluralism as it is, no one view will be able ultimately to control affairs of state and culture, not even with effective political organization or manipulation.

This chapter has shown how, even at the beginning of American history, considerable diversity existed around the question of the proper relationship between church and state. Colonies handled the question quite differently and with considerable diversity. Developments, however, moved in clearer directions as Founders considered the question of drafting a Constitution. The Constitution became a secular document, carrying the hopes of those who drafted it that it would recognize the rights of all American citizens, whether religious or not. The Bill of Rights made these rights even more explicit. As American pluralism has surfaced, in dramatic fashion, some have wanted to revisit these questions in new and creative ways, some fearing what this pluralism might mean and others wanting to assure that this pluralism is respected and incorporated into the rich matrix that forms American cultural life. The bottom line remains the same, however. There can be no establishment of religion in this country.

Americans possess both freedom for religious belief and freedom from religious belief. Religious diversity has always existed in this country, but now its presence is undeniable. Today, new studies reveal there are nearly 6 million Muslims in this country—more Muslims than Episcopalians, or members of the Presbyterian Church (U.S.A.), and as many Muslims as Jews. Hindus number nearly 1.3 million in America, and, if you count Buddhists born in America, there are nearly 4 million Buddhists in this country. It is interesting to note that Los Angeles is now the "most complex Buddhist city in the world."[61] This healthy diversity has resulted from America's historic commitment to religious freedom. You don't have to take a religious test to become an American, to run for public office, to vote, to join the military, or, for that matter, to die somewhere in the deserts of Iraq wearing an American uniform. There are good Americans who represent every kind of religion and no religion. You do not have to be a Christian to be a good American. Believe it or not, you don't even have to be a Christian to be a good Republican in this country.

Americans live in a country where the Constitution and the Bill of Rights guarantee that government can't dictate to citizens in matters of faith and conscience. Majority rule can't dictate in these areas. The actions of state or federal legislatures can't dictate in these areas. The President can't dictate in these areas. And, contrary to the hopes of some today, the courts can't dictate in these areas. America is the land of both/and. American Christians live in an inclusive country. The poetic words of a young Jewish woman, Emma Lazarus, found on the Statue of Liberty, make the point well:

> Give me your tired, your poor, / Your huddled masses yearning to breathe free, / The wretched refuse of your teeming shore. / Send these, the homeless, tempest-tossed to me. / I lift my lamp beside the golden door![62]

This nation welcomes people of all faiths and people associated with no faith. America is not the land of "Either you are a Christian, in fact, a particular type of Christian, or you are not a true American." No, America is the land of both/and, not either/or.

Religion is not just a private matter. It can be public too, without violating the separation of church and state. Many people possessing a strong religious commitment believe their faith compels them to work for justice in public ways. Many have used their faith to act and speak loudly in public ways to work for racial and gender equality, for the rights of the poor. Faith, for example, can speak loudly against the notion of preventive war.[63] People of faith can speak publicly and often do, serving the public good without violating the First Amendment.

Secular Americans also speak publicly. They express their commitments by using the best of the secular reasoning that stands behind them. These too serve the public good. Together, religious and secular Americans who respect one another's rights to contribute to our public discourse with both conviction and civility can model what it means to be a pluralistic America, a nation where people of many faiths and people of no faith can live and work together to better their common lives. This was the hope of the Founders and the wisdom behind the First Amendment. America needs that hope and wisdom more today than ever before.

Chapter 2

The Free Exercise Clause

". . . or prohibiting the free exercise thereof."

The last chapter indicates that accommodationists, particularly the nonprefer-entialists, want too cozy a relationship between religion and public life. Government should not play favorites between religions but, given American history, is allowed to favor religion over nonreligion. The nonpreferentialists, therefore, unduly privilege religious values over nonreligious values when it comes to matters important to the nation. Yet the last chapter also indicates that those who favor strict separation between church and state actually seek to privatize religion. Their defense of the metaphorical "wall" leads not only to the separation of the institutions of church and state but also to a separation of the ability of religious values to speak to matters related to public life. The strict separationists unduly privilege nonreligious values over religious values when it comes to matters important to the nation. Neither view is truly an acceptable interpretation of the First Amendment. One tends to violate the establishment clause; the other tends to violate the free exercise clause. This raises the question, Do these two parts of the First Amendment conflict with one another or speak against one another?

The bottom line is that there is but one First Amendment. Does this mean that there is only one purpose, whether one construes that one purpose as separation or as the free exercise of religion? There are advocates of both positions, where one of the clauses ends up, in practical ways, being subordinate to the other. The fact is, of course, that the First Amendment contains two clauses. The establishment clause deals with the relationship between church and state at the "structural" level. Therefore, it is a "structural clause." The free exercise clause is concerned with the "protection of individual religious rights." Therefore, it is a "rights clause."[1]

Founders created the establishment clause to ensure, on the one hand, that government could not use its power to give advantage to any particular religious expression, and, on the other hand, that no particular religious expression could control government or make use of governmental power. Neither government nor religion could use the other as a tool to achieve its purposes. The establishment clause, as Justice Black stated in *Engel* (1962), "rested on the belief that a union of government and religion tends to destroy government and to degrade religion."[2] Founders included the second part of the First Amendment, the free exercise clause, in order to make it clear that government could not restrain or hamper any particular religious expression. The free exercise of religion in America protects the rights of individuals to express themselves freely in matters pertaining to religion. It protects religious groups or organizations only in the sense that individuals who possess rights in religion make up the memberships of these groups.[3] Religious organizations are protected from the negative effects of government action through the establishment clause. Rather than understanding establishment and free exercise as competing interests, it is best to understand that these two clauses actually complement one another. They serve a unity of purpose. Neither clause controls or defines the other. Both have their areas of jurisdiction, and both are needed.

Strict separationists also stress a unity of the religion clauses. But their main concern is for separation between state and church. The overriding governmental interest, in their view, is to restrict religion from any access to governmental power. Marvin E. Frankel is a good example:

> Thrusting religion into the public square—always in the sense of "access" to the power and prestige of government—serves no worthy purpose and exacts the kind of toll against which church-state separation was designed to safeguard. It furthers no shared or ambiguous moral values. Far from promoting the freedom of anyone, it constrains and offends minorities in the very process for which it is designed: the pronouncement of the dominant religion's power.[4]

Leo Pfeffer is another example. He has long argued that there is no tension between these two clauses; neither are they two distinct clauses with separate emphases. Rather they are two sides of the same coin—the coin essentially possessing sides of separation and freedom. The stress for Pfeffer and other separationists is on the unity of the two clauses. There is no conflict between them. Ideally, neither clause is superior or subordinate. But, practically, "heads" on the coin is definitely separation, a "single, unitary mandate of stark neutrality, which equally prohibited laws favoring religion or those enjoining it."[5] Most separationists offer a broad application of the establishment clause and a more limited view of the free exercise clause. This sometimes comes out, among some separationists, as mandating a privatization of religion, where religion cannot really assume any meaningful voice in the public square because in doing so, it tends toward violation of the broad interpretation of the establishment clause.[6] Separationists generally "believe that a prominent public role for religion is incompatible with the practice of popular government in the United States."[7]

Accommodationists, on the other hand, argue that the unity connected with the two clauses is entirely understood in light of free exercise. Founders, they argue, meant for the establishment clause to protect the free exercise of religion. Richard Neuhaus makes the most consistent argument in this regard. He proposes a "rule of thumb: any use of 'no establishment' that restricts 'free exercise' is a misuse of 'no establishment.'" Free exercise is the "end" of the First Amendment, while nonestablishment is merely the "means" to that end. The separationists, he argues, have turned nonestablishment into an "end in itself." Neuhaus terms this the "Pfefferian Inversion," in honor of Leo Pfeffer, "the father of strict separationism," who has argued establishment cases successfully before the Supreme Court for forty years. For Neuhaus, the First Amendment is designed only to protect the free exercise of religion. In making this argument, Neuhaus states that he does not believe government should be neutral with regard to religion, but rather sides with those "who claim that religion has a 'privileged status' in the Constitution."[8] This is, however, rather an outrageous claim. When religion seeks access to government funding and power by claiming privilege, religion quickly crosses boundaries leading to some form of establishment. Madison understood that neither religion nor irreligion could be given constitutional privilege. In his "Memorial and Remonstrance," for example, he wrote,

> Whilst we assert for ourselves a freedom to embrace, to profess, and to observe the Religion which we believe to be of divine origin, we cannot deny an equal freedom to those whose minds have not yet yielded to the evidence which has convinced us. If this freedom be abused, it is an offence against God, not against man: To God, therefore, not to man, must an account of it be rendered.[9]

The differences between the separationists and the accommodationists in their interpretations of the First Amendment make clear the difficulties faced by the Supreme Court as it attempts to determine appropriate decisions in cases dealing with the intersections of religion and public life in America. The important thing to recognize, however, is that the Supreme Court, throughout its history, has tended to understand the First Amendment by emphasizing the distinguishing features of the two clauses. For the most part, the Court has not set them in tension with one another but has understood establishment and free exercise as having distinct jurisdiction when it comes to the law. There are occasions, however, as Chief Justice Warren Burger phrased it in an opinion written in 1970, when the "Court has struggled to find a neutral course between the two Religion Clauses, both of which are cast in absolute terms, and either of which, if expanded to a logical extreme, would tend to clash with the other."[10] In other words, Burger is arguing that when tension between the clauses exists, the Court tries to accommodate religious practice in neutral ways, without allowing government to promote religion directly. For the most part, the history of the Court has developed a distinct history of cases dealing specifically with either establishment or free exercise claims.

THE SUPREME COURT AND FREE EXERCISE CASES

As is true of the cases involving the establishment clause, cases using "free exercise" as the heart of a claim did not much appear in American jurisprudence until about 1940, over one hundred and fifty years after the approval of the Bill of Rights. As indicated in the previous chapter, this delay rests in the fact that Protestant power in American culture held sway throughout these years. The landscape, however, was changing more rapidly than most Protestants realized. Robert Handy has pointed out that Ezra Stiles, president of Yale, preached a sermon in 1783 predicting the absolute dominance of American religion by three particular denominations: the Congregationalists, the Episcopalians, and the Presbyterians.[11] Stiles predicted that by 1860 there would by 7 million Congregationalists. When 1860 arrived, there were about 250,000. By 1850, Presbyterians were around 350,000 in number and Episcopalians were somewhere around 100,000 strong.[12] Stiles could not have been more wrong.

The top three were Roman Catholics (approaching 2 million), Methodists (roughly 1.3 million), and Baptists (just under 1 million).[13] In 1776, Catholic membership stood at about 25,000, or one percent of the population. By 1900, Catholics would dominate all statistics for the big three denominations with over 12 million members (roughly 14 percent of the American population) compared to about 5.5 million Methodists and a little over 3 million for Baptists. At the time Stiles made his prediction, Catholics were barely on the radar screen, there was no Methodist church, and Congregationalists like Stiles "would have trouble seeing [Baptists] as other than a lower class sect."[14] The inaccuracy of Stiles's prediction simply indicates the difficulty anyone might have in foreseeing the shape of growth in American religion. Prior to 1850, most Americans gave Mormonism no thought, but by 1900 Mormons had surpassed 250,000 members and would grow exponentially in the twentieth century.[15]

As the shape of American religion changed, especially as new religious expressions appeared, the need to challenge cultural mores appeared among those who felt disadvantaged by them. The first Supreme Court case to make a challenge based on free exercise appeared when Mormons challenged laws forbidding more than one marriage. When Brigham Young declared that polygamy was an official belief within the Mormon community, public outrage led to a congressional response. In 1862, Congress passed the Morrill Act to prohibit polygamy in American states and territories. The first thing to notice about free exercise claims is that they appear when someone believes the law prohibits or criminalizes the free practice of what religious belief dictates. In this case, a court in the Utah territory convicted George Reynolds of polygamy in 1875. Reynolds ultimately appealed to the Supreme Court, and the case was heard in 1878. The Court used this case to create a test to apply in such cases. The Court argued unanimously that free exercise guarantees absolute freedom of belief but not of action. The First Amendment meant, declared the Court, that "Congress was deprived of all legislative power over mere opinion, but was left free to reach actions which were in violation of social duties or subversive of good order."[16] In this first free exercise case, the Court accepted Reynolds's claim that polygamy was a "religious practice" but concluded, without much examination of the evidence found within the Mormon practice itself, that it violated acceptable practices in a civilized society. This "belief-action" doctrine, defined by this case, "gave an extraordinarily narrow definition of the constitutional guarantee" of free exercise. This court-defined dichotomy between belief and action has not controlled the Court's decisions since that case.[17]

The 1940s brought a spate of cases, particularly involving Jehovah's Witnesses. In fact, Robert Miller and Ron Flowers count "approximately eighty cases" involving the Jehovah's Witnesses that have arrived at the Supreme Court since 1938. These cases, they argue, have given "greater clarity" and "greater breadth to the meaning of the Free Exercise Clause." The first case (*Cantwell v. Connecticut*, 1940) has special significance as the case that incorporated the First Amendment into the rights described by the Fourteenth Amendment, making them applicable to all states (see the discussion on incorporation in chapter 1). Newton Cantwell and his two sons were charged with violating the law when they played anti-Catholic records and distributed religious material in a heavily Catholic neighborhood. Using the belief-action doctrine, the Court could have sustained the conviction of Cantwell and his sons for disturbing the peace through religious solicitation without a license. Instead, the Court carefully examined the conflict between the state's interest to preserve the peace and the government's interest in protecting the free exercise of religion, and unanimously concluded that the conduct in this case did not constitute "a clear and present danger to a substantial interest of the State." This "clear and present danger" doctrine, first used by Justice Holmes in a free speech case in 1919, provided a much broader protection of free exercise.[18]

Other cases involving the distribution of religious tracts followed on the heels of the Cantwell case. The first of these (*Jones v. Opelika*, 1942) involved a law requiring payment of a tax to distribute literature. Jehovah's Witnesses lost the case in a 5–4 vote when the Court's majority argued that the First Amendment did not require the government to provide a fiscal exemption to religious groups affected by generally applicable legislation. In his dissent, however, Justice Murphy argued that the free exercise of religion was a "preferred freedom" that was more precious even than free speech or a free press. The next year, with a new member of the Court on board, the Court used the "preferred freedoms" doctrine to overrule *Jones v. Opelika*. In the new case (*Murdock v. Pennsylvania*, 1943), the Court ruled 5–4 that the distribution of religious literature was exempt from the tax.[19]

During 1943, the Court also reversed a more prominent ruling involving the Jehovah's Witnesses. Very shortly after *Cantwell*, the Court decided a case involving two children, Lillian and William Gobitis, who were expelled from school for their refusal to salute the American flag. In considering the conflicts present in this case, Justice Frankfurter, writing for the majority (8–1), stressed the importance of "national cohesion" and ruled that the children had to salute the flag. The law requiring the flag salute was "nondiscriminatory" and reflective of no intent to inhibit any person's religious beliefs.[20] In his lone dissent, Justice Harlan Stone argued that the "very essence" of the First Amendment protected the "freedom of the individual from compulsion as to what he shall think and what he shall say, at least where the compulsion is to bear false witness to his religion."[21] Justice Stone's words would be revisited just three years later.

In a remarkable reversal, considering an 8–1 majority in 1940, the Court changed its mind in 1943. There were two new additions to the Court in that span. Further, legal and religious scholars had attacked the Court for its opinion. A "wave of public violence against the Witnesses" also had taken place in the wake of the decision. Finally, legal action against the Witnesses took place in numerous locations. In West Virginia, after the first case, a new law required all school children to say the Pledge of Allegiance. When Witnesses again asked for relief in the courts, their case reached the Supreme Court by 1943. Using the "clear and present danger" test in this second case, the Court ruled the requirement to salute the flag unconstitutional. Echoing Justice Stone's words in his 1940 dissent, Justice Jackson, one of the two new justices on the Court, writing for the majority of six, stated,

> If there is any fixed star in our constitutional constellation, it is that no official, high or petty, can prescribe what shall be orthodox in politics, nationalism, religion, or other matters of opinion or force citizens to confess by word or act their faith therein. If there are any circumstances which permit an exception, they do not now occur to us.[22]

In addition to general laws that seemed to restrict or offend their religious sensibilities, alternative religions in America struggled against the way Protestant mores and practices found their way into American law. Across the country, there were various laws against drinking, swearing, smoking, and working on Sunday. All these laws had their origins in Protestant Christian piety and practice. In 1961, the Court heard two cases involving Orthodox Jewish businesses forced to close on Sunday. This meant these businesses could only be open five days per week, since they closed for Jewish Sabbath on Saturday. These cases involved both the establishment clause and the free exercise clause. The Court decided against the Jewish businessmen by claiming that what had once been a holy day had now taken on the importance of a secular holiday allowing for rest and time with the family. The state had developed an interest in the holiday, apart from religious considerations. Further, though it might pose an economic hardship for some because of their religion, the burden imposed on their free exercise of religion was minimal and "indirect."[23]

Moving from economic hardship affecting businesses to that affecting individuals seemed to make a difference in the Court's posture regarding burdens imposed on free exercise. Adele Sherbert, a convert to Seventh-day Adventism in the late 1950s, found herself in a difficult situation when the mill where she was employed decided to make all employees work on Saturday. When she refused to do so, she was fired. She applied for unemployment and was denied because she had voluntarily refused to meet the conditions of her job. The Supreme Court (7–2) reversed the decisions of the lower courts in the case. "To condition the availability of benefits," wrote Justice Brennan, "upon this appellant's willingness to violate a cardinal principle of her religious faith effectively penalizes the free exercise of her constitutional liberties."[24] In dissenting opinions, justices pointed out that Mr. Braunfeld, the Orthodox Jew from the previous case, suffered greater hardship than Adele Sherbert. Miller and Flowers point out that since *Sherbert*, most of the laws relating to Sunday "have been repealed or modified" so that "the weight of such laws is no longer so onerous to Sabbaterians."[25]

The *Sherbert* case created a new test used by the Court in subsequent years that replaced the "clear and present danger" doctrine with a more substantial examination. The "*Sherbert* test" involved three prongs. If the first of these is positively met, then the Court must investigate the second, and so on. (1) Does the action of the government place a burden, whether direct or indirect, on the religious exercise of this individual? (2) Is there a "compelling state interest" that provides rationale for placing a burden on the free exercise of this individual? If there is no "compelling interest," the case is decided in favor of the plaintiff. (3) In the case of "compelling interest," does another "least restrictive alternative means" exist that can achieve the same purpose without placing a burden on free exercise? If "alternative means" exist, the government must use them. If not, the case is decided in favor of the government. The *Sherbert* test meant that free exercise trumped the state unless the state could prove a "compelling state interest" and no other alternative means existed within which the state's interest could be met. This expanded the meaning of free exercise considerably. This test figured prominently in a case in 1972 when Amish parents withdrew their children from public schools after the eighth grade. Wisconsin law required all children to stay in school until age sixteen. The Amish believed that after eighth grade Amish children would face too many temptations that challenged the Amish way of life. The Court unanimously sided with the Amish. Chief Justice Burger wrote the opinion and, using the *Sherbert* test, argued "that only those interests of the highest order and those not otherwise served can overbalance legitimate claims to the free exercise of religion."[26]

The "compelling state interest" test found in these two decisions required the Court to determine whether free exercise might outweigh the governmental interest to enforce a generally applicable law without any exceptions. For example, the Court exempted both Adele Sherbert and the Amish from generally applicable laws without finding those laws to be unconstitutional. The Court held for exemption in another case involving a member of the Jehovah's Witnesses in 1981. A worker in a steel mill quit his job and applied for unemployment when he was transferred to an area making equipment for military tanks. When Indiana denied unemployment benefits because he quit, he filed suit using a free exercise claim. Using the *Sherbert* test, the Court concluded that the state had placed a burden, however indirect that burden might be, on Eddie Thomas's right to exercise his religious beliefs.

There are a couple of very interesting aspects of the *Thomas* case. First, there were other Jehovah's Witnesses working in the plant who did not quit and who did not believe working there violated their religious consciences. This was part of the state's argument in the case. The Court ruled that it could not get into who was practicing their religion appropriately, or who best represented the theological beliefs of Jehovah's Witnesses. As Chief Justice Burger phrased it, "Courts are not arbiters of scriptural interpretation." Free exercise of religion in this country means that the courts cannot become theologians.[27] Second, Justice Rehnquist, in his dissenting opinion in this case, provided a glimpse into the future of the Court's treatment of free exercise claims. In his view, the "tension" between establishment and free exercise was of "fairly recent vintage," brought about by modern social welfare legislation that largely affects individuals, the decision of the Court to "incorporate" the First Amendment into the Fourteenth Amendment, and the "overly expansive interpretation of *both* clauses." The tension, he argued, would "diminish almost to the vanishing point if the clauses were properly interpreted." He argued that the state of Indiana had merely been following generally applicable law, and that law happened to affect this one person financially because of his religious beliefs.

> Just as it did in *Sherbert v. Verner*, the Court today reads the Free Exercise Clause more broadly than is warranted. As to the proper interpretation of the Free Exercise Clause, I would accept the decision of *Braunfeld v. Brown* and the dissent in *Sherbert*. In *Braunfeld*, we held that Sunday Closing laws do not violate the First Amendment rights of Sabbatarians. Chief Justice Warren explained that the statute did not make unlawful any religious practices of appellants; it simply made the practice of their religious beliefs more expensive. . . . Likewise in this case, it cannot be said that the State discriminated against Thomas on the basis of his religious beliefs or that he was denied benefits *because* he was a Jehovah's Witness. Where, as here, a State has enacted a general statute, the purpose and effect of which is to advance the State's secular goals, the Free Exercise Clause does not in my view require the State to conform that statute to the dictates of religious conscience of any group.[28]

Nine years later, the Court abandoned the *Sherbert* test and adopted reasoning similar to that argued by Justice Rehnquist in the *Thomas* case. Galen Black and Alfred Smith, both members of a Native American church in Oregon who worked in the area of drug rehabilitation for a nonprofit agency, were fired in 1984 when their employers found they had used peyote in a sacramental ritual within a worship service. They applied for unemployment compensation, and Oregon denied their claim. When they sued, the Oregon Supreme Court concluded that the state had placed a burden on the free exercise of their religious beliefs. In 1990, the Supreme Court overturned the state court in a landmark 6–3 decision that greatly reduced the government burden in free exercise cases. Rather than arguing that the state had a "compelling interest" in regulating drug usage, Justice Scalia wrote an opinion that replaced the "compelling state interest" test with one that allows the government to enforce "generally applicable law" that prohibits "conduct that the State is free to regulate." No individual can be allowed to "become a law unto himself." Any state can, if it chooses, offer exemptions to generally applicable laws, but the state is not constitutionally required to do so on the basis of religious belief. Scalia's opinion recognized and accepted the fact that the practices of minority religions could be burdened by this understanding, but that burden, in his view, constituted an "unavoidable consequence" of democracy and could best be handled through political processes. "We cannot afford the luxury," argued Scalia, "of deeming *presumptively invalid*, as applied to the religious objector, every regulation of conduct that does not protect an interest of the highest order."[29]

Justice O'Connor agreed with the decision but preferred to use the "compelling interest" test to reach it. Scalia had essentially placed free exercise of religion in a secondary position when he argued that other cases decided by the Court in its history had been "hybrid" in that they combined concerns about free exercise of religion with "other constitutional protections, such as freedom of speech and of the press." She strongly dissented from the majority's opinion concerning generally applicable laws and argued that the previous test upheld the understanding that religious liberty "occupies a preferred position, and that the Court will not permit encroachments upon this liberty, whether direct or indirect, unless required by clear and compelling government interests 'of the highest order.'" "In my view," O'Connor argued, "the First Amendment was enacted precisely to protect the rights of those whose religious practices are not shared by the majority and may be viewed with hostility. . . . For the Court to deem this command a 'luxury,' is to denigrate '[t]he very purpose of the Bill of Rights.'" In dissent, Justice Blackmun (joined by both Brennan and Marshall), echoed O'Connor's opinion of the rejection of the *Sherbert* test, but also strongly argued that the Court made the wrong decision in the case. He condemned Scalia's opinion as a "wholesale overturning of settled law concerning the Religion Clauses of our Constitution."

> I do not believe the Founders thought their dearly bought freedom from religious persecution a "luxury," but an essential element of liberty—and they could not have thought religious intolerance "unavoidable," for they drafted the Religion Clauses precisely in order to avoid that intolerance.[30]

The *Smith* decision replaced the government's burden to prove compelling interest with a presumption of the state's right to legislate generally applicable laws without concern for religious exemptions. So long as a state did not intend to discriminate against religious behavior when it passed the law, the free exercise of individuals has not been violated when the law affects them individually. Justice Scalia's hybrid argument also considerably narrowed government protection of the free exercise of religion because it stated that the free exercise clause could only be used by the Court when generally applicable laws also seemed to have a negative effect on the freedom of speech, the freedom of the press, or the rights of parents. As Justice O'Connor noted, this removed the free exercise of religion from its "preferred position" as an independent and constitutionally protected right on its own.

The *Smith* case caused considerable protest to emerge among religious groups, constitutional scholars, and congressional leaders. Congress, in 1993, passed a Religious Freedom Restoration Act (RFRA) to counteract the effects of the *Smith* decision. The act required by law that the Courts must require governments, whether federal, state, or local, to demonstrate "compelling interest" in order to justify any burden to the free exercise of religion. The law took effect in November but lasted less than four years.

A Roman Catholic church in Boerne, Texas, hoped to build a larger sanctuary for its worship services. The church is located in a historic preservation district and city authorities denied the permit to expand. Patrick Flores, the archbishop of San Antonio, sued under the provisions of the RFRA. In its ruling (6–3), the Court ruled the RFRA to be unconstitutional. The majority argued Congress acted beyond its authority when it enacted this law. Congress claimed to be acting under section 5 of the Fourteenth Amendment that grants Congress "power to enforce, by appropriate legislation, the provisions of this article." The Court's majority opinion, offered by Justice Kennedy, argued that, while Congress has the power to enforce "the constitutional right to the free exercise of religion," the Fourteenth Amendment does not give Congress the authority "to determine what constitutes a constitutional violation" (519). Further, Congress cannot determine the manner the various states use in enforcing the content of the Fourteenth Amendment. Justice Kennedy concluded that the RFRA "contradicts vital principles necessary to maintain separation of powers and the federal balance" (536). The Court ruled in favor of Boerne, concluding that the city's zoning laws were constitutional.[31]

In her dissent, Justice O'Connor (joined by Souter and Breyer) argued primarily that the *Smith* decision used an "improper standard for deciding free exercise claims." Since the majority decision in this case rested on the assumption that *Smith* properly interpreted free exercise, O'Connor could not concur. She argued that the free exercise clause "is best understood as an affirmative guarantee of the right to participate in religious practices and conduct without impermissible governmental interference, even when such conduct conflicts with a neutral, generally applicable law" (546). The *Smith* decision, wrote O'Connor, "has harmed religious liberty" (547). Using a lengthy historical argument, she concluded that

> historical evidence casts doubt on the Court's current interpretation of the Free Exercise Clause. The record instead reveals that its drafters and ratifiers more likely viewed the Free Exercise Clause as a guarantee that government may not unnecessarily hinder believers from freely practicing their religion, a position consistent with our pre-*Smith* jurisprudence.[32]

Justice O'Connor believed the *Boerne* case should have been the occasion for overturning the standard used in the *Smith* case. The majority of the Court disagreed, leaving general free exercise questions largely to the mercy of local and state legislation.

In response to the *Boerne* decision, Congress again offered legislation. In 2000, Congress passed the Religious Land Use and Institutionalized Persons Act (RLUIPA). This act states that zoning laws and prison regulations will not be allowed to impose a burden on religious liberty unless the government proves a compelling interest. It also argued that government had to find the least restrictive ways to enforce such laws when it comes to matters involving religious freedom. The RLUIPA is much narrower than the RFRA, but it attempts to protect churches and prisoners from generally applicable legislation in these areas. Several court cases have arisen in its wake, some being upheld by the lower courts and some resulting in the conclusion that the RLUIPA is unconstitutional. A Muslim inmate in Wisconsin sued so he could be allowed to use prayer oil in his cell. A Virginia inmate sued because the prison refused to serve kosher meals. Prisoners belonging to minority religions in Ohio sued in order to gain access to religious literature and worship. These cases have slowly worked their way through the court system, with the Supreme Court agreeing to hear the Ohio case in 2005. In its decision, the Court unanimously upheld the RLUIPA stating that it reasonably accommodates the exercise of religious freedom without violating the establishment clause, and ruled in favor of the Ohio prisoners.[33]

This review of the Court cases dealing with the free exercise clause is not comprehensive. Many other cases could be included. But this overview is substantial enough to draw a few conclusions about the free exercise of religion in America. It should be clear that the trend in the Court is toward a much narrower protection of the right enumerated in the free exercise clause. Before *Smith*, free exercise claims were generally privileged in such a way that they often prevailed; since *Smith*, the authority of the government will prevail more often than not through appeal to generally applicable laws. As my colleague at TCU, Ron Flowers, has put it, "Whereas before *Smith*, religious freedom was the rule and government interference was the exception, now just the opposite was true."[34]

The one thing all these cases in free exercise have in common is the fact that each one involved a minority religious expression in America. The word "minority" is not meant pejoratively in this usage, as if to say "less important." In the

United States, the Constitution's First Amendment means to say that every religion and religious expression stands on equal ground and is equally important. Rather, it is used here to describe those religious expressions with small numbers of members compared to the majority expressions of religion in the United States, which are Protestantism and Catholicism. For the most part, members associated with religions other than Protestant or Catholic Christianity are the ones who have been forced to go to the courts to protect their right to the free exercise of religion in this country. Majority groups, particularly Protestant Christians, have rarely had to seek remedy for the violation of the free exercise of their religion, though this could change, especially if Christian expressions adopting serious engagement with science and philosophy and psychology begin to be viewed by the Court as more secular than religious, and therefore not protected.[35] Members of minority religions are more often than not among those whose rights to the free exercise of religion are most adversely affected by government action or by legislation passed by the majority.

The Supreme Court's position in the *Smith* decision has minimized the level of protection offered for minority religious expressions in America. By placing free exercise at the mercy of generally applicable laws and not allowing for individual exceptions, the Court has subjected minority religions to the majority understanding concerning law. Where the "controlling state interest" test allowed for checks and balances on a case-by-case basis, the new standard established by *Smith* does not. Though America is mostly past the days when "Blue Laws" could regulate what Americans can buy on Sunday and birth control laws reached into the bedroom, we still live in a culture where majority religious beliefs about appropriate practice might dictate to law in ways that seriously infringe upon the free exercise rights of minority religious expressions. Will Muslim employees be able to attend to their afternoon prayers during the workday, or their children be allowed to wear the type of clothing prescribed by their religious beliefs? Will the state be allowed to require autopsies when a family's religious belief understands them to be a mutilation that keeps the spirit of the loved one from being free, attaching it to a living member of the family?[36] Will individual Wiccans, Jains, Hindus, or members of Hare Krishna be able to enjoy the same rights to exercise their religions freely that Protestant or Catholic Christians enjoy in this culture? Minority religious expressions are now subjected to the legislative prowess of the majority culture in a way that is experienced quite differently than most Christians experience it.

Rather interesting is the fact that those justices on the Supreme Court (Chief Justice Rehnquist before his death, Justice Scalia, Justice Thomas, and Justice Kennedy) who are most inclined toward an accommodationist view of religion where the establishment clause is concerned, have been four of the justices who have most ardently defended narrowing the interpretation of the free exercise clause, making it less accommodating to religion. What does that mean? Rehnquist argued in *Thomas* for a narrower interpretation of both the establishment clause and the free exercise clause.[37] These interpretations work heavily in the favor of Christianity, the majority religious expression in America. Narrowing the interpretation of the establishment clause allows government to legislate aid to religion, so long as that aid is granted on a nonpreferential basis. This interpretation has opened the door to modern programs like Charitable Choice and Faith-Based Initiatives, where religious groups are beneficiaries of significant government funding. Since well over three-quarters of Americans are associated with Christianity, government aid predominantly ends up in the hands of those associated with Christian faith. A narrower interpretation of the establishment clause definitely favors Christianity.

On the other hand, narrowing interpretation of the free exercise clause rarely affects Christians but has a profound effect on the religious practices associated with minority religions. When thought through, the consistency represented in these positions makes much more sense, given the perspective of these four Christian accommodationist-oriented justices. Narrowing interpretation of both clauses benefits accommodation of Protestant and Catholic Christianity while significantly limiting accommodation granted to members of minority faiths. This kind of philosophy represents a sophisticated conservative vision designed to regain Christian ground lost to religious pluralism in this country. The subtlety of this approach to the religion clauses is near genius in its construction. The effects of this "narrowing" approach to the interpretation of both religion clauses will be especially friendly to the association of Christian faith and government, while it proves devastating to the free exercise claims of all minority religions in this country, the most religiously pluralistic nation in the world.

Finally, this brief discussion indicates the importance of the role played by Sandra Day O'Connor in cases related to the free exercise clause. Her analysis of cases involving the establishment clause has been equally discerning and impressive. She established a reputation on the Court for being a great friend to religious liberty and religious expression, whether found among the minority or majority religions in the United States. The record of Chief Justice John Roberts, before he joined the Court, seems to indicate a tendency to favor narrowing the interpretation of the establishment clause.[38] The confirmation of Samuel A. Alito Jr. to an appointment on the Supreme Court significantly changes the makeup of the Court in its approach to cases involving the religion clauses. Alito represents another of this particular kind of accommodationist voice on the Court. For example, during his fifteen years' service on the United States Court of Appeals for the Third Circuit, he argued for a narrowing of the establishment clause that would allow majority Christians to bring prayer into public school graduation ceremonies.[39] The appointments of these last few years have greatly increased the probability that narrower interpretations of particularly the establishment clause are likely to prevail in the foreseeable future. This trend will have implications both for Christians and for all other religious expressions in this country.

Persons of all religious faiths in the United States are often reflective about how they relate their religious understandings to the public life they experience in the United States. There are thinkers representing most every religion in America who write or publish in this area. For Christians who do this kind of thinking, this reflection has involved critical theological understanding. For that reason, before moving on to the remaining chapters in this book, it is appropriate to examine the question of how Christians have thought about the relationship between Christianity and public life from a broader theological perspective. But yet another question precedes this one.

Discussion of the free exercise clause should make it clear that the Founders expected that religion would assume public forms in this country. The one thing the free exercise clause does not do is push religion underground. Religion in America does not have to be merely private. It is public as well. Religious practices often gain public notice. For that reason, the second portion of the First Amendment guaranteed individuals the right to practice their religion, even though some religious practices might seem strange to the general public. The First Amendment, through the free exercise clause, guarantees religion the right to assume a public place in American life. In other words, though the institutions of church and state are separate, there is no constitutional separation between religious values and public life in America. Some religions may choose to separate their practices and beliefs from public life. That is their choice, and their religious belief may require it. But the Constitution does not require it. At this point, before turning to a Christian view of the public, it is helpful to reflect briefly on the way public life in America has developed.

THE NATURE OF PUBLIC LIFE
AND CHRISTIAN RESPONSE TO IT

The Development of Public Life

As we think about the nature of public life today, we must first reflect on a bit of history. At the time of the American Revolution and the formation of the Constitution, many of the traditional Christian groups were quite comfortable with the establishment of Christianity in various colonies. But two groups, pietism and rationalism, which represented much broader movements arising in the seventeenth century, were much less comfortable with it. Pietists, represented by Baptists like John Leland, and rationalists, represented by leaders of state like James Madison and Thomas Jefferson, found common purpose in their attempt to free the individual human mind from the bonds of tradition and outside authorities, whether church or state. Religious wars had dominated public life for centuries. Both rationalists and pietists were tired of them. Each, for their own purposes, wanted to create a public space free of the control of wrong-headed religious commitments. But they also wanted to protect the practice of religion in public ways. For pietists, no one, whether representing a state or a religious institution, should stand between an individual and God. For rationalists, each person possessed a capacity to use reason to find the truth, and the institutional interference found in organized religion often interfered with that capacity. If enabled to exercise itself freely in public debate, reason alone would lead to consensus in this country without coercion. Since rationalists designed the nature of our public life, with the consent and encouragement of the pietists, the tendency within American public life has been to move increasingly in two very different but simultaneous directions.[40]

On the one hand, individuality is not to be prized in public life. On the other hand, public life has increasingly served individual interests. What do I mean by these two seemingly contradictory statements? In the first place, the Enlightenment approach recognized that public life was for all persons. Of course, if we are honest with ourselves, we must also acknowledge that the Founders and other early Americans did not consider all persons as persons in quite the same way; this is especially evident in their treatment of slaves, Native Americans, and even women. The purpose of the national public debate about any issue of importance, for the rationalists, was to define policy through consensus building. This often meant that individual interests had to be set aside. Instead, individuals who enter public life are to work toward a consensus of beliefs that the largest number of people can accept as their own. In this way, public life in America has naturally emphasized "the lowest common denominator" approach to individuality. Only those aspects of individuality that the public as a majority can affirm belong in public life. Thus, those aspects of human existence that help to make individuals the persons they are, the things they take most seriously, the things that have helped to shape their moral values, especially beliefs rooted in religion, are safely left behind so far as the public is concerned.

During the 1800s, through at least half of the 1900s, American culture represented Protestant values in enough ways that most Protestants were not too worried about such things as "secularization." Protestants largely took public life for granted. As pluralism became more apparent, however, and as culture properly displaced Protestant values from their privileged status, Christians have been unclear about how to respond. In the meantime, the Enlightenment approach to public life, one that naturally bracketed out the importance of religious beliefs by emphasizing their role on the formation of individuals, has helped, over time, to create a United States described by phrases like a "culture of disbelief."[41] Of course, Christians have helped create this culture when they have abandoned efforts to relate their faith to the public life in which they live.

The Enlightenment created and perpetuated the myth of a public life controlled by a neutral and universal discourse, untouched by individual personal or religious biases.[42] Though many of the Founders possessed religious presuppositions and expected that religion would have a place in the public debates of the country,[43] their approach to public life increasingly relegated religion and its language to the private life. As pluralism has increased over these past five decades, the tendency to keep religion private increased as well. As a result, secular language has largely dominated public life in modern America. Richard Neuhaus coined the phrase "the naked public square" to describe this lack of meaningful religious language in the public life of the United States.[44] The public square is not as "naked" as Neuhaus claims it is, especially if, unlike Neuhaus but like Jeffrey Stout, one thinks of the public square not as a "place" but rather as a "sphere" that appears whenever "one addresses people as citizens."[45]

It is true that a good bit of the religious language that exists today in public life is either associated with the Religious Right and with very particular content, or it is without substantive content and associated with no clear religious tradition, other than the cultural and highly generalized religious expressions so common to American life. I'm speaking at this point of the language about God one finds on coins, or in the Pledge of Allegiance.[46] But significant religious language is still plentiful in public discussions between citizens, as citizens, in the United States. It is true, however, that Christian individuals and communities need to give careful and deliberate attention to both how they use such language and why or when they should use such language in public life.

So, to return to where this section started: on the one hand, individuality has not been prized in public life in America. On the other hand, public life has largely served the development of individual interests. As I have mentioned, both pietism and the Enlightenment valued the ability of individuals to stand before God without intermediaries. Rationalists, particularly, emphasized the Enlightenment presupposition that human beings were autonomous individuals bent on pursuing "their own self-interest." The liberalism found in the Enlightenment writings of Thomas Hobbes and John Locke emphasized the creation of a social contract, voluntarily entered into by these autonomous individuals, in order to "facilitate their personal security and private gain." The goal of public life was not to fulfill some particular vision of a common good; rather public life served to increase the ability of all individuals to "secure their private ends." Public life in America, therefore, often serves individual gain more than the common good. When this philosophical liberalism that emerged from the Enlightenment is connected to capitalism, the resulting culture places emphasis on individualism, wealth, and consumption. Public good, a notion of broader purposes with a strong sense of public virtue, is not high on the list of the priorities.[47]

This is reflected in many ways through the proliferation of special interest groups in American life today. There are not many places in our public life where the sense of the whole competes well with the desires of the particular parts. Legislators and senators seek special pork-barrel legislation for their own districts or states. If they don't, they won't be reelected. Lobbying groups, including Christian lobbying groups, lobby the public and Congress on behalf of their own special interests. And those in Congress, in their own self-interest, respond by pocketing the benefits offered by lobbyists to support special interests. Single-issue politics rule the day everywhere. They rule in government and in education. They rule the day in denominations, in congregations, even in seminaries. Is there a way to invigorate a greater sense of the whole? Is there a way to enable belief in the principle that securing a victory for the whole is more important than achieving a victory for any one part?

This was not always the case in American public life. In spite of their commitment to the Enlightenment value of individual autonomy, the Founders, including people like Washington, Jefferson, Franklin, and Madison, all had a fairly clear sense of public virtue. They spoke unashamedly of improving the commonwealth even if it meant significant self-sacrifice.[48] Over the past two centuries, however, this sense of public virtue increasingly has been lost. These days, as Robert Bellah and others lamented in *Habits of the Heart* and as Alasdair MacIntyre explored at some length in his book *After Virtue*, the language of the public is controlled by the language of "personal rights" and of respect for the "rights" of others. "Our rights talk," argues Mary Ann Glendon, "in its absoluteness, promotes unrealistic expectations, heightens social conflict, and inhibits dialogue that might lead to consensus, accommodation, or at least the discovery of common ground."[49] Public discourse today is devoid of language concerned with "virtues" and with "the good" that might conflict with the individual. This does not mean, as Jeffrey Stout has pointed out, that language concerned with rights and language concerned with virtues cannot coexist. It just means that they don't coexist much in today's public discourse.[50]

Further, there has been such a "confluence of capitalism and philosophic liberalism" that "personal success and consumption have become the primary ends of American life."[51] Even religion has become "a competitive item for sale."[52] As Carlyle Marney used to say so eloquently, Americans are addicted to "salvation by successing."[53] That statement might today be altered to include "salvation by consuming." The pursuit of private gain has become the great American sport in all walks of life. Of course, perhaps the greatest example is how the great American sport of baseball eclipses any notion of "team" by offering single players guaranteed contracts worth more than 250 million dollars; the team pales by comparison. Baseball mirrors the realities of American public life; a strong sense of the public community and its public virtues often gives way to the autonomy and worth of the individual.

Public Life from a Christian Perspective

A genuine Christian understanding of the word *public* must include a sense of the body of people and things that exist beyond concern for merely personal, private, or individual desires. For that reason, Christians, individually and corporately (as church), have had to be interested in developing, maintaining, critiquing, and supporting the public life of the nation. Each controversial issue of the past half century has pressed in its own way for American Christianity to modify its tendencies toward individualized Christian faith (where sin is viewed as an individual activity and redemption is understood as primarily personal) and to become more responsive to the claims of community (where sin is social as well as individual, and redemption inherently includes a concern for social justice). In very real ways, these controversial issues have forced American Christianity to wrestle with the meaning of the gospel in wider contexts, including what relevance the gospel might have for American public life.

Displaced in public life during the latter half of the twentieth century, Christians divided over what to do about it. On the one hand, some were excited about the ecumenical possibilities occasioned by a changing Catholicism and were tantalized by the prophetic opportunities brought about by their new displaced status in the culture. These moderate-to-liberal Christians supported pluralism and favored an active involvement of the church in the affairs of public life to secure justice for all. On the other hand, more conservative Christians mourned the loss of cultural unity caused by pluralism. They discouraged political activism on the part of the church but encouraged individual Christians to do their part to restore traditional values to their rightful place at the center of the culture. In response to modern pluralism and the new context presented by it, American Christians struggled to develop theological strategies for relating faith to public life. And they had to do it on the run, as suddenly they found themselves faced with one controversial issue after another. In both liberal and conservative camps, these theological strategies evolved over the past five decades quite differently than either had planned in the 1950s or 1960s.

But the most basic theological claim about public life for Christians has been that they must be concerned about it because God is concerned about it. A central Christian tenet throughout history is that God cares for more than just those who profess membership in the Christian community. Persons of other religions and of none, as much as Christians, constitute those who inhabit the public associated with God's love. Parker Palmer has described the public as inclusive of "all those people, those strangers, who share" the space in which we all live. The word "public" should contain a vision of our "interdependence upon one another." Christian or not, religious or not, all members of the public are related to one another, in fact, are interdependent. For Christians, the human unity found in public life is itself theological because "we are all children of the same creator God."

> Despite the fact that we are strangers to one another—and will stay strangers for the most part—we occupy a common space, share common resources, have common opportunities, and must somehow learn to live together. To acknowledge that one is a member of the public is to recognize that we are members of one another.[54]

Christians, in other words, cannot routinely accept, acquiesce to, or contribute to the kind of public life that ignores the stranger, the powerless, or concerns that speak to the common good of the whole community. As Parker Palmer puts it,

> At bottom, religion, like the public life, has to do with unity, with the overcoming of brokenness and fragmentation, with the reconciliation of that which has been estranged. . . . The God who cares about our private lives is concerned with our public lives as well. This is a God who calls us into rela-

tionship not only with family and friends, but with strangers scattered across the face of the earth, a God who says again and again, "We are all in this together."[55]

Martin Luther King stressed this notion when he used the story of the Good Samaritan to answer the question "Who is my neighbor?"

> "I do not know his name," says Jesus in essence. "He is anyone toward whom you are neighborly. He is anyone who lies in need at life's roadside. He is neither Jew nor Gentile; he is neither Russian nor American; he is neither Negro nor white. He is 'a certain man'—any needy man—on one of the numerous Jericho roads of life." . . . The Samaritan was good because he made concern for others the first law of his life. . . . In the final analysis, I must not ignore the wounded man on life's Jericho Road, because he is a part of me and I am a part of him. His agony diminishes me, and his salvation enlarges me.

King also emphasized that being a good neighbor is never limited to "the eternal accidents of race, religion, and nationality."[56] For Christians, loyalty is never given to the nation only, or first, but rather to God. Thus, when Christians think about the nature of public life, their thoughts also include the notion of a public beyond the public life of the nation itself. Christian commitment comes before patriotism. Therefore, the Christian's notion of public should always extend beyond merely the American public. In this way, Christians "are often concerned not only with the common good of the nation but also with the common good of all human beings."[57] Christian theology dictates that the Christian notion of public must be global as well as local or national. And the free exercise of religion in this country guarantees the ability of Christianity to offer this vision in public ways.

Given that an increasingly secularized public life in America has tended to relegate the importance of religion and religious values to the private sphere, and given that public life has tended to serve individual interests over community virtue or common good, what role might Christian faith play in revitalizing public life? Christian faith ought, at the very least, to critique the individualistic and consumeristic tendencies of American public life. Unfortunately, instead, much of today's public Christianity itself reflects these tendencies. A crucial question here is whether Christianity can itself become a "public religion." In Linell Cady's definition, "public religion refers to the way in which a specific religious tradition or community appropriates its distinctive resources to contribute to the upbuilding of the common life." She quotes Martin Marty, who has argued that "public religion" is more suitable than civil religion in a context as pluralistic as the United States is today:

> This term [public religion] from Benjamin Franklin fits the American pluralist pattern better than does Rousseau's civil religion because it took account of the particularities of the faiths that would not disappear or lightly merge to please other founders of the nation. These churches could,

however, contribute out of their separate resources to public virtue and the common weal.[58]

Most everyone who deals with the topic of Christianity and public life quotes Alexis de Tocqueville, the French traveler who visited America in 1830 to see firsthand what American democracy was all about. Tocqueville and a friend traveled the countryside, starting in New York, but traveling to Michigan, Wisconsin, and back to Boston, Philadelphia, and Baltimore, before heading west to Pittsburgh and Cincinnati, then turning south to Nashville, Memphis, and New Orleans, and finally back through the southeast to Washington and New York. While Tocqueville commented on the necessity of individualism within a democracy that stressed equality, he also clearly uttered his fear that it might, at some point, come to dominate the communitarian ideal. But more important than this prescient insight is Tocqueville's appreciation for the way that religion, particularly Christianity, has played an important role in forming the values associated with the public life of America. Religion is the "first of their political institutions; for if it does not give them the taste for freedom, it singularly facilitates their use of it." "I do not know if all Americans have faith in their religion," concludes Tocqueville, "—for who can read to the bottom of hearts?—but I am sure that they believe it necessary to the maintenance of republican institutions. . . . Despotism can do without faith, but freedom cannot."[59]

Robert Bellah and his associates have argued that Tocqueville recognized the "habits of the heart" for Americans in their family life, religious traditions, political involvement, and other public virtues. They found their strength, as Tocqueville understood them, in the American concern for equality. The habits of the heart for modern Americans, according to these authors, find their power in individualism. Americans have lost their connectedness, their sense of community.

> Perhaps the crucial change in American life has been that we have moved from the local life of the nineteenth century—in which economic and social relationships were visible and, however imperfectly, morally interpreted as parts of a larger common life—to a society vastly more interrelated and integrated economically, technically, and functionally. Yet this is a society in which the individual can only rarely and with difficulty understand himself and his activities as interrelated in morally meaningful ways with those of other, different Americans.[60]

In their follow-up book to *Habits of the Heart*, Bellah and his colleagues spoke of the way philosophical liberalism defined justice more in terms of individual rights than in terms of the common good. According to these liberals, they noted, "religious groups, with their strong visions of the good, tend to disrupt democratic politics by bringing into public life matters that should remain essentially private." But for Bellah and his associates, "organized religion can offer a genuine alternative to tendencies that we have argued are deeply destructive." The "public church" can help Americans learn to refocus their understanding of the "public" back on the common good, rather than on individual rights.[61]

Martin E. Marty, whose work is largely responsible for pointing sociologists, theologians, and historians to the importance of both public religion and public theology, coined the phrase "public church" in the early 1980s. His analysis of American religion caused him to recognize ways the Christian church in America had offered "a critical and constructive voice within public religion." As he put it, that "contribution has little to do with 'saving faith,'" but rather "focuses on 'ordering faith,' which helps constitute civil, social, and political life from a theological point of view." Based on his thorough study of American culture and religion, Marty concluded that America has "never . . . lacked the witness of the public church."

> The public church is a family of apostolic churches with Jesus Christ at the center, churches which are especially sensitive to the *res publica*, the public order that surrounds and includes people of faith. The public church is a communion of communions, each of which lives its life partly in response to its separate tradition and partly to the calls for a common Christian vocation. In America the constituency of this convergence of churches comes from elements within the old mainline, the newer evangelicalism, and Catholicism.[62]

The public church understands, says Marty, that God is "active beyond the story the Christian inherits." This leads the public church to an affirmation that "since God is present beyond the tribe, then the tribe engages in idolatry when its claims are in every way exclusive."[63] Therefore, the public church does not work dogmatically, but rather relates to the public life of the nation by engaging it, alongside the public religion of others representing different religious expressions, through its understanding of the "fitting response."

Those readers who are familiar with H. Richard Niebuhr will recognize the language of the "fitting response." Niebuhr believed ethics concerns itself with more than either the question of "right" or the question of the "good." Those who are concerned with the "right" ask themselves, "What is the law?" and then act. Those concerned with the "good" ask themselves, "What is the goal?" and then act. But Christians, said Niebuhr, should always ask first, "What is happening?" and then "What is the fitting response to what is happening?" This approach to ethics is based on the belief that any response to what is happening is, first, a response to God. In all their actions, Christians are accountable first to God. With this in mind, Christians must express their concern with anything pertaining to the "human moral life in general" (the public) by asking themselves what most responsibly constitutes a "fitting response" to God.

> Our action is responsible, it appears, when it is in response to action upon us in a continuing discourse or interaction among beings forming a continuing society. . . . When an Isaiah counsels his people, he does not remind them of the law they are required to obey nor yet of the goal toward which they are directed but calls to their attention the intentions of God present in hiddenness in the actions of Israel's enemies. . . . God to whom Jesus points is not the commander who gives laws but the doer of small and of

mighty deeds, the creator of sparrows and clother of lilies, the ultimate giver
of blindness and of sight, the ruler whose rule is hidden in the manifold
activities of plural agencies but is yet in a way visible to those who know
how to interpret the signs of the times.[64]

Some Christians have acted as if they know precisely "how to interpret the signs"
and, therefore, have acted exclusively or dogmatically. But Niebuhr stressed that
the "most pervasive form in which God acts as our Governor is in the human
experience of limitation, of finitude." This limitation, for the Christian, should
be, among other things, an "affirmation of the value of others . . . a life of pre-
liminary judgments . . . creative, sustaining, and liberating action in service to
others . . . knowledge of the fact that our action is never fully right."[65] The dark
side of religious experience in the world always emerges when it sets itself in the
place of God, as if it alone knows or speaks the truth.

The truth is, on any given issue, the public church will speak in a great variety of voices. In their study of the public church in America, Bellah and his colleagues pointed out that the churches are rarely unanimously pitted against the
secularists in any discussion related to public life. Often, denominations stand
against one another, or congregations within denominations stand on different
sides of the same issue. This is clear in the disagreements between significant
numbers of Protestant denominations and the Roman Catholics in America
about abortion, or the debates in the public church about homosexuality.[66] The
public church often stands against the public church on issues in public life in
this country. But "shared religious and political symbols allowed civil discussion
to continue." The fact that the public church does not speak with a single voice
"does not diminish its significance to our common life." It does, however, cause
us to recognize that the public church is not monolithic. When it joins the public conversation, it is not so overpowering that it should inspire fear in others.
Yet, even in disagreement with itself, it should be speaking on behalf of the "common good of all human beings and with our ultimate responsibility to a transcendent God."[67]

A number of different scholarly voices have made the same kinds of arguments. Michael Perry cites the strength of religious faith in general by saying it
"is best understood as trust in the ultimate meaningfulness of life—that is, the
ultimate meaningfulness of the world and of one's own life, one's own being, as
part of and related to, as embedded in, the world."[68] Parker Palmer stresses that
when Christians relate their faith to the public life of the nation, they help "to
infuse life with meaning, or to articulate the meaning with which life is already
ripe." As they do that, they "will help to revitalize our public realm."[69] Stephen
Carter emphasizes the role of religious groups as mediators "between the citizen
and the apparatus of government, providing an independent moral voice." In this
role, "they can serve as the sources of moral understanding without which any
majoritarian system can deteriorate into simple tyranny."[70]

In general, I agree with Parker Palmer's assertion that public life and politics are not the same thing.[71] Public life is much more than politics. What is at issue in public life is what it means to be fully human. Politics usually turns on the activities of government. However, if Christians are truly concerned with public life, they must also be concerned with politics. Political activity in this country gravely affects the quality of the nation's public life, the quality of what it means to be fully human. If Christians act publicly to further their concerns about public life, they must also be willing to take political actions when necessary. So, ultimately, there is a definite relationship between public life and politics. A relationship between Christian faith and public life, therefore, also implies a relationship between Christian faith and politics in America. How has the fullness of these relationships been mistreated? How have they been healthfully cultivated and lived out? How are these relationships to be understood in the context of today's postmodern world? Those topics are taken up in the next five chapters.

PART II
PUBLIC LIFE AND FAITH

Chapter 3

Iconic Faith

INTRODUCTION

When God-language is used by presidents, when Bibles are used in courtrooms, or when God is trusted on coins, the meanings are far different from understandings that operate in Christian communities. These kinds of uses of religious language form an iconic context that often affects how Christians understand the relationship between Christian faith and public life in America. We don't think much about this aspect of public life. We are so used to it that we take it for granted. But Christians must become more sophisticated in dealing with the iconic context surrounding the use of religious language in American public life.

What do I mean by the term *iconic*? Another word for *icon* is *image*. *Mirriam-Webster's Online Dictionary* reminds the reader that *icon* is a word very familiar to today's computer users, a "graphic symbol on a computer display screen that suggests the purpose of an available function." In the same way, icons operate within a culture as words, images, or sometimes "graphic symbols" pointing to particular meanings. Usually, icons are pictures or some other tangible item or items that people venerate for having some sacred significance. Sometimes, as pointed out by *Mirriam-Webster*, icons can be "objects of uncritical devotion" as in the sense of the word *idol*.[1]

What does this iconic context accomplish for Americans? First, Christians should understand that the iconic nature of America's public life helps us to make sense of who we are when we think of ourselves as Americans. Sociologists of religion have often explained that "the very nature of our thinking and our social behavior takes place in terms of symbolic boundaries." These symbolic boundaries enable us to "make sense of our worlds." Therefore, they are "fundamental to all of social life."[2] I do not think I do an injustice to this kind of description when I suggest that the lines of these symbolic boundaries are often drawn into our consciousness by the public use of icons.

The fact that there is a relationship between religion and cultural systems was clearly drawn by Clifford Geertz in his well-known essay "Religion as a Cultural System." For Geertz, every cultural system has its inherent religious dimension. Geertz defines *culture* as "an historically transmitted pattern of meanings embodied in symbols, a system of inherited conceptions expressed in symbolic forms by means of which [humans] communicate, perpetuate, and develop their knowledge about and attitudes toward life." And religion, wrote Geertz, is "(1) a system of symbols which acts to (2) establish powerful, pervasive, and long-lasting moods and motivations in [human beings] by (3) formulating conceptions of a general order of existence and (4) clothing these conceptions with such an aura of factuality that (5) the moods and motivations seem uniquely realistic." Cultural symbols, therefore, often operate religiously, as symbols that help citizens of the culture to understand reality in distinct ways, ways that carry with them "such an aura of factuality" that they arouse the belief among citizens that the symbols depict reality as it really is.[3]

In the late 1960s, Ninian Smart examined "religion and the human experience" and concluded that all religion contains at least six dimensions that make it "religion." These six dimensions include ritual, myth, doctrine, ethics, social institutions or communities, and experience.[4] The iconic dimensions of American culture, those that often challenge Christian commitments and understanding if uncritically affirmed and accepted within Christian communities, operate in all six of these dimensions of religious experience. The meanings portrayed in these six dimensions of iconic cultural faith often compete with the meanings contained within Christian faith in these six dimensions of religious understanding.

The iconic structure of our social world is necessary. Though it has tragically excluded groups over the years for one reason or another, it mostly serves to bring disparate people together. Christians, as citizens, sing the national anthem at ball games, make their trips to Washington, D.C., pledge allegiance to the flag, and celebrate national holidays, grateful for the heritage of freedom enjoyed in our contemporary national life. Yet these experiences of benign, even beneficial, iconic participation turn into iconic *confusion* when Christians fail to distinguish the iconic symbols used in public life from the symbolism and meaning associated with Christian faith.

Iconic confusion is represented in two particular circumstances: (1) where cultural icons are located and affirmed in the sacred spaces of Christian contexts; and (2) where Christians assume the use of Christian images or icons in public life witnesses to Christian faith when, in fact, these icons are created and used for purposes related explicitly to public life, not to Christianity.

American public life is filled with visual and literary symbols drawn from Jewish and Christian tradition. It has been this way from the very beginning of America's history. When early Americans were searching for a national symbol to define the new nation, Benjamin Franklin recommended the image of Moses parting the Red Sea and Thomas Jefferson volunteered the image of the children of Israel wandering in the wilderness. In 1856, Benson Lossing sketched the Great Seal proposed by Franklin, showing the children of Israel crossing the Red Sea, with the motto of the American Revolution around the outside.[5] Some early descriptions of George Washington as an American Moses are found in many colonial sermons and political documents.[6] Puritan preacher Cotton Mather was especially fond of the comparison. Much of the American myth associated with Washington depicts him as a pious Christian and, of course, a Christian who could never tell a lie.

The Founders settled on other images for the Great Seal, but these images continued to underscore the religious understanding of an America that somehow would serve divine purposes in the world. Look particularly at the two symbols pictured on the back of the dollar bill that represent the front and back of the Great Seal of the United States: On the right side of the bill is an eagle with the olive branch (for peace) and thirteen arrows (representing willingness to fight) with the words "E Pluribus Unum"—"out of many, one." On the other side is the image of the incomplete pyramid (all other considerations aside, this may be a particularly good image for a government project). At the top of the pyramid is the image of the eye of God. Above it all is a Latin motto: "Annuit Coeptis," meaning "God has favored our undertakings," a roundabout way of saying, "God Bless America." On the bottom runs another Latin phrase, "Novus Ordo Seclorum," meaning "A New Order for the Ages." The Great Seal, and these mottoes, seem to signify the spiritual meaning of America as a nation chosen by God to fulfill divine purposes.[7] And, of course, all American money, either coin or bill, carries the phrase "In God We Trust," a motto for the nation designated by a joint resolution of Congress in 1956.

Thanksgiving Day is a great holiday not of the Christian faith but rather a celebration representing this "iconic context." Its origins are found in the Thanksgiving fast days declared by various U.S. presidents back to colonial times. The day reached holiday status in 1863 when Lincoln issued a declaration. Congress confirmed the holiday in 1941. Of the many holidays of the ritualistic calendar belonging to "iconic faith," it is the one that finds a ready celebration in Christian churches. In some churches, July 4 is celebrated nearly as fervently. In addition, of course, the Christian holidays of Christmas and Easter have also become a part of our iconic context, symbolized more through

Santa Claus and the Easter Bunny than through recognition of either the birth
or resurrection of Christ.

Other symbols in American public life are shared with Christianity and point
to this belief in a sacred destiny for the life of the nation. Allusions to God appear
regularly in our patriotic songs. The second verse of our national anthem, "The
Star-Spangled Banner," says, "Blest with victory and peace, may the heaven res-
cued land praise the Power that hath made and preserved us a nation. Then conquer we must, when our cause it is just; and this be our motto: In God is our
trust." Remember the words to "America": "America, America, God shed his
Grace on thee." Or consider the "Battle Hymn of the Republic," a crusading
hymn for the North during the Civil War: "Glory, glory, hallelujah; Glory, glory,
hallelujah; Glory, glory, hallelujah; Our God is marching on!" Or consider the
last verse of "My Country, 'Tis of Thee," which begins "Our fathers' God, to
Thee, Author of liberty, to Thee we sing."

Every single presidential inaugural address—except George Washington's sec-
ond inaugural, which was a very short 135 words—has made some reference to
divine blessing or providence or God's hand in America's life. Historically, many
American Christians have heard these as Christian references. But are these truly
Christian references? When one examines the rhetoric of President George W.
Bush, as was also true with President Reagan, one would likely find that his frequent use of religious rhetoric often assumes that America is a Christian nation.
David Domke and Kevin Coe, writing for the Internet journal *Sightings*, recently
documented that President Bush mentioned God twenty-four times in his combined first-term inaugural and State of the Union addresses. In his second inaugural address and first State of the Union address of his second term, both in
2005, he added another eleven mentions of God. Currently, Bush is averaging
5.8 references per major presidential address. Only Ronald Reagan, among presidents, even comes close (at 5.3 references). But, perhaps even more interesting,
Domke and Coe also noted a difference in the way President Bush uses God-talk.

> Presidents since Roosevelt have commonly spoken as petititioners to God,
> seeking blessing, favor, and guidance. The current president has adopted a
> position approaching that of a prophet, issuing declarations of divine desires
> for the nation and world. Among modern presidents, only Reagan has spo-
> ken in a similar manner—and he did so far less frequently than has Bush.[8]

In his first inaugural, President Bush did extend his references to include mention of synagogues and mosques. The two prayers on either side of his inaugural,
however, were laced with explicitly Christian references. Franklin Graham, Billy's
son, actually offered his prayer of invocation to Jesus: "May this be the beginning
of a new dawn for America, as we humble ourselves before you and acknowledge
you alone as our Lord, our Savior and our Redeemer." Reverend Kirbyjon Cald-
well offered a benediction that closed with "We respectfully submit this humble
prayer in the name that's above all other names, Jesus, the Christ. Let all who
agree say 'Amen.'" By the time of the second inaugural in 2005, Reverend Cald-

well had softened his language and closed his benediction at the inaugural with the words "Respecting persons of all faiths, I humbly submit this prayer in the name of Jesus Christ, Amen." Public references to Jesus have been a trait associated with several members of this administration, including George Bush. President George W. Bush, at the time Governor Bush, even declared a "Jesus Day" in Texas on June 10, 2000. Former Attorney General John Ashcroft, speaking before the Christian Coalition in 1999, told his audience, "And because we have understood that our source is eternal, America has been different. We have no king but Jesus."[9]

What do Christian allusions by politicians or government officials in our public life really mean? Do they mean America is truly a Christian nation and that dedication to Christ and to Christianity naturally and meaningfully pervades our public life? This is, of course, not the case. Rather, even though these symbols are often derived from the Christian tradition, generally, in their meaning and in their use, they are not Christian. In most instances, the use of these symbols does not even represent a nominal Christianity. Even references to God in our early national history, such as in the Declaration of Independence and in our national mottoes, were not necessarily designed to be explicitly Christian in meaning. They were not references to a God who is related to Jesus Christ in order to redeem a wayward humanity. Rather, these symbols did generally convey a kind of deistic belief in the primacy of God over all human institutions and a widespread confidence among Americans that America stood for moral purposes in the world.

The immediate source for shaping this doctrine is the history of America or certain events of that history that have been judged revelatory. Religious images that depict God's deliverance of God's people, or God's demands upon the chosen people, are among images that have been applied to events in America's history. The Bible provides many of the images for these interpretations, but the events themselves come out of the American experience. Conrad Cherry emphasizes "two chief revelatory events" in American history: the Revolutionary War and the Civil War.

> The first was a moment when God delivered the colonies from Pharoah Britain and the "evils" of the Old World, revealed the purposes of the nation, and adopted the Young Republic as an example and instrument of freedom and republican government for the rest of the world. The Civil War was the nation's first real "time of testing" when God tried the permanence of the Union or, in some interpretations, brought judgment upon his wayward people. Documents like the Declaration of Independence and the Gettysburg Address function as scriptures that interpret these events and hence preserve the traditions of the civil religion.[10]

To Cherry's two revelatory events, I would add two others. The conclusion of the Cold War of the late twentieth century assured Americans that they were God's protection against atheistic communism in a world prone to revolution. Success in that effort has now enabled America, and the second President Bush, to believe more fervently in the myth that America, as the most powerful nation on earth, will be able to bring liberty and freedom to all nations in the world. This was a theme, or, perhaps more accurately, a goal, stressed by President Bush in his second inaugural address in 2005.[11]

Second, the events of September 11, 2001, have also proved revelatory for Americans. For many, it proved how vulnerable America and America's values were to attack by those who oppose them. Government response has often been similar to that expressed by William Bennett approaching the first anniversary of 9/11. Americans "must be willing to say that there are moral absolutes" and to stand firm in affirming them.[12] The resulting war on terrorism is the new Cold War, only it is a hot war, and, in that sense, much more dangerous. Americans are much more confident, after September 11, that God stands with America against the terrorism present in the world. In the aftermath of that horrific day, President Bush "pledged to pursue and destroy not just al Qaeda, but terrorism; not just terror, but evil" and "informed the world there could be no neutrality in the coming struggle."[13] This kind of division of the world into good and evil spheres, with America clearly and unambiguously standing on the side of good, is quite different than the posture assumed by the Founders in the eighteenth century, who hoped America would serve the good but never automatically assumed that the nation always did.

As time has passed in American history, politician and citizen alike have elaborated on doctrines growing out of these revelatory experiences and concluded that standing under God, an early affirmation of the Founders rooted in their recognition that America stood under the judgment of God, now routinely implies an inherent morality, a "chosen-ness," a "special" standing. This doctrinal understanding has often found expression in belief in a God especially identified with American institutions. Along the way, Americans began to emphasize a "God" who is especially interested in the success of the American experiment, one who makes no particular demands upon it other than that it continue to succeed and spread that success to the corners of the globe. As Sidney E. Mead has put it, "God, like Alice's Cheshire Cat, has sometimes threatened gradually to disappear altogether or, at most, to remain only as a disembodied and sentimental smile."[14] When iconic faith hardens into an explicit doctrinal confidence that God stands with America, everywhere and always, it moves more into the style of a priestly faith that can be especially threatening to the heart of Christian commitment and belief. These kinds of developments will be discussed in the next chapter.

The symbols of iconic faith, often finding their source in Christian tradition and widely used in America's public life, therefore always serve a practical rather than an explicitly theological purpose. Though the symbols may be borrowed from Christian tradition, the faith that utilizes them does not issue from Christian commitment. The primary objective of iconic faith is to serve the nation, not to serve God. Therefore, iconic faith celebrates the ideals of America, often as if those ideals were constantly realized. America's use of God-language, respect for icons like the Ten Commandments or various monuments in Washington, D.C., love of patriotic songs, and expression of high confidence associated with flying flags and pledging allegiance—all these things celebrate America and the heritage of liberty associated with things American. They are not meant to celebrate God or to underscore America's need to worship a God who cares about all the people of the world, a God who may, in fact, judge rather harshly some of the tactics associated with America's war on terror. Iconic faith serves a particular purpose, and that purpose is not primarily Christian.

Iconic faith is certain of the goodness of America. The role of leaders is to extol that goodness, not question it. The symbols associated with iconic faith are designed to bring the community together as well as to define its limits. The iconic, through its expressions or depictions, often signifies from the cultural perspective who is in and who is out as full members of the culture. Therefore, iconic faith is resistant to change and to the development of new understandings of truth. It prefers the status quo. When change does come that broadens a sense of what community truly means, as through civil rights or women's rights or a battle for gay rights, it does not come easily.

Iconic faith affirms pluralism, but that affirmation has its limits. Generally, those who affirm the public symbols that define iconic faith, and represent them well, are embraced. But it is not quite this simple. There is little doubt that African Americans, for example, represented American values as solidly as other groups in the twentieth century. They put on military uniforms and fought for their country. They sang patriotic hymns just as well as, or perhaps better than, other groups of people. They pledged their allegiance to the flag and expressed as well as most Americans their beliefs in both God and nation. But cultural norms, aided by iconic faith, still managed to separate them in significant ways. Thus, African Americans have long had a hate-love relationship to the iconic. Leaders like Martin Luther King, for example, have worked to transform the pragmatic and public understandings of it by prophetically pushing the culture to live up to the ideals contained within it, while, for the most part, cultural use of iconic language insisted they stay in their place.

Far more understandable, however, is the fact that those who do not embrace certain important iconic symbols often have difficulty garnering public acceptance and respect. Some groups, for religious purposes, voluntarily choose to maintain their distance from icons within the civil realm. Seventh-day Adventists and Jehovah's Witnesses, for example, have spent considerable time and money defending their faith from the intrusions of the iconic. Because this is the case, members of these groups, who are most often solidly patriotic individuals and good American citizens in their own right, have frequently been misunderstood by those who believe symbols like the flag, the Pledge of Allegiance, or even cultural protections of Sunday as Sabbath, are sacrosanct. Such transgressions against the iconic symbol structures of public life belong, in the view of iconic faith, in the category of sin. When one refuses to salute the flag, one sins. On a sliding scale of sins, it is most likely a venial sin. It would not necessarily deny the offender access to sanctifying grace that enabled the sinner to be counted among American citizens. Such a sin can, within our culture, be forgiven if one makes the clear case that personal religious belief hinders such an activity. While failure to salute the flag might arguably, among adherents of iconic faith in America, be considered a venial sin, the attempt to burn the flag is, no doubt, a mortal sin. There is no greater transgression, in the view of iconic faith, than this one. One of the features of iconic faith, then, is the ethical prescription to respect the flag and other icons important to American life.

In sum, iconic faith is always bound up with cultural norms and expectations. Over time, cultural norms and expectations change. Adjustments in iconic faith then become necessary as well. Theoretically, at least, it is now possible for an African American or a woman to become president. Iconic faith of a century ago would not have entertained either notion. But popular expressions of iconic faith in America today would likely still exclude the possibility that a Buddhist, an atheist, or a homosexual could sit at the helm of American government. This does not mean, however, that this will always be the case. Like the twentieth century, the twenty-first century will bring changes that affect the character of the ethical expectations and cultural norms associated with iconic faith in America.

Like all religious faith, iconic faith values the importance of both piety and personal experience. The spirituality of contemporary iconic faith is exhibited in public and private acts of piety that celebrate, or reverently recognize, American values. American public life possesses many tangible items that generate a notion of reverence that becomes attached to America's self-understanding as a nation and enables Americans to engage in forms of spirituality associated primarily with iconic faith. Many of these items are not necessarily Christian in their religiosity, but they carry a strong sense of sacred meaning nonetheless. Americans revere the eternal flame at Kennedy's grave, the Washington monument, the Lincoln and Jefferson memorials, the shrine of our major documents at the National Archives, and the Vietnam War Memorial. All of these sites in the nation's capital are icons of American civil religion that generate reverence and perhaps even a sense of awe among those who visit them. Americans also participate in iconic spirituality when they engage in such simple activities as standing at baseball games, removing their hats, and placing hand over heart to sing or listen to "The Star-Spangled Banner." Many Americans also hoist American flags on makeshift poles mounted on or near their homes. Some participate in party politics. Many take seriously their responsibilities to vote for the candidates of their choice. Others join the National Guard or some branch of the armed services. Patriotic devotion to country has, of course, demanded ultimate sacrifices from those who have died on battlefields from Normandy to Vietnam to Afghanistan and Iraq.

Social institutions also serve religious expressions. Iconic faith is no exception. Historically, public schools have exposed children to some level of familiarity with America's mission in the world and the multitude of symbols that convey its special meaning. Public schools convey much of the content of iconic faith by teaching students about the importance of patriotism, the history of American accomplishment, and the details of myths associated with it. They engage children in rituals and practices that help them understand their relationship to the country. Texas public schools, for example, are required by the state legislature to start each day with the Pledge of Allegiance. Children in most states first learn to sing patriotic hymns in public school music classes. In addition, public schools teach children the meaning of the holidays associated with American culture and inculcate within them the early habit of observing them. As Sidney Mead put it, when Americans separated church and state, public schools developed and assumed the role traditionally filled by churches, to educate citizens and "to make possible and to guarantee the dissemination and inculcation among the embryo citizens of the beliefs essential to the existence and well-being of the democratic society."[15]

Churches are another social institution that often serve iconic faith. When churches serve iconic faith, they reflect, promote, and act as repositories for the symbolic boundaries of American culture. They display the American flag in their sanctuaries and celebrate national events and holidays in their worship services. As Conrad Cherry has described it,

> to a great extent the churches of this land came to abide by the suggestion of the Founding Fathers that the different religious groups should not only exist for the sake of their own beliefs and practices, but should also assume responsibility for maintenance of the public order, the dissemination of the essential religious beliefs . . . and the promotion of the public welfare. The presence of the American flag in the churches, the celebration of national events by religious groups, the frequent mixing of biblical and "sacred" American history in sermons are some of the obvious signs that national religion has often found a home in the American churches.[16]

When Christian churches serve the iconic faith, they occasionally work at cross-purposes with Christian understandings of the work of churches. Churches, in Christian understanding, serve the purposes of the gospel, not those of any nation. When cultural icons are found in the sacred spaces of Christian churches, a kind of iconic confusion inevitably results. For example, displaying the American flag in sanctuaries of worship tends, symbolically, to contradict Christian belief in both the universal nature of the church and the universality of God's care and concern.

To clarify some distinctions between iconic expressions and Christian faith, it is helpful to look at the way three tangible iconic expressions drawn from the Christian tradition operate in American public life. These kinds of expressions also contribute to forms of iconic confusion found among Christians. We can get a better sense of the role of these expressions by briefly examining the use of the Bible, prayer in public places, and the symbol "God" in the Pledge of Allegiance.

THE BIBLE

In trying to explain why so many Americans have resisted or ignored the advent of biblical criticism, Martin E. Marty pointed out that Americans have a rather superstitious, quasi-religious reverence for the Bible that has little to do with any real knowledge of its contents. Americans resist biblical criticism not because they are familiar with the Bible's content but rather because they revere it as a supernatural book with which no one should be allowed to tamper. In American public life, the Bible is revered as icon, as object, not as source for Christian theology.[17]

In 1980, Marty offered statistics to back up his argument.[18] I've updated those statistics by using more recent Gallup polls: 34 percent of Americans believe the Bible should be taken literally, word for word, as the actual word of God, and 48 percent believe it should be understood, at the very least, as the inspired word of God. This means that, combined, 82 percent of the American people believe that either the Bible should be taken literally or is at least the inspired word of God.[19] Teenagers in America have similar views: 39 percent believe the Bible is the actual word of God to be taken literally, while 46 percent see the Bible as the inspired word of God (a combined total of 85 percent).[20] According to a 2004 ABC News poll, 61 percent of Americans understand the creation story of the Bible found in Genesis to be "literally true."[21] Polls show that 93 percent of all Americans own a Bible.[22]

While a large percentage of the American public, nearly every home, owns a Bible, and while more than four out of every five Americans view the Bible at least as inspired, and 65 percent of Americans believe the Bible "answers all or most of the basic questions of life," only 16 percent of Americans claim to read the Bible at least once daily. Twenty-one percent of Americans say they read the Bible weekly, 12 percent claim monthly reading, 10 percent say they read it less than monthly, and 41 percent say they rarely or never read the Bible. These statistics mean that while 93 percent of Americans own Bibles, 51 percent of them read it less than monthly or not at all. According to Gallup, the frequency of Bible reading among Americans has been steadily declining over the past decade.[23] As Walter A. Elwell put it shortly after the 1980 Gallup poll appeared, "It is apparently one thing to *believe* that the Bible is God's word and quite another to read it."[24]

As Marty pointed out in his essay, it would seem only natural that "the same Gallup poll that showed Americans believing the Bible to be beyond criticism, without error, would also find it being used and find it informing life." When Marty examined the polls, however, he found that this was not the case. Americans, in general, are not very familiar with the content of the Bible.[25] Not much has changed since 1980, when Marty wrote his essay. When asked in more recent Gallup polls to name the first book of the Bible, only 49 percent of the public came up with the book of Genesis. Sixty-five percent did not know the content of John 3:16. Sixty-five percent did not know who ruled Jerusalem at the time of Jesus. Only 40 percent could name the Trinity. Worse, only 34 percent of Americans knew who delivered the Sermon on the Mount. These statistics indicate clearly that the American public reveres the Bible much more than reads it.[26]

The Bible of iconic faith is rarely read. It simply is. It is everywhere and nowhere: "everywhere" in its presence, but "nowhere" in its content. Thanks to George Washington, who rarely mentioned the Bible in his lifetime of prolific writing, it maintains a prominent place in most political inaugurations. Washington brought along his Masonic Bible to his first inauguration and, after the oath was administered, he reverently kissed it.[27] The first President Bush used Washington's Masonic Bible for his inauguration. President George W. Bush had planned to use it but used a family copy instead. The content of the Bible plays no role in inaugurations or in "taking the oath of office." Rather, the Bible is an object that conveys seriousness of purpose and intent, and the candidate's pledge to speak truthfully.

For similar reasons, the Bible finds a home among most of America's voluntary organizations as well. Even though they are at opposite ends of the ideological spectrum, both the Ku Klux Klan and the Red Cross share the same basic ceremonial ritual to assure transition of leadership.[28] Many of America's courtrooms still use the Bible to swear in witnesses, along with the pledge to speak truthfully, "so help me God." Yet, again, where the Bible is used, it is used as an object representing truth, without any genuine concern for specific content of the book as representative of the revelation of God to human beings.

In 2004, District Judge James M. Honeycutt of North Carolina, a devout Southern Baptist, decided to remove references to God from his courtroom because, given America's pluralism, and the number of non-Christians who appear as witnesses in cases, he believed such explicit references to God were inappropriate for some witnesses. "I believe," Honeycutt wrote, "that the burden should not be on those individuals to speak up and request an oath that does not mention God or use the Christian Bible." The Supreme Court in North Carolina ruled that Honeycutt must return to the traditional rituals associated with swearing in witnesses required by state law, unless witnesses themselves asked for exceptions.[29]

In America, politics and political leaders like to use the Bible for their own purposes. The year 1983 stands as a kind of highpoint for the iconic use of the Bible. President Reagan and Congress proclaimed that year "The Year of the Bible." In announcing the decision during his speech to the National Association of Religious Broadcasters, President Reagan stated that the Bible "has great meaning for each of us and for our nation." But the year of the Bible actually celebrated the iconic use of the Bible, not the Christian use of it.[30]

The iconic Bible always subordinates biblical values to whatever American political thought might need at the moment. It takes phrases from the Bible that Christianity has applied to the church and applies them to the American nation, phrases like "a city upon a hill," "the new Israel," "a light to the nations," the "servant of the Lord," and "the chosen people." Speaking on the first anniversary of 9/11, President Bush closed his address to the nation from Ellis Island with the following words:

> Tomorrow is September the 12th. A milestone is passed, and a mission goes on. Be confident. Our country is strong. And our cause is even larger than our country. Ours is the cause of human dignity; freedom guided by

conscience and guarded by peace. This ideal of America is the hope of all mankind. That hope drew millions to this harbor. That hope still lights our way. And the light shines in the darkness. And the darkness will not overcome it. May God bless America.[31]

The last two sentences, prior to the benediction, are a direct quote from John 1:5, without any quotation marks or note or reference to that fact. That passage in the Bible describes the Word of God, in whom "was life, and the life was the light of all people" (John 1:4). But here Bush lifts the words of John 1:5 out of context and uses them to refer to America and its role in the world. They have been filled with new, and very different, content. When politicians address the content of this iconic Bible in the public arena, they are not primarily interested in espousing Christian themes. Rather, passages from the Bible serve as convenient proof-texts for expressing what one already believes to be true. The Bible is transformed into a supporting text for a political agenda.

Perhaps one of the more graphic examples of this form of eisegesis is found in President Reagan's early 1985 comments before 250 business and trade representatives who had been invited to the White House, and later the same day before 4,000 people at the National Religious Broadcasters annual convention. Reagan told his listeners that the Bible is "on our side" in advocating increases in the military budget. To make his point, Reagan provided those in attendance with a paraphrase of Luke 14:31–32, a passage addressing the costs of Christian discipleship. "Jesus, in talking with his disciples," said Reagan, "spoke about a king who might be contemplating going to war against another king with his 10,000 men. But he sits down and counsels how good he's going to do against the other fellow's 20,000 and then says he may have to send a delegation to talk peace terms." Reagan then commented: "Well, I don't think we ever want to be in a position of only being half as strong and having to send a delegation [under those circumstances] to negotiate . . . peace terms with the Soviet Union."[32] Like the previous example from President Bush, this is a classic example of quoting an iconic Bible for personal political purposes in a way that ignores Christian content altogether.

In 1963, the Supreme Court ruled in *Abington Township School District v. Schempp* that devotional reading of the Bible in public schools was unconstitutional. It is interesting that the attorneys representing the states, in this case Pennsylvania and Maryland, argued that requiring Bible readings in all public schools had "secular purposes," including "the promotion of moral values, the contradiction to the materialistic trends of our times, the perpetuation of our institutions and the teaching of literature." The Supreme Court, however, concluded that the use of the Bible was both sectarian and religious, even when read, as fitting its iconic status, without any form of interpretation or comment. And the Court noted that statutes requiring schools to open with morning prayers and Bible reading were "of quite recent origin."[33] In 1900, only Massachusetts required it. Within the next two decades, only eleven other states joined Massachusetts.[34] Though most of the public in America expressed the belief, after *Abington*, that the Bible belonged in public schools, polls again showed that a strong majority of American school districts at the time of the case did not read the Bible, devotionally or otherwise.[35]

For the Christian community, the Bible is not an iconic book. It is not merely a symbol of truthfulness or seriousness. Nor is it a book to be used for purely political purposes. Before it is anything else, the Bible is a record of the history of God's relationship with creation, of God's concern for human redemption and how God acts to bring it about. For this reason, the Bible speaks primarily to the community of faith, not only about the importance of redemption but also about the meaning of faithfulness. The Bible, because it addresses relationships—between human beings and God, and between human beings as individuals and communities—is a book that contains implications for the political sphere. But Mark Noll's word of caution is appropriate here:

> The key to using the Bible fruitfully for politics is to remember its character, to recall that it speaks first to men and women in their relationship with God. But then it is appropriate to go further and affirm that although the Bible speaks comprehensively to human beings in their relationships with each other, its general message about God and the human condition is an orienting message. It does not offer a detailed blueprint for action today, but it does offer a framework for a plan of action.[36]

Further, the Christian community historically recognizes (even though some American Christians have had difficulty recognizing the recognition) that the Bible is not any one nation's book. Nor does it address any particular nation's people as its primary constituency. The Bible reveals no special covenant between God and America. Growing out of the Jewish and Christian traditions, the Bible speaks primarily to the divine covenants God has made with those who make up these universal communities of faith, communities that extend well beyond the politics of any one nation. When the nation uses the Bible in iconic fashion, the nation honors the book as a symbol instead of taking the book seriously for its content. In this kind of context, politicians, and even ministers and Christian social activists, can easily slip into the political misuse of the Bible's content to suit their own purposes.

PRAYER IN THE PUBLIC SCHOOLS

Again, it is best to begin by looking at a few statistics related to prayer in America. Seventy-eight percent of Americans pray at least once a week, and 57 percent pray at least once a day. Thirty-two percent of Americans report having mystical prayer experiences. Even more surprisingly, 20 percent of atheists also report "praying" daily. What do these statistics prove? Well, for one thing, if what Americans report to be true is true, as Kenneth Woodward of *Newsweek* observed, there is more praying than there is sex going on in our country.[37] Of course, I suppose one has to admit that there may be a good deal of praying for sex going on as well.

Gallup asked people, in 1962, after the *Engel v. Vitale* court case, if they knew whether their local public schools used prayers and Bible readings. Only 30 percent replied that they knew that these kinds of observances took place. Forty-five percent said they did not know. But when asked whether they approved of "religious observances in public schools," 79 percent of those asked said yes. When Senator Strom Thurmond submitted, yet again, a proposal to allow voluntary prayer, or a "moment of silence," in the schools in 1983, Gallup showed that 67 percent of Americans favored the proposed constitutional amendment. In general, support for voluntary prayer in the public schools and the latest polls indicate that approximately 78 percent of Americans approve of offering non-denominational prayers at public school ceremonies, like graduations.

When *Jager v. Douglas School District* (1989) was appealed to the Supreme Court, the Court refused to hear the case. This action meant the lower court's ruling stood, declaring pregame prayers at high school football games to be unconstitutional. A few years later, in *Lee v. Weisman* (1992), the Court ruled as unconstitutional the practice of prayers led by clergy at public school graduation ceremonies. While the public widely believed (74 percent) that prayers should be part of these public school graduations, the majority (55 percent) was opposed to prayer "if it offends a large percentage of parents." In *Santa Fe Independent School District v. Doe* (2000), the Court ruled that even students could not lead prayers at public school functions.[38]

Representative Al Edwards, a Democrat from Houston and one of the authors of a bill on silent prayer in the Texas House, claimed that "since we took prayer out of the schools, we have seen a number of bad things happen."[39] This kind of approach is also the premise of David Barton's book *America, To Pray or Not to Pray: A Statistical Look at What Has Happened Since 39 Million Students Were Ordered to Stop Praying in Public Schools.*[40] The book amasses graphs and statistical analyses to prove that crime, venereal disease, premarital sex, illiteracy, suicide, drug use, public corruption, and other social ills began a dramatic increase after the *Engel v. Vitale* (1962) Supreme Court decision banning organized school prayer.

Relating the so-called decline of American culture to the Supreme Court decisions of 1962 and 1963 is about as relevant, as my colleague Joey Jeter likes to put it, as relating cultural decline to the fluoridation of water, which happened at the same time. In other words, it makes as much sense to claim that the increase in premarital sex is due to the fluoridation of water as to place the blame on banning organized prayer and Bible reading in public schools.[41] In the 1950s, when there was a great increase in religious understanding and in church attendance, Gallup polls revealed that only 34 percent of the public knew that Jesus delivered the Sermon on the Mount (about the same today). Daily Bible readings in the public schools did not seem to produce more serious Bible readers in the 1950s.

Prayer over loudspeakers at today's football games will not likely produce more serious pray-ers in the future either.

Christians should be clear about at least five issues when they discuss the question of prayer in public schools. On the first and fifth of these, I suspect, people on all sides of the issue would likely find basic agreement. The second, third, and fourth would likely be more controversial. One's response to these three middle propositions probably depends on prior attitudes about voluntary prayer in the public schools.

1. *Prescribed prayers, written by employees of the state or school system, do not belong in public schools.* Neither the state nor public school systems should be in the business of writing prayers for our children to recite. When government or largely secular institutions engage in explicitly religious activities they usurp religion's important functions and identity, and they usually get religion wrong.

2. *Prayer has not been kicked out of the public school system.* The 1962 decision does not mean that the Supreme Court is hostile to religion or to prayer. It is important to note the first sentence in Sandra Day O'Connor's concurring opinion in *Wallace v. Jaffee* (1985): "Nothing in the United States Constitution as interpreted by this Court . . . prohibits public school students from voluntarily praying at any time before, during, or after the school day."[42]

Any individual student can pray silently in school so long as she or he does not disturb anyone else. There is no constitutional backing for any school official to prohibit a student from reading the Bible, praying, or informally engaging in conversations about religious subjects, so long as no one else's right to be left alone is violated. Students may gather quietly for prayer on school property, including before, during, or after football games. But praying publicly at football games, through megaphones or by other amplified means, violates the rights of others who have gathered for the purpose of watching a football game. People who attend football games possess the right to watch the football game without having to experience this kind of Christian encroachment on a public event intended for another purpose.

In recent years, there has been a movement to enact moment-of-silence laws in many state legislatures. In many instances, the State Attorney General or State Supreme Court has ruled that these attempts violate the First Amendment because their intent is to reinstate school prayer. Alabama's law is the best example of this point. Passed in 1978 as period of silence for "meditation," it became in 1981 "for meditation or voluntary prayer," and finally in 1982 "willing students" were to be led in a prescribed prayer to "Almighty God the Creator and Supreme Judge of the world." An Appellate Court struck down the 1982 law, and the Supreme Court, in 1985, struck down the 1981 law.[43]

This leaves the question of "moment of silence" still hazy. The major determining factor of constitutionality is whether or not the "moment of silence" possibility has a religious purpose. For example, if a teacher instructs students to bow their heads, the constitutional "moment of silence" has suddenly become unconstitutional. The same would be true if a teacher suggested the time be spent in prayer. Further, the Court has clearly ruled in the Alabama case that if it can be determined that the "moment of silence" legislation has a religious motivation, it would be unconstitutional. Discussions in Texas have tried to avoid open religious sentiments. The result has been the law passed in Texas that mandates both the Pledge of Allegiance and the moment of silence to start the day. This is phrased like Virginia's law, and the Fourth Circuit Court affirmed the law as one without religious purpose. On October 29, 2001, the Supreme Court denied the possibility to review the Fourth Circuit's decision.

Americans United for the Separation of Church and State have produced "talking points" related to this trend to pursue "moment of silence" legislation. These points are helpful in clarifying some of the issues related to this kind of government activity.

- If moment of silence legislation passes, it will doubtless lead to the state sanction of religion. The Establishment Clause requires government neutrality toward religion. Because moment of silence legislation inherently promotes prayer or meditation, it amounts to a state sanction of religion over non-religion. In addition, moments of silence conform most closely to the Christian practice of silent prayer and meditation. In contrast, many religions require adherents to chant, pray audibly or to move when praying. A moment of silence thus prefers one religious tradition over others.

- A moment of silence may become coercive prayer. Any legislation that establishes a moment of silence must be sensitive to the likelihood that the school, teachers or students will actively or tacitly coerce non-religious children and believers in non-majority faiths to participate in prayer. Some legislation exacerbates this probability by requiring all students to participate in the moment of silence. Safeguards must be established so that those who do not wish to pray are not harassed or ostracized as being anti-religious, amoral heathens.

- Teachers will become the facilitators of religious practice. Under proposed legislation, teachers will be responsible for conducting the moment of silence during the school day. While teachers are prohibited from encouraging prayer, this is all but impossible to police and teachers retain the discretion to interpret and define the contours of the moment of silence. Some teachers may choose to refer to the moment of silence as a moment of reflection, of meditation, or of prayer or suggest that students comport themselves in an "appropriate and respectful" manner. In addition, some teachers may be prone to guide the students by suggesting a topic of thought such as morality, faith, or God. This is tantamount to putting the teachers in the role of quasi-religious leaders.

- Moment of silence legislation is completely unnecessary. Any person who needs 60 seconds in the day to organize their thoughts and prepare for the day's events can do so at any time during the morning. They can do so before rising from bed, while in the shower, before breakfast, or on the way to school or work. In addition, prayer and bible study are not prohibited in public schools; they simply must be voluntary, student initiated and non-coercive and must not bear the imprimatur of the State. For example, students may pray silently on their own during breaks or study periods.[44]

3. *Specific Christian prayers are not appropriate for either public schools or for events sponsored by public school districts* (and, by extension, at other kinds of public events like Chamber of Commerce meetings or presidential inaugurations). America's schools today are quite diverse in the kinds of religions students represent. Though nearly every religious expression on the globe today is represented in America's public schools, the vast majority of today's students are Christian. But the types of Christianity represented by students are dramatically diverse. Suppose a prayer amendment making oral prayer in school acceptable actually passed? Would that bring back a united, harmonious America? No. Instead, it would make more visible the differences that already exist. Once upon a time, communities were homogeneous. Catholics dominated Catholic wards, and a single Protestant ethos, be it Lutheran, Baptist, or Methodist, predominated in various Protestant towns. Today, more and more people of many faiths, including many different forms of Christianity, now must share the turf.

If a prayer amendment made it possible for oral prayer to be recited in public schools, who would control the style of prayers to be offered? Majority percentages of certain types of Christians still might be able to control prayer in certain portions of the country. In Utah, for example, it might be possible that prayers associated with Mormon identity would dominate. What would conservative Christians who are transferred there do? Would they be upset by Mormon-style praying in the public schools? With the passage of a prayer amendment, the Constitution could not really help them. What would Jews and Muslims do while prayers are offered in the name of Jesus Christ? The disgruntled could only begin to work on repeal. Specific Christian prayers are not appropriate for public school systems. They would explicitly exclude the many non-Christians found in public schools, and would likely lead to fights even among Christians over the kinds of prayers to be offered. Christian prayers belong in Christian contexts, not contexts where people, representing both many different kinds of faith and no faith, are gathered for purposes unrelated to Christianity.

4. *Christians ought to think twice, even when the law allows, before offering generic prayers in public schools or at events sponsored by public school districts* (and, by extension, at other kinds of public events like Chamber of Commerce meetings or presidential inaugurations). To honor change and pluralism, public prayers have had to change. While the courts in Virginia and Pennsylvania placed no limits on acceptable graduation prayers, the Sixth Circuit Court[45] held that only prayers which did not "say to some . . . students . . . we do not recognize

your religious beliefs, or our beliefs are superior to yours" were permissible. This court declared unconstitutional any prayers using any manner of "Christian theology," such as using the name of Jesus, or demonstrating sectarian bias in any other subtle ways. The Sixth Circuit explained that ceremonial prayer was acceptable; prayer that is " 'civil' or secularized . . . that does not go beyond the American civil religion."[46]

In other words, courts have tended to rule that when Christians pray in public, they can pray generically without violating the law. Christians can pray at public events or at public school graduations so long as they do not use any overt Christian connotations in their prayers. But when Christians pray in generic ways, can they honestly still call them prayers? Prayers are the expressions of a worshiping community, and worshiping communities necessarily have particular beliefs. Christian prayers belong in contexts where Christians can and do take prayer seriously. Generic prayers are merely performed for ritualistic purposes suitable to contexts of iconic faith. When prayers become rituals and are expressed in only the lowest common denominator ways, as at football games or graduation ceremonies, they lose their status as Christian prayers.

Thus, in one way, it is fully understandable, for example, why Reverend Kirbyjon would pray at President Bush's inauguration "in the name of Jesus." For him, prayer emerges out of a worshiping community who understands what it means to be redeemed by God through Jesus Christ. But those attending the inauguration and the millions in the nation and across the world who watch do not all belong to this worshiping community, and the inauguration itself has nothing to do with either Christian redemption or worship. Does an explicitly Christian prayer "fit" this kind of occasion and audience?

Meanwhile, politicians who have defended this specific reference to Christ in such public inaugural prayers occasionally do so by stating that this language merely points to the way the life of Jesus supports "a set of common moral principles" shared by all Americans. The name Jesus Christ, therefore, becomes just another symbol pointing to shared moral values, a symbol in prayer that serves a secular purpose and is thus acceptable.[47] It becomes another way in which something important to the Christian community becomes merely "ceremonial" or part of a public ritual that serves secular purposes. These are the kinds of arguments politicians and lawyers make about "Jesus" language to make it acceptable to judges who serve in places like the Sixth Circuit Court.

Some Christians recognize that praying in the name of Christ is offensive to many who are present at public occasions not associated with Christian worship or the Christian community. Therefore, many of these Christians pray generically at such occasions. As they do so, they should recognize that their prayers primarily serve a secular purpose. In such cases, their use of the name God (or "Divine Providence" or any other such name) is also "generic" in meaning and automatically becomes a receptacle for a symbolic content associated more specifically with America than with biblical content revealing a God who both judges and redeems human beings. Maybe Christians should question whether their prayers, prayers of any kind, truly belong in these kinds of occasions, where ritualistic and secular purposes and a secular audience overcome both Christian meaning and content. Those concerned with the integrity of Christian prayer might prefer to keep it largely within the contexts and expressions shared by a community of faith.

5. *The public school systems have done a woeful job, through adoption of bad textbooks and through inadequate teaching, of addressing adequately the serious role religion does play in human life.* Public schools have failed miserably at the task of objectively teaching about religion. The Court has argued for over thirty years that this was an acceptable, even necessary, endeavor for public schools. But schools have not done it. Probably due to fear of crossing the lines of church and state separation, textbooks have failed to address religion as a social and historical reality.[48] But a meaningful treatment of the role of religious faith in history, and even in the development of the nation, can be accomplished without violating the First Amendment. There is great room for improvement on this score, and Christians would be served better if they concentrated their attention on solving this problem rather than in lobbying for a meaningless "moment of silence" in public schools. Some have begun to undertake this effort successfully by working together, and across religious lines, to see that religion is treated fairly and with respect within curriculums in America's public schools.[49]

THE PLEDGE OF ALLEGIANCE

Francis Bellamy (1855–1931), a Baptist minister, wrote the Pledge of Allegiance.[50] As vice president of the Society of Christian Socialists, Bellamy was also a Christian Socialist who strongly opposed capitalism. In 1891, a series of sermons on "The Socialism of the Primitive Church" and a sermon entitled "Jesus the Socialist" led to a forced resignation from his Boston congregation. Bellamy joined the staff of *Youth's Companion*, a popular family magazine with a circulation of about 500,000. Daniel Ford, a member of Bellamy's congregation and supporter of his socialist views, owned the magazine.

Beginning about 1888, the magazine, in order to raise money, started a campaign to sell American flags to public schools. Prior to this time, school systems rarely displayed the flag in this country. By 1892, the magazine had sold flags to some 26,000 schools.[51] When President Benjamin Harrison researched ideas about how to celebrate the 400th anniversary of the discovery of America, James Upham, Ford's nephew, and Bellamy saw it as an opportunity to promote the use of the flag in the public schools. They lined up the National Education Association to support *Youth's Companion* as a sponsor of the president's event. Bellamy authored the program for the president's celebration, including writing a flag salute for the event. The original version was first published in the magazine on September 8, 1892, and read as follows:

> I pledge allegiance to my flag and the Republic for which it stands, one
> nation, indivisible, with liberty and justice for all.[52]

Bellamy originally wanted to use the word "equality" in his pledge. "Equality," he
wrote, "meant equal rights to an education on the part of poor children as much as
for rich children. Equality included the right of people to work and earn a decent
living for their families. And equality meant," Bellamy concluded, "that a person's
religious beliefs, or lack thereof, could not be dismissed or demeaned by the State."
Ultimately, Bellamy became convinced that, since so many people stood against
equality for women and blacks, including the word "equality" would be too controversial among the school officials he hoped would adopt the pledge.[53]

The "official programme" of the original "Pledge to the Flag," performed as
part of the National Columbian Public School Celebration on October 21, 1892,
read as follows:

> The pupils, in ordered ranks, hands to the side, face the Flag. Another sig-
> nal is given; every pupil gives the Flag the military salute—right hand lifted,
> palm downward, to a line with the forehead and close to it. Standing thus,
> all repeat together, slowly, "I pledge allegiance to my Flag and the Republic
> for which it stands; one Nation indivisible, with Liberty and Justice for all."
> At the words, "to my Flag," the right hand is extended gracefully, palm
> upward, toward the Flag, and remains in this gesture till the end of the affir-
> mation; whereupon all hands immediately drop to the side.[54]

Bellamy's pledge underwent several changes in wording over the years. The
word "to" was added before "the Republic" in October of 1892. Then, in 1923,
the words "my flag" were changed to "the Flag of the United States" at the urging of the American Legion's National Flag Conference. The next year (1924),
the pledge was altered again with the addition "of America" after "Flag of the
United States." It was this version of the pledge that was codified into public law
in June of 1942. Instead of the military salute beginning the pledge, the hand
was now to be placed over the heart before extending it toward the flag.

> That the pledge of allegiance to the flag . . . be rendered by standing with
> the right hand over the heart; extending the right hand, palm upwards,
> toward the flag at the words "to the flag"; and holding this position until the
> end, when the hand drops to the side.[55]

Objections to the salute became rather regular after this joint resolution in Congress passed. The Parent and Teachers Association, the Boy and Girl Scouts, the
Red Cross, and the Federation of Women's Clubs all objected to the salute as
"being too much like Hitler's."[56] In December 1942, Congress amended the code
by striking the words "extending the right hand" and the end of that sentence.
From that time on, the pledge called for placing "the right hand over the heart."[57]

In 1954, following several years of lobbying by the Knights of Columbus and
the American Legion to get the United States to accept the version of the pledge
used in their own gatherings since 1951, Congress amended the codified section

by adding the words "under God" after the word "Nation."[58] This became official on Flag Day, June 14, 1954. Therefore, the pledge is currently codified as follows: "I pledge allegiance to the Flag of the United States of America, and to the Republic for which it stands, one nation under God, indivisible, with liberty and justice for all."

The contemporary arguments about the Pledge of Allegiance began in March 2001 when an emergency room doctor named Michael Newdow filed suit in federal court that the words "under God" contained in the pledge were unconstitutional. Acting as his own lawyer, Newdow argued that his daughter's First Amendment rights were harmed because she was forced to "watch and listen as her state-employed teacher in her state-run school leads her classmates in a ritual proclaiming that there is a God and that ours is 'one nation under God.' " Since this flap started, the girl's mother, Sandra Banning, clearly stated that she shares the public outrage about what Newdow has done.[59]

The controversy became heated when, on June 26, 2002, the Ninth Circuit Court ruled in Newdow's favor, stating that the pledge, as currently worded, was "an impermissible government endorsement of religion."[60] One of the more interesting sections of the decision is the one dealing with the legislative history of changes made to the pledge. The legislative debates of the early 1950s demonstrate clearly that the words "under God" were meant to be normative: that good and patriotic Americans must believe in a deity. President Eisenhower, during the act's signing ceremony, demonstrated this fact well when he stated,

> From this day forward, the millions of our school children will daily proclaim in every city and town, every village and rural schoolhouse, the dedication of our Nation and our people to the Almighty.[61]

The majority opinion explains that the 1954 act's "sole purpose was to advance religion, in order to differentiate the United States from nations under communist rule." The act used the following language:

> At this moment of our history the principles underlying our American Government and the American way of life are under attack by a system whose philosophy is at direct odds with our own. . . . The inclusion of God in our pledge therefore would further acknowledge the dependence of our people and our Government upon the moral directions of the Creator. At the same time it would serve to deny the atheistic and materialistic concepts of communism with its attendant subservience of the individual.[62]

This language makes it quite clear that the supporters of the act intended for the pledge, with the words "under God," to convey that Americans believe in a creator who provides moral directions for the country over against the atheistic and materialistic concepts of communism. Therefore, the pledge, at that moment, assumed a religious purpose rather than just a patriotic or ceremonial purpose. To be a good American, one needed to recognize these religious beliefs. One could not be atheistic and be a good American.

These ideas in response to communism were carried further in the next two years. First Congress added the words "under God" to the pledge. A year later, in 1955, legislation added the words "In God We Trust" to all coins and currency. In 1956, Congress changed the national motto, "E Pluribus Unum," to "In God We Trust." E Pluribus Unum, meaning "Out of Many, One" had been suggested by Benjamin Franklin, Thomas Jefferson, and John Adams. It symbolized America's ability to bring people of different backgrounds and nationalities together as one people. The 1956 change in the motto, again occasioned by the threat of "atheistic communism," was not an insignificant one. In a sense, in response to the threat of communism, it narrowed the American willingness to accept difference by excluding atheists from being able, as American citizens, to represent the national motto.

The U.S. Ninth Circuit Court of Appeals in San Francisco ruled that Congress violated the First Amendment when it passed a law in 1954 that added the words "under God" to the Pledge of Allegiance. The court ruled, in a 2–1 decision, that it saw the 1954 action as governmental support of monotheism. Though this is the controversial part of the court's ruling, it is good to take a look at the ruling as a whole. The first thing to note is that the ruling does not make it illegal for school children to say the Pledge of Allegiance. Just like prayer, students can say voluntarily, within school, whatever they might wish to say. The ruling itself rules two things as unconstitutional: (1) the California statute that school teachers start every day by leading students in the Pledge of Allegiance; and (2) the language of "under God" within the pledge itself.

Concerning the first point, this is not the only time that a federal court prohibited school systems from coercing children to recite the pledge. The Supreme Court ruled in 1943 that making students recite the pledge constituted a violation of the First Amendment. This ruling came eleven years before the act of Congress that inserted the words "under God" in the pledge.[63] At that time, the Supreme Court justices wrote,

> The action of the local authorities in compelling the flag salute and pledge transcends constitutional limitations on their power and invades the sphere of intellect and spirit which it is the purpose of the First Amendment to our Constitution to reserve from all official control.[64]

One of the major issues in the Ninth Circuit Court opinion included the fact that California teachers are required to recite the pledge whether they can affirm all its contents or not. This is in violation of the 1943 court case. Though students are not required to say the pledge, they are put into the "untenable position" of choosing to participate or, by silence, to protest. The Supreme Court has ruled in school prayer cases that this kind of position is unacceptable.

Concerning the second point, the Ninth Circuit Court (two of three justices) ruled that the pledge constituted an "endorsement of religion" and "profession of a religious belief, namely, a belief in monotheism."

> To recite the Pledge is not to describe the United States; instead, it is to swear allegiance to the values for which the flag stands; unity, indivisibility, liberty, justice, and—since 1954—monotheism.[65]

Members of the Religious Right and conservative members of Congress do not necessarily disagree with the court's finding that this phrase is an endorsement of monotheism. As an editorial in the *Pittsburgh Post-Gazette* put it, "for all these people, the words 'under God' find favor precisely because they are religious; the pledge's reference to God exists to endorse America as a Judeo-Christian nation in an era when organized prayer has been banished from public schools."[66] But the justices see a different kind of problem. The pledge, the justices wrote,

> is an impermissible government endorsement of religion because it sends a message to unbelievers "that they are outsiders, not full members of the political community, and an accompanying message to adherents that they are insiders, favored members of the political community." Lynch, 465 U.S. at 688 (O'Connor, J., concurring).[67]

If this decision by the Ninth Circuit had been allowed to stand, it would have affected the Pledge of Allegiance in ten states (Alaska, Arizona, California, Hawaii, Idaho, Montana, Nevada, Oregon and Washington—the tenth state would have been Texas, which passed legislation to require the pledge after this court case began).

In his dissenting opinion, Justice Fernandez relied on the Seventh Circuit Court's previous consideration of the phrase "under God." That court determined that the phrase, in the context of the pledge, "is devoid of any significant religious content, and therefore constitutional." In Fernandez's words, "the danger that phrase presents to our First Amendment freedoms is picayune at most." Another phrase that has been used by the courts to describe this lack of serious content is the phrase "ceremonial deism." Phrases like "under God" do not necessarily carry deep or significant religious meaning but rather serve a ceremonial purpose. Fernandez, for his part, believed the words do convey "a vestige of the awe we all must feel at the immensity of the universe and our own small place within it, as well as the wonder we must feel at the good fortune of our country."[68]

The Supreme Court heard this case, due to an appeal, on March 24, 2004. The Court handed down its decision on June 14, 2004. During arguments, Justice Stephen Breyer asked Newdow if it was possible that including "under God" in the pledge is such a broad and generic use of religion by the government that it is meant to include even nonbelievers. Newdow replied,

> I don't think that I can include "under God" to mean "no God," which is exactly what I think. I deny the existence of God and for someone to tell me that "under God" should mean some broad thing that even encompasses my religious beliefs sounds a little, you know, it seems like the government is imposing what it wants me to think of in terms of religion, which it may not do.[69]

Justice David H. Souter, one of the Court's strongest defenders of church-state separation, also seemed to be leaning toward the "ceremonial deism" argument. "I think the argument is that simply the way we live and think and work in schools and in civic society in which the Pledge is made, that the—that whatever is distinctively religious as an affirmation is simply lost." When students recite the pledge, Souter said, that may be merely a way of "solemnizing" an occasion. Newdow argued against this point, claiming once again that the pledge constituted advocacy for a belief in God.[70]

It is also interesting to note the argument of the two attorneys on the other side, Terence J. Cassidy and Theodore B. Olson. Cassidy challenged Newdow's standing as a noncustodial parent, which carried the day in the Supreme Court's decision. The Court avoided the issue raised by the Ninth Circuit decision by concluding that Mr. Newdow, as a noncustodial parent, did not have the standing to sue.[71] Just before Cassidy finished his argument, he also dealt with the church-state issue. During rebuttal, Stevens asked him to respond to the friend-of-the-court brief filed by several members of the clergy. These religious leaders asserted that if "under God" isn't meant to be taken seriously, it forces children to take God's name in vain every day. Cassidy said in response, "I would disagree because we feel that the use of the term 'one nation under God,' reflects a political philosophy . . . and that is the philosophy that's now more enhanced, more reflected in the 1954 act." During his time before the Supreme Court, Olson, the Solicitor General of the United States, argued as follows: "Fourteen justices of this court since the Pledge of Allegiance was amended have indicated that [it] is not a religious exercise. . . . It is something different of a ceremonial nature."[72]

In other words, Olson's and Cassidy's responses return us once again to the argument made in the Ninth Circuit, the argument made by those who want to keep the words "under God" in the Pledge of Allegiance. The legal argument in these circles has been that the phrase "under God" should be understood as merely "ceremonial," or merely as a "political philosophy." The words "under God" in the context of the Pledge of Allegiance, these lawyers argue, possess no religious meaning whatsoever. The Ninth Circuit majority said that the pledge's history constitutes an attempt to establish belief in monotheism. The minority opinion sided with the lawyers and held that the threat contained in these ceremonial words was "minuscule."

Christians should stop and think about these two opinions for a moment. The majority opinion of the Ninth Circuit stated that the words "under God" constituted a belief in monotheism and were therefore unconstitutional because they excluded Americans who could not affirm monotheism. The minority opinion of the Ninth Circuit argued that the words contain minimal religious content, certainly no particular content that would constitute religious establishment. The words "under God" are more ceremonial in nature, meant to depict wonder and awe. The words are not particularly "religious."

In response to these positions, Christians might ask themselves two questions. If the majority opinion is correct, that the words carry significant, and particular, religious meaning pertaining to monotheism, is it right that they are ensconced in a pledge of allegiance to be recited and affirmed by all Americans, including those who belong to a wide variety of the world's religions (many of which are not monotheistic) and those who belong to none?

Alternatively, if the minority opinion of the Ninth Circuit Court is correct, is anything truly lost by removing the words "under God"? When religious language becomes merely ceremonial or ritualistic, or is used only to "solemnize an occasion," do Christians really lose anything when it is removed? Perhaps, more importantly, the religious leaders who filed a brief with the Supreme Court siding with Newdow are correct: to pledge allegiance daily using the name of God, when the name of "God" is merely ceremonial deism, is actually asking our Christian children to take the name of God in vain on a daily basis.

CONCLUSION

How are we to assess this iconic context and its relationship to Christianity? The symbol structure of American life all too easily becomes confused and intertwined with the symbol structure of Christianity. This does not just work one way. Not only do Christian symbols invade the public sphere, but American symbols also invade the Christian sphere. Tangible icons often find their way into Christianity. By our ready affirmation of the way Christian symbols are used in American public life, we increase the possibility that American symbols will appear in the life of the church. When public icons invade Christian life, they dilute the Christian message and fill it with American content.

Therefore, do icons of American public life rightfully belong in the sanctuaries of Christian worship? Should patriotic hymns appear in Christian worship services? Should the Pledge of Allegiance be recited in Christian Sunday schools or the American flag be displayed in Christian sanctuaries? Christians continue to struggle with these questions. On the one hand, patriotism certainly has its place. Christians stand and sing the national anthem at baseball games; they visit the Vietnam War Memorial and the National Archives. They do so because they rightfully identify with America. They value what America means to them and, in some ways, to the world. They value what America's approach to religious freedom means to the ability of the church to express itself. They also value what American democracy means to them personally as individuals. In other words, it is natural for American citizens, whether Christian or not, to participate in some expressions of the iconic. But Christians work to distinguish between the two, the iconic and the Christian, in order not to become confused when public figures or public life borrows from the reservoir of Christian symbolism.

On the other hand, Christian worship intentionally brings Christians into the presence of God, not as Americans, but as children of God concerned with the family of God the world over. That is why many Christians would answer all these questions in the negative. The church's task is not to teach patriotism.

Schools already do a decent job of that. Rather, in every country, the church calls worshipers to the recognition that God's purposes transcend the purposes of any one nation or people.

Much of the American Christian experience has been willing to adapt to culture. The iconic context has entered the life of the church in some very subtle ways. Learning is replaced by techniques and strategies. Attendance equals commitment. Membership rolls mirror the societal divisions between races and classes. A growth in church budget translates into God's blessing of the work, and the voice of the majority is often viewed as synonymous with the voice of God. In sum, Christians who regularly confuse Christianity with the iconic context can unwittingly express American values more than they serve Christian values.

In 1963, as Protestants were being displaced in culture, Martin Marty asked what mainstream Protestants could do now that they faced the loss of their cultural influence? In that year, in a book titled *Second Chance for American Protestants*, he described three potential options. First, as one alternative, Protestantism could simply stress "business as usual." This strategy would ignore pluralism in the hope that it would eventually go away. This approach pretends pluralism does not exist. Marty described this approach as "Protestantism without pluralism." A second alternative might take a more aggressive approach by implementing a counteroffensive. Such a Protestant endeavor would seek to "win back" the "ground-occupying" place in culture it used to hold. The activities of the Religious Right are called to mind. This is "Protestantism against pluralism." The third approach, the one Marty championed during those years, sought "redefinitions and a new course of action in the setting in which Protestantism will inevitably live."[73] That approach might be described as "Protestantism in pluralism."

Protestantism of the early 1960s, Marty argued at the time, had been given a second chance. With this book, Marty defined the "second chance" as "a change to a different set of ground rules," one that took seriously "the erosion and breakdown of one specific Christian bond with culture."[74] Marty's approach recognized that cultural displacement was a positive outcome of pluralism. In the intervening years, pluralism has helped churches take intentional steps toward a more inclusive and globally aware church life. Mainline Protestantism is now situated on the fringes of American religious life. There is nothing inherently negative about that location. The power of culture, and its accompanying iconic context, over the church's life is minimized when the church no longer stands at the center of culture. Further, the power and influence associated with the church's voice might actually be more significant when it speaks from the fringes rather than from the center of the culture. At least when it comes from the fringes, nobody can claim that the church's words and phrases are meant to be merely "ceremonial in nature."

Chapter 4

Priestly Faith

INTRODUCTION

A second style of interaction between Christians and public life in America appears in the form of priestly faith. Though often expressed as if the primary concern is God, this interaction is usually an attempt to "restore the nation" to the purity of its "Christian origins" or, alternatively, to describe the mission of the nation as somehow directly representing God's purposes in history. In other words, the primary concern is the nation itself and an attempt to represent the nation, its history and its purposes, in a particular way. This expression of the mixture of Christianity and public life takes a step beyond mere confusion of iconic symbols with Christian faith. It finds expression at the point where Christians transform generalized and confused iconic faith into either a systematic collection of values or a definition of cultural ethos, promote either one as if it fully represents the true meaning of both Christianity and America, and seek to persuade the government to protect its interests by legislative and political means. It also finds expression where government leaders transform national interests or initiatives into divine missions in the world.

Priestly faith confuses the nation with the church. This happens, for example, when Christians attempt to legislate what they consider to be Christian behavior for the nation as a whole. But it also happens when Christians understand important national values to be normative for the church. Throughout American history, members of the church have often accepted national values as if they were synonymous with God's will, whether these values expressed segregation, anticommunism, or the need to protect the family from the evils resulting from women joining the workforce in increasing numbers.

The tendency to connect God's will with national initiatives, whether dealing with domestic or foreign policy, is also, essentially, an idolatrous one. Priestly faith connects the national mission with the divine mission in the world. In doing so, it makes ultimate what is only relative. In the priestly case, ultimate loyalty belongs to the nation, rightfully conceived. Those who oppose that rightful conception of the nation and its mission are demonic and represent all that is evil in the world. This is true because opposition to the nation is understood to be opposition to God. Certainty pervades priestly faith. One always knows what is good and what is evil. Those who espouse the priestly vision of the nation understand it as God's vision for America. And America stands for all that is good in the world.

Christians in America who defend this kind of public theology stand in a tradition longer than they might realize. The first historian of the church, Eusebius, by the time of his death, had much in common with them. Eusebius was born, most likely, sometime during the 260s and died sometime around 339 or 340. His life was filled with either the memory of, or experiences of, serious persecutions of Christians in the Roman empire. Major persecutions occurred under Decius (250) and Valerian (257) before Eusebius was born. But one of the most severe, the "Great Persecution," occurred under Diocletian (303–305) and Galerius (305–311), a persecution Eusebius escaped around 309. By 315, Eusebius became bishop of Caesarea.

In the earlier portion of his career, prior to the victory of Constantine at the battle of Milvian Bridge (312), Eusebius judged emperors according to whether or not they persecuted Christians. Pagan emperors were the norm and could be considered "good" so long as they tolerated Christians. During these years, he supported a broad policy of religious toleration throughout the empire and believed the use of violence would never solve anything effectively in matters involving religion. Religious pluralism within the empire constituted the norm, and Eusebius did not expect or call for a change. By the time of his death, however, his viewpoint had changed considerably.

Eusebius, like many Americans today, found himself moved by the social context he experienced to see clearly who could be counted as good and who could be judged as evil. Horrible persecution, ended by Constantine's leadership and military force, led him to hail Constantine as "the Warrior of God." God chose Constantine to rid the world of evil. By the time he wrote the *Life of Constantine* on the occasion of the death of the emperor, Eusebius had concluded that God used emperors and empires to root out the pagans, destroy evil leaders and their nefarious designs upon humanity, and spread Christianity. Official and violent persecution of paganism and all who associated with it now seemed perfectly logical to him. The new Christianized Roman Empire fully represented the will of God within history. Eusebius expected Rome, as God's agent, to rule the world until the end of time. We all know how that turned out.[1]

Priests see America as a Christian nation and define its mission, both at home and in the world, according to these terms. The word *priest* means different things to different people. I am not using the term in a biblical sense or in a churchly sense. It has nothing to do with the ministry or with the church. Rather, I am relying on the way sociologists of religion have occasionally used the term *priest*. With this word, I am describing a sociological category operating in religious ways in the culture.

Max Weber indicated in the 1960s that "a distinguishing quality" of the priest in culture "is his professional equipment of special knowledge, fixed doctrine, and vocational qualifications."[2] Joachim Wach, another sociologist of religion, emphasizes the role of the priest as the "guardian of traditions and the keeper of the sacred knowledge . . . the custodian of the holy law, which corresponds to the cosmic moral and ritual order upon which the world, the community and the individual depend." He is the "interpreter of the law" and therefore may function as "judge, administrator, teacher and scholar" in order to "formulate standards and rules of conduct and enforce their observance."[3] Priests are always confident of the nature of their revealed truth. As priests, they teach the faith's precepts and guide the newer members into deeper knowledge. When questions arise, they are able to provide definitive answers consistent with other elements of the faith. Since there is only one true faith, they are not satisfied with ministering only to the converted. Thus priests in America are interested in rooting out heresy and keeping American public life and foreign policy pure and free from error.

The priests of this faith assume authority and know all the answers because they are experts in the American cultural tradition. For this reason, priests are generally resistant to new truth because that cultural tradition is all they need. Nothing can rival the faith received through the ages. For this reason, priestly faith is uncomfortable with cultural change and is therefore inherently conservative. Since pluralism brings change, priestly faith is mostly uncomfortable with it. If new types of Americans arrive, learn the tradition well, and adapt to it, they are likely to be welcomed. If newly minted American citizens challenge this tradition or question its legitimacy in certain areas, they will find their status as good Americans questioned by those who find the priestly faith to their liking. The important "tradition" here, however, is the tradition of American cultural faith, not the larger Christian tradition, ecumenically conceived.

We have seen a resurgence of this type of public faith among American Christians over the last three decades. Christian fundamentalists on the right edge of politics have been regularly drawn to this expression, though others, religious liberals included, have been known to practice it on occasion. These have been anxious times for many Christians. As we have noted, religious pluralism emerged in the 1960s in ways that threatened many American Christians. Some responded by resorting to a priestly perspective.

Expressions of priestly faith throughout the 1980s and 1990s were obviously evident in aspects of Christian fundamentalism and the Religious Right, represented in the declarations and actions of people like Jerry Falwell and Pat Robertson, and by organizations like the Moral Majority and the Christian Coalition. For most of the 1970s, no formally organized and politically active Religious Right movement existed. The Moral Majority was not formed until 1979–1980. And throughout the mid-1960s, Jerry Falwell had condemned the political activities of the Protestant clergy during the civil rights and anti-Vietnam movements. His inerrant Bible told him inerrantly that religion and politics did not mix. But cultural changes up through the 1970s led some Christians on the right to reevaluate their relationship to public life. The government had become far too liberal for their liking; it had become secular, perhaps even anti-Christian. Their inerrant Bible now told them inerrantly that they should use their religion to reclaim the traditional lines of public life in America.

"The mission of the Christian Coalition is simple," said Pat Robertson. It is "to mobilize Christians—one precinct at a time, one community at a time—until once again we are the head and not the tail, and at the top rather than the bottom of our political system." And, he continued, "We have enough votes to run this country . . . and when the people say, 'We've had enough,' we're going to take over!"[4] But, as is evident from a wide variety of editorial cartoons, the press loves to lampoon the priests of public life. A Pat Oliphant cartoon from 1980, for example, shows the "Celestial Reception" desk. The angelic clerk is yelling to God, who is behind the office door, "That pest, Jerry Falwell, from Moral Majority is on the line. Now he wants to know if you hear prayers from Jews, Muslims, unredeemed gentiles, left-handed agnostics, pantheists, vegetarians, blacks, Democrats and homosexuals!" "Oy," says God, "Tell him to stick to politics and leave the religion to me!"[5]

These Christian activists have shown a willingness to use legislation and coercive politics to achieve their priestly vision of Christian public life in America. They want a particular kind of America, one connected to narrowly defined Christian and Jewish values. "When I said during my presidential bid that I would only bring Christians and Jews into the government, I hit a firestorm," Pat Robertson recalled later. " 'What do you mean?' the media challenged me. 'You're not going to bring atheists into the government? How dare you maintain that those who believe in the Judeo-Christian values are better qualified to govern America than Hindus and Muslims?' My simple answer is, 'Yes, they are.' "[6]

The Moral Majority and Christian Coalition are not the only priest-like groups of recent decades. Christian Voice appeared as a Christian lobbying group that also kept tabs on how congressional representatives voted on particular issues. Low grades on these report cards meant, according to Christian Voice, that a person was voting against both the essence of America and Christianity. Randall Terry's Operation Rescue has also been in the news during the past couple of decades, especially in trying to shut down abortion clinics: "I want you to just let a wave of intolerance wash over you. I want you to let a wave of hatred wash over you. Yes, hate is good. . . . Our goal is a Christian nation. We have a Biblical duty, we are called by God, to conquer this country. We don't want equal time. We don't want pluralism."[7] These kinds of activities and statements are classic expressions of priestly faith.

Since the 1990s, many of the religious leaders on the conservative right, like Robertson and Falwell, have stepped back from visible political activities. Their direct involvement has become less necessary due to the political emergence of George W. Bush and other prominent Republican leadership, like Bill Frist in the Senate and Tom DeLay in the House, all of whom represent the ideas of the Religious Right in political discourse. Ralph Reed, formally a director of Robertson's Christian Coalition and, at the time of this writing, running for lieutenant governor of Georgia, has become a political mover and shaker among Republicans. As he put it in 2001, the organized Religious Right "no longer plays the institutional role it once did," in part because the movement succeeded in changing the political landscape in the country by electing friendly leadership. "You're no longer throwing rocks at the building," explains Reed, "you're in the building."[8] There may be a flip side to this kind of phenomenon, however. As Bill Keller, after describing Karl Rove's "master plan," put it in an op-ed essay in the *New York Times,*

> The interesting story, then, is not that Mr. Bush is a captive of the religious right, but that his people are striving to make the religious right a captive of the Republican Party.[9]

For the most part, those on the Christian religious right stand in a primitivist tradition, identifying with simpler times and a particular understanding of how America used to be, and working to make it that way again. Others, especially among political operatives like Reed, may have more complex reasons for pursuing their political goals. Walter Capps, in his book on the Religious Right, has put it this way:

> Instead of celebrating the varieties of religious experience that are available to human beings, the movement's leaders prefer to talk of normative faith, correct teaching, indispensable doctrine, enduring values, permanent truth, and of the absolute conditions of human salvation. Within this framework, New Religious Right religion appears to be a deliberate and calculated effort to reassert a particular way of life, yes, even a normative culture, against a variety of menacing threats. And, as the guarantor of its claim, it professes that the Christian faith and the democratic form of government (as practiced and championed within the United States) are thoroughly and absolutely compatible, both of which, in this precise combination, are intended for all people, wherever they live, throughout the world.[10]

Some of the work of early-twentieth-century optimistic social liberals might also be described in the category of priestly faith, particularly that of those thinkers representing the "new theology," like Lyman Abbott and Shailer Mathews, with their strong emphasis on the immanence of the kingdom and the importance of human actions in bringing it about. They defended a progressive, rather than primitive, priestly tradition, identifying with a divinely inspired and developing America. Their revelation about Christianity and public life did not come from an inerrant Bible but from a more scientific reading of both Scripture and history. Both the conservative at the end of the twentieth century and the liberal new theologian at the beginning of that century represented aspects of priestly faith, but with vastly different content.

In many expressions, priestly faith is equivalent to nationalism among Christians. With ultimacy attached to America and its cause, priests promote American culture, interests, and style of democracy as if they were synonymous with everything that is good, just, and righteous for the human community as a whole. This occasionally translates into an aggressive foreign policy or, as Conrad Cherry has termed it, "a muscular imperialism that cloaks American self-interest with platitudes about saving the world for democracy, a racist myth that justifies American actions abroad because of 'Anglo-Saxon superiority.' "[11] When Christians understand America as acting on behalf of God in the world, then their slide into national self-righteousness is quick and usually rather costly. In Cherry's words,

> It has been all too easy for Americans to convince themselves that they have been chosen to be a free and powerful people not because God or the circumstances of history choose in mysterious ways but because they *deserve* election. The blessings of success, wealth, and power are readily taken as signs of their having merited a special place in history.[12]

The last chapter noted that public life in America fills Christian symbols with meanings defined by political needs and concerns. In this way, icons important to Christianity, whether represented by things (like Bibles), in picture or sculpture (images of the Ten Commandments in our courthouses), or through language (like using "In God we trust" on our coins), take on associations different from those Christians would ordinarily connect with them in their own communities. Priestly faith, in the style of interaction I am presenting here, goes a step further than iconic faith.

Christians who represent priestly faith fill the symbols of public life with their own particular Christian understandings and then assert these meanings to represent the only true way of being both Christian and American. They require new tests of Christian commitment: how one votes on an abortion amendment, what one thinks about marriages among gays and lesbians, or how one stands on the question of preventive war in Iraq. Randall Terry provided a clear example in 1993 when he said, "If a Christian voted for Clinton, he sinned against God. It's that simple."[13] Or consider the more recent priestly example of Pastor Chan Chandler, of the East Waynesville Baptist Church in North Carolina, who kicked nine members out of the church in May 2005 because they voted for John Kerry instead of George W. Bush.[14] Christian commitment, in these priestly cases, is judged by some peculiar standards. The priest, therefore, perverts not only Christian faith but also the civil religious ideals represented in America's founding documents.

LESSONS FROM THE PAST

In order to put some flesh on the bones of this description of priestly faith, I want now to provide some examples of priestly behavior drawn from the pages of evangelical and mainline Christian journals over the past half century. It is worth mentioning that all these journals disagreed with the strategies of the Religious Right as it developed. None of them ardently sought to represent the role of the priest in their thinking about American public life. In this way, illustrations drawn from their pages demonstrate how priestly approaches to public life sometimes sneak up on the Christian community. Christians can become priests without consciously realizing they are doing so. When priestly behavior catches the Christian community by surprise, it stands in stark contrast to the activities of the Religious Right, where priestly behavior these days is regularly a trademark of identity. But it is equally damaging to the Christian witness.

In their emphasis on American values and cultural ethos, these magazines especially represented at least one dimension of the role of the priest. Priests often associate the status quo, or the way they currently understand the world, with God's way of doing things. When challenges from outside or from inside challenge their understanding of the world, or when new cultural issues reach prominence for the first time, Christians sometimes provide a "we have always done it this way" kind of response. God's will is then connected to the way Americans understand the world or the way they have always done things. Priestly behavior is almost sure to follow this attitude, because when this happens, contrary understandings of the world or change in general can all too quickly be associated with the demonic.

Democracy/Capitalism versus Communism

In February of 1956, Nikita Khrushchev denounced Stalinism for its domestic crimes against the Soviet people and appeared willing to accept different forms of communism within the Soviet republic. The communist world began to take "polycentrism" seriously. Though few nations within the Soviet orbit resisted an ideological affinity, many of them sought some freedom from Moscow domination. Khrushchev's expressed attitude spawned new resistance movements in Poland and Hungary. Such national resistance to Moscow, however, never fit into Khrushchev's agenda. Soviet force met both movements, the latter with especially brutal means.

American concern over the willingness of Soviet leadership to brutalize its own people quickly turned into fear that such brutality might soon reach American shores. In the late summer of 1957, the Soviets fired the first successful intercontinental ballistic missile (ICBM). On October 4, the Russians launched Sputnik, the first outer-space satellite. A month later, another Sputnik orbited the globe, this time with a dog aboard. At the time, someone commented that the next one would have cows aboard—"hence, the herd shot 'round the world."[15] Quips like these offered only a thin veneer covering a much deeper American anxiety.

Russian superiority in rocketry shook American confidence in its own technological program to the core. "All in all," the *Christian Century* (hereafter, *CC*) concluded in January 1958, "it would be an untrustworthy American who suggested that America's recently effervescent confidence did not go rather suddenly flat toward the end of 1957." Soviet accomplishment in space called into question, for many Americans, the "unspoken assumption of a kind of general, built-in American superiority." This meant that American superiority had to be reasserted.[16] In response, 1958 not only witnessed the creation of the National Aeronautics and Space Administration but the National Defense Education Act as well. Federal aid to education in the areas of foreign languages, science, and mathematics suddenly became a matter of primary national importance.[17]

As a result of Hungary and Sputnik, American concern about Soviet power reached an all-time high in 1957. For at least one contributor to *Christianity Today* (hereafter, *CT*), Sputnik represented God's judgment on America.[18] Several other events, however, seemed to weaken the Western moral condemnation of the brutal Soviet military action in Hungary. The nearly simultaneous invasion of Egypt by British, French, and Israeli troops did nothing to increase Western international credibility. Vice President Nixon's stormy "goodwill" visit to Latin American countries in the late spring of 1958 helped to instruct Americans about the strength of nationalist movements in the underdeveloped areas of the world, but Americans had a difficult time grasping the lesson, as events in Southeast Asia soon clearly demonstrated.

National consciousness in third-world countries, however, continued unabated. The years of colonial imperialism were finally coming to an end. In 1960 alone, eighteen countries recovered their independence. America dealt with all nationalist movements by running them through the filter of "communist influence." For Secretary of State John Foster Dulles, neutrality in the Cold War among developing nations meant that those nations harbored a procommunist sympathy and a distinctly anti-American posture. This kind of understanding did not endear America to any of those nations as they developed their independence. Dulles's refusal to accept the right of any nation to assert neutrality in the stand-off between the Soviet Union and the United States also served to model the posture of priestly nationalism for many American Christians throughout the 1950s.[19]

During the Cold War, *CT* routinely set democracy and capitalism over against communism. Part of the fabric of public life in America during those years, perhaps the cross-stitch that held the symbolic boundaries in place, was the anticommunism Americans shared. Editors shared it too. It seemed only natural to them to describe Jesus as the "great democrat."[20] Though *CT* editors condemned the raising of democracy to the level of religion,[21] they saw it as the natural consequence of Christianity. Editorials from the 1950s through the 1970s regularly linked communism to evil, as in the description of communist propaganda as "dedicated to the service of antichrist," or in the reminder that "Even the Devil Wears a Smile."[22] Editors most often pitched the conflict as one between "atheistic communism" or "materialistic atheism" and "Christian faith." Under these conditions, it seemed impossible to consider that a communist could ever be a Christian.[23]

J. Edgar Hoover, Director of the FBI, regularly wrote revival-oriented articles for the pages of *CT*. "An America faithful to God," he wrote, "will be an America free and strong." If America is "to meet this atheistic enemy," American ministers "must urge a rededication to Christian beliefs." "Communism," wrote Hoover, "is the bitter enemy of religion." It was either "Soviet Rule or Christian Renewal."[24] In cultural parlance, Christianity, particularly evangelical Christianity,[25] became the pragmatic first line of priestly defense against communism. For his part, Hoover's dedication to the revival did not go unrewarded; the Capitol Hill Methodist Church in Washington, D.C., dedicated a colored-glass window, twenty-two feet wide by thirty-three feet high, as the "J. Edgar Hoover Window" honoring "the Christian virtues of Hoover and other Christian statesmen."[26]

Priestly forms of anticommunism also, of course, made it impossible for editors at *CT* to sanction diplomatic recognition of the People's Republic, since to do so would certify "approbation" of an atheistic and immoral nation. Such an action would only sacrifice America's "moral courage and earnestness." Nixon's approach to China finally produced a change in position on this issue. By 1971, editors came to view China as contributing to a "balance of power" in the East over against the Soviets.[27] By 1974, while still supporting the spread of democracy, editors at *CT* also took the time to point out that evangelicals seemed "to be growing more sensitive to the need to distinguish the Gospel from the political and economic practices of their homelands."[28] The era of Gorbachev, combined with a more cynical approach to icons in public life, led editors at *CT* to take a more open view, even of the Soviet Union.[29] "The challenge of the 1990s," proclaimed a 1989 editorial on the "greening of communism's red flag," "may be to understand kingdom citizenship in a way that makes room for believers who follow Christ in different [economic and governmental] systems."[30] These kinds of adjustments helped to check the tendencies toward priestly responses to communism.

Prior to the Vietnam years, the *CC* also tended to link democracy with God and place it opposite the linkage made between communism and evil. The Soviet launching of Sputnik and ICBMs, the invasion of Hungary, the new and vitalized presence of the Russians in the Middle East—all these things are mentioned by editors who editorialize that war with Russia and that "evil man" Khrushchev might be very close on the horizon. Perhaps the worst of the journal's anticommunism in this period is displayed in a November, 1961, editorial called "Confronting Communism." The author, probably Harold Fey, described communism as a philosophy that must "obliterate religion. . . . Indeed, communism cannot remain communism and do otherwise." Though the editorial warned readers not to "commit the great blasphemy of confusing democracy with the kingdom of God," its author assumed absolute incompatibility between Christianity and communism. "Christianity and communism," according to the editorial, "cannot coexist in the same person any more than Christianity can share the same disciple with Buddhism or Islam."[31]

Under Fey's leadership, however, the *Century* could also hold positions that made it rather unpopular with average anticommunist groups and individuals. The journal strongly sought United Nations recognition of the People's Republic of China. On the issue of space, even given the threat of initial Soviet successes, Fey condemned American exploration as a "fantastic waste" of economic resources.[32] Just after the Cuban missile crisis, editors insisted that Americans look to the "enemy within" for part of the cause of the crisis itself, especially "the shameful history of [American] exploitation of Cuba." They also argued for de facto recognition of the East German communist regime in the Berlin crisis.[33] Clearly, the *Century*'s anticommunism had some sophisticated and reflective edges to it. Priestly faith is hard to maintain in these kinds of more critical contexts.

By 1968, editorials more regularly addressed the shortcomings of American life. The *Century* printed an editorial titled "Universal Moral Myopia." The Soviet Union had just invaded Czechoslovakia, but the editor was in no mood to engage in simple anticommunist banter. Instead he pointed to America's "two evils," racism and Vietnam, and stated that the Russian invasion should not serve as "a scapegoat for our own guilt." Though his editorial took seriously the situation in Czechoslovakia, it compared the invasion to both the American intervention in Vietnam and the U.S. invasion of the Dominican Republic. Communism, in other words, had no monopoly on immorality. The editor defended his position with solid theological reasoning. He pointed out that Americans "live as if the meaning of our lives was ours alone to create."[34] This theological approach to the culture enabled the *Century* to assume an occasionally prophetic, rather than priestly, posture toward American society as a whole.

But rereading the pages of these two journals, in fact, drives home the realization of just how much the anticommunism of earlier decades, in the popular mind at least, expressed a deep-seated belief that the Cold War represented more a religious battle than a political one. The first President Bush, in his State of the Union address in 1992, attributed America's victory clearly to God's purposes when he said, "By the grace of God, America won the Cold War."[35] Many American Christians shared these priestly sentiments, then and now.

Vietnam

Events in Vietnam were, of course, connected to these priestly anticommunism views and brought another major issue for priestly expression during the 1960s. The *Century* heralded the birth of the Republic of South Vietnam in November of 1955 and said not another meaningful word about it until April 25, 1962, when an editorial demanded that President Kennedy tell the truth about why "American soldiers [were] dying almost every day in South Vietnam."[36] It is interesting that editors at the *Century* did not respond in a priestly manner to American involvement in the war itself. By the mid-1960s, they were openly questioning the American role there.

In 1962, these mainstream liberals at the *Century* feared the implications of a communist takeover in southeast Asia as much as anyone else did. None of them questioned the fact that South Vietnam needed help. The domino theory made limited sense to them at the time. While recognizing the legitimacy of the cause against communism throughout 1963 and 1964, editorials in Christian journals like the *CC, America, Commonweal,* and *Christianity and Crisis* argued against expansion of the war and called for a peaceful, negotiated withdrawal.[37]

But the prospect of a national presidential election at such a crucial time frightened these editors. Just before the Republican National Convention in 1964, Harold Fey wrote a *Century* editorial titled "Goldwater? No!" Fey believed Goldwater's ideological bent "would inflame the cold war" and probably escalate the war in Vietnam. Just after Fey retired in September, Kyle Haselden, in one of his first tasks as editor, endorsed President Johnson for reelection (in an editorial titled "Johnson? Yes!"). He was confident that a Johnson/Humphrey team would handle Vietnam with wisdom and could be trusted to avoid the "hair-trigger action" of a Goldwater.[38] *Christianity and Crisis* joined the *Century* in believing that God wanted a Johnson victory.[39] The tone of these editorials, completely linking perceived Christian goals in Vietnam to the election of Johnson over Goldwater, placed editors at both journals solidly in the role of the priest. Given Johnson's quick escalation of the war after his victory in 1964, both journals quickly regretted their actions.

Not only did the *Century* endorsement cost the journal its tax-deductible status for a year; it also led to an editorial shift toward a more realistic understanding of politics, including less willingness to wed Christian goals to the election of particular leaders. Johnson's policies forced the *Century* editor to eat his words, something few editors ever enjoy doing. Haselden's profound disappointment found expression as early as May, 1965.[40] Later, *Century* editors Alan Geyer and James M. Wall pointed out the mistaken assumptions evident in the journal's pre-election editorial endorsement of Johnson. Wall, for example, writing in the context of the Religious Right's involvement in the 1980 presidential election, used the example of the *Century's* endorsement in the 1964 election to point out that Christian groups should refrain from the endorsement of particular candidates and, instead, trust the political process to work.[41] Assigning God a preference in an election, besides turning Christians into priests, can also backfire on Christians who then find it necessary to stand against the leader's positions after the election.

The Pentagon Papers revealed that Johnson, prior to the election, had already taken steps to escalate the war. By the end of 1965, troops in Vietnam numbered over 185,000; one year later they would number 385,000, building eventually to over 540,000 troops. That these developments jarred the *Century* is clearly evident in its stronger opposition to the war in Vietnam after 1965. The 1964 Tonkin Gulf Resolution authorizing presidential authority in sending American troops to Vietnam had originally brought barely a whimper. By early 1966, editors had decided the resolution had blown "a hole in the Constitution of the United States big enough to drive an undeclared war through."[42]

CT rightly criticized the priestly posture of both *Christianity and Crisis* and *CC*. "Increasingly it became clear," after the reading of these editorials, "that, if some ecclesiastical enterprises had ever understood the New Testament doctrine of election, they had now left it far behind for a kingdom at whose entrance stood a polling booth."[43] But the evangelical journal also could act the priest itself concerning Vietnam. *CT*'s mind-set, one of fervent anticommunism, led to uncritical support for American efforts during the Vietnam War, efforts occasionally connected with God's will. As the "greatest bastion for freedom," America could not avoid intervention.[44] The actions of those who protested the war, like those students who burned draft cards, editors claimed came "perilously close to treason."[45] Billy Graham even produced a film titled *Viet Nam Profile: Depicts the Drama of God at Work in the Midst of War*. An advertisement in the *CT*'s pages read,

> Fly over the battlefields; witness war's devastation; see the heroic work of the chaplains; thrill to answered prayer with courageous mountain tribespeople; meet the people of Viet Nam; watch missionaries and Vietnamese Christians in the Evangelistic ministry.[46]

By 1971, *CT* began to reconsider its position on Vietnam. This was at the time of the William Calley trial, when a Gallup poll revealed that "seven of ten Americans do not think the administration is telling the people all they should know about the Viet Nam war." The editorial called for honesty.[47] By May of that year, Harold Lindsell, the editor of the journal, admitted for the first time "that perhaps we should never have gotten into Viet Nam in the first place."[48] Publication of the Pentagon Papers brought more discomfort.[49] The changing stance, however, did not bring any greater empathy for the student protests; student marchers against Vietnam were described as "termites eating at the vital structures of American life and democracy."[50]

The events connected with the Vietnam War, however, brought insights that challenged the kind of priestly assumptions represented in the pages of the journal during this period. An editorial, published after the negotiated treaty in 1973, expressed a considerably different tone than had been common for the journal. The editorial asked whether America had learned these important lessons: that great nations have power limitations; that no nation can police the world, or make it safe against Communism; and that no country should resort to war unless its necessity and justification can be made plain and understandable to its people.[51]

Race

On a Sunday morning in October, 1955, visiting Father Gerald Lewis prepared to officiate at Mass in St. Cecil's Church in Jesuit Bend, Louisiana. But an unruly group of gentlemen, lay members of the parish, took it upon themselves to block his ability to officiate on that particular Sunday. The problem? Father Lewis was a "Negro" priest. Their church was segregated. They did not want a Negro priest to serve them communion. Archbishop Joseph Rummel of New Orleans responded quickly with an action of his own. He excommunicated the men involved in blocking the ministerial action of this priest and declared their activity a clear violation of the laws of the Church.[52] A simple solution for a simple problem of prejudice. The hierarchy of the Church was able to take a definitive action; no gray areas existed here. The priest had the "right" to perform the Mass in that white parish; the hierarchy clearly supported the right and excommunicated the offending parties who tried to prevent that right from being exercised. But did this simple action really take care of the problem encountered by this Catholic minister? Was this parish free of racism now that the offending parties in this one instance had been excommunicated? Of course not. Most American church leaders knew that, but, like most middle-class white people, they were unable to understand what to do about the less obviously attributed forms of racism. They were rarely even able to define those areas.

The problem of racial prejudice has always reached much deeper into church and, for that matter, into cultural life than simply the way it has affected the rights of individuals. The problem facing African Americans in 1955, at the beginning of the civil rights movement, was systemic, deeply woven into the cultural fabric of the nation. One might say today that racism had always been an essential ingredient of iconic faith in America. It ran through the whole religious, economic, and political structure of American life. Therefore, racism was not merely a problem of rights. If racism was to be eradicated, it would take more than the simple act of excommunicating (or imprisoning) the offending parties who kept minority Americans from exercising their ecclesial (or civil) rights; every aspect of American life would have to be addressed. And the white church, as one black church leader put it in 1963, would need to become "a revolutionary force committed to distinguishing and separating the Christian understanding of life from the idealizations and norms of middle class white society."[53]

Though many white Catholics and Protestants supported the civil rights movement as it began, what is missing during those years is much mention in the independent Christian journals of courageous and activist involvement of the institutional church itself. The vacuum of such literature stems from the fact that such activity did not much exist. Localized and individual acts of the church were

not very frequent either. Editors and authors lamented the fact that local congregations in crisis areas were not more involved. Future Senator Paul Simon, a
member of the House in 1958, quoted a black minister who condemned the
"silence of the good people," who are so "objectively analytical that they never
get subjectively committed." As for denominational groups, this young black
minister reported, there was "a high blood pressure of creeds and an anemia of
deeds."[54]

Father Andrew Greeley questioned whether justice was alive on Catholic campuses because Catholic students were largely absent from any forms of activism.
One southern minister, after looking in vain for news indicating an active white
Christian protest of the Emmett Till murder or the atrocities at Koinonia,
intoned, "God has been forced to call impromptu prophets in judicial robes and
baseball uniforms to summon the sinful to repentance." Meanwhile, Reinhold
Niebuhr hoped the church could "prove it is at least as good as sports in establishing brotherhood between the races." The fact that the institutional church
failed in these matters is why Gayraud Wilmore was probably justified in 1963
in describing the "New Negro's" image of the white Protestant as "at best a con-
descending, paternalistic gradualist and at worst a vicious wielder of power who
in the south opens White Citizens Council meetings with prayer and who in the
north champions conservative Republicanism."[55]

Few Protestants or Catholics questioned why forms of the institutional church
were not more heavily invested in the actual work of civil rights. In the Protestant case, most of them knew that the national bureaucracies were unable to commit resources and personnel to areas of controversy unless the local churches were
equally committed. Catholics generally acted through the Catholic Interracial
Councils or through bishops who issued orders of integration for parochial education. The Catholic record of accomplishment was a bit better, but none of the
local parishes or other institutional arms of the church distinguished themselves
through radical activism during these years either. Both Protestant and Catholic
leaders understood and generally honored the limited tolerance most American
Christians had for organized institutional activism in political matters.

During this first period of the movement, both Catholic and Protestant
church leaders seemed genuinely optimistic that things would work themselves
out over time, especially if the "Negroes" could continue to use nonviolent techniques effectively. Such feelings helped to reduce any sense of urgency to become
actively involved. After the first few years of the movement, they possessed
increased confidence that the self-interest motives operating against segregation
would eventually carry the day. Southern cities and states where segregation
remained most prominent, by 1961, had begun to experience economic difficulties directly attributable to their stance on segregation. As one Protestant minister put it, "in the end, the almighty dollar will determine the outcome."[56]

Occasionally, these Christian leaders also discussed realities that, in their view,
limited white Christian leadership in its ability to push the institutional church
toward an activist involvement in the quest for civil rights. Reinhold Niebuhr

and Waldo Beach liked to emphasize the congregational realities of Protestant life. Protestants simply did not possess the kind of authority that could enable a massive and activist response. Niebuhr also stressed the nature of sin, particularly the difference between individual sins and collective sins. When one has "a religious experience of repentance and conversion," that person is more likely to recognize the need to repent "individual sins which defy common standards of decency than collective sins that are imbedded in these common standards." For Niebuhr, the ability of the church to deal with "collective sins" offered "the real test of the redeeming efficacy of our Christian faith."[57] And the church always has trouble dealing honestly and forthrightly with the notion (and the implications) of corporate sin.

Niebuhr here made a distinction that not too many Christian leaders would make clearly when they struggled with the nature of Black Power after 1965. The collective sin embodied in "our peculiar cultural values, our 'Southern way of life,' or 'our American way of life,' " as Niebuhr variously phrased it, most often escaped the white line of sight. American Christians in white churches, both South and North, usually repented their own sins when they violated "common standards of decency," but few questioned whether those common standards themselves might be sinful. As Niebuhr put it elsewhere, this constitutes the very nature of the power of culture over faith. In response to events in Little Rock, for example, he wrote, "The Christian faith, in its collective expressions, is as liable to sanctify custom as to support the law even though it has more in common with the law than with the custom of a region." Kyle Haselden, a southern minister soon to join the editorial forces of the *Century*, emphasized this point as well: "Change at the deeper levels of life," he wrote, "is alien and is viewed with suspicion, as though a break with tradition were violation of a sacred heritage, repudiation of father and mother, desecration of the graves of ancestors, desertion of compatriots."[58] The priests of public life often firmly, and uncritically, defend "tradition."

Some, for example, among Protestant evangelical leaders found themselves greatly disturbed by both government action and the extent of civil disobedience in the South. Carl F. H. Henry, a Presbyterian and one of the most influential evangelical leaders in America, expressed serious reservations about the wisdom of government policy because it tended to demand too much change. Other evangelical authors agreed with him. The major outlet for their opinions was *CT*. Concerning questions of race relations, *CT* believed it needed to challenge some aspects of the status quo. Its editors never doubted that blacks deserved equal standing in society, complete with equal rights in voting, education, and other important areas of society. "Justice for all, regardless of race," declared one editorial, "is an inescapable outcome of the Gospel."[59] However, cultural assumptions and theological presuppositions combined in a way that kept these evangelicals from actually supporting the civil rights movement as it developed.

The arguments these evangelical editors and authors set out can conveniently be divided into social and theological categories. From a social perspective, they opposed growing governmental power and decried the tendency in this country to turn the Supreme Court into a "policy-making" body. They urged protection of individual rights above all else; in their dictionary, that meant the government should not step in to impose restrictions on what individuals could do with their own personal property, whether that property was home or business. With the events in the South, that position generally translated into a strong expression of support "for state's rights over an ever-increasing power of the federal government." One editorial, written during the struggles between James Meredith and the University of Mississippi, put it this way:

> Who will say race relations are better in Mississippi as a consequence of Federal force, or that bitterness has not been added to prejudice? . . . The indubitable fact of sprawling Federal power, and the national government's growing intrusion into the educational arena, helped to sharpen the Mississippi controversy. . . . Amid the hectic razzle-dazzle of swift-changing frontiers, the tear gas of Oxford has not hidden from view the long-range concern over Federal versus state powers.[60]

It is interesting, given its own evangelical pietism stressing the individual's relationship before God with no intermediaries, that *CT* often argued that segregation was a states' rights issue. The government had no right to become an intermediary.

In general, the magazine attempted to argue a separate but equal position. Editors and evangelical authors appeared not to doubt the equality of the black person with the white, but believed that government should not interfere with voluntary segregation of the races. As one early article put it,

> the white South desires—and holds it to be a right—to preserve its European racial and cultural heritage; this cannot be done if integration is enforced in social institutions. . . . Segregation has the potential to develop into a partnership of mutual respect; this partnership can never arise from a judicial force bill which is intolerable to one of the groups. . . . Segregation in America is, and should be, a fence not a wall, a division with many openings. . . .

From this perspective, editors often used the term "forced integration" to describe the process of desegregation. As one editorial expressed it, "forced integration is as contrary to Christian principles as is forced segregation." Forced integration, so the argument went, brought government intrusion and the violation of individual rights, and, hence, increased racial tensions. Interestingly enough, that was exactly the argument (and phrase) used by Governor Orval Faubus in Arkansas from 1957 to 1959.[61] A few voices in *CT* were gently raised in favor of desegregation,[62] but, for the editors, segregation was not all bad. The major cultural assumption negating full support of desegregation appeared mostly in the belief that the races were different enough that, in certain social circumstances, they should actually remain separated.[63]

Editors at *CT* charged that Protestants and Catholics who supported government efforts in desegregation were actually uncritically identifying Christian faith with secular goals (in other words, as evidence of priestly faith). Protestant and Catholic liberals, for their part, argued they did not equate political programs with the essence of Christianity itself. Rather, they believed the gospel led them to endorse certain political initiatives as "more Christian" than others. Walking that fine line was not always easy, and they did not always succeed. They certainly did, on occasion, give the impression that they were challenging whether those who defended segregation in the South could possibly be considered Christian. In other words, the liberal perspective also slipped into priestly faith, where opponents could be defined as "evil" or "unchristian." But progressive identification of Christian faith with the need for desegregation grew from Christian commitment to a gospel that understood all human beings as loved and affirmed by God. This led these Christians to challenge the iconic and cultural commitment to separating the races.

Evangelical theological arguments emphasized a need for the Christian to recognize a distinction between the kingdom of God and the kingdom of this world. As Carl F. H. Henry described it, the "universe is fallen and desperately wicked, and . . . supernatural redemption is its lone hope." Such a separation between history and the kingdom of God meant clearly that no secular programs should ever be identified as essentially or authentically Christian.

> Liberal Protestantism openly equated Christian social concern with support for specific modern enterprises and goals such as the League of Nations, the United Nations, giant labor unions, and integration.[64]

That was the problem of the social gospel in general, Henry asserted, in that it "was prone to equate the activities of unregenerate humanity at its best with authentic Christian achievements, and neglectful of the wholly proper priorities of supernatural revelation and redemption."[65] The church has no business attempting to transform the social order because "the depth of depravity" is too extensive for such efforts to be successful. But, at this point, by refusing to address the need for social transformation, theologians like Henry occasionally offered priestly endorsements of existing cultural values.

Incredible as it may seem, CT completely ignored the activities of Martin Luther King during the height of his activities. King's name was not even mentioned in those pages until 1964, when editors noted in two sentences that he had been chosen Time's "Man of the Year." In November, one sentence announced his winning of the Nobel Peace Prize. And in 1966, the example of King was used by editors to demonstrate concern with "lawlessness as a sign of our times."[66] In short, Martin Luther King was not highly regarded by the magazine. By way of contrast, Martin Luther King began publishing articles in the Century in February 1957, and the magazine named him an editor-at-large in October 1958. Later, the Century held the distinction of offering the first national publication of King's "Letter from Birmingham Jail" shortly after he wrote it in 1963.[67]

The evangelical understanding of integration represented in *CT* during these years serves to verify anthropologist Mary Douglas's insight that "people really do think of their own social environment as consisting of other people joined or separated by lines which must be respected."[68] These evangelicals did not consider themselves racists. But they were mostly blind to the immorality of segregation as a cultural practice. Part of the iconic symbol system operating at this time clearly defined where blacks stood in relation to the white culture. Though these evangelical voices defended equality for blacks, they usually meant an equality that did not or could not impact where they themselves lived. The power of the iconic assumption that blacks had "their place" and it was a place that whites did not enjoy, carried considerable weight with these editors, even though they never phrased it quite so blatantly. And it led to the magazine's priestly response to the civil rights movement, the connection between the cultural practice of segregation and God's will. The assumption, of course, was not limited to the evangelical community.

The mainline Protestant and Catholic churches demonstrated plenty of evidence of the pervasiveness of this assumption in their communities as well. Duke Divinity School and Candler School of Theology, both schools associated with the Methodist Church, retained their color bars during these years. In these cases the barriers were clearly defined. But even where barriers had fallen, invisible or ambiguous barriers remained in the form of white expectations of black behavior in the majority culture. Vanderbilt Divinity School, though integrated (in a token way, with three or four black students), offers one of the clearest examples of this reality.

The Divinity School entered crisis territory when one of their African American students, James Lawson, was arrested for his participation in sit-in demonstrations in Nashville. The administration of Vanderbilt University, which had no black students other than those in the Divinity School, rapidly acted to terminate Lawson's association with the school. Faculty at the Divinity School challenged the decision, eventually resigning in mass. For five or six months during 1960, the crisis boiled over at Vanderbilt. Eventually, the chancellor offered a way for Lawson to graduate from the Divinity School (through taking a battery of tests, and transferring some class credits) and for faculty to return to their jobs. Lawson refused the settlement because the dean of the Divinity School, J. Robert Nelson, was not allowed to remain. Such happenings probably should have convinced Christian liberals that their confidence in the role of education in overcoming racial injustice in this country was seriously misplaced.[69]

Protestants and Catholics also had to deal with significant differences in attitudes between clergy and laity that affected the church's willingness to act. Clergy were mostly educated in seminaries where questions related to ethics and justice were built into the curriculum. Laypeople, on the other hand, rarely had the opportunity to discuss or analyze serious ethical questions. Attitudes differed considerably. An early poll showed that southern Protestant ministers overwhelmingly favored integration. Not so among laypeople. In 1964, Catholic leaders were shocked to discover that 55.5 percent of Catholic ballots in a Maryland preferential election were cast for George Wallace in spite of the consistent teachings of Catholic leaders in that state dealing with race. As late as November 1966, a majority of laypeople in one of the most socially active and liberal Protestant denominations, the United Church of Christ, expressed the belief that blacks were moving too quickly. Less than half of the respondents were willing to accept blacks as neighbors, despite a consistent educational campaign about the merits of the civil rights movement being conducted within the denomination during these years. John Bennett commented the next year that Protestant and Catholic leadership increasingly reached consensus on most social issues; as this consensus developed, both found themselves growing closer to one another than to their own constituencies.[70]

By 1961, when white Protestant and Catholic leaders complained about gradualism or groused that progress came much too slowly, they most often did so because they understood the potential of black militancy. An acute fear of violence, sometimes veiled, sometimes not, usually accompanied their strong support for King's program of nonviolence after this time. White Christians worried about the outbreak of racial violence, and when black nationalism and the Black Muslim movement caught their attention in 1960–1961, that fear found regular expression. Young African nations emerged from colonial pasts and began to have an impact on the affairs of the United Nations. Actual and effective power among Africans caused an increasing impatience among young black Americans, especially among those for whom the setting of the urban ghetto seemed so hopeless. Black nationalism offered something tangible that could speak to their despair. Black militancy, once it appeared, loomed larger and larger in the white perspective with every passing year.[71]

Malcolm X spoke the language of black nationalism better than anyone. He frankly scared white Christian liberals. They appreciated the fact that King and other moderate middle-class African Americans shared their perception of him as dangerous, racist, and an advocate of black supremacy. But by 1963 James O'Gara of *Commonweal* incisively noted "the position of these [responsible] Negro leaders becomes more and more difficult precisely to the extent that Black Muslim charges against white society seem to be true."[72] When Malcolm X appeared in the viewfinder of white Americans (late 1959–1960), neither King nor most of the white liberals understood just how different the experience of racism was for blacks living in the urban ghettos of the northern cities from that experienced by blacks in the South. For their part, Black Muslims never made much headway in the South either.

It would be a few years before King understood much about the situation in northern ghettos, and most white Christian liberals were much slower to catch on. One of the rare, discerning white liberals, William Stringfellow, predicted in early 1962 that the racial "exploitation" and its accompanying "alienation" and "estrangement" of the races evident in Harlem could lead to a northern explosion of revenge: "To Negroes in the north, revenge may seem sweeter than equality and certainly seems more honorable than acceptance of further appeasements."[73] Beginning especially with the summer of 1965, the ramifications of black experiences in the North would be virtually impossible to ignore. Eventually, they represented a shift in focus for the civil rights movement, from the South to the North. Mainline Christian support ultimately disintegrated due to the seismic nature of that shift. The shift recorded a movement from an emphasis on "rights" to a severe questioning of the core values of the American culture itself. And a defense of those core values by white Christians often caused a lapse into priestly forms of response to public life.

A LESSON FROM THE PRESENT

Following these lessons from history, it might be worthwhile to take a quick look at a contemporary example of how priestly faith is operating on the American scene today. For this lesson, however, we'll flip the lens and examine how this style also shows up in political circles in ways that often draw Christians into it.

The Priestly Rhetoric of the President in the War Against Terrorism

September 11, 2001, is a date that few Americans will ever forget. Most likely, everyone over seven or eight on that day will remember exactly where they were when they first heard or saw the news of the airplanes and the towers. President George W. Bush's first response was measured and cautious. He spoke of an "apparent terrorist attack." A few hours after the attack, in comments at the Barksdale Air Force Base, Bush became more direct as he pledged "to hunt down and punish those responsible for these cowardly acts." By that evening, in his comments from the Oval Office, he began to use a rhetoric one scholar has described as Bush's "discourse of 'evil.'" Bush told listeners that

> America was targeted for attack because we're the brightest beacon for freedom and opportunity in the world. And no one will keep that light from shining.
>   Today, our nation saw evil, the very worst of human nature, and we responded with the best of America, with the daring of our rescue workers, with the caring for strangers and neighbors who came to give blood and help in any way they could.[74]

In this way, Bush began a rhetorical description of the attacks, and the resulting war against terrorism, that pitted Good against Evil, Light against Dark. On September 26, 2001, in a photo opportunity with the Prime Minister of Japan, he told reporters, "make no mistake about it: This is good versus evil." "These are evildoers," he told them. "They have no justification for their actions. There's no religious justification, there's no political justification. The only motivation is evil."[75]

When you describe this brand of evil, you must oppose it, or you are part of it. Like Secretary of State John Foster Dulles during the early years of the Cold

War, Bush declared there could be no "neutrality" in this war. On September 20, he told Congress, "Every nation, in every region, now has a decision to make. Either you are with us, or you are with the terrorists." There is no position in between. "I will put every nation on notice that these duties involve more than sympathy or words," President Bush told those gathered for the Warsaw Conference on Combating Terrorism on November 6, 2001. "No nation can be neutral in this conflict, because no civilized nation can be secure in a world threatened by terror."[76]

Bruce Lincoln pointed out in his analysis of Bush's rhetoric that he has not been "apocalyptic and, with a single unfortunate (if revealing exception), he never cast the conflict as a Crusade." The one exception noted by Lincoln came on the South Lawn of the White House on September 16 in responding to questions from the press after a brief statement. At that time, Bush told reporters, "The American people are beginning to understand, this crusade, this war on terrorism is going to take a while."[77] The press in America did not take much notice of the comment, but "it rang alarm bells in Europe" and in the Arab world.[78] When the word was translated for the Arab world, it came out meaning "war of the cross."

Shortly after President Bush's first use of the term "crusade," his aides suggested that he had only meant to describe the nature of a long struggle, without any of the historical religious baggage contained within the word. Even though his first use of the word brought some measure of embarrassment, President Bush actually did use the word a second time, again probably inadvertently, speaking off the cuff and without a script. He was in Alaska "rallying the troops" on February 16, 2002. Referring to the Canadian Armed Forces, he said, "They stand with us in this incredibly important crusade to defend freedom, this campaign to do what is right for our children and our grandchildren."[79] Reflecting back on Bush's use of the term the first time, James Carroll of *The Nation* wrote,

> For George W. Bush, crusade was an offhand reference. But all the more powerfully for that, it was an accidental probing of unintended but nevertheless real meaning. That the President used the word inadvertently suggests how it expressed his exact truth, an unmasking of his most deeply felt purpose. . . . Here is the deeper significance of Bush's inadvertent reference to the Crusades: Instead of being a last recourse or a necessary evil, violence was established then as the perfectly appropriate, even chivalrous, first response to what is wrong in the world. George W. Bush is a Christian for whom this particular theology lives.[80]

Whether there is any merit to the psychological interpretation provided by James Carroll, and there most likely is, the president has made it clear through his rhetoric that America's war on terrorism is a battle of good against evil. Peter Singer, a philosopher and professor of bioethics at Princeton, has analyzed President Bush's speeches and found reference to "evil" in 319 of them, 30 percent of the speeches he delivered between taking office and June 16, 2003. In most of those usages, evil is used as a noun, not as an adjective. For Bush, evil is an active power, visible and clearly identifiable. Evil, in Bush's usage, is rarely what people do; evil is either a "thing, or a force, something that has a real existence apart from the cruel, callous, brutal and selfish acts of which human beings are capable."[81] And people can be evil—in their very being. So you don't define their actions as evil; rather you define them as evil. In other words, his use of evil is theological, indicating a state of being that stands over against God and all that is good. His belief that America is called to eradicate evil (including evil persons), therefore, is equally theological, and places America clearly on the side of the angels, in the role of the "church," standing with God and with all that is good over against this massive evil in the world.

Many times, since September 11, he has also personified evil in the person of either Saddam Hussein or Osama bin Laden. The month after the attacks, he addressed business, trade, and agricultural leaders and told them, for example, that Americans "do know *the evil one* [Osama bin Laden] who hides [and] thinks in ways that we can't possibly think in America—so destructive, such a low regard for human life."[82] Use of this phrase "the evil one" is language that resonates well with conservative Christians in America. They hear clearly what Bush wants to convey to them by using it. But, truthfully, this kind of language provides a false cloak of morality around American military operations as if they were fighting Satan, demonic evil itself, personified in human form. This use of language is unfortunately not far afield from the rhetoric that surrounded the medieval crusades.

To describe the event of flying planes into populated towers as "evil activities" is different from depicting the men who flew the planes, or ordered their flights, as "evil" personified. The difference is more than merely a semantic one. When you describe "evil activities," you are led naturally to ask questions. What kind of environment produced these kinds of activities? Did our government, or our people, or the business world itself, symbolized by those operating in the towers, do anything, however great or small, that might have contributed to creating an environment within which these kinds of evil activities could emerge? In asking these questions, one is not trying to determine whether these evil activities are in any sense justifiable. Evil activities are not justifiable. But one asks these questions to understand better what kind of environment is conducive to the emergence of evil activities, and what kind of forces help to create and sustain this environment. What contributed to this context? However, when one simply describes the men who flew the planes, or the people who ordered the act, as evil, no other questions are necessary. The answer is contained in the description. These men are evil. They did this. If they had not been evil, this would not have happened. Get rid of the men, and all others like them, and you get rid of the problem. But it is never that simple. If we don't ask the questions behind the emergence of evil activities, we might only take more actions that contribute to creating contexts anew where evil activities will again emerge.

There is no ambiguity in President Bush's picture and no way to understand intent or motives of enemies as political; rather, they are simply absolutely evil.

This personification can justify just about any American action, by way of contrast, as representing all that is good against all that is evil, including, of course, preventive war in Iraq. This portrayal of American action as "good" compared with the "evil" we face is bolstered in the presidential rhetoric used by President Bush in his second State of the Union address, where he makes reference to the way America has been "called" to its mission in our day.

> We've come to know truths that we will never question: evil is real, and it must be opposed. . . . Deep in the American character, there is honor, and it is stronger than cynicism. And many have discovered again that even in tragedy—especially in tragedy—*God is near.* In a single instant, we realized that this will be a decisive decade in the history of liberty, that *we've been called to a unique role in human events.* Rarely has the world faced a choice more clear or consequential.[83]

These are clearly very religious words. Evil exists. We must oppose it. God is near, and calls America, in a vocational sense, to this "unique role in human events." With words like these, the American missions in Afghanistan and Iraq, and across the world, are clearly sanctified and carry divine significance in the ongoing battle for the kingdom of God.

Finally, on at least two occasions, President Bush has clearly used rhetoric during this war that, while not directly causing the dehumanization of prisoners so recently in the news, certainly can be seen as fostering the kind of mentality that allowed it. The first usage occurred on October 14, 2002, again on the South Lawn. Responding to an event when citizens were murdered in Bali, Indonesia, during a terrorist attack, President Bush told reporters that "those of us who love freedom must work together to do everything we can to disrupt, deny, and bring to justice these people who have no soul, no conscience, people who hate freedom."[84] To suggest that the enemy has "no soul" is to suggest that they are not human. President Bush used the phrase again in his April 2004 call to renew the U.S.A. Patriot Act. Speaking at the Hershey Lodge and Convention Center in Pennsylvania, the president told those gathered that

> We will never show weakness in the face of these people who have no soul, who have no conscience, who care less about the life of a man or a woman or a child. We've got to do everything we can here at home. And there's no doubt in my mind that, with the Almighty's blessings and hard work, that we will succeed in our mission.[85]

This kind of presidential rhetoric, describing the enemy as "people who have no soul," naturally leads to an ability to dehumanize the enemy among those who take these words seriously. Recent news has carried clear evidence of ways that troops have dehumanized prisoners by their treatment of them in captivity at Abu Ghraib. Photographs and videos explicitly revealed all manner of systematic physical and psychological abuse of prisoners. The behavior of guards shocked families and friends back home who described the offenders as solid citizens from whom they could never imagine this kind of activity. But the Taguba Report, ordered by the senior U.S. military official in Iraq, found clear evidence of "sadistic, blatant, and wanton criminal abuses." In most cases, the report indicated that guards "sought to degrade" detainees. The word "degrade" is interesting because it connotes shame or debasement, all characteristics of what it means to dehumanize, to treat people as if they have no souls. Beyond the fact that these particular individuals were "not adequately trained for a mission that included operating a prison,"[86] the fact is that these soldiers came to view the prisoners as somehow less than human. Only that kind of perspective permits this abusive behavior in the minds of otherwise sane individuals. Unfortunately, dehumanizing behavior follows naturally when the president and other political leadership in America offer such an unambiguous priestly response to the events on September 11.

President Bush's presidency is, among other things, nearly always very decisive about its actions. As Ron Suskind put it in an article in the *New York Times Magazine* in October 2004, President Bush's approach to all matters of policy and decision making can usually be described as "without a doubt." The administration is, in Suskind's words, "a faith-based presidency." There is nothing inherently wrong with a president taking personal faith seriously. President Carter, for example, is a recent president well known for taking faith seriously. In President Bush's case, it is the way his faith is connected to absolute certainty that some have experienced as problematic.

> The faith-based presidency is a with-us-or-against-us model that has been enormously effective at, among other things, keeping the workings and temperament of the Bush White House a kind of state secret. . . . This is one key feature of the faith-based presidency: open dialogue, based on facts, is not seen as something of inherent value. It may, in fact, create doubt, which undercuts faith. It could result in a loss of confidence in the decision-maker and, just as important, by the decision-maker.[87]

Of course, there is no doubt that the acts of September 11 were "evil." There is a difference, however, between recognizing certain acts as evil and using the nation as a self-appointed agent to remove all evil from the world. There is also a difference between recognizing activities as evil and concluding, with absolute certainty, that all human beings who oppose American activities in the world, or even those who resort to acts of terrorism for political purposes, are themselves purely evil. For that too easily confines evil in certain places and refuses to recognize the evil that might reside even in portions of America's foreign or domestic policies. James Wallis put it well in *Sojourners* when he examined what he described as President Bush's "Dangerous Religion."

> To fail to speak of evil in the world today is to engage in bad theology. But to speak of "they" being evil and "we" being good, to say that evil is all out there and that in the warfare between good and evil others are either with us or against us—that is also bad theology. Unfortunately, it has become the Bush theology. . . . In Christian theology, it is not nations that rid the world

of evil—they are too often caught up in complicated webs of political power, economic interests, cultural clashes, and nationalist dreams. The confrontation with evil is a role reserved for God, and for the people of God when they faithfully exercise moral conscience. But God has not given the responsibility for overcoming evil to a nation-state, much less to a super-power with enormous wealth and particular national interests. To confuse the role of God with that of the American nation, as George Bush seems to do, is a serious theological error that some might say borders on idolatry or blasphemy.[88]

It is also a near perfect example of contemporary priestly faith.

CONCLUSION

The 1960s had opened up an entire "Pandora's box" of issues that vied for attention within the Christian camp. Just as Protestants were being forced to accept their minority status within the culture and attempted to act out of it, they faced new challenges. Their self-definition through the 1960s remained too largely male, white, and middle class. By the end of the 1970s, the definition had been expanded to allow more significantly for female, black, Hispanic, and even, in some cases, homosexual expressions. Though largely still middle class by the end of that decade, Protestants had at least begun to incorporate some of the theological insights of the lower classes by way of liberation theology. Issues related to public life were no longer "those issues" outside the walls of the church (if they ever were); the late sixties through the seventies witnessed them crashing into the life of the church itself. The 1960s leadership (read here "white, male, and middle class") among Protestants and Catholics could no longer ignore them.

There can be little doubt that American Christianity has become fragmented since 1956. Social issues have certainly played a very important role in new understandings of both theology and church during these years. When the church has acted as priest, it has made this fragmentation worse. This chapter has briefly examined three events from the past (the Cold War, Vietnam, and the civil rights movement) that resulted in a variety of priestly assumptions in the Christian community. Many other examples could have been provided in some depth.

Christian priests struggled with the development of rock music and the birth of modern cinema, equating Elvis with the "depth of decadence" in society, or lamenting that Pat Boone, in the movie *State Fair*, engaged in "as torrent and violent love-making as is possible to depict on a screen. . . . It is to weep."[89] The sexual revolution and the emergence of the voice of gays and lesbians brought similar identifications between American culture as it was in the past and the will of God in these matters. As one editorial expressed it in 1970, "if God had wanted homosexuals, he would have created Adam and Freddy."[90] This is not too far removed from the "God Hates Fags" mentality expressed in some Christian rallies today.

Advocates of this position in the 1970s and 1980s were naturally tempted to connect AIDS to divine judgment on homosexuality.[91]

The chapter could also have provided the example of the church's response to the changing public role of women since the 1950s. Barbara Brown Zikmund lamented the failure of churches, until the 1960s, to understand and help the women who were called out into the workplace during the Second World War.[92] The indexes of the independent Christian journals during these years support her complaint. In 1956, in their national assemblies, both the Methodists and the Presbyterians voted to extend to women the same privileges men had in ministry. The *Century* celebrated the move. Yet the editors remained reluctant to support women working outside the home. They feared two developments: (1) women might take jobs needed by ethnic minorities; and (2) women working outside the home would likely have an adverse effect upon the family life of America. So while they supported women in ministry and the rights of women in the workplace, they feared that large numbers of women would leave their important positions in the home. *CT*, in 1963, called working mothers "a national problem" since "unhappy homes breed juvenile delinquency and reduce the efficiency of working husbands." Further, they tended to take jobs that were needed by men.[93]

Some of the items on this priestly agenda were derived primarily from cultural considerations and then found some expression in biblical rationale, like staunch support for democracy and capitalism, a strong anticommunism, certain aspects of race relations, and anti-Catholicism. Other items, like those involving changing sexual mores and the roles of women, were more easily grounded in various forms of Christian biblical interpretation, though even in those cases cultural influences are extremely hard to differentiate from the self-confessed biblical arguments. It is hard to determine the precise negative impact these priestly arguments had, either in the church or in society, during their heydays in American culture. One can at least affirm the fact that the merger of cultural assumptions with Christian and biblical justifications generally strengthened Christian adherence to the status quo that made it more difficult for Christians to support meaningful and significant change within both the church and the social order.

One of the telltale marks of positions taken as priests is the unmistakable way such positions are necessarily changed over time. The examples we have looked at all have one thing in common. In nearly every case, the editors have had to adjust their positions and take views considerably different than they once took. Usually, the generation following an expression of priestly faith is embarrassed by its expression, repents, and tries to recover a more truly Christian perspective on whatever the issue was that occasioned the priestly response in the first place.

On the contemporary scene, there are other examples we could have used as well. The Air Force Academy, throughout 2005–2006, has struggled with the penchant among some of its officers and senior cadets to connect fundamentalist Christian faith with the most acceptable way to serve in the air force.[94] There is also the case of Bishop Michael J. Sheridan, of Colorado Springs, who threatened to withhold communion from Catholic voters if they supported abortion or gay marriage. Other Catholic bishops in 2004 indicated that a vote for John Kerry constituted a sin that must be confessed before communion. Rev. Andrew Kemberling, a Catholic pastor in Colorado, had a ready response to those who might accuse him of telling Catholics how to vote. "We are not telling them how to vote. We are telling them how to take Communion in good conscience."[95]

Roy Moore, former Chief Justice of the Supreme Court of Alabama, provided another excellent public example of priestly faith from 2001 to 2003 as he tried to keep his 2.5–ton granite monument of the Ten Commandments in the Alabama Judicial Building. As a judge, his action went well beyond merely iconic faith through his efforts to use the monument to represent "the sovereignty of God" in America, and to denote the fact that "this country was established on a particular God and His divine, revealed laws; it [display of the Ten Commandments] reflected the Christian faith of our founders."[96]

This chapter could also have addressed in some detail the Terri Schiavo case and Congress's response to it. In one of the worst examples, Representative Tom DeLay told a conference organized by the Family Research Council that "God has brought . . . Terri Schiavo, to help elevate the visibility of what is going on in America." He meant by this that it helped raise awareness of the fact that Democrats, the national news media, and other "do gooder organizations" had formed a "whole syndicate" and started a "nationwide concerted effort to destroy everything we believe in."[97] Using God-language to claim God intended Terri Schiavo's tragic case to be used for the purpose of bringing political gain for conservative leadership in the Republican Party is an unfortunate example of priestly faith.

The divisions in American life are palpable today, both in politics and in the church. What will heal these divisions? What will bring the unity that "special issue" theology has lost for the church? This appears to be the major question of our time. If Christians cannot address public life with any degree of unanimity, how can they expect to influence its development toward Christian objectives of peace and justice? Yet, as always seems true for those who affirm the gospel, there are signs of hope in the midst of despair.

As hinted earlier, many Christians from among evangelicalism, post-Vatican II Catholicism, and mainstream Protestantism have found themselves growing closer together rather than further apart in the 1980s and 1990s, in spite of all the "culture wars" rhetoric.[98] Black theologians, feminist theologians, and theologians of third-world liberation have also discovered mutual commonality. Many of their expressions have crept into the vocabulary of both evangelical and mainstream Christianity in the last two decades. Perhaps most importantly, these last twenty to twenty-five years have also witnessed a deep and ecumenical concern among many Christian groups to return to the importance of Christian tradition for ethical reflection. The "post-traditional" world advocated by Robert Bellah in 1970 has given way to one in which he has more recently expressed his belief that "only living traditions make it possible to have a world at all."[99]

As diverse as those within the Christian movement in America are, this common and self-critical search for the relevance of Christian tradition to the way we live together as Americans within a shrinking world holds great promise for a more unified Christian witness in the modern world. But Christians have to find a better way than simply falling into the practice of priestly faith to express it. This concern forms the topic of our next two chapters.

PART III
FAITH AND PUBLIC LIFE

Chapter 5

Public Christian

We have been talking about how public life engages Christian faith in American life. The last two chapters chronicle the temptation among Christians to affirm uncritically the nature of their cultural surroundings. As H. Richard Niebuhr noted in the first few decades of the last century, culture has always affected the practice of faith.[1] The encounter with public and cultural life in America has led Christians to read their Bibles and express their personal faith in particular ways. Occasionally, Christians have confused public life and faith at key points and offered biblical and theological rationale for assumptions more important to culture than to faith. Once in a while, these occasions surface as a firm commitment to the status quo as if it somehow represented God's will for all people in all places. At other times, they surface as arguments for change that benefit wealthier and more powerful members of the culture in ways that actually seem counter to the gospel when subjected to a more critical examination. Through these activities, Christians have exhibited characteristics reminiscent to the kinds of categories I have described as "iconic faith" and "priestly faith."

In any attempt to understand how Christianity relates to public life in America, theological beliefs must not be ignored. For some Christians in America, theological understanding enables a thoughtful response to events in public life. Clearly articulated theological reflection provides Christians with ground rules for participation in public life. It bestows content and meaning for the kind of response Christians might have to controversial issues when they arise. It is important, therefore, to consider different theological strands in relating faith to public life. This chapter examines a theological perspective that believes a right relationship between the two requires that the church, first of all, must tend to salvation and not to politics. This does not mean, within this theological understanding, that Christian individuals should not be active in the public or political life of the nation. Christians are encouraged, outside the church, to participate fully within the public life of the nation. They vote; they run for office; they participate in lobbying organizations; they are as active as other responsibilities and commitments allow them to be. But their congregations are not. For this reason, I call this posture that of the "public Christian," rather than the "public church" (the topic of the next chapter). To gain a sense of the theological tradition within which this theology stands, I begin with an examination of Augustine's theological influence. That influence has not always ended up the way Augustine, Bishop of Hippo in Africa (386–430), himself might have preferred if he were around to define it, but the influence of his work has played a significant role for many Christians.

AUGUSTINE AND THE "CITY OF GOD"

Historically, when Christians have thought about faith and public life, they have often couched their reflections in the language of two cities. Augustine's *City of God* helped to secure this language in the church. But the talk of two cities actually exists within Scripture and is found especially in Revelation. In this apocalyptic literature of the Bible, the new Jerusalem, descending from heaven (Rev. 21:2, 10) is depicted as the city of God (Rev. 3:12), "prepared as a bride adorned for her husband." In these passages, the cities of earth, represented at their worst in the city of Babylon, "a dwelling place of demons" (18:2), are destroyed. Gerard O'Daly points out the possibility that these passages are influenced by "the Jewish apocalyptic tradition, in particular their dualism, and the antithesis between this world or age and the one to come."

> The antithesis Babylon-Jerusalem is used. It is also found in the so-called New Testament Apocrypha, which speak of the kingdom of God, Satan's reign, the city of Christ, and two "metropoleis". . . . Similar imagery is found in a work of apocalyptic literature written in the first half of the second century . . . the *Shepherd of Hermas* [which] develops an antithesis between two cities, and the theme of the Christian's alien status.[2]

According to Johannes van Oort, it is Augustine who combines several aspects of existing tradition and brings them to bear in creating an understanding among Christians that these two cities are opposed to one another throughout human history, from creation to the end of time. Part of the tradition Augustine draws on to make his case includes non-Christian sources. This included writers from the Stoic tradition, thinkers associated with Platonism, and even Jewish writers like Philo, who spoke of a homeland not of this world and the hope of returning there after spending time as an alien in this world.

Manichaeans, particularly, spoke of two cities and also of two kingdoms, the heavenly kingdom and the kingdom of this world. Manichaeism was a Gnostic sect opposed by the early Christian church. Augustine had been a member of the sect for a number of years before his conversion to Catholic Christianity. Manichaeans understood evil to be ontological, eternal, and always opposed to the good. Evil is not and has never been a part of the good. Instead, evil eternally fights the good. Christian tradition, on the other hand, described how evil developed as a result of fallen angels, led by Satan, himself an angel who fell away from the good. For Augustine, Satan was "under God's jurisdiction" and defeat of evil would certainly occur at the end of history.[3] But this was God's business, not ours. Unlike Eusebius, Augustine did not believe God used emperors to destroy evil. After all, God not only allowed Constantine to rule; God had also allowed all the persecuting emperors to have their day in the sun. Augustine believed such turns of events should teach Christians that neither earthly kingdoms nor Christian rulers were going to solve the world's problems or bring in the kingdom of God.[4]

Tyconius, a prolific thinker associated with Donatism in the last quarter of the fourth century, also wrote about such things. The Donatists opposed the Catholic Church, believing it to have gone astray by following too closely the ways of the world. Donatists understood the church "sojourning as an alien in the midst of hostile surroundings." Tyconius spoke primarily of two bodies, the body of Christ (the church) and the body of the devil. But later thinkers like Augustine, who depended on the work of Tyconius, spoke more in terms of two cities. It is possible that the commentary Tyconius wrote on the book of Revelation, lost to the contemporary world, also did so. The commentary work of those who followed him emphasized this "antithesis" between the two cities. But in his main body of work, Tyconius describes the body of Christ to contain both "salvation and disaster, blessing and curse, . . . both good and evil," and these will remain undistinguished until the end.[5] In other words, even Tyconius did not contain the total and absolute separation, historically, between good and evil that will be so characteristic of Augustine's work.

> Although Augustine was aware of their intermingling in this age of the world, he emphasized the absolute antithesis between the two cities. Both in the model catecheses and in the *City of God* he narrates the history of the world from creation to end as the history of the two antithetical cities, and says that the two *civitas*, each with its king and angels, form one society.[6]

As Augustine put it,

> accordingly, two cities have been formed by two loves: the earthly by the love of self, even to the contempt of God; the heavenly by the love of God, even to the contempt of self. The former, in a word, glories in itself, the latter in the Lord.[7]

Van Oort's study also examined the tradition of early Christian apologists who preceded Augustine.[8] Ambrose, Bishop of Milan (374–397), spoke of the two cities but usually "spiritualized and individualized" them. For Ambrose, the soul of Christians was to be the city where God or Christ lived. It should be the city of Jerusalem. The human passions that opposed God and also sought control of the soul were represented by the city of Babylon. In other words, Ambrose did not use these two cities in order to depict a conflict in human history but rather the ethical conflict fought within each individual human soul.[9] Origen (185–253 or 254), a theologian whose work significantly influenced both Ambrose and Augustine, also spoke of the two cities. He equated the city of God with the church, which was composed of individuals who practiced the good virtues. And here is where Ambrose learned his lessons from Origen well. Each virtuous soul practicing the virtues was a city of God. Thus, the kingdom of God bears fruit in each individual soul first. The most important battle was the struggle over control of the inner self within each human being. Who will rule in the soul, God or the devil? This is quite different than the description of the cities in Augustine, where the reader will find the two cities locked in a cosmic struggle set to determine the course of human history.

Other Western writers preceding Augustine, like Lactantius (early fourth century) and Cyprian (mid-third century), made little use of the imagery of the two cities, but they did develop theologies that contrasted the way of darkness (associated with the world and with the devil) and the way of light (associated with the church and with God). These negative views of the world were quite influential in Christian circles prior to Constantine. Official persecution produced a strong sense of alienation from the world. Cyprian admonishes, "We should consider, dearly beloved brethren, and again and again remember that we have renounced the world and are sojourning here temporarily as guests and aliens."[10] Van Oort also analyzed the use of military language found in Cyprian, who often described the camp of God as being locked in conflict with the camp of the devil.

Before Cyprian, Tertullian (late second, early third century) distinguished himself as a significant theologian in the West. He lived in Africa and eventually joined the Montanists, a strict movement among early Christians. They believed in the strong presence of the Holy Spirit and practiced ecstatic prophecy associated with rigid and ascetic lifestyles. The Catholic Church condemned Montanism as heretical in the late second century. Even though Tertullian eventually broke with the Catholic Church, his theological influence remained. For him, baptism meant the end of any meaningful association with the world. Christians must leave everything behind. "Nothing is more foreign to us than the State," wrote Tertullian. "What, indeed, has Athens to do with Jerusalem? And the Academy with the Church? . . . But as for you," he wrote his fellow Christians,

> you are an alien in this world and a citizen of Jerusalem, the city above. . . . Incompatible is the oath to serve God with the oath to serve man, the standard of Christ with the standard of the devil, the camp of light with the camp of darkness. No one can serve two masters, God and Caesar.[11]

Though he did not regularly use the language of two cities, Tertullian's writings clearly describe Christians as aliens in the world, opposed to the darkness associated with the devil's rule. Van Oort draws the following conclusion:

> It is this apocalyptic atmosphere of antithesis to the surrounding world, the heathen culture and pagan Rome in particular, that is constantly found in the West in the centuries preceding and following Constantine. This antithesis is characteristic of a theology of the two cities. It is encountered especially in the writings of Tertullian and Cyprian; furthermore to a greater or lesser degree in various other authors belonging to the tradition of Western Christianity prior to Augustine. With reason, therefore, it has been observed: "The theology of the Two Cities, Jerusalem and Babylon, was never to die out completely in western Christian thought."[12]

Ultimately, however, van Oort's work reveals that Augustine's theological approach has most in common with writings prior in time to the musings of the early Christian theologians like Tertullian, Cyprian, or Origen. Those works, "in which archaic Christian concepts closely related to Judaism had an important place," included the book of Revelation, the *Shepherd of Hermas*, and the *Acts of Peter and the Twelve Apostles*. Van Oort also examined the earliest catechetical literature and found that much of it discusses an antipathy between darkness and light. The discovery of the Dead Sea Scrolls (1947), and especially the *Manual of Discipline*, revealed that members of the Qumran community, a Jewish ascetic community in existence before the beginning of the Christian era, learned of such things.

This idea of two ways and two societies or kingdoms is also found in early catechetical documents associated with Christianity, including especially the *Didache*, the *Epistle of Barnabas*, and the Latin document *Doctrina apostolorum*. Each of these teach their readers, in the style of the Jewish *Manual of Discipline*, about the two ways: one is associated with light, Christ, and Christians while the other is associated with darkness, Satan, and the world. In the early Christian community, these teachings were associated with baptism. Once you learned of the existence of the two ways and two spirits, you chose the one and renounced the other by entering the baptismal waters.

Obviously, these concepts existed in Jewish and early Jewish-Christian communities and continued in some fashion throughout the development of Western theology up through Augustine, and, of course, beyond. But Augustine added distinctive touches. As van Oort put it,

> Augustine was the only one to present a comprehensive doctrine of two anti-thetical *civitas* [cities]. Only he described the entire history of the world as the history of the two cities. It was Augustine who emphasized that each of the two cities contains angels and people and that these two societies are engaged in a gigantic struggle.
>
> . . . Augustine placed the two cities opposite each other. For the differ-ence between the two is great: the society of the believers is in opposition to that of the wicked; the two societies are allied with angels, the good ones or the evil ones. And although the two cities are intermingled in this temporal existence, there is fundamentally an absolute antithesis, an unbridgeable gap. . . . There is nothing in between. . . . There is only belief or unbelief; a middle course does not exist.[13]

Augustine lived from 354 to 430. It is important to keep in mind that Augus-tine's great work on the city of God is set in a context where a Christian controls the empire. Augustine believed that the Christian ruler, those in the genre of the great Constantine, kept his power and authority in the proper perspective, as sub-ject to the one true God.[14] Even within history, Augustine asserted, God main-tains power over all the earthly kingdoms as they exercise their own desires and fulfill their own lusts for power. In other words, God is in control. Kingdoms that do not recognize it will not know anything of true community, even though God still governs their affairs more than they know.

Perhaps for this reason, Augustine is not predisposed to condemn the impor-tant and necessary activities related to the social sphere. In an age before nation-states, and before religious freedom became a constitutional principle anywhere in the world, Augustine could go so far as to laud the benefit of Christian lead-ers who "could protect the church by suppressing its rivals."[15] He also recognized that wars must be fought to provide for the social needs of human beings under the care of government. Such things pertain to states, not to the church.[16] And whether the government is run by Christians or not, it is still the earthly city; its peace is earthly peace, not the heavenly peace that is everlasting and represented in "the perfectly ordered and harmonious enjoyment of God and of one another in God."[17] Augustine argued that the earthly city is never the heavenly city, no matter who rules or how completely the ruler or the people connect the city with Christianity.

One can note, therefore, that there are several themes in Augustine's book rel-evant to the discussion of the relationship between Christian faith and public life. As already evident in the paragraphs above, the only proper end for human life is "the contemplation of God." This is, of course, the task of the church and Augustine's book is much more about the church than it is about the world.[18] Augustine makes it clear that public life is not the first priority for the church. The church exists for God and for the worship of God. Further, Augustine stresses that the Christian is, as a result of regeneration, an "alien" or "stranger" in the world. The Christian's true home is not in this world but in the city of God, far away from this world. The Christian knows that all of life finds its com-plete happiness and end in the one true God.

But Christians also exist, for the time being, in this world, this "earthly city." The two cities, Augustine argued, are "entangled together in this world, and intermixed until the last judgment effect their separation."[19] Even though a citizen of a different city, the Christian lives in this one. Therefore, "the heavenly city . . . while in its state of pilgrimage, avails itself of the peace of earth, and, so far as it can without injuring faith and godliness, desires and maintains a common agreement among men regarding the acquisition of the necessaries of life."

> The earthly city, which does not live by faith, seeks an earthly peace, and the end it proposes, in the well-ordered concord of civic obedience and rule, is the combination of men's wills to attain the things which are helpful to this life. The heavenly city, or rather the part of it which sojourns on earth and lives by faith, makes use of this peace only because it must, until this mortal condition which necessitates it shall pass away. Consequently, so long as it lives like a captive and a stranger in the earthly city, though it has already received the promise of redemption, and the gift of the Spirit as the earnest of it, it makes no scruple to obey the laws of the earthly city, whereby the things necessary for the maintenance of this mortal life are administered; and thus, as this life is common to both cities, so there is a harmony between them in regard to what belongs to it.[20]

While the church values earthly peace because it facilitates its ability to make a witness, and individual Christians participate in finding commonalities that make for better conditions on this earth, obey the laws, and provide "the service due to his neighbour [*sic*],"[21] both church and Christians yearn for the next life. For Augustine, the church is the city of God within history.[22] Therefore the distinctions between church and world are sharp and irreconcilable. This city, even in the midst of a "Christian empire," is "like Egypt, like a desert," akin to "the seventy years of captivity in Babylon."[23] For Augustine, this world was the place to travel through. Christians must not become too attached to it. The world is temporary, passing, and without ultimate meaning. Yet, Augustine does not disdain the world; rather, for him, it is all a matter of perspective. Christians had work to do in the world to make it a better place, but it was not their final home.[24]

For Augustine, too many human beings love the world primarily. They love the world, and things of the world, instead of loving God. The world and all its beauty "is indeed a good gift of God; but that the good may not think it a great good, God dispenses it even to the wicked."[25] Christians must maintain the proper perspective. Gifts of God, things related to the world itself, can be appreciated, used, or even loved but always with a love secondary to the love one has for God. The church is not connected with any one kingdom, Christian or not, but rather counts its citizens from every kingdom.

> The heavenly city, then while it sojourns on earth, calls citizens out of all nations, and gathers together a society of pilgrims of all languages, not scrupling about diversities in the manners, laws, and institutions whereby earthly peace is secured and maintained, but recognizing that, however

various these are, they all tend to one and the same end of earthly peace. It therefore is so far from rescinding and abolishing these diversities, that it even preserves and adapts them, so long only as no hindrance to the worship of the one supreme and true God is thus introduced.[26]

Martin Luther, writing over a thousand years after Augustine, carried on this tradition of understanding the work of the church as the "city of God" and contributed his own work emphasizing a separation between the two kingdoms. Given his belief that the medieval church had lost its way, Luther, however, began to express greater confidence in the role secular authorities could play even in reforming the church. God gave a precise role to governing authorities to restrain the evil in the world. "If all the world were composed of real Christians, that is, true believers, there would be no need for or benefits from prince, king, lord, sword, or law."[27] In other words, God intended temporal government for those who belong to the kingdom of this world. "Real Christians," those who truly hold membership in the kingdom of God, did not need it. The church attends to the business of salvation while the government keeps the peace and restrains evil deeds. Each have their place in God's design and need one another. Christians do not wield the sword as Christians; rather they act as hangmen, or soldiers, or princes in order to fulfill God's purposes for secular authority.[28]

In his best moments, Luther believed, with Augustine, that governments had limits. They could not constrain the soul of the individual or put an end to heresy. Though Luther was not entirely consistent with this principle when it came to the peasants, he consistently opposed trying to connect God's will to all the activities of temporal government. The kind of "civil righteousness" governments might accomplish maintained its significance only within time and history. It meant nothing when one stood before God. God is only concerned with the justifying righteousness found in Christ.[29] Christians must "take heed and first fill the world with real Christians" before they "attempt to rule it in a Christian and evangelical manner." Both the church and the government, the kingdom of God and the kingdom of this world, had their distinctive tasks. Ultimately, however, there is only one righteousness that means anything and that belonged exclusively to the kingdom of God.

> Therefore it is out of the question that there should be a common Christian government over the whole world, or indeed over a single country or any considerable body of people, for the wicked always outnumber the good. . . . For this reason one must carefully distinguish between these two governments [kingdoms]. Both must be permitted to remain; the one to produce righteousness, the other to bring about external peace and prevent evil deeds. Neither one is sufficient in the world without the other. No one can become righteous in the sight of God by means of the temporal government, without Christ's spiritual government. Christ's government does not extend over all men; rather, Christians are always a minority in the midst of non-Christians.[30]

What kind of theological legacy in the relation between faith and public life, represented to a considerable degree in Luther as well, has Augustine left for Christians who followed him? A summary is probably in order. First, God reigns over both cities, whether recognized or not. Second, the city of God is never to be equated with the earthly city. In fact, in Augustine, though not the case as much for Luther, the two cities, though "entangled," are in complete antipathy with one another, throughout all history. They serve entirely different ends. Third, the church's primary task is to worship God. Augustine understood the church in light of its idealized state as the eschatological church; in this way, the church should live based on its future condition as completely at home in the city of God, not really concerned with matters related to the earthly city. Fourth, love of anything in this world (country, spouse, children, self, democracy, creation itself), for the Christian, must always be secondary to the love one has for God. Fifth, Augustine makes no distinction between Christian empires and other empires; all are in fact representative of the earthly city that stands in antipathy to the heavenly city.[31] Sixth, no empire is the city of God; all earthly kingdoms are temporal and ultimately bound for destruction. Seventh, the city of God, even as it exists fragmentarily within history as the church, draws its citizens from all nations, all languages, and all cultures. Finally, Augustine's view of human history is apocalyptic. Human beings cannot save themselves. Human history is the story of the sin of humanity and its consequences. Its public life contains no permanent justice or ultimate good.

For these reasons, Christians who have been influenced by Augustine and his theological legacy in their thinking about faith and public life, whether they themselves recognize the influence or not, tend to emphasize the nature of two separate kingdoms. They believe the kingdom of this world, or the earthly city, stands in complete antipathy to the kingdom of heaven or the city of God. For American Christians in this camp, this means the church has little to do with the public life of the nation, unless that public life threatens the ability to worship "the one supreme and true God." These Christians recognize, however, that the church, as a representative of God's kingdom, the city of God, lives "entangled" in this world. Thus, the church's best form of service is to be an example of the kind of community that is promised within the kingdom of God, the kind of community that awaits all Christians after history ends. The church, therefore, does not act publicly or politically except as a witness to the truths associated with faith.

These modern American Christians, on the other hand, bring their theological understanding into their relation to public life on a daily basis. Their faith informs their vote, their vocational goals and aspirations, their everyday life in the world. Augustine recognized that Christians might be politicians, even emperors. Luther particularly stressed the message of Romans 13 that Christians are subject to the governing authorities because there is no authority unless it comes from God. Christians work responsibly to cooperate in the welfare of neighbors and the keeping of the temporal peace. They join political action groups and political parties. As they work in these endeavors, however, Christians should remember, if they follow the theological models set by Augustine or Luther, that their use of earthly things or involvement in temporal undertakings is always secondary to their love of God and their citizenship in the heavenly city. In this Christian approach to public life, individual Christians respond to the public life of the nation, as individuals, in more comprehensive ways than does the church. For that reason, I am calling this type of Christian response that of the "public Christian." During the past fifty years, many Christians who identify themselves as "evangelical" have represented this theological understanding well in relationship to public life.

PROVIDING CONTEXT AND A DEFINITION OF TERMS

The terms *liberal* and *conservative* are, of course, relative terms. They do not possess clear and concrete meaning that allows precisely locating the person who is dubbed either liberal or conservative. To illustrate the point, I often tell students that some of my relatives think I'm conservative and others are sure I'm a liberal. Such a diagnosis is entirely relative and depends on where my relative stands theologically. Though the terms *liberal* and *conservative* are problematic, they are shorthand for differences between individuals and groups of Christians. My use of the terms carries with it the recognition that, though they are not totally useless, they are often foggy and ambiguous.

The terms *evangelical* and *mainline* (or *mainstream*) are themselves troublesome in many respects. By using the term *evangelical*,[32] I mean to denote those church groups who traditionally have not been active in the National Council of Churches of Christ in America (NCC). Evangelicals generally stress biblical authority and emphasize the need for individuals to experience personally the grace of God leading to salvation, usually described by such terms as new birth or conversion, or being "born again." They place high value on an individual's relation to God and promote evangelism as probably the most effective tool in the church's fight against the sins of society. There are, however, vast differences between and among evangelicals on many issues. Evangelicals themselves cannot agree precisely about what it means to be an evangelical.[33]

The term *mainline* is difficult to get a hold on as well. If one means by it to describe those churches possessing large memberships and powerful identities, the groups described by the term have certainly changed since the 1950s. By this definition many of the evangelical churches in America today would definitely qualify as mainline. Richard G. Hutcheson Jr. suggested the following definition in 1981: "Large historical denominations having membership reflecting great diversity, but leadership and official positions putting them generally in the liberal, ecumenically included and socially concerned wing of Christians."[34] Since that time, many of these denominations have lost significant numbers of members to today's megachurches, which are largely evangelical in orientation. These Protestant mainline traditions in America were there at the beginning of the ecumenical movement in America and most participated in the founding of the Federal Council of Churches of Christ (FCC) in 1908. Generally, they have remained active participants through the development of the World Council of Churches in 1948 and the transformation of the FCC into the NCC in the United States in 1950.

Today's postdenominational context has made lines between evangelical Christians and mainline Christians harder to draw. The dominantly evangelical denominations have traditionally included the Southern Baptist Convention, churches associated with the Holiness and Pentecostal traditions of American Protestantism, Anabaptist denominations like the Mennonites, and Reformed churches, including the Presbyterian Church in America.[35] Some individuals among evangelical congregations and denominations might define themselves as mainline, though this is more unlikely since the latter term has fallen into such disrepute in recent years. For the most part, these groups remain solidly evangelical in orientation. Mainline denominations have included the American Baptist Church, the Christian Church (Disciples of Christ), the United Church of Christ, the United Methodist Church, the United Presbyterian Church, and the Episcopalian Church. Many of these traditional mainline churches today contain individuals who ardently define themselves as evangelicals. Most of them have strong organized factions within the denomination that self-identify as evangelicals and often oppose the social positions taken by the denominations. The American Baptist Convention, for example, has a strong contingent of members and pastors who primarily identify with the evangelical tradition spawned by fundamentalist reform during the 1940s and 1950s.

The truth is that both mainline Protestantism and evangelicalism, as coherent movements, have pretty well disintegrated. As David Wells pointed out a number of years ago, evangelicalism has developed a rather "sprawling empire," rather comfortable within American culture, that makes a consistent system of theological commitments between all groups who self-identify as evangelical hard to define.[36] On the whole, clear lines of division and definition do not work very well these days. With these caveats in place, I will still use these terms to distinguish between the "conservative"-leaning Christian groups and the more generally "liberal" ones.

Another set of categories that require a bit of definition includes those swirling around the theological notion of millennialism. Most early Christians anticipated the second coming of Jesus, believing that he would establish a millennial kingdom on earth. The term "premillennialists" describes those who believe Christ will inaugurate the millennium with his literal second coming. This interpretation depended on a particular reading of the book of Revelation. Through history, there have been varying types of premillennialism, but all have held the view that the coming of Christ preceded the inauguration of the millennium. Especially during times of crisis, Christian voices have found premillennial beliefs attractive. Earliest Christianity planted some of its deepest roots among the poorer peoples in Jewish Palestine who were attracted by the association of the kingdom of God with the poor and dispossessed over against the wealthy and socially situated.[37]

During the second and third centuries, when Christians faced intense persecution, most readers of Revelation emphasized that Christ would soon return to establish God's reign. Church history describes these Christians by the name "Chiliasts" (from the Greek word *chilioi*, meaning "thousand"). This chiliastic perspective gave Christians hope in the midst of suffering, much like the original book did for its initial readers. Most of today's scholars date Revelation from the 90s, during the Domitian persecution, or from the early 100s, during the reign of Trajan. Some conservative scholars argue that the book dates from the mid-to-late 60s, during the reign of Nero.

Early Christians were outsiders. This status, borrowing a term from Victor Turner, can be described as living in "liminality," a state marked by a strong tendency to create intimate communities, huddling together in the midst of hostile surroundings. Early Christian premillennialists, convinced that history and society conspired against them, sought close community with one another. Nearly all early Christian literature demonstrates this concern for stable Christian congregations and fellowships. At the same time, early Christian communities abolished social distinctions, emphasized communal ethics and care for one another, showed very little interest in addressing or changing the public life outside their communities, and demonstrated very little concern for developing social structures of their own.[38]

Since early Christians assumed the end was near, they and their children had to adjust Christian belief because the end did not appear. Immediate millenarian expectations began to disappear as the failure of their millennial vision became evident to them. Once Christianity became the religion of the empire, during the time of Constantine, chiliasm became much less fashionable. In fact, the church over the next few centuries was slow even to accept the book of Revelation as Scripture. By 400, the Western church had finally accepted it, but it took nearly a century longer for Greek Christianity to accept it. Syrian and Armenian churches were even slower to accept it. With the passing of chiliastic tendencies, new interpretations of the millennium were bound to appear. Augustine's book *City of God* brought a figurative understanding to Christian interpretation of apocalyptic literature. Christ's resurrection (or, for some theologians, Christ's birth) brought about a new millennium in a figurative sense that is associated with heaven and represented by the church's presence on earth. Many Christians after Augustine did not look for a literal millennium on earth within human history. For this reason, they have been known as "amillennialists." Some amillennialists through Christian history have described the millennium as a past event or as merely a symbolic allusion to God's action, either in final events or even in the present.[39]

Finally, there have been Christians within history who came to believe that the Christian witness would succeed in converting the world to Christ. This more optimistic view of the success of Christianity emphasized that Christ would return as this mission concluded, thus leading to a description of these Christians as "postmillennialists," since they emphasized a return of Christ following the establishment of the millennium. Early American Puritans, most notably Jonathan Edwards, defended a postmillennialist view. Its most influential advocates arose in the eighteenth century outside of America. During the late nineteenth century and early twentieth century in America, many of the more liberal-leaning Protestants clearly represented this view as they worked to transform the world into the kingdom of God.[40]

Defenders of this view have emphasized that the success of the church would bring in a millennium without any need for a supernatural event. In its better theological representations, postmillennialists emphasized that the millennium resulted from the grace of God rather than human action. But the view often degenerated into emphasis on the ability of the human church and Christians to bring in the kingdom of God. In general, to offer a quick summary, premillennialists have been pessimistic about history and its outcomes, amillennialists have emphasized the need for the church to become the example of light within a world that needs the witness of the city of God, and postmillennialists have been confident that the world is getting better and better because of the transforming power of the church in the world. The optimism of postmillennialism is harder to find in a world rocked by the holocaust and the dropping of atomic bombs.

Among these views of the millennium, there are those who emphasize that the author of Revelation presents a prophetic interpretation that makes sense of the panorama encompassing the whole church's history. This "church historical" or "continuous historical" view is found among those who represent each of these types of millennialism. Yet others read Revelation from a mostly "futurist" perspective, emphasizing the prophecies as a key to understanding events at the very end of time. The most popular form of the futurist type is found most clearly today in that form of dispensationalist premillennialism currently embodied in the *Left Behind* series written by Tim LaHaye and Jerry Jenkins. This series of novels tells the story of the Rapture, the belief among dispensationalists that God will take all Christians who are alive near the end of the world up to heaven in a single miraculous event.

This millennial view began among Plymouth Brethren in Great Britain during the nineteenth century. John Nelson Darby (1800–1882) provided the intellectual leadership for dispensationalism and for early versions of theological affirmations that get carried into twentieth-century American fundamentalism.[41] One can draw a line from John Nelson Darby through *The Scofield Reference Bible* (1909); popular revivalists like Dwight L. Moody (1837–1899), a respected revivalist who preached culture-denial but had supporters and friends in wealthy circles, and Billy Sunday (1862–1935), a wilder and more colorful character who attracted those kinds of crowds; the best-selling book of the 1970s, *The Late Great Planet Earth*; to modern bumper stickers ("In case of Rapture, this car will be driverless" and the counter "In case of Rapture, I'm going to steal your car") and the tremendous cultural success of and financial blockbuster status enjoyed by the fundamentalist literary work of LaHaye and Jenkins. There is a touch of irony in that observation for those who understand the "culture-denying" features of early American fundamentalism.[42]

In the mainline or more liberal-leaning churches, these views of millennialism hold less currency today. Most Christians in these churches are unfamiliar with the terms much less the ways in which these terms are defined. The *Left Behind* series does have readers among these churches and the series' influence may actually lead to significant numbers of Christians adopting a dispensationalist view simply because they are unaware of both the development of its history and the alternatives. The vast majority of today's scholars in the mainline church prefer a "preterist" reading of the book of Revelation. This view, sometimes called the "contemporary-historical" view or simply the "historical" view, emphasizes how the author of Revelation wrote a message of hope for Christians who were undergoing persecution at the hands of the empire.[43] In this understanding, the book of Revelation is a product of its time. It is not intended to reveal the whole history of the church or to predict the future of history. This historical reading of the book challenges the legitimacy of all these other forms of millennialism. For this reason, views of the millennium that fall into categories like "pre" or "post" or "a" are found mostly among more conservative Christians who continue to believe the book lays out a blueprint of either all history or the future.

In the twentieth century, a large number of American Christians representing the type I am calling "public Christian" have been evangelical and either premillennial or amillennial in their theological orientation.[44] Some of them are dispensationalists while others stress more of a "church-historical" view of Revelation, either of the premillennialist or amillennialist variety. They rely less on precise predictions concerning the end of time and more on the way Revelation tells the story of the travails of the church through time. Contemporary evangelicalism is of the sort that is most important to our consideration in this particular chapter. It emerged out of American fundamentalism during the 1940s, by which time many fundamentalists had concluded that the world was spiraling downward and Christians were living in the final days. These fundamentalists felt compelled to evangelize fervently to prepare for the return of Christ.

During the 1940s, a cadre of young fundamentalists felt that many with this view had abandoned God's call to attend to social issues. They tempered the kind of dispensationalist theology associated with much of fundamentalism by seeking expression of an intellectually responsible form of orthodoxy that could speak to the real problems of society. Though they did not abandon a dispensationalist view of the world completely, they believed in the possibility of Christians making a difference in the world. Major figures among these young fundamentalists included Harold J. Ockenga, Edward John Carnell, and Carl F. H. Henry. Even though he was not a scholar, Billy Graham contributed significantly to this new movement among fundamentalists. He worked closely with these theological scholars and lent his growing influence to help create new academic centers where those who held to Christian orthodoxy could develop a new level of academic respectability. For example, Fuller Theological Seminary in Pasadena, California, grew out of this movement. Graham also came up with the idea to create *Christianity Today* (*CT*) as a counterpart to the more liberal journals found among mainline Protestants and Catholics. In the founding of *CT*, these newly named "neo-evangelicals" contributed to the development of what Mark Noll has described as an "awakening Evangelical mind." The magazine called "for an intellectually responsible evangelicalism" that could more reflectively engage the modern world.[45] Carl F. H. Henry (1913–2003), its first editor, quickly developed into evangelicalism's most influential theologian and the one among them who pushed, for theological reasons, these new evangelicals to apply their faith to social concerns.

CARL F. H. HENRY: AN EVANGELICAL THEOLOGIAN FOR THE PUBLIC CHRISTIAN

Carl F. H. Henry, theologian and founder of *CT*, published a body of work that encouraged evangelical Christians to engage American public life. He expressed well the view of these young theologians that fundamentalism had become so isolated that no one much cared what it thought or did. Fundamentalism had lost its ability to influence the world. Henry described dispensationalism's belief that "world doom seemed inevitable" as "fundamentalist negativism."[46] He addressed this weakness directly in an early book entitled *The Uneasy Conscience of Modern Fundamentalism* (1947). The book "exploded like a bombshell in the fundamentalist camp."[47] Students at Wheaton, Henry noted, argued vigorously about whether the game of Rook should be included in the fundamentalist prohibition against card playing. Congregations railed against personal sins like dancing, smoking, watching movies, and drinking but had nothing to say about the larger issues facing society. In response to the social gospel of the liberals, fundamentalism had recoiled from addressing society "and because of its prophetic cheerlessness about the present age came more and more to narrow its message for the 'faithful remnant' that would be called out of the godless world context."[48]

Henry called for a contemporary version of Augustine's *City of God* and lamented the fact that twentieth-century fundamentalism would be unable to provide it due to its current retreat from society.[49] He emphasized that the kingdom of God is both present and future. It is present in the redemptive activity of Christ in the world, but the kingdom of the world is not yet the kingdom of God (Rev. 11:15). That vision will only be realized when Christ returns. Until then, the kingdom of God is not to be identified with any earthly government. These governments play their appointed roles, and as long as they do "not interfere with the *summum bonum* in the lives of regenerate believers," they can be "quite compatible" with the present kingdom of God.[50] For their part, evangelicals need to speak and act with a united and ecumenical voice by applying their redemptive message to the problems faced by the world. According to George Marsden, "Henry worked out more clearly than did most of his evangelical colleagues the puzzling question of how social and political efforts could be kingdom work" even though the kingdom "could never be equated with social, political, or national programs."

> His solution was essentially a version of Augustine's two cities conception. . . . Kingdom principles can influence the earthly city but can never be fully realized there in this age. In the meantime, however, Christians owe some allegiance to both cities, although the allegiance to the civilization of the earth is always relativized by the higher loyalty. Still, though the absolute good is unattainable, our Christian duty toward civilization is to work for the relatively better. . . . Christians should support the United Nations' efforts for world justice, even while protesting the non-Christian frame of reference on which such efforts were based. . . . So for Henry, evangelism remained the first task. Yet he and other reformers revived another dimension of evangelicalism: that evangelism is the necessary first step toward a second task—the improvement of society.[51]

In his hope that Christians would take seriously the problems of their societies, Henry did not include a major social role for the church, except as teacher. "The Church's primary duty," he wrote in his book on Christian ethics, "is to expound the revealed Gospel and the divine principles of social duty, and to constrain individual Christians to fulfill their evangelistic and civic responsibilities."[52] In his view, the church should never act politically but should help educate individual Christians to work conscientiously to fulfill their duties as citizens. Above all else, the church must preach the gospel, for "what the social order most needs is a new race of men." Counter to the mainline approach to social ills, Henry argued that the church should never "lend its moral prestige to particular, detailed politico-economic measures by official endorsement." He feared that churches entering the political fray will always lose their theological perspective. But he also took the evangelical churches to task for not "openly challenging race discrimination."[53]

What precisely is it that the church is to do? Henry took up the topic in general ways. Beyond its primary concern with evangelism, the church should stress "basic principles" relevant to social problems.

> These pertain to the divine source and sanction of human rights; the accountability of men and nations to objective justice and transcendent moral law, and the servant role of the State as a minister of justice and order in a fallen society; the permanent significance of the social commandments of the Decalogue; the inclusion of property rights as a human right; and so on.[54]

In 1984, he included "protection of monogamous marriage" and "capital punishment for murder" in his list of "the social imperatives of Scripture."[55] However, the task of specificity did not, in Henry's view, belong to the church. Rather, individual Christians carried that responsibility. "While the Church is not to seek secular political power," he wrote, "its members may and must exercise an influence in public affairs." The church preaches broad ideal principles drawn from biblical revelation, but it leaves their specific application to individual Christians.

> On the battleground of political decision and action the layman must carry the full share of responsibility. His political inaction itself can be a form of action, an unwitting approval of the status quo. According to his ability and opportunity he must fulfill his civic duty in local, state, and national activities, whose direction decides the quality of public life. By active means he must support and promote those legislative policies most compatible with biblical principles. He must distinguish and evaluate the live options as completely as possible from the standpoint of a just political order.[56]

In this way, Henry brought a renewed emphasis on the Christian's role in politics and public life. He encouraged fundamentalist Christians to participate fully in the public life of the nation. While he warned them not to identify the kingdom of God with any political system or nation, he stressed the importance of making political decisions based on biblical imperatives. He encouraged "young Christians" to "regard a career in government fully as legitimate a Christian vocation as medicine and missions." His son, Paul, listened carefully to him and served for Michigan in the U.S. House of Representatives from 1984 until he died in 1993.[57]

Henry was proud of the "evangelical philosophy of politics" he brought to *CT* during his years as editor (1956–1968).[58] Fairly early in his tenure with the magazine, he offered readers a brief "evangelical strategy" for social action. He argued that social action always had to be set in the context of mission. Social reform, for Christians, must never be "an end in itself." Due to the evangelical emphasis on sin, evangelical activity always "throbs with the evangelistic invitation to new life in Jesus Christ." Henry emphasized that all social problems "are in the last analysis a commentary on the disorder of private life." Collective sin was not on the evangelical agenda; these leaders believed sins could only be addressed individually. As Henry put it most clearly,

> evangelistic social action throbs with the evangelistic invitation to new life in Jesus Christ . . . a regard for social evils first in the light of personal wickedness. The evangelical recognizes that social disorders are in the last analysis a commentary on the disorder of private life, and that the modern dilemma is essentially a predicament involving persons who need to be addressed individually.[59]

This theology reduces social sin ultimately to the sins of individuals, and naturally understands the solution to sin to rest in bringing individuals to Christ. The accompanying theological belief that no social program or meritorious effort could successfully transform "unregenerate human nature" ran through most evangelical editorials in *CT* during the civil rights period. Editors opposed active civil disobedience because it smacked of compulsion rather than persuasion, which their evangelical souls much preferred. In their view, the solution to racism lay in changed hearts, one at a time.[60]

Much of lay southern Christianity, mainline and evangelical, shared these characteristics. Waldo Beach made the interesting observation in 1964 that the rural South presented a "sad paradox" because it constituted "the most pious, church-going section of the nation yet [was also] the most resistant to racial change." These Christians held Christian love in high esteem and cultivated "private charities and acts of kindness to the poor." But "charity" was about the extent of their understanding of justice. Beach found it ironic that African Americans heavily involved in civil rights activism shared much of the same theological tradition.

> This contradictory use by white and Negro churchmen of the identical theological tradition, the one privatized and escapist, the other active in ful-filling the corporate demands of the Gospel, is one of the ironies in the present racial revolution. It is also a sign of the stirrings of God's grace and newness of life in the Church.[61]

Henry did, of course, argue that God's demand for social justice extends to the whole human race, not just Christians or the church. This theological claim requires that Christians be concerned about social justice. But, for Henry, church involvement, as compared to the involvement of individual Christians, in working toward justice was served best by its status as example. In the church, God has given the world a "mirror" reflecting "the realities of a new social order." Members of the church belong to God's kingdom. Therefore, all aspects of social justice should be found within this community. The church must show the world, by example, how to live more justly. As a community, it engages in social service, feeds the hungry, and so forth, "with its eye on the value of the individual." But it does not become engaged politically. When the church "enters the secular arena and exerts political pressures for righteousness in the social order, then the church is prostituting her mission and adding to the confusion of the world." The church "exists to serve the kingdom of God." And since the kingdom of God "is not of this world, the church as an institution should be spiritual." The general cry issued from this corner has been "Let the Church be the Church."[62]

For these evangelicals, "the principle that the Church may not enter into politics" did "not mean that either the individual churches or their ministers and members may remain comfortably aloof from injustice and remote from human oppression and suffering."[63] Even though pastors must use the pulpit to urge acceptance of Christ, they may also proclaim the "ethical principles" found within the Bible. This kind of preaching, in Henry's view, never connected God's will with political solutions or parties, but rather proclaimed the general principles found in Scripture.[64] Greater expectations were placed on Christians as individuals. They must learn to discriminate between various "specific options for social reform and change" and apply these discriminations to their involvement in public life. Every Christian is "a citizen of two worlds," Henry told the readers of *CT*.

When Christians go to work, they are required to interact "with others outside the circle of redemption." Here they have an opportunity to demonstrate both their understanding of work as a divine calling and their support for "the state as an instrument of justice subordinate to the revealed will and purpose of God."

If evangelicals followed this theological approach to public life, they would, Henry claimed, avoid the kinds of deviations that have plagued others. Here he had in mind the isolation of the fundamentalists and the secularized versions of involvement found among Christian liberals who emphasized social gospel themes. From this theological perspective, Henry argued, Christians cannot become indifferent to the culture that exists outside the church. They also know that they cannot impose Christian ideals on an "unregenerate humanity" and hope that this is somehow going to lead to social stability. Further, evangelicals should be able to avoid the temptations affecting those who have claimed that secular programs are "authentically Christian." No social program involving non-Christians, argued Henry, can ever be completely Christian. Finally, given their theological commitments, evangelicals should know they cannot coerce society into love and righteousness; no amount of propaganda, education, or legislation will make it happen. At the end of the day, only redemption in Christ holds the potential to increase true love and righteousness in the world.[65]

Henry's theological approach to public life has remained influential among evangelicals. Alister McGrath believes "Henry's argument was unquestionably of major importance in encouraging a new generation of evangelicals to engage society."[66] It is hard, however, to track how successful it has been in actually making a social difference. Individual accomplishments resulting from the application of faith to public concern are not easy to document. The history of *CT* represents well, however, the type I have described as the public Christian, one that emphasizes the separation of the two cities but understands God as sovereign over both cities, connects personal sin with social problems, rejects any involvement of the church in the work of social transformation (except through evangelism), and encourages individual Christians to be seriously involved in the political and public life of the nation.

The history of the magazine's dealing with hot topics like abortion, race, human sexuality and homosexuality, war, and feminism also reveals some of the weaknesses associated with a public Christian approach to public issues.[67] When one's theological emphasis on sin is primarily defined in terms of human action, rather than on sin as a state of being that no human being or social structure can escape, depiction of sin can be isolated mostly in the actions of others, those with whom one disagrees or identifies as servants of the other kingdom. When this happens, the public Christian slips into priestly faith. When one understands Christians as "aliens" in this world, the temptation to become pessimistic about public life is strong. In these instances, finding motivation to contribute to public life might be difficult to muster. Further, when one takes the theological notion associated with "alien" status seriously, there is an accompanying temptation to turn toward sectarianism. If one takes that turn, the Christian witness can become

ghettoized, largely irrelevant, and easily ignored. Christianity, as it was for fundamentalism in Henry's early days, can become primarily a private matter.

As advocates for public Christians, *CT* has been concerned mostly with maintaining the important distinctions between church and world. For this reason, its
pages have focused on private sins in the area of personal morality, a strong witness for the necessity of individual salvation, and advocacy for those portions of
American life deemed in line with God's will. However, this posture did not keep
either editors or authors from offering a strong encouragement to integrate private and public life in meaningful ways. *CT*'s brand of faith has represented an
understanding of Christian wholeness that expects individual participation in
political and public processes.

Among the more telling pieces of evidence that demonstrate Henry's influence
on the development of American evangelicalism is the statement treating evangelical social responsibility known as the "Chicago Declaration of Evangelical Social
Concern." Paul Henry, son of the elder Henry and at that time a political science
professor at Calvin College, was among the organizers of the event that produced
the declaration. Planners invited both older and younger evangelicals. The meeting included people like Carl F. H. Henry and Frank Gaebelein, representing older
evangelicals, and Ron Sider and Jim Wallis, representing younger evangelicals who
were considered to be more radical in their social and political views. They spent
the weekend after Thanksgiving in 1973, at the YMCA Hotel on South Wabash
Street in Chicago, talking about evangelicals and social justice. The event ended
with drafting and signing the Chicago Declaration. Through the statement these
evangelicals confessed "the historic involvement of the church in America with
racism," attacked "the materialism of our culture and the maldistribution of the
nation's wealth and services," challenged "the misplaced trust of the nation in economic and military might—a proud trust that promotes a national pathology of
war and violence which victimizes our neighbors at home and abroad," and
acknowledged that "we have encouraged men to prideful domination and women
to irresponsible passivity." In typical public Christian fashion, the statement called
for "Evangelical Christians to demonstrate repentance in a Christian discipleship
that confronts the social and political injustice of our nation."[68]

Joel Carpenter, thirty years later, indicated some of the factors behind that
particular weekend. Many of the mainstream leaders in evangelicalism had lost
confidence in the Nixon administration. The civil rights movement, the Vietnam
War, and especially the Watergate scandal had shaken their previously optimistic
attitudes about Nixon and their access to the White House through evangelical
leaders like Billy Graham. They were beginning to doubt their previous assumptions that evangelicals could concentrate on salvation and Christian formation
and leave government to good Christians like Richard Nixon. Carpenter also
emphasized the success attending many other evangelical efforts at the time.
Evangelicals were gaining considerably in cultural prominence and visibility.
Billy Graham enjoyed tremendous respect and popularity; colleges across the
nation had thriving Campus Crusade programs; and even "one of the White

House conspirators, Charles Colson, announced his conversion to evangelical Christianity." Evangelicals seemed to be entering the mainstream of American life, and this "new visibility," Carpenter observes, "came with a growing sense of social responsibility." New ministries among evangelicals followed. Carpenter stresses "the heirs of the Chicago Declaration have been those who want to say that evangelical does not equal conservative."[69]

The Declaration is often recalled and referred to among those organizations associated with the younger evangelicals of 1973. For example, through organizations like Evangelicals for Social Action, founded as a result of the Chicago Declaration and headed by Sider, and the *Sojourners* Community and Call for Renewal, headed by Wallis, the clarion call of the Declaration can still be heard.[70] This shift in generational leadership is natural, however, and no doubt still connected historically in important respects to Henry's 1940s call for an awakened evangelical social conscience. The Chicago Declaration, if anything, marked a passing of the torch to a younger generation of evangelicals who would fulfill Henry's call in ways he had not really ever imagined.

About the time of the Chicago Declaration and just after, things looked great for evangelicals in America. Some hoped that evangelicalism could present a powerful influence through creative organization and the creation of a variety of coalitions of influence. But, as Henry reflected back on developments in the 1970s, "the prospect of a massive evangelical alliance seemed annually more remote, and by mid-decade it was gone." As George Marsden put it,

> by 1976, when *Newsweek* proclaimed "The Year of the Evangelical," the hopes of the neo-evangelicals for unity under their leadership had dissipated. Having a Southern Baptist and a Democrat elected to the White House did not advance their party's cause. In addition, for them 1976 brought increasingly open internal strife, centered on "the battle for the Bible." As evangelicals gained some of the national prestige they had once only dreamed of, the neo-evangelical leaders could no longer agree among themselves as to what an evangelical was.[71]

The younger evangelicals were pushing the edges of evangelicalism into new and considerably different expressions and the movement's self-assured sense of itself disappeared.

Even during the heyday of the older generation's evangelical confidence, however, one must remember that editors at *CT* did not often encourage coercion in matters they regarded as growing out of a specifically Christian view of the world, but preferred to rely on persuasive expression of their faith. And that persuasive work should primarily be done by Christians rather than by church bodies.[72] Readers of the journal through its history, therefore, find strong opposition to the church-sponsored social involvements of both mainstream Protestants and the Religious Right. Interestingly enough, the journal regularly reported on the political resolutions of the National Association of Evangelicals (NAE), a national association of evangelical denominations and individuals, without offering the same kind of chastisement.[73]

ORGANIZED PUBLIC CHRISTIANS

It is only natural, I suppose, that the call for individual Christians to join organizations outside the church to promote a Christian vision for American public life would lead to the formation of various Christian lobbying organizations. At a meeting in St. Louis in April of 1942, 147 evangelicals met to plan an evangelical alternative to the mainline Federal Council of Churches (FCC). The American Council of Christian Churches (ACCC), founded by fundamentalist leader Carl McIntire in 1941, regularly attacked the FCC leadership and its activities. These evangelical leaders were uncomfortable with the strident voice of the ACCC. They hoped to keep their focus on Christ and planned an organization that would be less divisive and less combative. In 1943, in Chicago, over one thousand evangelicals gathered in the first constitutional convention of the NAE. At this meeting, delegates adopted an evangelical faith statement composed of seven points that is still in use.[74]

Practical concerns drove this organization as well. NBC and CBS had indicated to the FCC a willingness to donate radio time to recognized faith communities. Since they had no national body, evangelicals were perceived as "unrecognized." Within a year, the NAE had organized the National Religious Broadcasters (NRB), a related service organization to promote evangelical broadcasting. One of the first efforts of the NRB successfully challenged the virtual monopoly held by the FCC for Protestant broadcasting over the two radio networks. Further, the NAE quickly formed separate commissions to help evangelical chaplains in the military and provide humanitarian relief across the world. Adding to the early success experienced by the NAE was its ability to bring Holiness, Pentecostal, and Anabaptist groups together in the same coalition. But the organization remained relatively small in its early years, attracting only about fifteen denominations composed of about 500,000 members. The NAE did not allow denominations holding membership in the FCC to join.

During the 1950s, following the growing status of Billy Graham and closely associated with him, the NAE began to grow. It also began to change. President Eisenhower's invitation to the White House is still touted on the NAE's Web site as evidence of its achieving "new heights." This invitation nurtured existing seeds of ambition to gain in national and cultural status and attention. By 1960, membership grew to thirty-two denominations with about 1.5 million members. But during the 1960s, the NAE struggled to maintain consistent leadership and rarely captured any national attention. As the Web site puts it, "No wonder when *Newsweek* marked 1976 as the Year of the Evangelical, the magazine had very little to say about NAE." By the late 1970s, the political activism of these evangelicals began to awaken, largely due to the fallout associated with the *Roe v. Wade* decision of 1973. Under new leadership, the NAE turned its attention on Washington and became much more politically active while, at the same time, trying to educate evangelicals about what was happening "inside the Beltway."

With the election of Ronald Reagan, the NAE experienced unprecedented access to White House functions and events. It was in his address before the 1983 NAE convention in Florida where President Reagan denounced the Soviet Union as "the Evil Empire." During these years, the NAE trumpets numerous "legislative victories," including passage of bills dealing with drunk driving and the provision of equal access to all religious organizations to public school facilities. By 1990, an additional fifteen denominations had joined and membership in NAE stood at around 4.5 million constituent members. Today, fifty-two denominations are members of the NAE, including in the neighborhood of 30 million members. Concerning its political activities, the Web site includes the following statement:

> The lobby arm of the NAE is a potent force in the arena of state, national and international politics. The force of 30 million Americans united under a common banner is an effective and powerful tool in shaping legislation. Under the leadership of Richard Cizik, the Office [of] Governmental Affairs has been instrumental in promoting, amending and sometimes defeating key legislation regarding religious liberties and moral issues. There is a battle for the public arena and the front line lobbyists are crucial to advancing the agenda of conservative, evangelical Christian America.[75]

Given this kind of approach to political activity, I think it is fair to conclude that the NAE no longer fits Carl Henry's original vision of its work or of his evangelical political philosophy. In describing the work of the NAE in his 1964 book, Henry argued that the "awakening interest" in government affairs represented by the NAE among evangelicals "begins with the premise that while the institutional Church ought not to engage in politics, individual churchgoers must fulfill an active political role."[76] But the one thing the present NAE does well is to bring institutional conservative evangelical denominations as "Church" squarely into the political role. It does so in the same way the National Council of Churches of Christ (NCC) does for mainline Protestants. The kind of direct lobbying described by the NAE is similar to those activities by the NCC that Henry criticized when he argued that

> the dignity of the Church is damaged when ecclesiastical leaders appear before political bodies to plead special cases. . . . When taking sides on politico-economic issues, moreover, policy-making bodies of large denominations, and special committees or boards of the National Council of Churches, so plead their partisan commitments in the name of broad moral idealism and spiritual concern that, wittingly or unwittingly, they imply that clergy men who do not share these endorsements lack social awareness and ethical concern.[77]

While commending the NAE in 1981 "for its many constructive activities," Henry criticized it for, among other things, playing "too small a part in accelerating a cooperative evangelistic thrust." Henry had always hoped for a large evangelical witness about the meaning of Christianity to the culture, and in many ways, the present NAE has provided precisely that.

James Reichley noted that as the Religious Right declined in its cultural influence during the early 1980s, the NAE began to play a larger role in Washington. He cited a study by Clyde Wilcox that "has found evidence that the longer evangelical activists participate in politics, usually on the Republican side, the more willing they become to compromise with others in the Republican party to advance common electoral interests." While this may make the institutional arm of evangelicalism more effective in its influence of American politics, it will do little to further Henry's original concern for the purity of the evangelical mission, bringing people to Christ, which he always associated with the primary work of the church itself.

Evangelicalism in America has changed considerably during the past fifty years, as described by the president of Fuller Theological Seminary five years ago:

> For decades we had been schooled in a cultural outlook characterized by three features: a remnant view of the church, an ethic of "over and against," and an apocalyptic view of the future. Now suddenly we were building megachurches and talking about moral majorities and strategizing about winning the culture wars—and most of this without serious theological reflection on why we now were seeing things in such different ways.[78]

In many ways, *CT* represented these trends as well. Comparing the magazine's content in 1959 to that found in 1989, David Wells concluded that although "the magazine had formerly looked outward, offering biblically informed and incisive critiques of church and society, it now looked inward, and its analyses of church and society read more like journalistic dispatches from the cheering section." The magazine, in some respects, had arrived. It became a mirror of the culture by responding to "sophisticated marketing surveys" and lost "its moral and intellectual fiber" and "its ability to call the evangelical constituency to greater Christian faithfulness."[79]

But the story does not end here. Increasingly, in evangelical circles, in addition to the Great Commission, many began to talk of the "cultural commission." Here, evangelicals referenced Genesis 1:28: "God said to them, 'Be fruitful and multiply, and fill the earth and subdue it; and have dominion over the fish of the sea and over the birds of the air and over every living thing that moves upon the earth.'" These evangelicals wanted to move beyond a theology only concerned with saving souls or one that merely reflected culture. Many among them now seek to save culture itself.

In a 1990 NAE survey, 83 percent responded that evangelicals should focus on converting individuals if they hoped to change society. In 2000, only 30 percent responded that way, while 64 percent expressed support for the view that transformation had to occur among both institutions and individuals. Along with this change, evangelicals and evangelical church bodies became more willing to build coalitions with nonevangelicals to seek broader objectives.[80] Some evangelicals have done this through participation in organizations like the Center for Public Justice, an evangelically oriented political action organization with a mission "to serve God, advance justice, and transform public life." The Center defines Christian politics to mean, "among other things, that Christian citizens, without any public privilege, will seek to live at peace with all people and will work to build states and an international order to promote justice for everyone."[81] The phrase "without any public privilege" is an important one, and could help these active evangelicals who seek social transformation to avoid the temptation to turn toward a priestly faith. James Skillern, the executive director, takes a mild accommodationist view toward the relationship between church and state.[82]

Theological reflection of a different type has accompanied many of these new developments in evangelical circles. The NAE today touts a theology more representative of the public church (addressed in the next chapter) than that of the public Christian. It remains in the middle range of conservative evangelicalism on matters of family life and other kinds of personal moral issues. However, it seeks broader engagement of the church and public life with a keener sense of the dangers of priestly faith than earlier fundamentalist counterparts. In October 2004, its Board of Directors unanimously endorsed a document issuing a call for evangelical political engagement. Ron Sider, president of Evangelicals for Social Action, cochaired the process leading to this development. The document, titled "For the Health of the Nation: An Evangelical Call to Civil Responsibility," says nothing about two cities or two kingdoms. It does not distinguish between the response of the church and the response of individual Christians. Its theological rationale follows more in "the tradition of the Hebrew prophets" than the book of Revelation. Along with Amos, it announces that God's kingdom "would be marked by justice, peace, forgiveness, restoration, and healing for all."

According to the NAE, the task of Christians and churches is to move contemporary society in these directions. While the document states that social problems are, on the one hand, caused by "personal sinful choices," it also stresses that "unjust social systems also help create social problems." In response, Christ "calls the church to speak prophetically to society and work for the renewal and reform of its structures." As Christians and the church act politically, they must remember "that biblical faith is vastly larger and richer than every limited, inevitably imperfect political agenda and that commitment to the Lordship of Christ and his one body far transcends all political commitments."[83] The theological groundwork laid by Carl F. H. Henry, though inevitably of a different sort than contemporary theological work in this area among evangelicals, led ultimately to a new strand of theology among evangelicals that attempts to relate faith and public life, one with a greater emphasis on the role of the church.[84]

The most prominent voice relating faith and public life among evangelicals today is that of Jim Wallis, the editor of *Sojourners*. There are many points of disagreement between Wallis and *Sojourners*, on the one hand, and the NAE, on the other. Wallis has regularly criticized the work of the NAE. This illustrates yet again the wide diversity present in evangelical circles revolving around the question of how to relate evangelical faith to public questions. Throughout his career, Wallis has been committed to linking concern for social justice with evangelical passion for personal salvation. Though neither Wallis nor Henry might appreciate the comparison, in many ways Wallis's work to bring social justice and evangelical conviction together has been a kind of natural extension of Henry's original goal to expand evangelical influence in American life.

Wallis was an antiwar activist in college and headed to Trinity Evangelical Divinity School in 1970 with a belief that the American church had failed to serve Christ. The first issue (Fall 1971) of the *Post-American*, the original name for *Sojourners*, carried a postcrucifixion image of Jesus wrapped in an American flag with the words ". . . and they crucified him" printed beneath. The image conveyed the idea that the surrender of the American church to culture had crucified Jesus anew. In his initial lead editorial, Wallis urged Christians to be members of "a new order who live by the values and ethical priorities of Jesus Christ and His kingdom." He called for a radical discipleship dedicated to "applying the comprehensive Christian message to all areas of life" and "committed to reconciliation, justice, peace and faith which is distinctly post-American."[85]

After a few rough years, including the breakup of much of the initial community associated with the magazine, the group moved operations from Chicago to Washington, D.C. At the same time, the editors renamed the magazine *Sojourners* to indicate that "the people of God . . . live in the world as strangers, pilgrims, aliens, and sojourners because of their loyalty to the kingdom of God, because of their identity as those who have entered into a new order of things."[86] In the early years, editorial arrogance and antiestablishment self-righteousness marred the magazine's call for a radical form of Christianity. Wallis and other members of the staff seemed blind to their own cultural limitations and believed wholeheartedly that their approach to faith marked a new turning point in the history of Christianity. They took themselves a bit too seriously. This weakness, however, also proved to be a strength. Passion for their mission and their sense of self-importance saw them through times when lesser-committed people might have given up.

Over the years, the editorial staff became more aware of their own involvement in human sinfulness. They assumed a stance of genuine humility and arrived at a more-sophisticated understanding of the struggles of the church in history. They connected their own renewal movement with the actions of other Christians through time. They wrote appreciatively of the revival movements in eighteenth-century England and nineteenth-century America as those movements witnessed against slavery and industrial exploitation. Editors connected with the history of the Franciscans, the Anabaptists, and other renewal movements. The magazine became more positive, more anxious to celebrate what it means to be the people of God located in the world. Well-known writers began to contribute to its pages, including people like Senator Mark O. Hatfield, William Stringfellow, Will Campbell, Dan Berrigan, Walter Brueggemann, Allen Boesak, Henry Nouwen, and Garry Wills. By the 1990s the list of contributing editors began to include people like James H. Cone and Rosemary Radford Ruether.

In its early years, the magazine spoke against American involvement in Vietnam, though the war was nearing its end by then. More recently, articles have provided a strong voice denouncing policies and politicians defending a "preventive war" against terrorism in Iraq.[87] Throughout its history, *Sojourners* has provided an articulate and impassioned Christian voice against racism. Editors were slower to accept the full implications associated with a growing commitment to feminism found among younger evangelical Christian women. They also found it difficult to speak much about the difficult issues related to human sexuality that were swirling in church circles throughout the 1970s and 1980s. Pages in more recent years have confronted the debate about homosexuality head on, calling, for example, for support for gay civil rights and civil unions but maintaining a traditional position that marriage should only be between a man and woman. *Sojourners* articles and editorials contain cogent criticisms of a capitalist economy and perceptive analyses of political situations in Latin America and the inadequate American response to them. Nuclear energy and nuclear weapons, global hunger, urban decline, gun control, the death penalty, tax resistance, human rights sanctuary, apartheid, and countless other topics regularly have filled columns in its pages. In all these cases, *Sojourners* has effectively argued an evangelical and Christian version of arguments more often associated with liberal Christians or secular persons with liberal social views.[88]

The *Sojourners* community practiced what it preached when it moved to D.C. They worked in an active, systematic political engagement to empower oppressed peoples. They developed a large day-care ministry for neighborhood children and a food program. They followed these ministries by creating a Neighborhood Center Building and forming a housing union to fight "gentrification" in D.C. neighborhoods. By participating in protest marches and withholding portions of their taxes designated for weapons or defense, they witnessed to their pacifist leanings. Members of the community have consistently lived simply, shared resources, and offered personal witness to the life they tried to encourage all Christians to follow through their writings in the pages of *Sojourners*. In 1995, *Sojourners* and Jim Wallis created Call to Renewal. Wallis continues to serve as its convener. The organization unites a national network of churches and faith-based organizations working to change social policies to favor antipoverty initiatives and to grow a Christian community dedicated to overcoming poverty.[89]

In 2005, with the publication of his book *God's Politics: Why the Right Gets it Wrong and the Left Doesn't Get It*, Jim Wallis hit the lecture-and-talk-show circuit with his "new vision for faith and politics in America." His book challenges Christians on the "Right" who have connected God too easily with war, wealth, and the Republican Party. Wallis equally chastises Christians on the "Left" for their seeming abandonment of faith when they address public issues. *God's Politics* is an engaging, persuasive, and effective common-sense statement of the fact that faith can enter the public square without violating the First Amendment. Though *Sojourners* and Jim Wallis stood squarely in the public Christian camp when the magazine began, Wallis and his community have clearly created a theological program that calls for "prophetic churches" to become engaged in political activities. "The truth is," Wallis writes, "that there are more churches committed to justice and peace than belong to the religious Right. It is time the voice of those congregations be heard and their activism be mobilized to become the conscience of American politics in a time of crisis." This posture, represented in the prominent evangelical voice of Jim Wallis, is yet another example of how effective public Christians occasionally morph into advocates for a public church.[90]

Chapter 6

Public Church

Those who represent a "public church" understanding of the relationship between Christian faith and public life share with public Christians a deeply rooted belief that God acts in history and that Christian people ought to recognize transcendent purposes in history, those things that lie at the heart of Christian identity. To borrow Paul Tillich's phrase, when Christian faith meets public life, it should actively represent the "principle of prophetic protest." In Tillich's words, this principle is "to be expressed in every situation as a contradiction to man's permanent attempts to give absolute validity to his own thinking and acting." "It is," Tillich writes, "prophetic judgment against religious pride, ecclesiastical arrogance, and secular sufficiency and their destructive consequences."[1]

In line with classical Christian tradition, the public work of Christians at its best has reminded all sides of an issue that human beings are finite and ultimately responsible for their actions in the world. When they are true to their theological beliefs, Christians who articulate this faith in the public arena include themselves among those who could be wrong and among those who are to be judged. In addition, this kind of faith sets forth a vision of a biblical God before whom everyone in the world is related as the human family of God. This faith does not speak in its own behalf, in the behalf of the status quo, in behalf of Christians only; rather it raises a compelling voice for those who do not have the power or the means to speak for themselves.

Like public Christians, but unlike those who practice a priestly faith, representatives of the public church do not demand that the American public conform to biblical revelation. Some churches, for example, through the last forty years, have translated their moral and religious claims into familiar and public forms of discourse completely removed from any theological foundations.[2] Others, perhaps best exemplified by American black ministers and churches involved in civil rights, have publicly affirmed theological foundations and believed that the insights gleaned from those foundations would be recognized as true, even by those who do not share the theology behind the insights. In either case, the public church affirms the importance of respecting the realities of American religious pluralism. Christians who seek to affect public life, whether as individuals or as a church, must always recognize that the political arena, like the religious one, is peopled with finite human beings. Therefore, Christians and churches must be prepared to live with some measure of ambiguity, doubt, and brokenness, as well as with the compromises necessitated by these kinds of realities.

Though the public Christian ideally shares all these presuppositions, the public Christian often differs from the public church in how this belief finds expression in public life. First, public Christians place priority on the church and its members to stand as witnesses both to God's salvation and to authentic human life in the world. It must, as its primary mission, bring lost individuals to Christ. The church represents the concerns of the "city of God" as an example for the human city, but should not, as church, join the political fray to try to accomplish social change. The public church, on the other hand, expects the church to engage social life in America, especially wherever political realities exploit human beings or deny them justice. In contrast to public Christians, the public church declares that the mission of the church includes the use of political wisdom, effective methods, and critical reason to establish a greater degree of relative justice in American public life. The adjective "relative" is important here. Christians recognize that absolute justice is impossible in our world. The best human beings can accomplish is an approximation of justice.

Second, where public Christians largely understand sin as resulting from the activities of individuals, the public church also emphasizes that human beings exist within a context where sin is systemic in nature. They argue that both good and evil are collective as well as individual. Evil resides within systems as well as within individuals. This means that judgment falls on societies and the collective institutions created by politics. The public church recognizes that social groups and institutions can sponsor and embody evil. The church cannot afford to ignore its concern for justice in these contexts. Both Christians and church are obliged, therefore, to work toward social redemption as well as individual redemption.

Third, the public church's approach to public life is essentially prophetic, defined by the way these Christians traditionally have asserted the unity of God's kingdom and have acted on this assumption either as if present (even though affirmed as eschatological) or as already somehow begun (from creation, or through the work of Christ). What I mean by the phrase "the unity of God's kingdom" is that these Christians believe strongly in God's care and concern for the world and all that it means to be in the world. For them, there is not a "kingdom of this world" that stands over against the "kingdom of God." Instead, God's concern encompasses all of creation, including those forces within it that, for the time being, stand in opposition to it. Those forces do not constitute a kingdom or a city over against, or separate from, the kingdom of God. Rather, they exist within it. This contrasts with a view of the kingdom of God that stresses its otherworldliness, its condemnation of material life, or even, in some cases, a condemnation of both nature and history. Christians in the public church believe God is concerned with all aspects of what it means to be human. This means it is not always easy to categorize what is purely a secular or a political concern from what is mostly a religious concern.

Over the past thirty to forty years, biblical theologians have begun to emphasize the significance of a theology of creation for these kinds of reflections. My colleague at Brite in Hebrew Bible, Leo Perdue, believes "creation integrates all other dimensions of God-talk."[3] Creation is not secondary to redemption in theological reflection but must actually be a primary theological consideration, "for God is the God of the world and all its inhabitants." In his commentary on Proverbs, Perdue stresses that wisdom in the Hebrew Bible "operates . . . within a universal framework where God is the God of the world, not only of a specific people."[4] God's concern extends to every creature and to nature itself, not simply to human beings in need of redemption. Terrence Fretheim, in his new book on this topic, credits this "salutary development" of renewed emphasis on creation to, among other things, "the emergence of an ecological consciousness":

> Other factors are equally important, such as a greater appreciation of the value of ancient Near Eastern creation thought; an openness to a greater range of texts that have to do with creation (not just originating creation), especially Wisdom literature; the welcome expansion of the conversation between science and religion; an increased awareness of the global scale of environmental issues; and an intensified sense of the deep relatedness and interdependence of all creatures.[5]

Fretheim's book argues that a biblically informed view understands creation is not merely past but also is continuing, allowing for "the emergence of genuinely new realities in an increasingly complex world." This clear theological claim, "that God's continuing creative activity enables *the becoming of the creation*," reveals divine and continuing concern for all aspects of the physical world. Fretheim argues that

> creation, while centered in the physical world in many ways, has to do with the continuing activity of God in all spheres of life whereby the world, often threatened by the presence of sin and evil, is ordered, maintained, evaluated,

and renewed. Generally speaking, those spheres of life include the historical, social, political, and economic—everything that is important for the
best life possible for all. . . . Given the realities of sin and evil, such continuing creational activity will not proceed without significant opposition. But
God will be creatively at work in the often tragic effects of such overt and
covert resistance, unrestingly seeking to bring "good" out of evil, to liberate
the captives and to build up communities.

When biblical texts speak of continuing creation, they do so in ways that
emphasize a role for human participation. The texts "speak of God using both
human and nonhuman creatures in this ongoing creative activity." And, concludes Fretheim, all creative work points to God's ultimate concern for the eschatological completion of creation.[6]

When Christians truly stand in a public Christian or a public church orientation to public life, they represent a strand of Christian understanding and
theological concern not primarily rooted in cultural identities. They don't
speak or act primarily as Republicans or Democrats, or even as Presbyterians
or Baptists. They do not speak as Christians who are primarily concerned with
American or denominational politics. Rather, they speak as Christians who
believe in the meaning of the gospel. They also believe that the gospel carries
with it implications for how human beings, in all their individual and social
relationships, treat one another and the created order. Thus, when they speak
or act in public life, they seek to move it toward a greater realization of both
the fulfillment of creation and the kind of justice found in the Hebrew Bible
and Christian gospel.

Since the gospel can be defined in a variety of ways, I want to be explicit
with what I mean by it. I like Clark Williamson's understanding that "the
gospel is an ellipse with two foci, the grace and command, gift and claim of
God, neither of which may be forgotten." The gospel, therefore, is the promise
that God loves each and every human being and creation and the command
that justice be done for each and every human being and in relation to creation.
The biblical witness contains the promise of God's grace and love extended to
all human beings and even to all of creation, including nature. It also contains
the command and claim that human beings must tend to the kind of justice
that will reflect and respect the meaning of God's love. Williamson claims that
both foci "are definitively made clear in Jesus Christ."[7] For those in the public
church, Christians, whether acting as individuals or as church, should seek a
shared community life that reflects both the gift of God's love and the claim of
God's concern for justice—not only as these pertain to human beings but also
as they relate to the whole of God's creation. Most Christians throughout history have attempted to pay attention to these strands of the gospel by creating
a theological understanding of the kingdom of God. To understand theological differences between the public Christian and the public church, it is important to note how the notion of the kingdom of God has itself undergone a shift
in theological understanding.

A SHIFT IN THEOLOGICAL UNDERSTANDING
OF THE KINGDOM OF GOD

Some Christians, as noted in the last chapter, have tended to stress a separation of the kingdom of God from the kingdom of this world and have urged Christians and the church to represent the kingdom of God rather than the kingdom of this world. This particular theological approach to the kingdom has especially emphasized God's control over the spiritual life of Christians and the church. The church's emphasis, in this understanding, is to enhance devotion to God and bring attention to the individual's relationship to God. Though the public Christian allows for individual political concern and activity, the church's goal is to develop a sanctuary where salvation exists in the midst of a sinful world.

In the theological tradition of Martin Luther, this form of Protestantism has emphasized God's direct rule in spiritual matters and a willingness to let government handle what seem to be purely material issues, with, of course, the confidence that God ultimately is sovereign in those affairs as well. H. Richard Niebuhr, in his discussion of these matters, stressed Luther's confidence in the freedom of the Word of God. He believed so long as "the Word is not shackled it will convert rulers and rich men and so produce a paternal, loving, reasonable rule on earth." But this reasonable rule would come through individually converted rulers, not through some form of church action, other than that taken to protect the freedom of the Word.

There is, however, another theological understanding of the kingdom of God that has operated in Christian history. This view has emphasized the need to act within history in light of an eschatological vision, an understanding of the ultimate purposes of God for creation. What does the kingdom of God value and how can human beings help the world to move in that direction? This has sometimes led to too much optimism about what human beings can actually accomplish. But that has not always been the case, especially when theologians have maintained an emphasis on the initiative of God. H. Richard Niebuhr compared Luther's understanding of the kingdom of God with that of John Calvin. Like Luther, Calvin emphasized that all authority associated with the kingdom belonged to God. However, as Niebuhr put it, "he was more acutely aware than Luther had been both of the necessity of restraining evil and of the danger which lay in giving human agencies unlimited powers of restraint." Calvin feared that both church and state could attempt to lay up too much power for themselves. Each must be subject to the kingdom of God, which transcended both of them. And each should attempt to live in view of values associated with God's kingdom. In Calvin's Geneva, the

> leaders of the church were doubtless the interpreters of Scripture, but they had no power to compel magistrates to adhere to the interpretation offered. The clear-cut separation of church and state, with both dependent on the kingdom of God, implied an organization of life wholly different from that which the Roman theory of the kingdom of God brought with it.[8]

In Calvin's Geneva, ministers served on a level equivalent to the magistrates, and both served the kingdom of God.

Calvin, like Luther, stressed distinctions between the kingdom and the world. But he denounced "certain fanatics" who "shout and boast" that Christians "have died through Christ to the elements of this world." Instead, Calvin argued that the "spiritual government" of God "is already initiating in us upon earth certain beginnings of the Heavenly Kingdom." He placed certain obligations upon civil government that related to religion. For example, the government should prevent "idolatry, sacrilege against God's name, blasphemies against his truth, and other public offenses against religion from arising and spreading among the people." In other words, Calvin gave civil government, in some respects, the responsibility to protect religion "from being openly and with public sacrilege violated and defiled with impunity." This is why Calvin believed magistrates had a "calling"— "the most sacred and by far the most honorable of all callings in the whole life of mortal men."[9]

What is important for our purposes here is not Calvin's granting to government the right to protect true religion against false ideas. Subsequent history has clearly revealed the attendant problems associated with that idea. In fact, the struggles in Calvin's Geneva after 1541 illustrate well those problems. Struggles between magistrates and ministers, riots, the execution of Michael Servetus, the break with Swiss Protestants—all these things revealed that the transformation of Geneva into a "Calvinist camp" was not entirely without consequence or a glaring lack of Christian character.[10] What is important is Calvin's theological belief that all aspects of human life fall under the purview of the kingdom of God. God has not written off the civil affairs of human beings, or any other aspect of human existence. As Niebuhr put it, Calvinism

> resolutely refused to give up any part of human life as beyond hope of redemption. Not economics, nor politics, nor church, nor the physical life could be regarded as merely temporal in significance, as not involved in corruption or beyond need of restoration to the harmony of God's kingdom. . . . Calvinism insisted with the thoroughness of the Hebrew prophets that God was king over every creature.[11]

This kind of theological approach expects the church to pay attention to all aspects of human life and to seek actively, in every area of human life, the values and ideals associated with God. In this way, Calvin reintroduced an idea largely abandoned in medieval Christianity. The medieval church had adjusted to the long delay of Christ's return by spiritualizing the kingdom of God. Medieval Christianity deferred true happiness and justice until the end of time. Only then could the deficiencies of the social order truly be addressed. Within this kind of theological understanding, one has a difficult time challenging the status quo. Calvin's theology clearly hailed an understanding of the kingdom of God that had immediate relevancy. "Justification was *now* to be apprehended; assurance of salvation was *now* to be received; the rule of Christ was *now* to become effective."[12] There is no theology of distinction located here that expects the world to carry on business as usual. Instead, for Calvin, God expects the world to change and reflect more adequately the fact of God's love for all creation.

This theological shift represented in Calvin is, in some ways, a recovery of the message found in the New Testament Gospels and in the Old Testament Prophets. As the Gospel writers recorded the sayings of Jesus, they presented a strand of theology claiming that the kingdom of God had established a foothold on earth. The kingdom of God is not merely future but is somehow present.[13] For Jesus, the kingdom of God contained some element of understanding and expectation that human life on earth, in all its features, would be redeemed. This included a belief that the activity of God had already somehow assured the defeat of evil and the reclaiming of creation. Jesus, thus understood, stands in the line of the prophets of Israel.

Prior to the appearance of the prophets, Israel remembered and celebrated God's saving acts in history, through festivals like Passover, bringing remembrance of God's saving activity in the exodus to current experience. The prophets brought a new emphasis to Israel. They preached a God who also was active currently, working in contemporary events in Israel. They proclaimed that God is active now to bring redemption in the future. God acted in history in the past, is entering history in the present, and will always enter history on Israel's behalf. Through this activity, God is challenging Israel in the present. The prophets refocus Israel's concern with salvation from past to future in a way that profoundly affects the present. This is not history moving toward a preordained climax, as is true of an apocalyptic approach. But rather, as with Jesus, the emphasis is "upon the sudden and unexpected manner of God's in-breaking into history and human experience and upon the responsibility of men to be prepared to respond to this crisis."[14]

Modern understandings of the importance of the kingdom of God as a theological theme began in the late nineteenth century. Albrecht Ritschl argued that the kingdom of God must be central for Christian theological understanding. He built on the argument of Friedrich Schleiermacher but criticized it for not connecting the kingdom of God to either God's purposes for creation or to the importance of the role of Jesus. For Ritschl, Christ brought redemption, and from the midst of redemption the kingdom of God arose. In Christ, the redeemed joined God in the effort to establish the kingdom within which human beings would be united by love. For Ritschl, the theology of the kingdom of God stressed an ethical imperative to be followed by all Christians. Human beings must work to establish a moral community.

Scholars like Johannes Weiss and Albert Schweitzer challenged the interpretation offered by Ritschl. Weiss, who was Ritschl's son-in-law, believed that Ritschl placed too much stress on human action in establishing the kingdom. Jesus, he argued, placed all his emphasis on God as king. God would bring the kingdom, not human activity. Jesus had little interest in establishing a new moral order in history, Weiss argued. This was not a call to social reform because society as history knew it would soon be no more. Political reform is the furthest thing from the mind of Jesus. Instead, Jesus saw himself as standing at the end of history. He stressed an imminent kingdom, one that was coming soon. In this understanding, then, Jesus urged followers to live in the vision of the future as if it were already present. His message was not so much to future generations, since the end was imminent. He urged followers to get their act together now. If they hoped to share the kingdom, they had to do something. They should repent and love one another while there was still time.[15] This early-twentieth-century argument troubled some Christian scholars because it concluded Jesus was wrong. The end, and the kingdom, did not come.

Other scholars, like C. H. Dodd, have argued that Jesus claimed the kingdom was actually present in his ministry. The kingdom has, at least to some degree, arrived. The eschatology of Jesus was "realized" in his ministry. Jesus was not mistaken about when the kingdom would arrive; it did arrive. The parables of Jesus, in this view, challenge hearers "to take great risks" in light of the crisis represented by the presence of the kingdom of God. In the ministry of Jesus, the kingdom of God had broken into this age and now is actively "grappling with the evil power of this age."[16] For Jesus, then, the kingdom of God requires a personal response; it requires faith. Ever since the ministry of Jesus, the kingdom has been present, but Christians following the first generation lost their sense of the dynamic presence of the kingdom and began to think of it as "located exclusively in the future." They thought of the present as a battle where the kingdom of the world maintains some degree of power and presence over against the kingdom of God. The "Christian's confident and joyous assurance that the age to come has already broken into the present age has faded into the background."[17]

Scholars after Dodd tended to discount Dodd's fully present kingdom. In its place, they emphasized a tension between present and future in Jesus' teaching about the kingdom of God. Norman Perrin, in his earlier work on the kingdom of God, represented this view. In Jesus, the kingdom is present "in that the power of demons is broken, sins are forgiven, sinners are gathering into an eschatological fellowship around Jesus." These "historical events" are "present to human experience."[18] So, the kingdom of God is, in some very real sense, present. This tension between present and future highlights an ethical emphasis for Perrin. How must the Christian respond to the challenge of God's kingly activity? What do Christians do in the midst of this tension?

Brian Blount places the African American approach to theology and ethics in the context of Gospel passages related to the kingdom of God. Jesus, Blount emphasizes, operates in each of these texts as representative for a future reality that exists within the midst of his present ministry. Jesus is "representative of a future kingdom that drives the present and all those who live in it toward the kind of historical transformation that prefigures and therefore inspires the liberation of those who are oppressed." This kingdom is a "force" not a "place" and is "a powerful, sweeping indication of God's rule that cuts into the path of human time and overwhelms it."[19] The kingdom is the compass of Christian life. If we lose sight of it, we are in danger of losing our bearing. . . . Of course, there are always dangers in trying to apply an apocalyptic symbol to a time that clearly envisions, and should envision after two millennia, an ongoing history. But Luke shows us that the kingdom emphasis can be ethically applicable even, and perhaps especially, in such a reality. It is the only foundation that can retain its ethical meaningfulness into an ongoing and apparently boundless future. That is because its existence is itself part and parcel of that future.[20]

Later in his career, Perrin turned to understanding Jesus' use of the kingdom of God more as "symbol" than as something that is either present or future. Jesus proclaimed the kingdom of God to evoke "the myth of the activity of God on behalf of his people." The symbol "is a challenge to the hearers to take the ancient myth with renewed seriousness," wrote Perrin, "and to begin to anticipate the manifestation of the reality of which it speaks in the concrete actuality of their experience."[21] For Perrin, the symbol "proclaims God as king for the existential realities of human life, jolts the hearer with the challenge of this experience, and compels commitment."[22]

All these understandings of the kingdom of God as expressed by Jesus have ethical implications. Whether one emphasizes the impending crisis associated with God's activity in Jesus, the kingdom of God actually present in the ministry of Jesus, or the kingdom of God as a symbol that evokes an anticipation of the kingly activity of God, people who experience the kingdom of God must respond to it. The reign of God contains a proleptic edge. In this sense, the future represented in justice complete in God is anticipated in ways that assume its presence (as if it is already accomplished, even though it is not). It becomes a part of contemporary experience. In each of these views, the cosmic reality of the kingdom of God informs the life of those who encounter it, both individuals and communities. They must forgive as they are forgiven; they must love as they are loved. The activity of God, both within history and that which is expected, demands human response. It makes a difference in human life for those who experience it.

There is another dimension in the Bible, found both within the Gospels and especially in the writings of Paul, that must be taken into account. It is clear that early Christians, living within the clear example of Jesus, were not all that interested in working to resolve questions of social justice. Jesus did not demand a thorough reform of society as a result of his understanding of the kingdom of God. The ethics and values of the kingdom are not easily transformed into a blueprint plan for civil government or society.[23] What are we to do with that reality? Does this mean that contemporary Christians should not be active, especially as church, in dealing with issues related to our public life together? Franklin Gamwell has taken up this question in his most recent book, in which he argues that Christian faith challenges Christians to relate their faith to politics and to understand political work as a Christian vocation.[24]

Gamwell begins his argument by recognizing that the "early account" of Christianity clearly believed that God ordained government. Paul, in his many writings, did not address the subject of governmental injustice and the nature of Christian response to it. His focus was on the nature of the Christian community and its extension into the world. Therefore, he was generally "accommodating" to the political order around him. There were Christians in the early years, as we have seen in the last chapter, who completely rejected and condemned the political order around them. The book of Revelation is the prime example. But, as Gamwell points out, that book does not advocate revolution. It focuses on the "passive resistance" of the Christian community. When the demands of the political community challenged the faith of Christians, martyrdom sometimes resulted, but early Christians did not try to overturn the rule of those in authority.[25]

Gamwell then turns to the question of whether this "early account" is in some way authoritative for contemporary Christians. There are Christians today who claim that the church's concentration on the Christian community, its love of God and love of neighbor, is part of the "essence" of Christianity. H. Richard Niebuhr, in a treatment of the "purpose of the church," identified "the increase of Love of God and Neighbor" as the church's central purpose in the world.[26] Time and the context of governments are irrelevant. The church, as Carl F. H. Henry believed, must be the church, not a political organization. Since the "early account" reflects this important element of faith, it is as relevant for Christians today as it was then. Gamwell's book offers a different response. While he affirms the "abiding content" of Christian faith, he believes that the "peculiarities" associated with various political contexts can actually demand different applications of the same Christian content. For Gamwell, the basic essence of Christian faith is wrapped up in the Great Commandment, to " 'love the Lord your God with all your heart, and with all your soul, and with all your mind, and with all your strength . . . [and] love your neighbor as yourself' " (Mark 12:28–31).

> The call through Jesus to love without reservation the God who loves all the world defines the abiding content of Christian faith, in the sense that anything else belonging to its essence must be everywhere consistent with this calling. No other meaning essential to Christian belief, in other words, can be in any circumstances inconsistent with the Great Commandment given with God's love.[27]

What Gamwell does not note is that concern for social justice is not completely absent in the church near the time of Augustine. Basil the Great (329 or 330–379), the oldest of the so-called Cappadocian fathers, for example, served as the Archbishop of Caesarea from 370 until his death. His friend, Gregory of Nazianzus, and his younger brother, Gregory of Nyssa, were the other two Cappadocian theologians so important to the life of early Eastern Christianity. He wrote of the necessity of desire as one of the "nonrational faculties" that, when properly directed, serves as a motivation for love of God and neighbor. He also spoke of *thumos*, perhaps translated as passion or assertiveness, as a "nonrational faculty" that seeks justice and the rejection of evil. In his work, he emphasized human connectedness and interdependence, and urged Christians to order their lives by orienting themselves to values associated with the kingdom of God in the teaching of Jesus. Christians who lived in this proleptic fashion could seek the reform of the entire society to reflect priorities associated with God's kingdom, especially love of God and neighbor.[28]

Even earlier than Basil in the East, some Christians in the West dealt somewhat differently in the late second or early third century with the delay of the return of Christ than Augustine would in the fourth century. After Augustine's theological work, Christians in the West often expressed their understanding of Christian relationship to the world in light of it. Earlier Christians recognized they were primarily oriented toward heaven, just like Augustine would be in his time, but they did not develop an elaborate theology that pitted the kingdom of heaven against the kingdom of this world. Instead, these Christians began to see that the delay of Christ meant living with the reality of being "in the world" even though they believed they could no longer be "of it." But since they could not escape being in it, they might as well address some of the problems associated with the world.

During these years, the well-known *Epistle to Diognetus*, written by an anonymous Christian to the tutor of Marcus Aurelius, attempted to describe something about who Christians were. In order to describe the Christian relationship to the world, he used the analogy of the soul to the body: "The soul dwells in the body, but is not part and parcel of the body; so Christians dwell in the world, but are not part and parcel of the world." Even though the flesh wrongs the soul, and occasionally makes war upon it, "the soul loves the flesh" and "is the very thing that holds the body together." When Christians "are reviled" they turn to "bless." When "they are insulted," they "render honor."

> The fact is, God loved men, and it was for their sake that He made the world; at their service He placed everything on earth . . . he who takes his neighbor's burden upon himself, who is willing to benefit his inferior in a matter in which he is his superior, who provides the needy with what he himself has received from God and thus becomes the god of the recipients—he, I say, is an imitator of God.[29]

This kind of theological understanding runs somewhat counter to what seems to be an inherent Christian disdain for the world that runs through theology in Christianity from Paul to Augustine.[30] Politics and involvement in social change, for early Christians, is irrelevant, perhaps even dangerous. And, even in Diognetus, while there is an affirmation of the world and the role Christians play in it, there is no call for active political engagement. In fact, Christians are to "endure all things as if foreigners." Gamwell asks the question, Is this "early account" of Christianity found in Paul and Augustine consistent everywhere with the Great Commandment to love God and neighbor, "or is that account an application of that love to particular historical circumstances"?[31] He examines Augustine's appreciation for the theological conviction that God created the world, and everything in it—also an inherent part of Christian theology. In other words, Augustine recognized that God loves the world. Yet he also stressed the world has turned toward sin and now threatens Christian development.

In Augustine's context, resistance to evil in political systems would have meant anarchy, the creation of even greater evil and a greater threat to Christianity. Government in the Roman Empire meant the rule of one or the few. Even the selection of rulers involved only one or the few. Citizens were effectively without power except through either "passive engagement" or "some form of rebellion."[32] Christian commitment, therefore, required political accommodation and a dedicated concentration on heavenly things. But this kind of response was not inherently a part of the essence of Christian faith. Rather, it resulted from an application of the essence of faith to the specific political context represented in the Roman Empire.

Gamwell then makes the argument that the political context, particularly in modern democracies, has changed dramatically from that found in early Christianity. Participation in politics and in government is expected as a part of citizenship in America today. Since there is nothing in the essence of Christian faith that prohibits democracies, an assumption Gamwell defends well within the book, Christians can work toward change in ways that do not create greater evil but in fact create possibilities for greater good. These kinds of activities are theologically in keeping with a Christian understanding of God's investment in the creation of, and care for, the world. The "early account," with its understanding of a Christian faith divorced from politics, is not applicable in current contexts of modern democracies. The possibilities that the "early account" may become applicable again, in future political contexts, or that it could very well be applicable today in other parts of the world, are not necessarily denied by this approach.[33] In the meantime, Christians can, as a Christian vocation, fulfill their call to love God and their neighbors in effective and practical ways through involvement in the nature of public life in modern democracies. This helps to explain, in part, why Christians in America have nearly always advocated some public role for Christianity.

A BRIEF HISTORY OF POSTMILLENNIALISM
AND PUBLIC LIFE IN AMERICA

Jonathan Edwards (1703–1758) holds the distinction of being among the earliest and most prolific postmillennialists in America. He stands, on the one hand, in the tradition of Augustine in recognizing an ongoing battle between the forces of good and the forces of evil. On the other hand, contrary to Augustine, Edwards believed that God would win this struggle within history, not after history had ended. He stood on the lookout, seeing signs all around him that God was winning. Thus, Edwards believed the glass to be at least half full. History was making progress. Again, in some respects, Edwards's perspective was a return to that of the Old Testament prophets. Though they were by no stretch of the imagination cockeyed optimists with respect to history, they did believe God worked within history every bit as much as God worked through individuals. Edwards believed God's "work of redemption" was like a "machine," moving through time completing the various stages of redemption. As righteousness gains strength in history, even society will begin to reflect its triumph.[34] As the First Great Awakening dawned in America, Edwards interpreted the events as a sign that God was on the move toward accomplishing the final stages of redemption.

But God did not accomplish this work alone. Though the kingdom being accomplished on earth centered in the work of Christ, God used the Holy Spirit's direction of the "human instrumentalities of the church."[35] The church had great responsibilities to fulfill that it could not ignore, and these responsibilities were deeply concerned with the world, with all of creation. For Edwards, however, the work was always God's work. As H. Richard Niebuhr has emphasized, "the coming kingdom appeared not as a goal toward which men were traveling but as the end which was hastening toward them; and now it was no longer simply the great happiness which men might miss but also the great threat which they could not escape."[36]

Another related theme in Edwards had to do with a consideration of the purposes of creation. For Edwards, God created the world in order to testify to the glory of God. God is both the "alpha and the omega, the beginning and the end of creation." Therefore, God's glory was "being communicated by God to creation, and reflected back by creatures to their Creator." This theological perspective highlighted the importance that the whole creation should reflect the purposes of God. Ultimately, nothing in creation could be left under evil's control.[37]

As the American Revolution neared, many American Protestants linked their postmillennialism more directly to the American cause of liberty. The grandson of Jonathan Edwards, Timothy Dwight, later to become President of Yale, delivered the valedictory address at that school in 1776. Living in the optimism of his postmillennialism, he declared,

> From the first of these remarks, it is evident that the empire of North America will be the last on earth; from the second, that it will be the most glorious. Here the progress of temporal things towards perfection will undoubtedly be finished. Here human greatness will find a period.[38]

These priestly connections between Christianity and America, and the accompanying confidence that God had a great plan for this new territory, carried the day for most of the Christian communities at the time of the American Revolution. Patricia Bonomi documented how "patriotic clergymen" urged hesitant colonists to take up arms by telling them "that failure to oppose British tyranny would be an offense in the sight of heaven." She concluded, "Ministers did the work of secular radicalism and did it better; they resolved doubts, overcame inertia, fired the heart, and exalted the soul."[39] Mark Noll noted the problem with these kinds of connections: "It was the unreserved embrace of the cause, the all-or-nothing identification of the patriot position as *the* Christian position." The problem here, Noll opined, "is religious" more than political because "[it] concerns the effect of such political action on the content of the faith."[40] The content of the Bible lost its independent meaning and Christians reinterpreted its content to serve America's revolutionary purposes.

While many Christians, like Timothy Dwight, hoped that established Christianity would remain after the revolution, they had to begin to face the facts of disestablishment. The defeat of the public support of Christianity did not dampen their belief that Christian faith remained vital to the social health of the country. Nearly all forms of Christianity, regardless of millennialist views, emphasized the need for Americans to turn to God, to be personally converted. Christianity, strengthened by various outbreaks of revival throughout the century, maintained a primary emphasis on evangelism.

But revivalist outbreaks also led to other activities. For example, following the Second Great Awakening, Christians found many ways to relate faith to society. Their goal remained, in essence, what they had represented during the American Revolution: they hoped to extend Christian civilization. As Robert Handy has put it, "they did not precisely define what they meant by civilization, but assumed the conventional usage of the time as meaning an orderly, well-mannered, and moral society based on a broadly Christian system of values and code of behavior."[41] The point here is that Christians in America throughout the nineteenth century regularly connected faith to public life and its endeavors.

Protestants were generally optimistic about the prospects of Christian civilization. Alexander Campbell, founder of the Disciples of Christ, named his journal the *Millennial Harbinger* in 1830, hoping to herald, as he put it in the first issue, the "development and introduction of the political and religious order of society called THE MILLENNIUM, which will be the consummation of that ultimate amelioration of society proposed in the Christian Scriptures."[42] Christians like Campbell supported the separation of church and state, but "strongly resisted any sense of the separation of religion and morals from public well-being."[43] They worked hard to create institutions of public education where these morals could be taught to the children of the developing nation. Protestant denominations, largely competing with each other on every religious front, were able to form a consensus about morals and values within the culture. And the culture, during most of the nineteenth century, largely reflected these values. In America, at least, one could describe the 1800s as a postmillennial century, bounding with Protestant confidence and priestly identifications between faith and public life.

A minority of Protestants during the nineteenth century held either to premillennial views or to millenarian views connected more directly to expectations that Christ was coming soon. Though these Christians did not share the optimism about history found among the majority, many did contribute to "the work of Christianizing society" nonetheless.[44] When some of the followers of William Miller, who expected the end of history in 1844, recovered from their "great disappointment," they became Seventh-day Adventists, created cereal as a health food, turned to building hospitals, and worked hard on behalf of Sabbath reform in American society. In the wake of the Second Great Awakening, Protestants formed voluntary societies focusing on distributing Bibles, creating Sunday schools, observing the Sabbath, curbing the sale and consumption of alcohol, and various other activities. In an examination of the "evangelical origins of social Christianity," historian Timothy Smith put it this way:

> The quest for perfection joined with compassion for poor and needy sinners and a rebirth of millennial expectation to make popular Protestantism a mighty social force long before the slavery conflict erupted into war.[45]

Christians sought to persuade Americans concerning proper social development. In some matters where persuasion did not seem to work, many of them turned to coercion and law to make it so. With the influx of immigration, particularly of the Roman Catholic variety, Protestants embraced rather nasty forms of nativism and anti-Catholicism.[46] They turned quickly to priestly styles of faith where only one kind of Christian expression suited American society, and it was, of course, their kind. On this, again, most Protestant denominations could readily agree. In the expansion westward, Protestants expressed a confidence in God's purposes for the nation through "manifest destiny." They presented a united front that tried to protect the cultural Protestantism they hoped to create, along with its accompanying values and objectives.

Other developments in early-nineteenth-century life, however, conspired against this Protestant unity. Many Christians in the North believed slavery constituted a horrible blight on their Christian civilization. Protestant Christians who were strongly influenced by revivalism in the early nineteenth century took the lead in this endeavor. People like Harriet Beecher Stowe and Theodore Dwight Weld sought to awaken Christian concern about slavery among evangelicals in America. Unitarians in Boston, like William Lloyd Garrison, also sought to reach more liberal thinkers with the message of antislavery. Timothy Smith shows how the connection in the North that more liberal Christians made between antislavery and women's rights in the late 1830s began to drive a wedge between even those who opposed slavery. And the majority of Christians in the South had little use for either the evangelical or the Unitarian versions of antislavery. As the Civil War approached, the major Protestant denominations all split. They found their effectiveness to speak to public life severely hindered.[47]

The conclusion of the Civil War brought social concerns in new areas. Since slavery had ended, most white Christians turned attention elsewhere.[48] For the most part, the interests of the churches remained firmly grounded in issues related to personal morality and education. When white Protestants gave any attention to the "Negro question," it usually focused on these areas. Some northern churches struggled to help educate freed slaves, while others were involved in vengeful efforts to reconstruct the old south in the image of the north. With rising Catholic immigration, American Protestants remained concerned about the rapid development of the alternative Catholic school system. Many Christians remained active in the battle to keep the Sabbath holy. Others struggled to respond to social crises created by new industrialization in America's cities.

Besides struggling with labor issues, churches worked to advance the cause of temperance, culminating in the national prohibition contained in the Eighteenth Amendment (1918). In the wake of Darwin's scientific theories and the rise of historical consciousness his work helped to occasion, some Christians adopted forms of Social Darwinism, popularized through the teachings of Herbert Spencer, and began to apply "survival of the fittest" to various social problems.[49]

In many cases, these kinds of social activities were clearly grounded in a post-millennialist view of the kingdom of God that, over the years, had lost Edwards's emphasis in divine initiative and had cast all confidence in the call to human action. By the end of the century, Protestants like Lyman Abbott, who followed Henry Ward Beecher (in 1888) in the pulpit of the prestigious Plymouth Congregational Church in Brooklyn, argued that a minister "is to be the herald of a new social order; he is to aim at nothing less than making a celestial city out of the City of Destruction; he is to be the inbringer and the upbuilder of a new earth wherein dwells righteousness."[50] As might be inferred from words like these, the nature of politics itself took on a divine significance. In a sermon preached in October of 1891 at Plymouth, Abbott claimed that the task of politics involved the attempt "to embody the justice of God" for the building "up of the kingdom of God."[51] Protestantism also used its understanding of the kingdom of God as theological justification for its increasing social standing and for the accumulating wealth attached to Christianity in late-nineteenth-century America.

The activism associated with this priestly confidence in the church's work for God also became associated with the nation's work. The birth of American foreign missions occurred in this century and combined notions drawn from post-millennialism, American imperialism, the development of Christian civilization, and evangelism. On the whole, as Charles Howard Hopkins concluded about these years, "progressive orthodoxy rendered specific service to the rising social conscience of the gilded age not only in its humanistic leanings but in its conception of the kingdom of God as an actuality realizable on earth."[52] Through its efforts to extend liberty in the world, America came to embody God's purposes for human history. By the turn of the century, and especially illustrated through the rapid success of the Spanish-American War in 1898, churches and their clergy gained confidence that America would play an important role in bringing in God's kingdom.[53]

As this brief historical overview of the nineteenth century illustrates, Christians subjected the kingdom of God metaphor to a few perversions during this period. Some churches and ministers secularized it by emphasizing that the church (more than God) was responsible for transforming human lives. This tended to detach the metaphor from the biblical emphases found in Jonathan Edwards that stressed the importance of faith in the sovereignty of God and the experience of grace found in Christ. Further, Christians tended to transform the Puritan confidence in the role God intended Christians to play in history into a general Christian confidence that the American nation could play that role better. In this way, some Christians nationalized the kingdom and used it to support a belief in American superiority and manifest destiny. Finally, Christians attached the kingdom of God to their belief in the inevitable progress of Christian civilization. Christians carried an Americanized Jesus and American mores to the foreign mission field. Reconciliation with God "now meant to be reconciled to the established customs of a more or less Christianized society." As H. Richard Niebuhr has put it,

> evolution, growth, development, the culture of the religious life, the nurture of the kindly sentiments, the extension of humanitarian ideals and the progress of civilization took the place of the Christian revolution. In similar manner the idea of the coming kingdom was robbed of its dialectical element. It was all fulfillment of promise without judgment.[54]

The developing social gospel movement at the end of the century shared many of these theological weaknesses. The movement's greatest theologian, Walter Rauschenbusch, however, attempted to restore the dialectic to American understanding of the kingdom of God. His early scholarship returned to the teachings of the Hebrew prophets and to Jesus. He was primarily interested in the prophetic strain found in these teachings. As the church turned toward institution, shortly after Jesus, he argued, it lost its prophetic voice. He recognized that Jesus delivered his message primarily to individuals but believed it contained social power, power to overturn societal values and to disrupt all existing relationships.

Like Jonathan Edwards, Rauschenbusch understood, and helped the social gospel movement to remember, that all human beings stand under the judgment of God. He also emphasized an equally important point with respect to judgment: not only does God judge individuals, but ultimately God judges the social institutions human beings have created. He stressed that human life, though beset by individualism, is essentially social and "insisted that the church had room for a theology that included the necessity of both personal and social conversion."[55] Contrary to Edwards, however, Rauschenbusch did not believe that the kingdom of God would fully arrive within history. He did not expect the social order to be fully Christianized. Near the conclusion of his first major book on the topic, published in 1907, he wrote,

> In asking for faith in the possibility of a new social order, we ask for no Utopian delusion. . . . We shall never have a perfect social life, yet we must seek it with faith. We shall never abolish suffering. There will always be death and the empty chair and heart. . . . Imperfect moral insight will work hurt in the best conceivable social order. The strong will always have the impulse to exert their strength, and no system can be devised which can keep them from crowding and jostling the weaker. . . . At best there is always but an approximation to a perfect social order. The kingdom of God is always but coming.[56]

This theological belief, rightly understood, provides Christian foundation for the public church. Whatever it contributes to public life, the church recognizes the shortcomings. The kingdom of God is transcendent to all such activities but is not unrelated to them. The public church attempts, through its efforts in public life, to move social relations toward a greater "approximation" to the gospel, where persons are treated justly, and in a way that honors the fact that all are children of God, whether all recognize it or not.

Five years later, Rauschenbusch published *Christianizing the Social Order* (1912).[57] Generally, he did not use the term "Christianizing" in a priestly sense, but rather he sought ways Christians could work to transform social institutions to reflect the teachings of Jesus. The book criticizes the sins of capitalism (one chapter is titled "The Case of Christianity Against Capitalism"), particularly the American quest for profits, and stresses "the rights of the working-class Americans to receive a just wage and to unionize." Chapters cover such things as education, family life, women's suffrage, and the need for corporations and government to provide a safety net for the poor. Though he reminded readers of the dangers of believing the work can ever be done completely, his tone seemed a bit too optimistic in light of impending world war.[58]

Near the end of World War I, Rauschenbusch published his most substantial book, *A Theology for the Social Gospel* (1917).[59] Through its pages, he supplied a theological treatment of sin, salvation, and kingdom of God, and challenged Christians to take social reform seriously as an imperative of faith. He emphasized what he called the "superpersonal" forces of evil: the way sin infects social organizations and develops a power for evil that far exceeds that wielded by any individual. Christians, he argued, too often believe sin is only individual or personal. When Christians, and churches, neglect corporate or social sin, they ignore the kind of sin that radically affects people in every aspect of their social lives. Rauschenbusch knew the effort to build a just society must involve radical conflict with evil. The power of sin touched everything, every human being and every social system. It is the theological foundation for Rauschenbusch's belief that no system would ever be perfect and that the kingdom of God could never fully arrive in history. History will always be affected by sin. "If our exposition of the superpersonal agents of sin and of the Kingdom of Evil is true," wrote Rauschenbusch, "then evidently a salvation confined to the soul and its personal interests is an imperfect and only partly effective salvation."[60] Society stands in need of redemption just as fully as individuals do. Capitalism and corporations and governments stand in need of redemption. The Christian church needed to help them live into it.

A major component of Rauschenbusch's criticism of historical theology rested in his contention that the visible church had become synonymous with the kingdom of God. As the theology of the kingdom of God faded into Christian confidence in the church, the transcendent vision and power of the kingdom of God disappeared. But the kingdom of God is always larger than the church. It "embraces the whole of human life."[61] The church, he argued, became more concerned with its own power and survival than it was with the transcendent judgment of righteousness contained within the theology of the kingdom of God.

The church and Christianity lost their bearings when they lost sight of the importance of their proleptic vision of the kingdom. The kingdom of God, he wrote,

> is the energy of God realizing itself in human life. Its future lies among the mysteries of God. It invites and justifies prophecy, but all prophecy is fallible; it is valuable in so far as it grows out of action for the Kingdom and impels action. No theories about the future of the Kingdom of God are likely to be valuable or true which paralyze or postpone redemptive action on our part. . . . It is for us to see the Kingdom of God as always coming, always pressing in on the present, always big with possibility, and always inviting immediate action. We walk by faith. Every human life is so placed that it can share with God in the creation of the Kingdom, or can resist and retard its progress.[62]

Rauschenbusch was not immune to the assumptions of his age. He argued equality for women and supported women's suffrage, but believed women should stay at home and care for children. His work, for the most part, neglected the issue of racial justice. He believed in the equality of all human beings, but generally understood that the problems of African Americans would largely be resolved, as Christopher Evans has put it, "by the wisdom and example of the white middle class." Evans described these paternalistic and stereotypical views as "neither exceptional nor intentionally malevolent—they were tragically typical."[63] To some degree, Rauschenbusch also shared the optimistic, somewhat nationalistic, belief that Anglo-Saxonism would, with the blessings of God, lead in both Christianizing and civilizing the world.[64] In all these ways, Walter Rauschenbusch revealed his own participation in the sinful contamination that affects all history.

Yet beneath all this was his understanding of God. Rauschenbusch firmly believed God always stood "on the side of the poor."[65] This, for him, was the great revelation contained within Christianity because it runs counter to the common sense found in social structure. Perhaps it was this conception of God, connected as it was with his concern for social reform, that represented his greatest legacy. As early as 1908, Rauschenbusch's influence had helped to create the Federal Council of the Churches of Christ in America (FCC). Eighteen million American Protestants, hailing from thirty-three denominations, formed the FCC's initial membership. One of its first acts, in 1908, was to create a Commission on Church and Social Service and to adopt the "Social Creed of the Churches," a social manifesto originally set forth by a group of Methodists (Methodist Federation for Social Service) to address problems associated with the industrial age. In 1912, the FCC modified the Social Creed to include other social concerns. For mainline Protestantism, the FCC, eventually replaced by the National Council of the Churches of Christ (NCC) in 1950, served as the national instrument demonstrating its commitment to the social gospel and the nature of the public church.

The practical accomplishments of the social gospel movement cannot be traced with absolute precision. Certainly, the movement brought awareness to the plight of the common laborer in America and provided crucial support for unions during a time when they had very little cultural support. In addition, the movement worked with progressive politicians early in the twentieth century to bring more political power to the American voter. Social gospel leaders created social awareness and encouraged more active social reform, especially among the Baptists, Congregationalists, Episcopalians, Methodists, and Presbyterians. The social gospel also revitalized interdenominational work in America and, through the work of the FCC and ecumenical missionary organizations, developed an appetite among American Christians for understanding the concerns of Christianity elsewhere in the world. Further, the movement's leaders had a direct impact on the development of seminary curricula, contributing the new fields of ethics and the sociology of religion to theological education. Through advocates like Richard T. Ely and Albion W. Small, the movement contributed to the development of the secular disciplines of economics and sociology, respectively.

The 1920s, and the interruption occasioned by World War I and its aftermath, brought decline for the social gospel movement. The liberal foundation of the movement faced criticism from all sides. A new and contagious fundamentalism critiqued leaders of the movement for abandoning doctrine in favor of ethics. Ethics without doctrine, they argued, could only be secular. Many Christians were attracted to the pessimistic view of history and the longing for the second coming of Christ that were associated with the rise of dispensational premillennial interpretations of the kingdom of God, especially those associated with the *Scofield Bible*. From a considerably different vantage point, some Christian scholars, later known as neoorthodox realists, began to criticize the liberalism of the social gospel as shallow and overly confident of human ability. Though the depth of Rauschenbusch's theology clearly contradicted these critics, the criticism rang true for many of those associated with the movement. The social gospel's influence waned during the 1920s, but the indigenous American movement nevertheless contributed themes that remain important to American Christianity.

Many who had been schooled in the social gospel would make greater contributions in this area than the movement itself was able to make. The NCC, through its Commission on Religion and Race developed in 1963, helped mainline Protestantism recover the social gospel in practical ways. After that date, the NCC finally provided institutional activity and support for social progress in the area of racial justice.[66] Several denominations, but most notably the United Presbyterian Church U.S.A., the United Church of Christ, and the Protestant Episcopal Church, followed suit and created active commissions to work in this area. Presbyterians chose Gayraud Wilmore to head their commission, while the NCC chose a white minister, Robert Spike, from the United Church of Christ. All these are examples of the work of the public church in this area.

As examples of the public church, one could turn to any number of locations, such as the story of Catholic involvement through bishops and their actions with issues involving peace and war, economic justice, or even abortion. Or one could turn as well to an analysis of the work of lobbying agencies like the Baptist Joint

Committee for Religious Liberty in Washington, D.C., or to a study of denominational involvements, or, perhaps, to the history of particular congregations like the Riverside Church in New York City and their activities as public church.[67] There is, however, no better place to look for an example than the black church. Somewhat ironically, due to the fact that the early leadership of the social gospel never adequately addressed racial problems in America, the social gospel found especially vital life in the black church during the 1950s and 1960s.

LESSONS OF THE BLACK CHURCH AS PUBLIC CHURCH

Martin Luther King Jr. connected with the Rauschenbusch legacy during his student days at Boston University. King, in later years, cited very few books when discussing his religious and theological development, but one of those he cited was *Christianity and the Social Crisis*. As Taylor Branch pointed out, a professor named George W. Davis, "son of a union activist in the Pittsburgh steel mills," introduced King to the work of both Rauschenbusch and Gandhi. Both profoundly affected him. He even managed to refer to Rauschenbusch in his wooing of Coretta Scott, to give her the clear impression that he had intelligence and possessed "substance." Branch recounts their first meeting, over lunch, where King "launched into discussion of topics from soul food to Rauschenbusch."[68]

In an autobiographical essay published in 1960, King spoke of his increasing disenchantment with Protestant liberalism's understanding of human nature. He attributes to the work of Reinhold Niebuhr his recognition of "the complexity of man's social involvement and the glaring reality of collective evil." But, he wrote, it was Rauschenbusch who schooled him of the necessity of Christian work to address it.

> Not until I entered theological seminary, however, did I begin a serious intellectual quest for a method to eliminate social evil. I was immediately influenced by the social gospel. In the early '50s, I read Rauschenbusch's *Christianity and the Social Crisis*, a book which left an indelible imprint on my thinking. . . . Rauschenbusch gave to American Protestantism a sense of social responsibility that it should never lose. The gospel at its best deals with the whole man, not only his soul but his body, not only his spiritual well-being, but his material well-being. Any religion that professes to be concerned about the souls of men and is not concerned about the slums that damn them, the economic conditions that strangle them and the social conditions that cripple them is a spiritually moribund religion awaiting burial.[69]

King's seminary years gave him focus, but Rosa Parks brought his focus to action. He knew her as the secretary with the local chapter of the NAACP. Her refusal to move and her willingness to continue to resist the criminal case served both symbolically and practically to create a new urgency in the black church. In the wake of the Parks event, black ministers met and formed the Montgomery Improvement Association. Due to political realities between and amongst the ministers, as much as to King's obvious gifts, the ministers chose King, the new-comer, as the organization's president. Under his leadership, segments of the black church rallied around a new version of the social gospel that launched the modern civil rights movement.[70]

Luther Ivory has argued that King appropriated two particular notions from Rauschenbusch that helped him articulate his concerns for justice in ways that made sense to both church and society. These notions were the "beloved community" and the "kingdom of God." King used them to preach an "eschatological vision for public consumption." He placed the image of the beloved community against the realities of the status quo and urged Christians to move toward its establishment in history. The beloved community, marked by integration and justice, served as the historical goal. While it was not the kingdom of God, the beloved community "both *pointed to* and *participated in* the realization of God's radical future." This is the point pressed by King's "I Have A Dream" speech. "Like the Old Testament prophets," Ivory concluded,

> King believed that this type of ordered community represented a partially realizable eschatology, which would materialize in several flawed institutional arrangements at some future point in human history. . . . Situated as it was at the intersection of the "is" and the "ought," the horizon of King's "dream" was inclusive of both present needs and future hopes. The vision represented both divine gift and human task. . . . The power of this prophetic vision to inspire hope and radical participation in God's future acted to prevent his eschatology from becoming captive to an other worldly focus. Conceived and articulated in concrete, social, political, and economic terms, the radical future vision of King was decidedly this worldly in focus. The future was both now and later.[71]

King said it best himself in a Christmas sermon in 1967: "It really boils down to this: that all life is interrelated. We are caught in an inescapable network of mutuality, tied into a single garment of destiny."[72] All God's children must depend on one another, and all exist in relation to the kingdom of God.

The story of the black church and its quest for civil rights must be understood as the story of congregational activism, truly the story of a public church across all the manifestations of what is meant by the term "church." The leadership of people like King proved essential, but it would have meant nothing had the memberships of black congregations not responded. The role of women, especially, was crucial even though it had been long ignored. Book-length studies have revealed just how significant their activism proved to be within these congregations.[73] The active involvement of congregations, however, owed much to King's style and his concern for connecting the dots between faith and action. All his public speeches are laced with theological themes stressing these connections. Organizations like the Southern Christian Leadership Conference kept the identification central in every detail, right down to the way they were named.

In other words, the Christians in the pews did not have to labor to make the connections themselves. The leadership made it clear that what they did, they did because they were Christian. James Cone has stressed that King always understood civil rights as vitally connected to his understanding of his ministry at Dexter Avenue. Whether he was in the church or in the streets, King understood his activities as the essence of a vocation in ministry. "The civil rights movement, therefore," writes Cone, "was not thought of as something separate from the church; rather it *was* the church living out its obedience to Jesus Christ's calling 'to preach good news to the poor,' 'to proclaim release to the captives,' and 'to set at liberty those who are oppressed' (Luke 4:18, RSV)." This understanding is what gave the movement its power. The social gospel has never had as clear an embodiment before or since than it had in the black church acting as public church. Cone offers personal testimony of what those years meant to him as a young college student at Shorter College: "As I participated in the black church, I believed, as did others I knew, that fighting for justice was as important as preaching the gospel on Sunday morning. . . . Martin King was my primary resource on how to think about the gospel and the black struggle for freedom." Simply put, this identification between the gospel and the quest for freedom crossed all black denominational boundaries and unified the black church.[74]

At this point, however, it is important to emphasize that the black church is not monolithic or one-dimensional in how it approaches issues related to public life. Robert Franklin has offered a taxonomy of the black church that lists at least five different types of responses to relating Christian faith and public life. The two most relevant for this portion of the discussion are those he describes as the "pragmatic accommodationists" and the "prophetic radicals." The accommodationists primarily seek social change by "making deals." They do not seek change through radical activity, but rather by playing the political game effectively. During the civil rights era, and afterward, some of the largest black denominations have represented this kind of understanding. Franklin argues that their understanding of God is largely an emphasis on "God as Creator," the one who provides plentiful resources to be shared among all living creatures. "God as Sovereign" might be more the theological note that is played here. The Sovereign God works through both politics and the church to accomplish God's purposes. This perspective can be described as the public church because the church, as church, is often involved in this form of political response. Politicians seeking office appear in congregations and seek support. Compromises and political strategies are devised and enacted, and occasionally social reforms are accomplished "that would accrue to the benefit of excluded, less-advantaged groups." The "prophetic radicals," on the other hand, are represented by leaders like Martin Luther King Jr. They "uncompromisingly" seek social justice more through "confrontation and negotiation." They were the prime movers in the quest for civil rights. Their theological emphasis is upon the God who acts in history, "God as Liberator and Judge."[75]

The civil rights movement was not the first time in history that black churches answered the call to social action. The formation of black denominations in the late eighteenth and early nineteenth centuries was itself a social statement, a rejection of "the ethical behavior of whites," as James Cone put it.[76] Early in their history, these churches actively opposed social injustice. Mother Bethel, the founding congregation of the African Methodist Episcopal Church in Philadelphia, hid slaves in its basement in the early nineteenth century. The African Methodist Episcopal Zion Church provided extraordinary leadership for abolitionist activities prior to the Civil War through people like Frederick Douglass, Harriet Tubman, and Sojourner Truth.[77]

Bishop Henry McNeil Turner of the AME church declared in 1898 that "God is A Negro," giving early expression to a theological understanding of God that has found important expression in later theologians like Albert Cleage and James Cone. Turner's early depiction of God as black attempted, theologically, to break the ties connecting blackness with inferiority. As a radical and a nationalist, and thus a predecessor to Malcolm X, Turner believed America would never change. He sought reparations from the government for the sin of slavery as a way to finance removing blacks to Africa, where they could be truly free. He preached black liberation and led his church to connect theology to both politics and the world. His death in 1915 left a serious void in national leadership seeking liberation for the black church.[78] Turner and Malcolm X represented another one of Franklin's types within the black church, the "redemptive nationalist." Generally, this segment of black church involvement has sought separation from, rather than engagement with, the public life of the nation. Their emphasis is on "God as Redeemer," the one who redeems them from the oppressor by delivering them to their own land where they are in control. Franklin notes that, in more recent years, some among this group have entered politics more intentionally seeking election of their own candidates. In doing so, they represent yet another version of the priestly faith I have described in chapter 3. They do not seek an inclusive or pluralistic vision, but rather invest themselves in politics to impose very narrow aims on the rest of the population.[79]

After Henry Turner, the black church aided in the creation of some of the more important secular organizations dealing with political issues affecting black people. The connections between the black church and the founding in 1909 of the National Association for the Advancement of Colored People (NAACP) have been well documented and discussed. Church worship services often concluded with prayer and immediately opened meetings of the NAACP. Congregations generally left political activities to these organizations, even though membership was shared between them. While such organizations sought civil rights through political means, they were largely moderate in orientation and tended toward cultural accommodation in their early years. After World War I, the black church largely turned toward the survival mode. Scholars generally agree that social protest or activities genuinely defined as public church were rather sporadic between the turn of the twentieth century and the civil rights movement among black churches. The profound economic pressures associated with the Depression combined with "the brutality of racism" and overwhelmed many a congregation's spirit. Gayraud Wilmore has described these years as "the deradicalization of the

Black Church." There were exceptions. There were congregations, like the AME church in Chicago led by Reverdy Ransom and the Abyssinian Baptist Church in New York, with Adam Clayton Powell in the pulpit, that continued the prophetic tradition of black church radical activism.[80]

A spate of academic literature, especially among social scientists, appeared during this period to argue that religion caused blacks to turn away from social activism. This perspective found its origins in the work of Karl Marx, who argued that religion served as "the opium of the people," causing them to accept their status in the world by urging them to turn to otherworldly considerations. Studies in this vein that began in the 1920s culminated in the work of Gary Marx in 1967, who provided the argument that sociological surveys confirmed this "opiate theory" rather convincingly. According to his survey of urban blacks in 1964, the more one attended church, the less committed one became to the civil rights movement. Alongside these arguments, other scholars, like John Brown Childs and Charles V. Hamilton, have insisted that religion has served as an inspiration to black political activity. A recent study, titled *Something Within: Religion in African-American Political Activism*, has challenged both sides of this decades-long debate. Frederick C. Harris has charged that both have neglected the importance of "the multidimensionality" of both religious beliefs and political practices.[81]

One of the more interesting aspects of Harris's argument involves his belief that the religious culture and churches of marginal groups actually serve dual, somewhat contradictory, purposes in a democratic society. On the one hand, they serve as laboratories of democratic culture, enabling both the cultivation of skills and knowledge of prevailing norms and values that lead to greater success and integration within the culture. In this way, even "radical" black congregations can play roles within the culture that seem "accommodationist" in orientation. On the other hand, the culture and institutions of dominated groups serve as a seedbed for material resources and ideas that challenge the domination of the majority culture and call for change. Harris describes this dualistic orientation as "an oppositional civic culture."

Using this concept, Harris examines civil-rights-era poll data to reveal the effects of religion on both conventional (political activism acceptable to the dominant political culture, like voting, education, giving to political campaigns, etc.) and unconventional (protest or demand activism) modes of political participation. Generally, these modes of participation are both "inclusive" of the civic order. Harris also sought to examine black views of participation "exclusive" of the civic order by giving attention to questions measuring approval of black nationalists, Black Muslims, the creation of a separate black state, and blacks' resorting to violence to accomplish their goals. By analyzing data this way, Harris is able to present a rather systematic understanding of the multidimensionality of African American political thought and action during the 1960s.

Harris also examined poll data to measure the impact of five religious characteristics (sectarianism, church attendance, denominational affiliation, membership in church, and membership in church-related groups) on the type of activism practiced by African Americans during the period. His findings again point to the multidimensionality of religion's influence on activism. "Afro-Christianity," as he describes it, during the civil rights period, fostered both loyalty to the American democratic society and opposition to certain aspects of it. In subtle ways, Harris's description of the dual function of churches joins the historic discussion between the priestly and prophetic functions of the black church as it has functioned in American culture.[82] But this study contributes to a much clearer, more informed understanding of the fact that blacks have developed a rich oppositional culture, immeasurably influenced by their faith, that has assisted in their struggle for political power within the culture.[83]

In later chapters, *Something Within* analyzes the effect of religion's organizational and psychological resources for political action since the 1960s. Using a quantitative analysis of the 1987 General Social Survey, Harris shows that the "more blacks are psychologically devoted to their religion, the more they think about politics and feel politically empowered."[84] Harris also offers a qualitative investigation of the influence of religious culture as a microresource for political activism. One chapter illustrates how African Americans have used sacred symbols, religious language, and rituals to make sense of political goals and construct meanings drawn from shared cultural experiences and worldviews. The power of these kinds of symbol systems, however, cuts two ways. Another chapter argues that these cultural resources, while resisting the dominant culture, have also constructed a patriarchal system of gender inequality that has restricted the ability of women to exercise both religious and political leadership in the black church.

In his epilogue, Harris briefly examines emerging trends in African American religious life and their potential impact on political activism. As Afro-Christianity gains strength among Pentecostals and Catholics, and loses numbers among traditional black Baptist and Methodist churches, religious inclinations supporting a movement toward political activism are likely to weaken considerably. Franklin's fourth type in his taxonomy describes those black congregations primarily interested in revivalist activity. He calls them the "Grassroots Revivalists" who primarily emphasize "God as Savior." The church's task is to bring God's salvation to individuals.[85] Congregations eschew contact with the political order, but most among them would likely fit the category I have described as "public Christian." The church's task is to represent God's kingdom by preaching an evangelistic gospel. Meanwhile, individual Christians vote and associate with other forms of political or public activity.

Harris also points out in his epilogue that the development of black megachurches will probably diminish the ability of members to practice politically relevant skills in their church life. The theologies of material prosperity and positive thinking often associated with such churches could also undermine collective efforts associated with black political activism. Tony Pinn also cites the "megachurch phenomenon" as a challenge to black social activism. The "prosperity thrust" present in many of these churches stresses economic empowerment and individual growth "over national consciousness." Members of the black middle class have occasionally assumed material comfort will bring comfort in all other areas of life.[86]

Robert Franklin's fifth and last type within his taxonomy is descriptive of this phenomenon. He describes these congregations within the black church as the "Positive-Thought Materialists." They emphasize "individual empowerment and have few ideas about community economic revitalization." Their theological understanding stresses "God as Provider." This understanding of God leads to emphases on self-improvement, personal mental and spiritual health, accumulation of wealth, and accomplishment of success in all spheres of life.[87] There is no emphasis on how the church assumes a prophetic role in public life. Yet, again, individual Christians involved in these churches are often involved politically in ways that serve their understanding of the gospel. This involvement can surface in ways that might fit either the public Christian or priestly faith categories, depending on the issues addressed by these individual Christians in public life.

Harris argues additionally that entrenched theocratic and autocratic norms in many congregations (read here "God as Sovereign") may ultimately frustrate black participation in democratic processes in both church and political life. He also mentions that government funding of faith-based charities, allowing in many cases for the hiring of social service professionals, may threaten the ability of black churches to nurture the skills of volunteers. In general, Harris does not paint an optimistic picture of the trends in the black church for the continuation of the alternative and empowering black "oppositional culture" that his book so convincingly demonstrates actually exists. Since the movement for civil rights, the social activism of the black church has declined to levels generally comparable to those before Rosa Parks refused to change seats on that Montgomery bus. Tony Pinn emphasizes the change in generations; over half of all black Americans living in 1998 were under age 30. They don't remember the movement, and, for many of them, the black church seems socially irrelevant today, perhaps due ironically to its success in securing socioeconomic and political advances since the 1950s. Pinn claims that church burnings during the 1990s (over ninety of them) and other events evidencing continued racism in American culture, however, have renewed interest among many blacks to return to churches in the hope that they can once again prove to be the strength of the black community.[88] The struggle to recover this strength will not be a short one.

C. Eric Lincoln and Lawrence H. Mamiya, in their landmark work on the black church, asked why so many black people in America were not even registered to vote. In 1983, for example, only ten million of seventeen million eligible blacks were registered. Gary Marx has argued it is because the church has taught them to ignore the realities of this world for the hope of the next. But Lincoln and Mamiya emphasize the "depth of alienation" among lower-class blacks in America. They deeply distrust the system that has kept them chained to poverty and discrimination. Social research done for their book revealed that only 8.4 percent of black clergy believed the black church should avoid politics, and

91.6 percent of black clergy across the nation, and across denominational lines, "advocated church involvement in social and political issues." All sociological surveys confirm that both clergy and laity in black churches affirm an activist role for their churches in much larger numbers than is true for white churches. These findings, along with other scholarly research produced by Frederick Harris and others, demonstrate that the black church tradition has actually acted as a "cultural broker" leading to increased participation in politics and the public life in America. The black church has not generally advocated revolution but has consistently emphasized making progress in social reform. Church programs provide education for civic activity and actually serve the black community by helping members overcome their deep feelings of alienation. Between 1980 and 1984, as Jesse Jackson prepared his run for the presidency, the black church registered more than one million voters.[89]

But the black church, as public church, still struggles to recover the voice it had during the two decades in the mid-twentieth century. Somehow, the black church must recover the kind of theological connections made so effortlessly by Martin Luther King. Lincoln and Mamiya have described a natural worldview of African Americans that King seemed to represent especially well theologically. Historically, black Americans have resisted making clear delineations between sacred and secular. Like their ancestors in Africa, for them, "the whole universe is sacred." As slaves, they incorporated Christianity into their understanding of this black sacred cosmos and found themselves drawn, by obvious circumstances, to "the Old Testament notion of God as an avenging, conquering, liberating paladin." Slavery led black preachers and people to pick up particular scriptural themes, and those related to God's active involvement in history on behalf of the oppressed naturally became prominent among them. The picture of a suffering Christ, who is nailed to a tree, created obvious resonances with the slave community in America. The eventual triumph of Jesus over horrific oppression provided hope that, one day, he would lead slaves to their own triumph in freedom, to "the absence of any restraint which might compromise one's responsibility to God." For black people, "freedom has always been communal in nature." Their Christian faith is naturally communal as well. Their common religious experience has been especially related to the "core values of black culture like freedom, justice, equality, an African heritage, and racial parity at all levels of human intercourse."[90]

The development of black theology over the past forty years has recovered these themes and given them more substantial theological expression than found within the civil rights movement. These theologians have aggressively asserted God's preferential option for the oppressed; they have brought a renewed emphasis to the theological understanding of "God as Liberator." Cone's bold declaration in 1970 that "God is Black" made clear his commitment that "either God is identified with the oppressed to the point that their experience becomes God's experience, or God is a God of racism."[91] Christians, white or black in America, must also become "ontologically black."

> The blackness of God means that the essence of the nature of God is to be found in the concept of liberation. . . . Those who want to know who God is and what God is doing must know who black persons are and what they are doing. . . . Knowing God means being on the side of the oppressed, becoming one with them, and participating in the goal of liberation. We must become Black with God.

Christians cannot work to become black like God; rather, argued Cone, it is the gift of God. It is salvation. "God comes to us in God's blackness, which is wholly unlike whiteness. To receive God's revelation is to become black with God by joining in God's work of liberation."[92]

Peter Paris has indicated that the peculiar history of black Americans has led the black church to its "quest for human freedom and justice, that is, the equality of all persons under God." The black church represents "the historical embodiment of [this] universally significant principle."[93] Paris makes the important case that the black church is indeed theological in its approach to social problems, but that theology must always be seen as closely connected to history; therefore, false cleavages between history and theology must be avoided.

> Implicit in this viewpoint is the understanding that the religious content of the black churches (as well as that of all churches) must be grasped and developed within a historical context, because even that which transcends history is dependent upon history for its transmission. In other words, there can be no sharp cleavage between the substance of religion and that of historical experience. . . . In fact, the [principal] idea the black churches sought to institutionalize—the parenthood of God and the kinship of all peoples— was not the creation of the black churches themselves. They merely sought the means of embodying it in their practice and as a moral claim on white churches to affirm in thought and practice the "kinship of all peoples" as the practical inference of the parenthood of God.[94]

This message becomes more important in our postmodern world. The message of the black church, born in the midst of African American experience in the United States, is especially relevant for the "entire human family." As J. Deotis Roberts puts it, black theology shares commonalities today with, for example, expressions of "Dalit Theology in India and Minjung Theology in South Korea."[95] These developing subaltern theologies (theologies from beneath), born through human struggle, recognize significant connections between theology and human experiences in ways that long to connect God's concern for history to more just ways to live in the midst of human community.

Today, one of the problems facing the black church is the lack of connection between black theologians and people in the pew. As black theology has found a home in the American academy, some have begun to question whether black theologians are beginning to be more concerned with publication and tenure than with their connections to the black church.[96] These are natural developments. Womanist theology, emerging over the past two decades, has thus far been conscientious about making connections between the experiences of women in the church and outside it with the way the black church should be thinking about God.[97] But these theologians and ethicists face the same pressures to turn increasingly to the academy. In 1994, the Black Religious Scholars Group (BRSG) was created to forge more meaningful linkages between black theologians and womanists and the black church. Meeting each year concurrently with the American Academy of Religion, the BRSG gathers in a black congregation in the host city and brings church and academy together to talk about important issues facing the black church.[98] Conversations like these may be the beginning stirrings of a recovery of the important witness of the black church as public church.

Cornel West, in his recent book *Democracy Matters*, points to the strong heritage of the "black prophetic Christian tradition." I believe he is correct when he argues that "much of prophetic Christianity in America stems from the prophetic black church tradition." Yet, this does not stop West from worrying that this tradition is suffering today and losing ground to "Constantinian Christians" who are attempting to suffocate "prophetic voices and viewpoints that challenge their status quo." Wealth, comfort, all the trappings of the American empire—these conspire against and tempt even black Christians in contemporary life.[99] The antidote for a disempowered black church and, for that matter, for the disempowered prophetic Christian tradition more generally, exists in the recovery of an ability to relate Christian faith to public life. Martin Luther King spoke the language of faith, informed by the gospel, and connected it powerfully to a call for the reform of public life. He did so in very public ways. Christians must learn again to stand in the tradition of King. The final chapter argues that today's postmodern context in the United States invites just this kind of Christian contribution.

PART IV
POSTMODERN CONTEXT

Chapter 7

Faith and Public Life
in a Postmodern Context

THE ROLE OF RELIGION IN A POSTMODERN CONTEXT

The free exercise of religion ultimately means the right to the full and free expression of religion. Jeffrey Stout describes this as "the right to make up one's own mind when answering religious questions . . . the right to act in ways that seem appropriate, given one's answers to religious questions—provided that one does not cause harm to other people or interfere with their rights."[1] This right to the free exercise of religion, as we saw in chapter 2, is one protected by the Constitution in this country. It applies not only to private expressions of religion but to public ones as well. In other words, the free exercise of religion also protects the right to express connections between religious understandings and the political or public implications or conclusions drawn from them.

Not everyone has agreed with this conclusion. Richard Rorty, a leading philosophical pragmatist, has argued that the nature of contemporary liberal democracy requires a strict separation between the private and the public. And he places religion securely in the private category, that area where "idiosyncratic loves" prevail. In response to Stephen Carter's book *The Culture of Disbelief,* which argued that religion should have a voice in public life, Rorty responded, "The main reason religion needs to be privatized is that, in political discussion with those outside the relevant religious community, it is a conversation-stopper." According to Rorty, people like Thomas Jefferson believed that religious believers should be "willing to trade privatization for a guarantee of religious liberty."[2] He referred to this as the "Jeffersonian compromise," a compromise between the Enlightenment and those who were religious. This perspective, however, fails to recognize just how strongly Jefferson and other founders believed in the value of religion and religious ideas.[3]

Nicholas Wolterstorff, a retired professor of philosophical theology from Yale, took Rorty to task for his response to Carter. Wolterstorff argued that he had the personal right to quote Psalm 72 in support of his own public endorsement of redistributionist social legislation if he wanted to, believing it reveals that God cares for the poor.[4] Jeffrey Stout also challenged Rorty about this essay.[5] There is nothing "essential" about religion that makes it a conversation-stopper in public debate. When religion does stop the conversation, wrote Stout, it has nothing to do with a Jeffersonian compromise aimed at keeping religion out of the public conversation. Rather, when religion enters the public debate, makes a faith claim, and then, when pressed for demonstration or elaboration, simply says, "Don't ask me for reasons," it tends to stop the conversation. Stout emphasizes as well, however, that many secular "hard-liners" in politics may also "claim to know that their answers are right" without being able to provide reasonable support for them.

Rorty responded to both Wolterstorff and Stout in a brief essay published in 2003. In an action he described as "back-pedaling," Rorty argued for at least two distinctions. First, he tried to distinguish between the public contributions of individuals who were members of congregations and those of "ecclesiastical organizations," those groups that "accredit pastors and claim to offer authoritative guidance to believers." The latter, he argued, don't belong in the public conversation because they do the most "damage." They fail to show respect for both the public conversation and for those who differ with them. Here he has in mind "the Catholic bishops, the Mormon General Authorities, the televangelists, and all the other religious professionals who devote themselves not to pastoral care but to promulgating orthodoxy and acquiring economic and political clout." Rorty's second distinction admitted that Wolterstorff had the right to base his commitment to particular social legislation on Psalm 72. Rorty said he would cite John Stuart Mill's *On Liberty* to support the same legislation. "Neither law nor custom," he explained, "should stop either of us from bringing our favorite texts with us into the public square." But Rorty explained that some religious appeals, especially those that quote biblical texts to restrict the rights of other citizens, create problems in the public sphere. Rorty argued all citizens should be able to provide reasons for public positions other than through simply appealing to any singular authority, whether "scriptural or otherwise." When one says, "The Bible says it, that settles it," there is no public conversation. In his response to Stout, Rorty agreed that the ability to stop conversations is not confined to the religious. The public conversation demands, Rorty concluded, "that citizens of a democracy should try to put off invoking conversation-stoppers as long as possible."[6]

Rorty is tending here to confuse two issues. His argument assumes, rather than demonstrates, that the essence of "ecclesiastical organizations," or what I am describing as public church, requires that they speak only in ways that stop the conversation. On this point, Rorty confuses the public church with what I have described as priestly faith. For Rorty, the public church, *essentially*, can only speak in priestly ways. Rather than using a philosophical argument to defend this claim, Rorty has defended his argument with the generalization that "it is mostly religion above the parish level that does the damage." Yet the damage to public conversation and to public life is done when churches, secular institutions, or individuals—whether religious or secular (including the president or other political leaders)—claim sole ownership to the truth and wish to promulgate or legislate that truth in ways that affect the rights of others at home or abroad or that violate the protections provided by the Constitution to all citizens in this country, whether they are religious or not. The problem is not one caused by religion entering the public conversation; rather, the damage is done when people or institutions, whether self-identified as religious or not, act absolutely because they claim to know the truth in absolute ways.

Reinhold Niebuhr's understanding of the relationship between irony and evil is helpful here. His profound emphasis on irony's role in human history resulted from his strong Christian theological sense of both the nature of human finitude and the power of human participation in sin. Human beings are situated in history. They cannot escape it. They are finite creatures who live and die. They possess only partial understanding, no matter how wise they may become during their relatively short lifetimes. Therefore, all human virtue is tainted by the inherent weaknesses contained within the human situation. The best-laid plans of human beings, then, often fall short of their desired goals. Often, if not usually, some unforeseen irony surfaces wherever human activities are involved. History is filled with irony.

> If virtue becomes vice through some hidden defect in the virtue; if strength becomes weakness because of the vanity to which strength may prompt the mighty person or nation; if security is transmuted into insecurity because too much reliance is placed upon it; if wisdom becomes folly because it does not know its own limits—in all such cases the situation is ironic.

Irony, according to Niebuhr, only turns dangerous when human beings refuse to recognize what it means. If its presence does not lead to a recognition that the virtue contains vice, or the reliance on security measures actually contain potential insecurities, then the situation turns dangerous. "Once one realizes the hidden vanity or pretension," Niebuhr concluded, "then it must lead either to an abatement of the pretension (by contrition), or else the vanities are accentuated to the point where irony turns into pure evil."[7] If one truly believes a particular virtue contains no hidden weakness, then pursuing that virtue without contrition and recognition of the weakness contained within it could lead to purely evil results. Priestly faith operates without any sense of irony. That is why it stops the conversation so easily.

The term "postmodern" is a difficult one to define precisely. Many things attach themselves to it. In order, however, to define it as a context within which discussions today exist, I want to emphasize postmodernism as a rejection of modernism. A postmodern context claims that the modernist project, the one shaped by the Enlightenment, was an attempt by thinkers to escape their finitude and to define "secure foundations for knowledge."[8] Modernism had great confidence in the power of reason to uncover ultimate and universal truth. Some modernist thinkers believed that certain moral beliefs are required by the structure of the human mind. Postmodern thinkers reject that possibility. Instead, they affirm that all thought is shaped by its historical context. Every community is shaped by its traditions and by the symbols it uses to illuminate meaning. Therefore, a postmodern context generally questions the existence of a universal common morality. Feminists, for example, have revealed that much of what we thought was universal was actually a male perspective. African Americans have revealed it as a white perspective. Can there be any perspective that furnishes universal agreement? The postmodernist says no. Perspectives are simply too much shaped by history and by the nature of the languages and communities that create and sustain them.

One of the reasons Richard Rorty wants to limit the public role of religion is due to his belief that religion is essentially involved with certainty, with creating grand theories that attempt to describe reality accurately. Religion believes it can transcend the limitations imposed by history, by language, by communities. In other words, religion is concerned with truth as if truth exists as an objective reality that can be understood and claimed within history. In the same way, Rorty condemns philosophy that seeks foundations or explanations for truth. Instead, in all his work Rorty stresses the influence of history. Neither philosophers nor religionists can "escape from the finitude of one's time and place,"[9] despite attempts to do so. For Rorty, people simply cannot ever claim to have discovered a direct one-to-one correspondence between truth and the reality one attempts to describe by reference to truth. Truth is always a human enterprise, created by, and contained within, the confines of human language. Does this mean that everything is relative? The relativist says that moral beliefs only apply to one's own community, and that all communities are equally justified in their own particular moral beliefs. Though Rorty's perspective can lead in relativist directions, he tries to avoid an absolute turn in that direction by emphasizing that a comparison of moral judgments leads to the recognition that some actually work better than others. In other words, as a pragmatist, Rorty determines value or quality by examining how well particular moral judgments work in comparison to other moral judgments.

Jeffrey Stout, in *Ethics after Babel*, more conclusively rejects relativism, but he has also emphasized that no community is likely to represent universal morality.

Stout makes a distinction between justification and truth. Justification is relative. Truth is not. One may be justified to believe something that is not true. In a particular historical context, say over one thousand years ago, persons may have been justified, given knowledge and human understanding in a particular location of the world, to believe slavery was acceptable. But the relative truth of that justification does not deny the ultimate truth that "slavery is evil" everywhere and in all time. Stout believes in the existence of universal moral truths, but human beings, given human finitude, just can't be absolutely sure what they are, and they are prone to error when they believe they have absolutely identified them.[10]

To believe in the existence of moral truth is one thing; to believe that one has perfectly described it is a different matter. When we humans describe a truth, we do so in the language and traditions of our own human communities. When we do that, we are not describing the truth; rather we are describing our beliefs about the truth. These two things are not the same. Once we take on the human task of describing whatever truth we think we may have discovered, we color that truth with human finitude. All of our knowledge, even knowledge about things that might be true, is affected by our human context, the inadequacy of human language, and, in Christian theological terms, our sin. The important thing to recognize, as Stout puts it, "is that doubts about explanations or criteria of moral truth are not necessarily doubts about moral truth."[11] Jeffrey Stout's perspective is not offered as a Christian perspective on postmodernism. His is a secular, rather than theological, piety.[12] But his philosophical ruminations about how to engender conversation between very diverse communities are very important for Christians who are concerned about maintaining the quality of public life. Christian responses to the claims of postmodernism have been quite diverse.

CHRISTIAN RESPONSES TO A POSTMODERN CONTEXT

There are those among Christians who simply deny the legitimacy afforded to views that take seriously the existence of a postmodern context. For some, postmodernism merely equates with relativism. Nothing good can come out of it. But this approach oversimplifies the complexities associated with postmodern perspectives. As evidenced in the previous brief description of Richard Rorty and Jeffrey Stout, there are differences between philosophers who represent postmodern perspectives. And when one compares their work to the work of scholars like Jacques Derrida and Michel Foucault, whose work represents even more fully the shift into philosophical relativism, even greater differences emerge. Not every postmodernist can be accurately portrayed as a "relativist" or an enemy of religion. Some Christians, however, conclude that all postmodern perspectives stand in opposition to Christian faith.

Among evangelicals, there have been at least two broad responses, or "loose coalitions." On the one hand, traditionalists stand firm for the truth that has been once-for-all delivered to the saints. There are varying degrees among traditionalists regarding how they might define the precise boundaries of faith, but there is, among them, a confidence that truth is contained within the Bible and the tradition, and that this truth is absolute and reliable. On the other hand, evangelical reformists prefer to leave boundaries open by emphasizing the center of evangelical beliefs rather than precisely defining the borders of acceptable belief. Reformists "recognize the fallibility of every human tradition and the need for ongoing reformulation of human perceptions of truth." Reformists are open to insights that a context defined as postmodern might offer to Christian theology. Roger Olson, who sets forth these categories, puts it this way:

> Traditionalists focus on postmodernism's sometimes subtle but definite denial of absolute truth. To them, theology's task is to expose this new philosophy in all its forms and manifestation as antithetical to belief in truth and certainty. . . . Reformists find postmodernity to be much broader than deconstructionism or even relativism. These, to them, are merely manifestations of postmodernity that evangelicals, of course, cannot endorse uncritically. But they see postmodernity in general as a new emphasis on holism in life and thought—a rejection of modernity's obsession with analysis and rationality as the summit of methods of discovery. They applaud postmodernism's recognition that something like faith is involved in all human thinking and see some benefits to postmodernism's discarding of the rationalistic mindset of the Enlightenment and modern secularism in favor of community-shaped perspective as a necessary ingredient in all knowledge.[13]

Since most evangelicals who are interested in responding positively to some of the elements found in a postmodern context are also, in some way, connecting to the work of Alasdair MacIntyre, there are some similarities in their approach to those among mainline Christians who refer to themselves as "postliberal."[14]

In the narrative that follows, I describe two different responses among mainline Christians to the postmodern context. Both groups take seriously what some have called the "historicist turn" in theology. Each understands that human beings are bounded by a historical context that is contingent, unpredictable, and dynamic. Sheila Greeve Davaney speaks of two shifts accompanying this historicist turn that have had particularly important religious implications. Pluralism has led theologians "to acknowledge the particularity of traditions and progressively to forego attempts to reduce various religious or cultural traditions to some common denominator." Few now claim a "common essence" or "universal experience" that all share. This shift has also led to the recognition that human judgment about the value or significance of religious traditions, or the comparison between them, is always historically situated. A second shift is the loss of belief in history as a progressive "salvation history." Christian theologians find it hard today to speak of history as "progress." History lacks a "clear direction." As Davaney has put it, "if the historical is our only context, it is a context which we do not control but for which we are, in good part, responsible."[15] Both these mainline theological responses take seriously the import of this historicist turn in theology. Both have an impact on how faith and public life interact and on the character of both the witness of the public Christian and the public church, two Christian styles of interaction that existed long before the development of a postmodern context.

The Postliberal Response

One of the effects of a postmodern context is to negate the claim that theology and moral philosophy rest in different realities, the former in faith and the latter in reason. An essential aspect of postmodernism is the belief that all claims, whether those made by religion or those made by philosophy, exist within specific communities of discourse. Each has their view of the human condition and of the world. Alasdair MacIntyre defends this understanding in his book *After Virtue*. He connects this view with the argument that the Enlightenment has failed to produce the good society. Instead, the principles associated with it and its liberal confidence in both reason and its ability to discover universal foundations for moral behavior have bred individualism and diminished the ability of modern individuals to practice the virtues that are necessary for the development of the good society. "There seems," he concludes, "to be no rational way of securing moral agreement in our culture."[16]

Since there is no agreement in modern society about common good, MacIntyre urges the "construction of local forms of community within which civility and the intellectual and moral life can be sustained."[17] The "postliberal" response among Christians insists that Christian communities should focus primarily on how Christians relate to one another and how Christian belief should function within the midst of a particular community. The most recognizable names here are those of George Lindbeck, Stanley Hauerwas, and William Willimon. Lindbeck's book, *The Nature of Doctrine*, presents the postmodern case for this position. The primary task of Christian theology is to think about the world from a Christian perspective. The Christian community should not attempt, however, to make universal claims for its thoughts. The postliberal theologian describes "the language and practice" of the Christian community and how that community sees the world rather than defending that view by appealing to universal standards of "human rationality or experience."[18] Such a rationality or experience simply does not exist. Finding some way to communicate in a universal language of morality is impossible, so Christians should not even try.

In making this argument, Lindbeck sets forth a "linguistic-cultural model of religion" and compares it with the "experiential-expressive" one. In his model of religion, "cultural and linguistic forms" are responsible for shaping religious beliefs. In other words, culture and language form inward religious experience rather than convey it. How one experiences religion is driven not by internal experiences of God but rather by one's "becoming skilled in the language, the symbol system of a given religion." When one learns the story of Jesus, one begins "to interpret and experience oneself and one's world in its terms." Where an experiential-expressive understanding of religion stresses a precognitive experience of faith, an experience of faith that causes one to think about it afterwards, the linguistic-cultural understanding emphasizes how external influences create the ability for faith to emerge at all. In the former model, the Holy Spirit acts on the soul, and human beings learn to express that activity in different and various ways through the languages and cultures of their human communities. In Lindbeck's model, the Holy Spirit enables human beings to hear the truth and internalize it through the languages and cultures in which they live. Thus, Lindbeck rejects the belief that "different religions are diverse expressions or objectifications of a common core experience . . . present in all human beings."[19]

Lindbeck develops this description of a postmodern context to undergird his own understanding of the importance of the Christian community. He defines the primary task of the church to be one of "absorbing the universe into the biblical world."[20] The postliberal or narrative theologies associated with George Lindbeck and Stanley Hauerwas are narrowly focused on the good of the Christian community. They do not exhibit much interest in what God is doing elsewhere or how the church might participate in transforming public life to be more representative of God's universal community. As Linell Cady has put it, "a Lindbeckian construal of tradition generates a clear mandate to the theologian to return to the originating grammar rather than to engage the tradition as a whole in its varied complexity."[21] It privileges the original Christian community, which itself was situated in a culture and language that shaped it. The development of Christian history since then is much less important.

> Lindbeck's confessional move has some serious flaws. It turns interpretive traditions into insulated entities, falsely imputing a kind of constancy to them. . . . Without some implicit assumption about the adequacy of the biblical worldview, however, it is difficult to see why this tradition of interpretation should be singled out from all the other operative traditions and used as the lens through which to interpret reality. . . . The dizzying acknowledgment of the multiple worlds produced through linguistic expression is a far cry from the fideistic appropriation of one of those worlds. . . . Lindbeck appropriates a postmodern framework to serve his primary role as a caretaker of Christianity, not to serve as a device to interpret and critique this tradition.[22]

When one looks at Christianity from Lindbeck's perspective, the task of Christian theology moves away from trying to correlate Christian faith with all those things that all human beings share in common. Instead, the task of theology is to set forth Christian ideas and understandings, formed through the language and culture of the Christian community. The attempt to defend or explain Christian theology by reference to universal criteria is doomed to failure from the start. There are no universal criteria. Christian theology should simply define the nature of itself, using the Christian community's self-understanding. Stanley Hauerwas has explored and defined the ethical position associated with these theological views.[23] In *Resident Aliens*, written with William Willimon, he argued that the task of the church is not to make the gospel credible to the modern world, but rather for the church to represent the gospel in the way it lives out its faith. "We argue," they wrote, "that the political task of Christians is to be the church rather than to transform the world."[24] Their focus is not on a public life including all, but rather on the life of a Christian community that finds meaning through its own symbols and narratives.

One of the interesting things to note here, then, is that Hauerwas and Rorty share the same belief that religious language does not belong in the public debate, attempting to influence the development of public policy. For Hauerwas, the church that lobbies in public life for any particular issue abandons its ability to practice Christian ethics. Christian ethics cannot be practiced except in the Christian community. "We serve the world," Hauerwas and Willimon write in *Resident Aliens*, "by showing it something that it is not, namely, a place where God is forming a family out of strangers." Individual Christians may find themselves supporting particular political efforts that might ease the troubles faced by American society, but the task of the church is to serve as the best example of what God can do with human community.[25] For Christians, "the world has ended." Instead, they should concentrate on ordering their "life in the colony" so that the world might look at it "and know that God is busy."[26] Hauerwas is among the most prolific Christian writers today. His exposition of an ethics of virtue has been extraordinarily influential among Christians.[27]

Hauerwas is not a fan of the liberal experiment known as American democracy; it is, he concluded recently, "in deep trouble."[28] In a review of Hauerwas's prodigious work, Jeffrey Stout concluded that Hauerwas is a Christian scholar whose work "inflames Christian resentment of secular political culture." In Stout's view, Hauerwas too loosely equates terms like liberal, secular, and democracy. They are "his names for what the world has become in an age of fragmentation after the demise of virtue and tradition." The result is a dualistic system that places liberalism and democracy on one side and Christianity and tradition on the other. This creates awareness of a great chasm between world and church. The world for Hauerwas, explains Stout, is "in a doubly darkened condition . . . not only outside the church, but also after virtue."[29] The only hope for the church is to concentrate on its own identity.

The church serves the world by being true to itself. Hauerwas, when he argues that Christians must remember "the call for the church to be the church," uses language about the church that is strikingly similar to the language used by Carl F. H. Henry.[30] When he criticizes liberalism, Hauerwas intends to warn Christians of what happens when they buy into the liberal agenda. You simply can't do it without losing your Christian voice.

> The increasing loss of social and political influence of Protestant Christianity has not meant Christian theologians and ethicists have abandoned the attempt to make America correspond to some assumed ideal. Faced, however, with America's increasingly diverse population, such an endeavor has been disciplined by the assumption that when Christians enter the public realm they cannot use Christian language. Rather, some mediating language is required and assumed to be justified in the name of common morality or by natural law reasoning.[31]

Though Hauerwas eschews using the term postmodern to describe himself, he certainly rejects the modernist project. And, at this point, in his discussion about Christian language and public life, he is right to describe liberalism's belief that religion is best kept out of the public discussion but wrong to conclude that American-style democracy requires it.

Liberally minded Christians have often made the same mistake. Through most of the 1970s and 1980s, editors at the progressive journals represented by the Catholic *Commonweal* and the ecumenical *Christian Century* mostly argued that Christians needed to make this kind of translation. They agreed with the general liberal Christian wisdom that it is best to keep Christian language and origins out of the public debate.[32] The basis for decisions in American public life must certainly be broader than merely the insights derived from Christian faith; such decisions are and should be informed by science, philosophy, political thought, and history. Christian language, however, should not be excluded from the public debate simply by virtue of its being Christian.[33] Nor should public life exclude the insights and language of Hinduism, Islam, Judaism, or any other religious community. Evidence began to appear in journals around 1990 that liberal Protestants were beginning to change their views on the use of religious rhetoric in public life. James Wall, for example, began arguing, in response to the Michael Milken scandal on Wall Street, that "without input from our religious traditions we have no common moral language to refute St. Milken's secular religion of greed."[34]

Hauerwas's resident alien lives in a democratic culture that possesses few redeeming features where Christians are concerned. For Hauerwas, "the fundamental presuppositions that shaped much of American life and government were meant to destroy or at least marginalize the church." Thus he has no interest in participating in the democratic life of the nation by urging the church to apply its faith to public life in public ways. For Hauerwas, any attempt on the part of the church to make America "work" leads to a collusion among Christians with the story America promotes, that God is "at home in America." When Christians become concerned with helping America become better, they become more interested in promoting a kind of Christianity that will serve America, rather than the Christian faith that serves the gospel.[35] The church cannot work to effect transformation in American life without becoming just another example of "Constantinianism."

In essence, Hauerwas believes that what I describe as priestly faith necessarily follows whenever and wherever Christianity, through the work of the church, attempts to play a role in public life in America. I do not agree. These are certainly temptations facing the public church, but they are not the inevitable results of Christian activity in public life. For Hauerwas, American-style democracy is the product of the secular liberal agenda. It will never be anything different from that, and Christians serve God best when they concentrate on their own identity. This is why Stout claims that Hauerwas has left behind biblical and theological concerns with justice. It is part and parcel of a larger move in Hauerwas that has transformed Barth's "ever-shifting boundary between church and world . . . into a rigid and static line between Christian virtue and liberal vice."[36]

While postliberals like Stanley Hauerwas believe it is impossible for Christians to participate in the public realm without sacrificing their Christian voice, Jeffrey Stout argues otherwise, for he views the development of democracy in America quite differently. Stout defines a philosophical posture that answers both sides of the deeply divided debate between antireligious liberalism and the "authoritarian version of a new religious traditionalism." In one corner of the ring stands Richard Rorty (or others like him); in the other corner stands Stanley Hauerwas (or others like him). "Each of them," writes Stout, "needs a 'force of darkness' to oppose" in order to portray their own cause as the "force of light." These two opposing forces, however, share more than they might recognize. They both defend the proposition that secular liberalism, with its antipathy toward religion, has won the day in creating a democracy that represents a thorough secularization of American culture. One celebrates this fact; the other laments it. In Stout's telling of the story, secular liberalism did not build this democratic house. The realities occasioned by pluralism did. Instead of understanding secularization as the result of a carefully orchestrated conspiracy to remove religion from all areas of life except the private, Stout urges readers to see its development as a pragmatic response to the realities of pluralism.

> My account of secularization concerns what can be taken for granted when exchanging reasons in public settings. . . . What makes a form of discourse secularized, according to my account, is not the tendency of the people participating in it to relinquish their religious beliefs or to refrain from employing them as reasons. The mark of secularization, as I use the term, is rather the fact that participants in a given discursive practice are not in a position to take for granted that their interlocutors are making the same religious assumptions they are. This is the sense in which public discourse in modern democracies tends to be secularized.

Stout emphasizes that this understanding means that there is no essential commitment in modern democracy to secularism. Individuals and groups "are free to frame their contributions to it in whatever vocabulary they please." They simply cannot reasonably "expect a single theological perspective to be shared by all of their interlocutors." Pluralism is an essential, and positive, feature of American democracy. It is not something that must be imposed on it from the outside, or something that demands pure secularization.[37] While Stout's belief that pluralism is a force tending toward secularized discourse might not give due consideration to the power of secular activists or the cultural elite in American history, it helps to bring into "focus the mediating ground occupied by liberal Christians sympathetic to new intellectual and moral currents."[38]

Stout's response to Hauerwas is at least two-fold. The world is not as bent toward secularization as you think it is, and the church does not possess a monopoly on the virtues. Both propositions can lead to an "excessive pride in the visible church as a virtuous community . . . and excessive certainty that one possesses the virtue of discernment, the capacity to tell the difference between the way of the world and the stirrings of the spirit."[39] Liberals are the wrong enemy, says Stout. The danger posed by the influence of a thinker like Hauerwas, he argues, is found in his reinforcement among Christians of what the Republican Party and Fox News are telling people: "that they are a beleaguered minority in an evil, liberal order." If you believe that, asks Stout, why would you want to "confront the fact of being a majority complicit in injustice"?[40]

Hauerwas has responded at length to Stout's criticisms in an appendix to a recent book. There he draws attention to the argument he made in *Resident Aliens* that "Christians have no other means of accurately understanding the world and rightly interpreting the world except by way of the church."

> Big words like "peace" and "justice," slogans the church adopts under the presumption that even if people do not know what "Jesus Christ is Lord" means, they will know what peace and justice mean, are words awaiting content. The church really does not know what these words mean apart from the life and death of Jesus of Nazareth. . . . It is Jesus' story that gives content to our faith, and teaches us to be suspicious of any political slogan that does not need God to make itself intelligible.

The vocabulary of the church makes sense only to those who inhabit it. People will only understand the meaning of words like sin and justice in light of the cross. Christian theology gives these words their substance. But Hauerwas stresses that he does not mean to say that "Christians cannot work with non-Christians to try to make our world less violent and more just."[41]

Critics often tag Hauerwas with the "sectarian" label. Hauerwas is right to refute it by stating, "If I have 'withdrawn' from 'public' debates surely I am not worth the time they spend in attacking me." Hauerwas has not genuinely withdrawn from public theology. Instead, he is one of today's most recognizable public theologians.[42] That is why his critics level the charge of sectarianism against him. They believe he is so influential that he will lead Christians, both as church and as individuals, to abandon the public conversation. The irony is that he may do so by acting as a public theologian, reflecting publicly, using theological categories and vocabulary, on most every issue of the day. Hauerwas claims regularly that he is not telling Christians not to be involved in government. "No! I just want them to be there as Christians."[43]

He is among the most public of voices presenting arguments on behalf of Christian pacifism. He is well known for his theological and ethical reflections advocating better care for the mentally disabled and the aged and infirm. He speaks regularly in public ways about marriage, human sexuality, and abortion. His theological ethics note the moral dilemmas associated with neonatal intensive care and suggest Christian solutions. His work regularly considers questions related to bioethics and defines medicine as a "tragic profession." Anyone who has seen him in action knows he does not shy away from public debate. Stories about his debating are legion, like the one in which he asked a medical researcher defending tests on fetal tissue, "What if it were discovered that fetal tissue was a delicacy? Could you eat it?"[44] In response to Stout, he wrote,

> I am not sure what to make of Stout's pleasant surprise that I participated in a panel about the impending war against Iraq in Washington. I have never thought my theological commitments required me not to be public. Given my arguments against the sequestering of theological claims, I have thought it my duty as an advocate of nonviolence to accept opportunities to speak when asked in any context. I would like to think this might give pause to those who accuse me of "withdrawing," but if the past is any indication I am sure that will not be the case.[45]

Hauerwas is a public figure. Though he would restrict the work of the church to "the formation of a people constituted by the virtues necessary to endure the struggle to hear and speak truthfully to one another," he knows "the One who is the Truth is the living God who often meets us in the face of the stranger."[46] This requires Christians to be open to the stranger, and even holds them accountable to the responsibilities that accompany citizenship in the space we share as Americans. In short, Hauerwas, in spite of his efforts to keep the church and the world radically separate, fits the mold of the public Christian, one who desires to speak about God in public ways that influence how citizens, not just Christians, think about things.

He's a religious despiser of American-style democracy and culture but, also ironically, an astute and effective participant within the context provided by it. You don't get named "America's Best Theologian" (2001) by *Time* magazine, a prime media representative of what American-style democracy and culture stand for, unless you are an all-star on the public playing field. Though I'm sure he would not agree with the overly simplistic generalization, I'd have to say that Hauerwas, the postliberal, is, in many ways when it comes to the topic of faith and public life, a late-twentieth- or early-twenty-first-century incarnation of Carl F. H. Henry. This is true in spite of the fact that Henry expressed serious disagreement with early expressions of the narrative theology and postliberalism that are so clearly found in Hauerwas's work.[47] It is also true in spite of the fact that Hauerwas sees himself moving more in a Catholic than evangelical direction.[48] But, like Hauerwas, Henry emphasized the church as the location where Christian identity is formed, with a mission to represent the gospel and to provide the example of what it means to be children of God by avoiding the taint of the world. Like Henry, Hauerwas is neither sectarian nor irrelevant; he is an intelligent, highly visible and public, consistently theological reminder that Christian liberal perspectives can never afford to rest too comfortably. The work of both these public Christians disdains the life of the public church. Though I respect and share their concern for Christian identity, I'd have to agree with Cornel West: "To be a prophetic Christian is not to be against the world in the name of church purity; it is to be in the world but not of the world's nihilism, in the name of a loving Christ who proclaims the this-worldly justice of a kingdom to come."[49]

The Revisionist and Broadly Historicist Response

The "revisionist" response to a postmodern context among mainline Christians insists that Christians and the church should relate Christian belief to experiences that all people share and be ready to defend those beliefs in public ways. The most recognized names in this category may be David Tracy, James Gustafson, and, in a broadly historicist way, Linell Cady, though one could name many others. These are among the major public theologians writing today who support the work of the public church. While Lindbeck sees theology as an internal Christian conversation, revisionist theologians understand theology as a public conversation that engages science and the broader culture. These revisionist theologians believe that Christianity, in order to be taken seriously by the world, must encounter pluralism through open communication and must attempt to engage public life in theological ways.

All these theologians are critical of the postliberals. In their view, postliberals have "ghettoized" Christianity by insulating it from the world. James Gustafson has labeled Lindbeck's approach as a "pernicious . . . sectarian temptation."[50] If the church followed that "perilous" approach, its theology has nothing to say to human life and experience. Postliberals, the revisionist argues, make both Christians and Christian faith irrelevant to public life. Liberation theologians have also criticized postliberalism for being "more concerned with Christian catechesis, formation and liturgy than with the struggle for social justice."[51] The postliberal invests nothing in the active creation of a larger common life and largely ignores the fact that Christians are shaped by a multiplicity of communities rather than a single community of faith.

David Tracy, a Catholic theologian teaching at the University of Chicago Divinity School, used the term "revisionist theologian" to describe the efforts of theologians who believe they can articulate in a postmodern context a sophisticated Christian theology that reasonable and intelligent non-Christians could affirm as reasonable and intelligent. Tracy has stressed that theologians of the church should be able to address the experiences that all human beings share under the same ground rules observed by non-Christian arguments.[52] He recognized as well that theology is distinctive from other disciplinary reflections in that in addition to the two publics served by all disciplines—the academy and the general culture—theology serves a third public, the church. Theology thus faces the dilemma of trying to be faithful to three publics at once—not an easy task, especially where these three publics seem to use such different criteria for determining what is meaningful and important. Tracy proposed that there are three related disciplines within theology: fundamental theologies that relate to the academy, systematic theologies that relate to the church, and practical theologies that relate to society.[53]

Part of the historicist turn is to recognize that human beings regularly face the limits of their historical existence. Religion, Tracy argues, ordinarily tries to "provide responses to questions at the limits of human inquiry and human experience." All human beings ask these kinds of questions.

What, if any, is the significance of such positive experiences as a fundamental trust empowering the fact that we continue to go on at all, as distinct from all our other trusts? What is the significance of such profound negative experiences as a fundamental anxiety in the face of no specific object (No-thing) as distinct from fear in the face of some specific object? What is our primordial response to finitude, to contingency, to death as our ownmost destiny, to radical oppression or alienation, to joy, love, wonder and those strange experiences of a consolation without a cause?[54]

Religions provide responses to these kinds of questions in those things Tracy defines as the religious "classics." Classics emerge through expressions like images, events, doctrines, texts, persons, rituals, symbols, or myths. They might be embodied in a musical expression or a beautiful exhibition of art.[55] To be designated a classic, such things must contain meanings that transcend the limitations of their origins. In some way they point beyond themselves to something else, to illuminate some sense of the whole. Religious classics, in distinction to classics that reveal some particular feature of reality, disclose something of the "whole" of reality. Tracy talks about the way "the event of Jesus Christ," a Christian classic, does precisely this:

> Yet we learn that we may honestly, *in spite* of all, now yield to that other clue, that other faith, disclosed in the fundamental trust we live in the everyday by going on at all, that trust disclosed decisively in the revelation of the graciousness of God and the graced reality of self and world in the event of Jesus Christ. As thus released, we are not freed to some new knowledge, some new gnosis which we now possess for ourselves alone. Rather we are finally freed to embrace a fundamental trust in the whole, to demand of ourselves, by that trust, a hope for the sake of the hopeless, to risk a life in the impossible gospel possibility of a faith and hope working through a love given as pure gift and stark command.[56]

Christian theology "serves an authentically public function," claims Tracy, "when it renders explicit the public character of the meaning and truth embedded in the Christian classical texts, events, images, rituals, symbols and persons."[57]

Tracy's theology emphasizes the importance of hermeneutics, of interpretation. To be human is to interpret. There is no experience without interpretation of experience. Human beings, therefore, should not be passive recipients of the classics. They must interpret the meaning of the classics. Everyone approaches interpretation with some "preunderstanding of the questions addressed by a classic text." They must be willing, says Tracy, "to put that preunderstanding at risk by allowing the classic to question the interpreter's present expectations and standards." For most human beings,

> Reality is what we name our best interpretation. Truth is the reality we know through our best interpretations. Reality is constituted, not created or simply found, through the interpretations that have earned the right to be called relatively adequate or true. In science, language inevitably influences our understanding of both data and facts, truth and reality. Reality is neither out

there nor in here. Reality is constituted by the interaction between a text, whether book or world, and a questioning interpreter.[58]

Though Tracy understands that truth exists behind the classics and that there is an encounter with truth through the classics, he also recognizes the importance of correlating the experience of the classic with the present contemporary situation. This is the task of conversation, a conversation that involves human beings, their interpretations, and the preconceived notions they bring to every experience. The conversation also involves the classics themselves, and they contain a plurality of meanings. In seeking truth in answer to questions that test the limits of human knowledge, we can never be sure we have absolutely found it. Rather than finding standards that can be applied in all times and places, one is transformed by the experience and finds answers that speak critically to the moment.

This conversation in the search for truth involves conversing not only with the classics but with others who interpret the classics wherever they may be found and in whatever religious traditions they are claimed. "Persons willing to converse," writes Tracy, "are always at one major disadvantage from those who are not. The former always consider the possibility that they may be wrong." A conversation "is not a confrontation. It is not a debate. It is not an exam. It is questioning itself. It is a willingness to follow the question wherever it may go."

> Conversation is a game with some hard rules: say only what you mean; say it as accurately as you can; listen to and respect what the other says, however different or other; be willing to correct or defend your opinions if challenged by the conversation partner; be willing to argue if necessary, to confront if demanded, to endure necessary conflict, to change your mind if the evidence suggests it.[59]

Given the context of pluralism in America and across the world, and even the pluralism present within contemporary Christian theology, Tracy has developed what he calls the "correlational model of theology." This correlational approach lifts up the power to create hope, work toward justice, and affirm plurality and ambiguity in the midst of the public life that defines a community. His combination of conversation and correlation is, in essence, a response to the reality of pluralism. When attempting to interpret the classics and the way they illuminate human experience and respond to human questions, one has to recognize the importance of "a pluralism of interpretations and ever new reinterpretations for an ever changing personal, social, and historical situation." Since not every interpretation is equally acceptable, it is also important that every theologian

> must try to set forth a model of theology and a set of criteria which can help the wider community spot the better and worse interpretations of the same reality of mystery. . . . There is no doubt, therefore, that theology should function in the public realm even to fulfill *its own* task of interpretation *as correlation*. For what is that task? It is nothing less than the risk of an interpretation of the Christian tradition for this, our situation. We cannot but interpret as the same selves we are—now open to the challenge of Chris-

tianity and thereby open as well to the challenge of all other insights into who those listening, questing, questioning, interpreting selves might be. . . . It is not by chance that both theology and public life find themselves needing one another. For both are peculiar. Both emerge fundamentally from the need to respond to human suffering. Both attempt to transform that suffering through models of the good life as grounded in justice or love—indeed, both. . . . Publicness is not a luxury for theology; it is intrinsic to the whole task.[60]

This is why Tracy's work has come to emphasize the importance of pluralism. His work over the past fifteen years has turned toward the importance of interreligious conversations.[61] His recognition that contemporary life is defined more by "polycentrism" than by the old Western center has led him to a greater engagement with theologies that have emerged from other locations present in this polycentrism, including black and womanist theologies and feminist interpretations of theology. Neither the old foundationalism (where truths are objectively known and clearly defined) nor a new relativism will suffice.

> The theological alternative is clear: a fidelity to the ever-greater God in a new cultural and religious situation where the realities of otherness and difference are critically and religiously appropriated by all Christian theologies that dare to move beyond any form of intellectual foundationalism and its institutional counterparts, cultural imperialism and ecclesial triumphalism, and beyond any exhausted model of liberal modernity that can promise only relativism.[62]

Some revisionist and historicist theologians believe Tracy's approach is too connected to philosophical foundations or experiences presumed to be universal. These theologians generally do, however, recognize how Tracy's work has developed. In a sense, all revisionist theology possesses roots connected to the liberalism of the nineteenth and early twentieth centuries. It has, however, clearly moved beyond those identifications. Even Tracy's early work showed a clear historicist perspective and an awareness of the developing postmodern context for religion. In more recent work, Tracy has emphasized the limitations, the narrow angles of vision, represented by Western theology. He has also recognized how power and authority often create classics, classics that can lose their status once these origins are discovered and exposed. All classics are ambiguous.[63] Christian classics, for example, contain "sexism, racism, classism, and anti-Semitism" and their effects. This is why "the readings of the oppressed—however different and even uncivil by some tired standards of what can count as civil discourse—must be heard, and preferably heard first."[64] The power of traditions in forming both classics and us must be recognized and critically assessed. Yet the fact that Tracy's work still emphasizes the classics that have survived, often through the aid of privilege or power, when other texts, rituals, symbols, or myths could not, raises suspicion for some about whether these classics "carry a freight—indeed perhaps an ontological freight—that separates them from the other events and processes of this particular history."[65]

Another theologian often categorized as a revisionist is James Gustafson, retired from Emory University in 1999. Though he and David Tracy are friends and were once colleagues at the University of Chicago, Gustafson dissents from Tracy's belief that the theological enterprise must include something different from systematic theology—a "fundamental" theology—that presents the academic theory for how Christians can or should relate to public life. For Tracy, "fundamental theologies" are necessary in order "to provide arguments that all reasonable persons, whether 'religiously involved' or not, can recognize as reasonable." In response, Gustafson writes,

> It is interesting to note that the bishops did not need to forge a hermeneutical theory, or a theory about a "public theology," or a moral theory on which all rational persons could agree . . . in order to write a document that has been taken very seriously by some important persons in public life. Nor is it clear that if the bishops had had such theories their efforts would have achieved either lesser or greater public impact.[66]

Yet Gustafson has spent considerable time thinking about theological questions that relate to how Christians should approach public life. He stresses an "interactional view" of human agency that is thoroughly historicist in its orientation. His theology stresses the fact that human beings, as finite beings, possess limited capacities and are influenced by things that have preceded them and by the culture that surrounds them. They must interact with an environment that is not always benevolent, whether hurricanes like Katrina or tsunamis in Southeast Asia. To be human is to recognize limits. No matter what their accomplishments, no matter how they might extend their ability to master particular forces, no matter what "our biological capacities and our cultural developments make possible," human beings will never overcome finitude. "Though we may not agree on how best to describe human uniqueness," writes Gustafson, "I take it to be unassailable that man is not God."[67] A strong sense of human situatedness in history, human finitude, is a strong antidote to falling prey to the temptation of priestly faith.

When human beings live authentically with the reality of their limits, they begin to experience genuine religious affections. Among these affections, Gustafson describes the "sense of dependence" as one of the most "primal." This sense develops when human beings truly recognize their finitude, the extent to which their very existence testifies to the need for others. We are dependent on parents, on oxygen and rain, on plant life, on the social arrangements all around us. Among those who recognize their finite dependence on all that supports the mystery of life, there also develops a sense of wonder or awe. This kind of understanding develops other religious affections or pieties, like a sense of gratitude and of obligation. These lead to a sense of guilt and a sense of repentance.

> Religions build upon human senses of direction, and incorporate them into their ritual, cultic, and moral activities. Both Augustine and Thomas Aquinas assumed that to be human was to have a natural orientation toward

an end; most human activities were explainable to these great fathers of the church in terms of the ends that persons sought, the desires that they had. They shared with many other Christians through the centuries the notion that this natural directedness was toward the supernatural end of communion with God, the vision of God. . . . [T]he eschaton, the coming of the reign of God, has been for many Christians not merely the mark of the *finis*, the temporal end of history, but also for the *telos*, the final goal of life. . . . [T]hey have been exhorted to organize human societies so that that Kingdom is actualized as much as possible in particular historical conditions.[68]

One of the key features for Gustafson's theology is the "displacement of the salvation of persons as the principal point of reference for religious piety and for the ordering of theological principles." In its place, he gives priority to the "moral imperative" that Christians "are to conduct life so as to relate to all things in a manner appropriate to their relations to God." This means, writes Gustafson, that

the warm and friendly deity of a great deal of contemporary piety is displaced; the assurance that regardless of how difficult and tragic human life is, God will make it right, at least for persons who trust in him, is brought under serious questions. . . . Human purposes and human conduct have to be evaluated not simply on the basis of considerations derived from reflection about what is good for man. . . . It may be that the task of ethics is to discern the will of God—a will larger and more comprehensive than an intention for the salvation and well-being of our species, and certainly of individual members of our species.[69]

Gustafson is not saying that God stands opposed to the activities and welfare of human beings. But he is saying that not every activity of God can be understood by how it serves the good of human beings. To do that is to make God anthropocentric, completely centered on the good of human beings. God's purposes are no doubt larger than that. For Gustafson, God stands with human beings "in the sense that the possibilities of any human flourishing are dependent upon what we have received and on forces that are not ultimately under our control." But human beings are not "the measure of all things."[70] God, not us, is the "center of gravity."

In Augustine's terms, to love God as the supreme good is to reorder our other affections so that we can love others and all things in relation to God. To love other things as the supreme good is to have the wrong center of gravity; it is to be basically disoriented in the proper valuations of other things. . . . It is my position that God in relation to man and the world is an appropriate center of gravity; orientation to God will govern and order the heart in a way nearer to what human life is meant to be.[71]

Therefore, for Gustafson, the church's public theology must be explicitly theological. God is the primary reference point for Christians. God is the center and all things relate to God. God is God; we are not God. The church must relate its activities to an interpretation of God's purposes for the world. Since we can never be sure exactly what God's purposes are (emphasis is on interpretation), we can never be absolutely sure about our own moral conclusions. The church must also give proper attention to the meaning and significance of human experience and human communities and to the circumstances in which individuals and communities act. This means the church must especially stress human finitude and the historicity of all human life as it addresses public questions. The church must always readily acknowledge the possibility of error. This stance is especially appropriate in a postmodern context, for, as Gustafson put it, theological ethics "itself develops, and . . . as changes in the world . . . occur, traditional principles need to be extended in their applications, may need to be revised, and in some instances may need to be radically altered."[72]

Gustafson believes the church's task is to convey publicly the best that Christian tradition has to offer. Theology joins the conversation without apology, using its own tradition of reflection and its own language. Yet it must be accountable to the conversation. This means theological ethics involves the use of the best that human reflection has to offer, whether the insights come from philosophy, science, the Bible, Christian tradition, other religious traditions, or human experience, broadly conceived.[73] The church must make clear why these sources offer something important when they do, and defend why what they use has significance. The church must describe why some sources are relevant and others are not. When sources conflict, the church must be clear about why certain sources are decisive while others are not. And the church must describe how the content is to be interpreted. Finally, in light of these things, the church must be willing to reflect critically about its own tradition.

The church, as part of its public theology, must offer an interpretation of people and communities that takes seriously their activities as moral agents. This means that the church must interpret how persons and communities ought to make moral choices and how they ought to judge their own acts, those of others, and the affairs of the public life the world shares.[74] In his second volume on theocentric ethics, Gustafson turns to specific moral issues. He discusses marriage and family, suicide, population and nutrition and offers moral criteria related to biomedical research. Throughout the book, he relates Christian moral understanding to a particular concern for the common good. "A theocentric piety," writes Gustafson, "motivates and issues in a readiness to restrain particular interests for the sake of other persons, for communities, and the larger world." He quotes Paul, writing to the church at Philippi, "Let each of you look not only to his own interests, but also to the interests of others."[75] Gustafson's approach to applying theology to public life affirms the possibility for the church to act in spite of its finitude. It represents a historicist revision of the old liberal notion of the public church that takes seriously the postmodern context. He paraphrases Romans 12:1–2 to define what is at the heart of his notion of theocentric ethics:

> Individually and collectively offer yourselves, your minds and hearts, your capacities and powers in piety, in devoted and faithful service to God. Do not be conformed to the immediate and apparent possibilities or require-

ments of either your desires or the circumstances in which you live and act. But be enlarged in your vision and affections, so that you might better discern what the divine governance enables and requires you to be and to do, what are your appropriate relations to God, indeed, what are the appropriate relations of all things to God. Then you might discern the will of God.[76]

The last person in this lineup of public theologians who illustrates revisionist and historicist thinking about these kinds of issues is Linell E. Cady. A professor in religious studies at Arizona State University, Cady has devoted considerable attention to questions relating to "religion, theology, and American public life." She criticizes the liberal assumptions that characterized Enlightenment confidence in the human ability to use reason to define objective truth. In Cady's view, for example, Tracy's confidence that fundamental theology can deal with religious questions in ways that all reasoning persons can understand depends too readily on the assumption that reason is itself "a universal, ahistorical capacity that all persons share in common." She emphasizes that reason "is inextricably rooted in a specific historical and cultural matrix." Human thought always "reflects the assumptions, values, and interests of a particular place and time." In other words, Cady stresses the historicist perspective even more emphatically than Tracy.

Where modern thought since the Enlightenment has understood reason as a "universal capacity" present within all human beings that is able to transcend historical influences in order to make judgments by using empirical data, a postmodern context has stressed the particular social and cultural location of every knower. This means that human judgment about common good, or about right and wrong, does not emerge from a universal sense that is contained within each person but rather from, as Cady explains, a context "that is influenced by the assumptions, needs, and interests of the interpreter." Making judgments is not, therefore, a process of trying to find an objective position, because all positions are a matter of perspective. The implications are clear. When philosophical liberals, nonreligionists like Richard Rorty, claim that religion is private and the public must be secular, the assumption is that religion is parochial and therefore must be private while secular thought is objective and can therefore be public. A postmodern context challenges the elitism associated with secular discourse. All thought is contextual and contains culturally influenced assumptions, expressed in the language of some form of tradition. The thought of secular liberals is no exception.

Cady argues, however, that Christian thinkers must recognize all the implications associated with the postmodern context in the same way that philosophical liberals must. This means that Christian thinkers cannot become public with their reflections in any way that claims privilege for their sources.[77] If theologians enter the public arena arguing that the public must listen to them because their sources of understanding are better, more authoritative, or more privileged than others, they are not truly recognizing the way religious understanding is also affected by cultural settings and the language associated with a particular tradition. In short, if public Christian and public church enter public life to dictate to it, their position is no more defensible than that of secular philosophical liberals who want to keep their voices private. In fact, they contribute to the rationale for why their voices should not be heard. They also cease to be public Christians or public church and have become representatives of priestly faith. A postmodern context levels the playing field for all participants in the public debate. It means that Christians and secular philosophical liberals all have an equal voice. Neither can claim that their voice is privileged because of its sources. Every participant in discussions about public life must be open to the arguments of others in public life. Nobody possesses a privilege or perspective that shuts all other arguments down. For those who affirm the reality of sin's influence on human life, like Christians for example, this principle underlying appropriate public debate ought to be easy to grasp and support.

Using models developed by Ronald Dworkin as a typology for judicial reasoning and applying it to theology, Cady defines what she regards as both inappropriate and appropriate forms of public argumentation for theologians and the church. *Conventional* arguments try to determine how Christian authorities have argued positions in the past, based on either the Bible or tradition, and argue from these precedents. The past arguments are "privileged and unassailable." This posture is not open to "the forms of open inquiry and persuasion that constitute public reflections" and usually ends up relating faith and public life in some form of priestly faith. An *instrumentalist* approach more readily dismisses the past and attempts to reach decisions based purely on what kinds of actions or activities should be affirmed in order to create the best possible future. Cady believes Dworkin's third alternative, *extensionalism*, best fits theological argumentation because it "helps break down the misperception that the theologian's choice is between a heteronomous appeal to past authorities or a forward-looking indifference to tradition." Extensionalism is a form of argumentation that takes tradition seriously, but instead of interpreting a tradition narrowly, it attempts to interpret the tradition "as a whole." Extensionalism also values "the current insights and values of the theologian."[78]

As an example of this approach, Cady offers an analysis of theological reflection about the ordination of women. An extensionalist argument would need to counter the conventionalist argument by providing a "broader context" for the historical fact of male discipleship as presented in the Bible.

> To this end, such an argument might contend that: (1) the patriarchal character of first century Palestine made male discipleship the norm; (2) historical research discloses women were active disciples of Jesus but were written out of New Testament historical accounts; (3) Jesus' overall attitudes and actions toward women counteract the cultural disvaluation of women, thereby functioning as judgment upon continued sexist oppression; (4) the biblical message as a whole asserts the equality of all people under God and hence takes precedent over distortions which inevitably crept in to limit

such equality. My point is not to suggest that any of these strategies is deter-
minative, but to identify the sort of wider considerations that are demanded
by the extensionalist appeal to the past.

Since all use of reason is culturally and historically conditioned, Cady highlights
the fact that interpreters will use "current beliefs and values" when they interpret
past materials. This is "unavoidable given the nature of interpretation, conventionalist denials notwithstanding." The dialectic between interpreter and materials interpreted is always present.[79] In the process of interpretation, the
extensionalist will always attempt to consider the whole rather than give essential value to some particular part of the tradition. Extensionalism makes it possible for theology to join the public conversation.

Cady's approach to theological interpretation also affirms a public life that
cannot properly be defined as either a collection of self-interested individuals or
a homogeneous community. Instead the public realm should be regarded "as an
all-encompassing common life that embraces substantial diversity—in regard to
values, beliefs, and behaviors—amongst all its members. Such diversity, however, does not go all the way down."[80] There are areas where common agreement
exist. These areas are reached through conversation. The pursuit of what a society regards as truth cannot be merely an individual task; it must be a "social
process." "Although what now enjoys a social consensus is dignified by the des-
ignation 'knowledge,' or 'truth,' we recognize a difference between what is
shared according to current lights and that which is valid 'in the long run.'" The
discovery of truth is a continual process, and one that should "be committed to
the cultivation and extension of a common life that is, at least hypothetically,
radically inclusive in its scope."[81] Cady's emphasis is on the need to expand our
notions of public life to include more global associations, those that can "rela-
tivize our strident nationalisms and temper our anthropomorphic proclivities."
But conversations within the public life must always respect "local sources of
meaning and identity" for these are crucial to our formation and understanding
as persons.[82]

Here is where Cady places the contribution theology offers to public life. The
Christian vision of God emphasizes God as "creator, sustainer, and redeemer."
Christians believe in the value of a proleptic vision, living within the recognition
of "the disparity between the present order of creation and a redeemed common
life, the eschatological community of being." Christian devotion to God, she
argues, "is not compatible either with a retreat from the public realm or, as
importantly, with indifference as to its configuration." Instead, Christians will
seek to affirm and work toward those ends that coincide with "the redemptive
activity of God within the historical arena." There are always dangers in identifying specific activities with God's redemptive work. These must be recognized.
"God's redemptive activity should not be narrowly linked with any single cause
despite the rhetorical and political efficacy it may yield."[83] Yet Christians must
try to address those forces of our common life that distort justice or prevent some

from full participation in the community. This involves more than merely tending to the life of the Christian community, in good Hauerwasian fashion, as if that community can stand apart as an example "over against the wide society." A public theology, argues Cady,

> will need to look closely at the current social order, seeking to discern the attitudes, assumptions, and practices that undermine the mutuality and integrity of our common life and prevent the transformation into the universal community of being. For God's redemptive role will be linked with the actions directed toward removing the obstacles to genuine community.[84]

A postmodern context helps Christians to understand that all human communities represent and promote only partial truths. This recognition actually fits well with a theological tradition that understands sin and its effect upon the human condition. Therefore, when Cady writes about public religion, she means the way "a specific religious tradition uses its resources to build up the common life." Christian public theology uses Christian resources and Christian understandings and "seeks to contribute to the upbuilding and critical transformation of public life." However, it can't do so by claiming its sources are privileged and uniquely authoritative. Instead, it must use a form of argument that is public. Theology is "situated in a tradition, a context."

> Public theology, eschewing the impossible ideal of universal intelligibility, will situate itself within a recognizable tradition and communicate primarily, although not exclusively, to inhabitants of that tradition. For a public theology, however, this inevitable situatedness does not legitimate confessional or authoritarian modes of reflection. . . . If theology is to expand its audience and influence, it will need to attend to the variety of its features that undermine a public character.[85]

Today's postmodern context recognizes that all communities, religious or not, are "situated in a tradition." Therefore, the old "Enlightenment framework that has interpreted reason and public in terms of what is common, objective, and unaffected by historical and social location" no longer works today.[86] However, Cady does not want to throw out the proverbial baby with the bathwater. Today's cultural context must retain "the Enlightenment distinction between engaging in open inquiry and citing heteronomous authorities."[87] The temptation for some Christians is to retreat into confessional corners where they can be comfortable with the sole authority of their own traditions. Christians who truly want to engage the public life of the nation must be willing to risk their comfort for discussion and dialogue; they must be willing to make their arguments in a context where counterarguments are made and all who participate are held accountable to the critical analysis of ideas. Public theologians will recognize there is no such thing as objectivity, but they will also respect, through their conduct and presentation, the "difference between critical inquiry and dogmatic citation."[88] Those with an historicist perspective, those who seek to bring theology into the public sphere, know both that they have something of value to contribute and that they do not have all the answers.[89]

CONCLUSION

Until very recently, both philosophical liberals and mainline Christians agreed that Christian theological expressions did not belong in public life. The philosophical liberal argued that religion is a private affair. The public church, usually associated with mainline Christian churches (both Protestant and Catholic) believed the church should be involved in shaping public life but should do so by using the language everyone shared. Most liberal mainline journals bought hook, line, and sinker the view that theological language was inappropriate for public life.[90] The public Christian has held that the church should stay out of public life because translating Christian conviction into language appropriate to the public would only secularize the church.

Today, Christians recognize that "common secular thought patterns of the whole community" do not exist and never really did. The secular rationality that Christians of yesteryear thought was objective and neutral was as much "a time-bound, metaphysically unstable, uncritical faith" as any other expression of truth.[91] For nearly two centuries, what passed for secular neutrality looked a good bit like what a white, male Protestant might say. As Robin Lovin put it in 1989, "the practical effect of the belief in public reason was a demand that everyone in politics talk like a Presbyterian lawyer."[92] When the separation of church and state is used to prohibit public theological participation in public life, we make it impossible to explore policy in light of moral ideals. All moral ideals are connected to a particular community of discourse. Those associated with religious communities belong in conversations about public life along with all others. The only alternative is to decide all policy matters "in terms of economic and technical criteria."[93] A postmodern context recognizes that all knowledge, whether secular or religious, is affected by history and culture. Every voice emerges from a community that shapes and forms it. No criteria exist that justify placing secular viewpoints above religious viewpoints as if the former were objective and the latter merely subjective. This means that the Christian community has the same right to participate in public life enjoyed by any supposedly secular community. There should be no question today, in our setting, about whether or not hospitality should be extended to religious voices in public life.

Today's public Christians, represented by people like Stanley Hauerwas, are concerned that even the slightest connection of the church with public debates or any attempts to transform public life toward some greater approximation of what it understands through faith to be the eschatological community is to place Christian life at the service of democracy. For Hauerwas, the church's first task is to be the beloved community, not to serve American-style democracy. Individual

Christians participate; they vote, perhaps work in political parties or with social-service agencies; but the church must be the church. Other theologians and ethicists, as represented in the work of David Tracy, James Gustafson, and Linell Cady, argue that it is in fact part of the essence of Christianity to work toward the transformation of the public life of the nation and of the global community, to move them both in the direction of God's "universal community of being," as Cady put it, where all are valued and where progress is made toward the kind of justice God intends for all creation, whether human or animal or environmental or ecological.

It is true that Christian communities involved in public discussions will have to make compromises. Reinhold Niebuhr described the way all people of faith are involved in the tragic dimensions of human experience. The tragic arises when human beings must make "conscious choices of evil for the sake of good."[94] Human beings simply cannot make decisions that always and absolutely serve only the good. This is especially true where public policy is concerned. Decisions, for example, made one way about social security or medicare will help some and harm others. The harm caused to some is an evil that results from the choice to improve the situation as it stands today in ways that bring a measurable improvement in the lives of a larger number of people, or in the relative justice provided by the social security or medicare programs. Conscious choices must be made. So while these choices might elicit admiration, they also involve guilt. Christians should be contrite about their involvement in tragic situations. But they cannot avoid them if they engage in matters important to public life. This is why a significant number of Christians want to keep the church out of these affairs. Yet the choice not to become involved, not to play a role, is also a choice. It is a choice with consequences, often tragic consequences. People who could be helped by involvement are also harmed by noninvolvement. This active choice to remain passive must also involve contrition on the part of the Christian community. Sheila Greeve Davaney, writing from her own position of pragmatic historicism, speaks an insightful word that is relevant to all Christians who recognize the realities present within a postmodern context:

> It calls us to choose without perfect choices, to justify them when finality is impossible, in terms of consequences that are never fully clear. . . . it acknowledges that our power to choose comes from resources that we have been given by all that proceeds us . . . it continually affirms the margin of creativity that we do have . . . it wagers on, not a promise of victory in or beyond history, but history's openness and generosity. . . . [I]t realizes that it too will be superseded some day. . . . [I]t holds that we are in part creators of the future and it calls us to create that future with care.[95]

If Christian faith, considered and reviewed within the context of accumulated human wisdom and knowledge, gives us insight into matters affecting our shared public life, it is good to claim that it does, and then to help others arrive at the insight any way they might be able to do so. Entering the public discourse, whether as public Christian or public church, entails a willingness to be persuaded by arguments of others, just as we hope they are persuaded by our arguments. Ideally, if we have erroneously confused for Christian insight what in fact is due to cultural conditioning of our tradition, we should be willing to be convinced by the public conversation that this is the case—whether the arguments attempting to convince us come from other Christians, or from others who share this space. We must be open to hearing about better ways of viewing the issue, to recognizing them, and to affirming them. Public "God-talk" does not have to be used as a bludgeon over peoples' heads, as priestly faith uses it, or merely as symbols filled with content redefined by American culture, as iconic faith uses it. It can, however, raise important questions and contribute to discussions about both the "plurality and ambiguity" of our common life together, to use David Tracy's phrase, that are relevant and important for everyone.

Jeffrey Stout is confident about the prospects of modern democracy. He believes in a democratic tradition best represented in the work of people like Ralph Waldo Emerson, Walt Whitman, and John Dewey. It is a style of democracy that encourages the development of the virtues and places emphasis on conversation, open debate, and mutual accountability. It is not inherently secular. Instead, Stout argues that the kind of environment provided by modern democracy is only benignly secular, in that all who participate in it must take for granted that not everyone shares the same religious assumptions. This means, writes Stout, that "one can participate in it wholeheartedly without implicitly discounting one's theological convictions."[96] In public conversation, the kind of "discursive exchange essential to democracy is likely to thrive only where individuals identify to some significant extent with a community of reason-givers."[97] Though Stout may be a bit too idealistic in his understanding of both human nature and democracy and in his belief in their natural inclinations to seek virtue, and though he may be a tad too dismissive of the role the cultural elite has played in developing a secular democratic culture, he presents a convincing and, I believe, accurate argument that American-style democracy is not, and has never been, inherently antireligious in nature.

> Democracy . . . takes for granted that reasonable people will differ in their conceptions of piety, in their grounds for hope, in their ultimate concerns, and in their speculations about salvation. Yet it holds that people who differ on such matters can still exchange reasons with one another intelligibly, cooperate in crafting political arrangements that promote justice and decency in their relations with one another, and do both of these things without compromising their integrity. . . . Among the most important democratic movements in American history were Abolitionism and the Civil Rights movement; both of these were based largely in the religious communities. . . . If religious premises had not been adduced in support of them, it is unlikely that either movement would have resulted in success.[98]

American history indicates that religion has always had something to do with the democratic creation of public life. Religious values and public policy are, and can remain, related to one another. Whether as public Christian or public church, the voice of Christian faith has often found its way into public life. There is nothing in the establishment clause that forbids it, and the free exercise clause clearly supports it. The question left to consider for the immediate future, I suppose, is what public Christians and the public church will do with it. Will they become more reflective about that voice? Will they link it more intentionally to their understandings (these being both self-critical and always in process) of who God is, of who human beings are, and of what serves creation? Will they use their voice to contend for a greater degree of relative justice for all God's children who are trying to discover how to live together and how to listen to and learn from each other, in what seems to be ever closer proximity to one another—or will they use it to echo either the vacuous claims common to iconic faith or the absolute dogmatism and exclusivity associated with priestly faith? Hope springs eternal, but, as is true about everything in history, only time will tell.

Appendix

Styles of Interaction between Christian Faith and Public Life in America

	Iconic Faith	Priestly Faith
General Description	(1) Where cultural icons are located in sacred spaces of Christian contexts (2) Where Jewish or Christian images or icons are used in public contexts to serve some public interest (3) Where these icons are venerated as having special or sacred significance	Where Christians transform iconic expressions into either a systematic collection of values or a definition of cultural ethos, promote either one as if it represents the true meaning of both Christianity and America, and seek to persuade the government to protect its interests by legislative or political means; where leaders absolutize the relative, or where government leaders transform national interests or initiatives into divine missions in the world or wrap them in God-language

	Iconic Faith	*Priestly Faith*
Approach to public truth, intellect, education	Uncritical; wants authority to provide answers; generally closed to new truth; prefers status quo and is resistant to change	Assumes authority and provides answers; generally closed to new truth; prefers status quo and is resistant to change
Spirituality	Practiced most meaningfully within homogeneous groups; self-fulfillment through identification with community identified by symbolic boundaries	Legalistic; seeks conformity with the correct form of spirituality; self-fulfillment through successful evangelization of Christian American tradition
Acceptance of pluralism	Within symbolic boundaries; those outside the boundaries must adapt to the meanings of the symbols before being accepted	Within traditional norms; if pluralism begins to threaten existing social norms, it must be contained
Notion of sin	Transgression against the iconic symbol structures of public life; i.e., burning the flag	Behavior inappropriate to the norms defining a Christian America or the America understood to be on a divine mission
Role of church	Reflects, promotes, and acts as repository for the symbolic boundaries of culture; generally not activist except in terms of celebration; can contribute to the power of culture's symbolic boundaries by participation/promotion	Activist; protector of cultural values by identifying heretics; the institution that best represents the *only and true* tradition of America's public life; works toward legislation to protect and ensure the continuance of the proper American tradition; does not distinguish clearly between role of the nation and role of the church
View of God and public life	God is favorably disposed toward things American	The priestly vision for America is also God's vision for America
Attitude toward political activity	Celebrative; individual and institutional	Legislative and focused; often single issue; individual and institutional
Goal for public life	To reflect order, stability	To reflect the great tradition
Evidence for regeneration of public life is present when	Symbolic boundaries are observed and reinvigorated.	Tradition is upheld and protected.
Self understanding	Keepers of the symbols that bind the community and interpreters of their meaning	Custodians of knowledge; protectors and defenders of the truth

	Public Christian	*Public Church*
General Description	When Christians emphasize the existence of the two kingdoms (kingdom of God and kingdom of this world) and affirm the radical discontinuity that exists or, as some prefer, that should exist between church and world. The church is to avoid activity intending to transform public life, but individual Christians are encouraged to participate through voting, or as politicians, or in any other appropriate way consistent with Christian faith. Priority is placed on the church and its members to stand as witnesses both to God's salvation and to authentic human life in the world, and to bring individuals to Christ.	Where Christians assert the unity of God's reign, and God's equal concern for all things sacred and secular, and act on this representation or assumption either as if presently existing (even though affirmed as eschatological) or as already accomplished (from creation or through the work of Christ). They believe strongly in God's care and concern for the world and all that it means to be in the world; expect the church to engage social life in America, especially wherever political realities exploit human beings or deny them justice; declare that the mission of the church includes the use of political wisdom, effective methods, and critical reason to establish a greater degree of relative justice in American public life.
Approach to public truth, intellect, education	Assumes transcendence and judgment of God and is therefore essentially prophetic; seeks word from God for self; ranges from closed to cautiously open to new truth; acknowledges the possibility of error and the distinction between justification and truth.	Assumes transcendence and judgment of God and is therefore essentially prophetic; seeks truth from others as well as from God; open to new truth even when from non-Christian sources; acknowledges the possibility of error and the distinction between justification and truth.
Spirituality	Derived from the community of faith and expressed through the piety and practice of the individual; respects diversity within clearly defined Christian limits; seeks self-transcendence for individuals who are primarily related to the church in the reign of God (as distinct from the world); sees theology primarily as an internal Christian conversation; recognizes human limits imposed by history	Celebrates the experience of God in the Christian community but also in all members of the world's community; usually respects differing ways of experiencing the sacred; seeks affirmation of diversity; seeks self-transcendence as a community (church) that is primarily related to the reign of God (including creation); sees theology as a public conversation that openly engages science and the broader culture; recognizes limits imposed by history

	Public Christian	*Public Church*
Acceptance of pluralism	Within reason; somewhat threatened by radical pluralism; priority is to communicate Christian identity within pluralistic conversations	Within reason, tolerant of pluralism where all are equal participants in the conversation; willing to put pre-understandings at risk for the sake of conversation and new understanding
Notion of sin	Pluralistic (emphasis on sins) and activistic (actions taken by individuals); personal and conscientious failure of each individual in relation to God and others	Monistic (emphasis on sin as state of being), an aspect of human finitude; resides within systems as well as individuals; judgment falls on societies and the collective institutions created by politics
Role of church	Primary task is not public; rather, it rests in identity as a community of faith and ability to witness to, or provide example for, the world as to the integrity or wholeness of the life of faithfulness, and to teach the divine principles of social duty and to represent the gospel in a way that lives out its faith; the church's first priority is salvation, not politics, but it should help educate individual Christians to work conscientiously to fulfill their duty as citizens.	Mission is inherently public in seeking out and working toward connection between the imperatives of the gospel and the establishment of relative justice in matters of public life; Christians and church must work toward social redemption as well as individual redemption.
View of God and public life	God is best served by integrity of church's mission as the community of faith; some encourage individuals to work for justice in politics.	God is best served by integrity of church's action seeking justice for each and every member of a creation loved by God; God is concerned with all aspects of what it means to be human.
Attitude toward political activity	Ranges from noninvolvement to open encouragement of individual political activity; no church activity in public life; the political task of church is to witness to the "city of God" rather than to transform the world	Sees political activity as an essential aspect of Christian identity; activist; part of the mission of the church

	Public Christian	*Public Church*
Goal for public life	To model itself after the witness of the community of faith	To embody relative justice; to relate to all things in a manner appropriate to their relations to God
Evidence for regeneration of public life is present when	Individuals are redeemed and brought into the community of faith; the church serves the world by being true to itself.	Relative victories on behalf of justice are won, and the sinfulness of social structures is addressed in redeeming ways; public life is moved forward to reflect the fulfillment of creation and the kind of justice found in the Hebrew Bible and the Christian gospel.
Self understanding	Expounders of the gospel; role models of and witnesses to the life of faith; shapers of Christian identity and the Christian community	Seekers of relative justice for the voiceless, oppressed, and marginalized; transformers of society; expounders of the gospel with attention to implications for how human beings, in all their individual and social relationships, treat one another and the created order

Notes

Introduction

1. Leonard I. Sweet, "The Modernization of Protestant Religion in America," in *Altered Landscapes: Christianity in America, 1935–1985,* ed. David Lotz (Grand Rapids: Wm. B. Eerdmans, 1989), 24.
2. Martin E. Marty, "The Year the Revival Passed Crest," *Christian Century* (hereafter *CC*) (December 31, 1958): 1499–1501.
3. For example, Colleen McDannell, *Material Christianity: Religion and Popular Culture in America* (New Haven, CT: Yale University Press, 1995).
4. The term *displacement* is one Martin E. Marty used to discuss pluralism's "displacement" of Protestantism as a "ground occupying" entity in American life in his early book *Second Chance for American Protestants* (New York: Harper & Row, 1963). Marty's preferred title for the book was *The Displaced Christian,* but the press preferred the more "upbeat" title.
5. Martin E. Marty, "The Constitution and the Congregation: Time to Celebrate," *CC* (June 3–10, 1987): 523.
6. Diana Eck, *A New Religious America: How a "Christian Country" Has Become the World's Most Religiously Diverse Nation* (San Francisco: HarperSanFrancisco, 2001). This book is an outstanding resource for understanding religious pluralism in America and its relation to discussions about religious freedom. Her "pluralism project" is located on the Web at http://www.pluralism.org.

7. This is an overly brief summary of the argument made convincingly by Eck in *A New Religious America*. The term "relative opening" of the borders comes from Alejandro Portes and Rubén G. Rumbaut, *Immigrant America: A Portrait*, 2d ed. (Berkeley: University of California Press, 1997).

8. William R. Hutchison has provided an illuminating history of the pluralist ideal in America, and tension surrounding it, through his book *Religious Pluralism in America: The Contentious History of a Founding Ideal* (New Haven, CT: Yale University Press, 2003). Martin E. Marty has also recently addressed the topic of engaging pluralism through risking hospitality and promoting engagement in his book *When Faiths Collide* (Malden, MA: Blackwell Publishing, 2005).

9. James Davison Hunter, *Culture Wars: The Struggle to Define America* (New York: Basic Books, 1991).

10. Robert Wuthnow, *The Restructuring of American Religion: Society and Faith Since World War II* (Princeton, NJ: Princeton University Press, 1988), 225, 227.

11. See, for example, my essay examining the response of Christianity to homosexuality in Toulouse, "The Muddled Middle: Protestantism's Encounter with Homosexuality since the 1960s," in *Sex, Religion, Media*, ed., Dane S. Claussen (Boulder, CO: Rowman & Littlefield, 2002), 43–63. Many of my conclusions summarized in this paragraph are supported in other essays written over the last ten to fifteen years. See the last full paragraph on xxii, and the footnote accompanying it.

12. The phrase appeared in the *CC* in 1951 in response to emerging developments in American culture: see *CC* (June 13, 1951): 701–3. Also see Martin E. Marty, "Peace and Pluralism: The *Century* 1946–1952," *CC* (October 24, 1984): 979–83 for a discussion of the conservative nature of some of the magazine's viewpoints; and "Protestantism Enters Third Phase," *CC* (January 18, 1961): 72–75, for an editorial by Marty affirming "fully realized pluralism."

13. R. Laurence Moore makes this argument in the second chapter of *Touchdown Jesus: The Mixing of Sacred and Secular in American History* (Louisville, KY: Westminster John Knox Press, 2003). One might also look at the role of Jewish contributions to popular culture, for Jewish businessmen were instrumental in developing mass-produced housing in the late 1940s (Bill Levitt and Levittown houses) and the new phenomenon of discount stores (Eugene Ferkauf and his Korvettes stores); see David Halberstam, *The Fifties* (New York: Fawcett Books, 1993), 131–54.

14. C. Stanley Lowell, "If the U.S. Becomes 51% Catholic," *Christianity Today* (hereafter *CT*) (October 27, 1958): 8–12; and "Should Americans Elect a Roman Catholic President?" *CT* (October 26, 1959): 22–23.

15. A Former Jesuit Trainee, "America's Need: A New Protestant Awakening," *CT* (October 28, 1957): 3–6.

16. Michael Daves, "Religious Fracas in Dallas," *CC* (October 12, 1960): 1181.

17. "The Candidate's Religion," *CC* (March 3, 1959): 251–53. "Moratorium on Bigotry," *CC* (April 27, 1960): 499; and "Religious Debate Must Continue," *CC* (May 4, 1960): 533. See letter written by Richard Yaussy, "A Catholic President?" *CC* (July 7, 1960): 829. Editorials dealing with the question of JFK's religion and his candidacy are numerous. Some samples include "Candidate's Religion Remains a Proper Consideration," *CC* (May 27, 1959): 636; "Why Senator Kennedy Withdrew as a Speaker," *CC* (January 27, 1960): 93; "Religion Plays Part in Wisconsin Vote," *CC* (April 20, 1960): 460; "Planned Politics Pays Off," *CC* (July 27, 1960): 867–68; "Religious Affiliation," *CC* (August 17, 1960): 939–40; "When Is a Catholic President Not Free?" *CC* (August 24, 1960): 966.

18. See the following unsigned editorials on Kennedy: "No Political Messiah," *CC* (August 10, 1960): 915–16; "Kennedy Clarifies Stand to Houston Ministers,"

CC (September 28, 1960): 1109; "Nixon Wins Round One," CC (October 12, 1960): 1171, where the editor confesses he feels better about the "presidential caliber" of both men; the essay by Winthrop S. Hudson is "The Religious Issue in the Campaign," CC (October 26, 1960): 1239–40.

19. Herberg, *Protestant-Catholic-Jew: An Essay in American Religious Sociology*, rev. ed. (Garden City, NY: Anchor Books, 1960), 38–39.

20. Martin E. Marty, *The New Shape of American Religion* (New York: Harper & Row, 1959), 2.

21. Ibid., 69 and 71. This book is Marty's first book-length treatment of the "post-Protestant age."

22. Ibid., 27–28, and 32. Sidney E. Mead challenges the post-Protestant concept in his essay entitled "The Post-Protestant Concept and America's Two Religions," in Mead, *The Nation With the Soul of a Church* (New York: Harper & Row, 1975), 11–28. Mead's point is that the "constitutional and legal structure" of the United States had never been Protestant. This is certainly true; but prior to the 1950s, Protestants took that structure for granted and most Americans interpreted it in ways fully consistent with Protestant values and beliefs. After the late fifties, such interpretations were challenged. See also Marty, *New Shape*, chap. 4, 67–89, "America's Real Religion: An Attitude," esp. 73f., and 37–39.

23. "Gallup Names Five Most Admired Men," CC (March 11, 1959): 285. Early in his career, Graham had difficulty distinguishing bween things important to American culture (anticommunism, democracy, etc.) and those important to Christian faith. In his autobiography, he stated that he regretted not being able to do graduate work in religion. It is a tad ironic that the most well-known cultural representative of the essence of American Christianity had nothing more than a bachelor of arts degree. Had he been able to pursue graduate study in religion, Graham might have avoided some of the "semblance of involvement in partisan politics" that plagued his career, particularly during the Nixon administration. In listing his regrets, Graham wrote that he would avoid partisan politics if he "had it to do over again." He also said he "would speak less and study more." Graham did learn from experience, however. After Watergate, Graham began to discern much more carefully between American culture and Christian faith. For Graham's take on his career, see Billy Graham, *Just As I Am: The Autobiography of Billy Graham* (San Francisco: HarperSanFrancisco, 1997), esp. 135, 723–24.

24. Marty, *Second Chance*.

25. E. Harold Breitenberg Jr. has recently provided an excellent analysis of the use of terms like public theology, public church, etc., and of their origin; see "To Tell the Truth: Will the Real Public Theology Please Stand Up?" *Journal of the Society of Christian Ethics* (2003): 55–96; he gives Marty credit for being the first to use both the terms "public theologian" and "public theology" (see 73, note 13). The first use of "public theology" is found in Martin E. Marty, "Reinhold Niebuhr: Public Theology and the American Experience," *Journal of Religion* (October 1974): 332–59.

26. John Courtney Murray, *We Hold These Truths* (New York: Sheed & Ward, 1960), 21–23, 28.

27. Robert N. Bellah, "Civil Religion in America," *Daedalus* 96 (1967): 1–21. An early resource that covers many aspects of the resulting debates over civil religion is *American Civil Religion*, ed. Russell E. Richey and Donald G. Jones (New York: Harper & Row, 1974); see also Phillip E. Hammond, "The Sociology of American Civil Religion," *Sociological Analysis* 37 (1976): 169–82; and Robert N. Bellah and Phillip E. Hammond, *Varieties of Civil Religion* (New York: Harper & Row, 1980). For an early and important critical analysis of civil religion, see John

F. Wilson, *Public Religion in American Culture* (Philadelphia: Temple University Press, 1979).

28. Abraham Lincoln, "Second Inaugural Address," in Conrad Cherry, ed., *God's New Israel: Religious Interpretations of American Destiny,* rev. ed. (Chapel Hill: University of North Carolina Press, 1998), 201–2. Regarding civil religion as seen through a more prophetic lens, see Robert N. Bellah, *The Broken Covenant* (New York: Seabury, 1975); and Sidney E. Mead, *The Lively Experiment: The Shaping of Christianity in America* (New York: Harper & Row, 1976). Martin E. Marty's essay "Two Kinds of Two Kinds of Civil Religion" offers an accessible, entry-level discussion on the complexity of civil religion and the way that it can operate in both "priestly" and "prophetic" ways; the essay is found in Richey and Jones, *American Civil Religion,* 139–57, and is also published as "Civil Religion: Two Kinds of Two Kinds," in Martin E. Marty, *Religion & Republic: The American Circumstance* (Boston: Beacon Press, 1987), 77–94.

29. I am indebted to Martin E. Marty's use of the term "iconic" in this way to describe how the culture in America views the Bible. See Marty, "America's Iconic Book," in *Humanizing America's Iconic Book,* Society of Biblical Literature Centennial Addresses, ed. Gene M. Tucker and Douglas A. Knight (Chico, CA: Scholars Press, 1980). Originally, Marty delivered the address at the centennial meeting of the Society of Biblical Literature in Dallas, at the Loews Anatole Hotel, in November 1980.

30. The term "public church" was first used by Martin E. Marty in his book *The Public Church* (New York: Crossroad Publishing Company, 1981); see the discussion in chapter 2.

31. H. Richard Niebuhr, *Christ & Culture* (New York: HarperCollins, 2001). I recommend this particular edition because it has a foreword by Martin E. Marty, a preface by James M. Gustafson, and an introduction containing an essay H. Richard Niebuhr wrote on the "Types of Christian Ethics" that was not included with the original publication of his book.

32. For the original ATS Luce project, I have focused on a particular body of primary source materials, though I have devoted attention to relevant secondary materials as well. For primary materials, I chose to examine editorials and articles in six major independent Protestant and Catholic periodicals from the mid-1950s to the mid-1990s (*Sojourners* and *CT* to represent the Protestant "evangelical" community; *CC* and *Christianity & Crisis* to represent the Protestant "mainline" community; and *America* and *Commonweal* to represent the Catholic community). This book includes some material drawn from a few paragraphs found in papers I have previously published. This material appears in somewhat revised form in the introduction and in chapters 4 through 6. Paragraphs are drawn from "*The Christian Century* and American Public Life: The Crucial Years, 1956–1968," in *New Dimensions in Modern American Religious History,* ed. Jay Dolan and James Wind (Grand Rapids: Wm. B. Eerdmans Publishing Co., 1993), 44–82; "*Christianity Today* and American Public Life: A Case Study," *Journal of Church and State* (Spring 1993): 241–84; "*Sojourners,*" in *Popular Religious Magazines of the United States,* ed. Mark Fackler and Charles H. Lippy (Westport, CT: Greenwood Publishing, 1995), 444–51; "Liberty and Equality: Christian Faith and the Civil Rights Movement," in *The Papers of the Henry Luce III Fellows in Theology,* vol. 4, ed. Matthew Zyniewicz (Pittsburgh: Association of Theological Schools, 2000), 135–73; "Muddling Through: The Church and Sexuality/Homosexuality," in *Homosexuality, Science, and the "Plain Sense" of Scripture,* ed. David Balch (Grand Rapids: Wm. B. Eerdmans Publishing Co., 2000), 6–41; and review of Fredrick C. Harris, *Something Within: Religion in African-American Political*

Activism (New York: Oxford University Press, 1999), in *Church History* (June 2003): 431–33. I am grateful for permission to use this material. Other published essays related to this project include "A Climate of Optimism: The Origins of the *Christian Century,*" *CC* (January 26, 2000): 80–83; "Progress and 'Relapse': The *Century* and World War I," *CC* (March 8, 2000): 260–62; "Socializing Capitalism: The *Century* during the Great Depression," *CC* (April 12, 2000): 415–18; "The 'Unnecessary Necessity': The *Century* in World War II," *CC* (July 5–12, 2000): 726–29; "Indirect Action: The *Century* and Civil Rights," *CC* (October 18, 2000): 1044–47; "Days of Protest: The *Century* and Vietnam," *CC* (November 8, 2000): 1154–57; "Feminist Gains: The *Century* and Women," *CC* (December 20–27, 2000): 1341–43; "Perspectives on Abortion in the Christian Community from the 1950s to the Early 1990s," *Encounter* (Autumn 2001): 327–403; and "The Muddled Middle: Protestantism's Encounter with Homosexuality since the 1960s," in *Sex, Religion, Media,* ed. Dane S. Claussen (Boulder, CO: Rowman & Littlefield, 2002), 43–63.

Chapter 1: The Establishment Clause

1. Oral arguments in *Thomas Van Orden v. Rick Perry*—the transcript is found in PDF at http://wid.ap.org/documents/scotus/050302perry.pdf. The case reached a decision in June 2005. The case originating in Kentucky is *McCreary County, Kentucky, et al. v. American Civil Liberties Union of Kentucky et al.*

2. This is an argument often made by those associated with the Religious Right. However, the argument has been made by others as well. See, for example, A. James Reichley, *Religion in American Public Life* (Washington, DC: The Brookings Institution, 1985)—this book has been revised somewhat and republished as *Faith in Politics* (Washington, DC: The Brookings Institution, 2002); see also Stephen L. Carter, *The Culture of Disbelief: How American Law and Politics Trivialize Religious Devotion* (New York: HarperCollins, 1993).

3. For more detail on the nature of religious establishments in New York and in New England, see Leonard W. Levy, *The Establishment Clause: Religion and the First Amendment* (New York: Macmillan Publishing Co., 1986), 1–62. Levy covers well the ambiguity and complexity associated with these establishments.

4. Figures on numbers of families are found in Winthrop Hudson and John Corrigan, *Religion in America,* 5th ed. (New York: Macmillan Publishing Co., 1992), 34.

5. Levy, *Establishment Clause,* 26.

6. Sidney E. Mead, *The Lively Experiment: The Shaping of Christianity in America* (New York: Harper & Row, 1976), 36.

7. Edwin Scott Gaustad and Philip L. Barlow, eds., *New Historical Atlas of Religion in America* (New York: Oxford University Press, 2001), 69.

8. See Hudson's and Corrigan's discussion, *Religion in America,* 129–30.

9. James E. Wood Jr., "Religion and the Constitution," in *The First Freedom: Religion & the Bill of Rights,* ed. James E. Wood (Waco, TX: J.M. Dawson Institute of Church-State Studies, 1990), 3–4.

10. Isaac Kramnick and R. Laurence Moore (*The Godless Constitution* [New York: W. W. Norton, 1997]) argue this case well; see also Edwin S. Gaustad, "Religion and Ratification," in Wood, ed., *First Freedom,* 47. Gaustad's essay examines the impact of religious arguments on the ratification of the Constitution.

11. This is quoted in Edwin Gaustad and Leigh Schmidt, *The Religious History of America: The Heart of the American Story from Colonial Times to Today* (San Francisco: HarperSanFrancisco, 2002), 131.

12. Gaustad, "Religion and Ratification," 57. The quote is from Madison's "Memorial and Remonstrance." Justice Rehnquist has made the case, in his dissent in *Wallace v. Jaffree* (1985), that Madison acted pragmatically rather than from principle. I believe, along with others, that Rehnquist's argument is without merit on this point. See David Little, "The Reformed Tradition," in Wood, ed., *First Freedom*, 22.

13. This association quickly changed its name to The National Reform Association. In 1864, it tried to create a new constitutional preamble, one "humbly acknowledging Almighty God as the source of all authority and power in civil government" and "The Lord Jesus Christ as the Governor among the Nations." Attempts in the mid-twentieth century were by the National Association of Evangelicals, in 1947 and 1954, to add to the Constitution the affirmation that "this nation divinely recognizes the authority and law of Jesus Christ." Kramnick and Moore, *Godless Constitution*, 146–48.

14. William Lee Miller, *The First Liberty: America's Foundation in Religious Freedom* (Washington, DC: Georgetown University Press, 2003), 108.

15. Bernard Bailyn describes the process that finally brings the Bill of Rights to fruition: "There would be no Constitution unless the corpus of powers that had been created were balanced by an equally powerful enumeration of rights; unless it were explicitly stated that all powers not specifically delegated to the federal government were reserved to the people or to the states; and unless the enumerated rights were understood not to deny or disparage or limit all other rights, whatever they were, which were reserved in their totality to the people." Bernard Bailyn, *To Begin the World Anew: The Genius and Ambiguities of the American Founders* (New York: Alfred A. Knopf, 2003), 98.

16. There is, in American history, a strong tradition of theological arguments for separating church and state from one another, beginning with the serious work of Roger Williams informed by his Protestant and Reformed tradition. Theologically, the idea is rooted in the Protestant belief that God had divided the spiritual and temporal worlds, giving each a portion of authority and power separate from the other. See particularly David Little, "The Reformed Tradition and the First Amendment," in Wood, ed., *First Freedom,* 17–40; for book-length treatments of the topic, see Mark DeWolfe Howe, *The Garden and the Wilderness: Religion and Government in American Constitutional History* (Chicago: University of Chicago Press, 1965); and Timothy L. Hall, *Separating Church and State: Roger Williams and Religious Liberty* (Urbana: University of Illinois Press, 1998).

17. Miller mentions the "endlessly mischievous" activities of Patrick Henry in this regard. Miller, *First Liberty*, 111. For the story of how Madison overcame a defeat for a Senate seat to win the House seat in this "Henrymandered district" over James Monroe, see Lance Banning, *The Sacred Fire of Liberty: James Madison and the Founding of the Federal Republic* (Ithaca, NY: Cornell University Press, 1995), 265–73.

18. Banning, *Sacred Fire*, 274–75.

19. Bailyn, *To Begin the World Anew*, 124–25.

20. Comparison of this wording and other content about the nature of the arguments in Congress during this process is found in Banning, *Sacred Fire*, 285–90.

21. This written response to the Rev. Adams is quoted in John F. Wilson, *Public Religion in American Culture* (Philadelphia: Temple University Press, 1979), 3–6.

22. This case involved the right of Jehovah's Witnesses (Newton Cantwell and two sons) to witness for their faith in New Haven, Connecticut, without having to apply for the appropriate city permit. When the anti-Catholic tone of some of their teachings caused some disturbances among Catholics, the Cantwells were

arrested for disturbing the peace. The Supreme Court cleared the Cantwells of all charges. Chapter 2 discusses this case in a bit more detail.

23. See *Cantwell v. Connecticut*, 310 U.S. 296 (1940), at 303–4. Justice Roberts's opinion is reproduced in Robert T. Miller and Ronald B. Flowers, eds., *Toward Benevolent Neutrality: Church, State, and the Supreme Court*, 4th ed. (Waco, TX: Baylor University Press, 1992), 60–63. The relationship between the Fourteenth and First Amendments had been explored in a previous case dealing with rhetoric used by a socialist who called for the establishment of socialism through strikes or other means. The case was *Gitlow v. New York* (1925). Justice Sanford wrote the opinion of the Court and stated, "For present purposes we may and do assume that freedom of speech and of the press—which are protected by the First Amendment . . .—are among the fundamental rights and 'liberties' protected by the due process clause of the Fourteenth Amendment from impairment by the States." Though this case had nothing to do with religion, its application of the Fourteenth Amendment provided some inkling of what was to come. See *Gitlow v. New York*, 268 U.S. 652 (1925), at 666.

24. Banning, *Sacred Fire*, 288.

25. *Everson v. Board of Education of Ewing Township*, 330 U.S. 1 (1947), at 15–16 and 18; or Miller and Flowers, eds., *Toward Benevolent Neutrality*, 626–29.

26. *Everson v. Board of Education of Ewing Township*, 330 U.S. 1 (1947), at 31–32.

27. Quoted in Daniel L. Dreisbach, "Mr. Jefferson, A Mammoth Cheese, and the 'Wall of Separation Between Church and State': A Bicentennial Commemoration," *Journal of Church and State* 43 (Autumn 2001): 735.

28. For the story of the campaign of 1800 and the role of religion in it, see Mark A. Noll, *One Nation Under God? Christian Faith and Political Action in America* (San Francisco: Harper & Row, 1988), 75–89.

29. Quoted in Dreisbach, "Mr. Jefferson," 732–33.

30. *McCollum v. Board of Education* (1948); *Zorach v. Clauson* (1952); *Engel v. Vitale* (1962); and *Abington Township School District v. Schempp* (1963). All these cases are found in Miller and Flowers, eds., *Toward Benevolent Neutrality*.

31. Breyer filed his own opinion concurring in the Texas case but dissenting from the analysis of the plurality (the opinion written by Rehnquist and joined by Scalia, Kennedy, and Thomas). The full opinions of both these cases are found in *Journal of Church and State* (Autumn 2005); *Van Orden v. Perry* is found on 915–58 and *McCreary County, Kentucky, et al. v. American Civil Liberties Union of Kentucky et al.* is found on 959–1003.

32. John Witte Jr., *Religion and the American Constitutional Experiment: Essential Rights and Liberties* (Boulder, CO: Westview Books, 2000), 182. Another very good, and accessible, treatment of these cases is found in Ronald B. Flowers, *That Godless Court? Supreme Court Decisions on Church-State Relationships* (Louisville, KY: Westminster John Knox Press, 1994). See particularly his treatment of the *Lemon* test, used by the Court for cases involving establishment questions (66–67, 136–137).

33. Mary C. Segers and Ted G. Jelen, *A Wall of Separation? Debating the Public Role of Religion* (Lanham, MD: Rowman & Littlefield, 1998), 5. Jelen argues the separationist position, while Mary Segers argues the accommodationist position.

34. Carl H. Esbeck, "A Typology of Church-State Relations in Current American Thought," in *Religion, Public Life, and the American Polity*, ed. Luis E. Lugo (Knoxville: University of Tennessee Press, 1994), 5–15. This paragraph and the quotes contained within it come from Esbeck's descriptions.

35. Examples of strict separationists would include Leonard W. Levy (*The Establishment Clause: Religion and the First Amendment* [New York: Macmillan Publishing

Co., 1986]); Leo Pfeffer (*Church, State, and Freedom* [Boston: Beacon Press, 1987]); and Ted G. Jelen, *To Serve God and Mammon: Church-State Relations in American Politics* (Boulder, CO: Westview Press, 2000).

36. Esbeck provides only one particular example of freewill separationists. He lists Robert Linder and Richard Pierard (*Twilight of the Saints: Biblical Christianity & Civil Religion in America* [Downers Grove, IL: InterVarsity Press, 1978]). I believe Stanley Hauerwas and William Willimon's book *Resident Aliens: Life in the Christian Colony* (Nashville: Abingdon Press, 1989) would probably also fit in this category, loosely considered.

37. Again, Esbeck offers few resources here. He does mention Max Stackhouse, "An Ecumenist's Plea for a Public Theology," *This World* (Spring/Summer 1984), but I'm not sure he fits in this category more than the former one. Theoretically and theologically, the following books mentioned by Esbeck fit this category more than the other categories he describes: James Gustafson, *Ethics from a Theocentric Perspective* (Chicago: University of Chicago Press, 1981); Martin E. Marty, *The Public Church* (New York: Crossroad, 1981); and John Wilson, *Public Religion in American Culture* (Philadelphia: Temple University Press, 1979). In addition, one might list the practical examination of religion and politics in a book edited by James E. Wood Jr. and Derek Davis (*The Role of Religion in the Making of Public Policy* [Waco, TX: J. M. Dawson Institute of Church-State Studies, 1991]). The work of the National Council of the Churches of Christ in America and organizations like the Interfaith Alliance would likely fit here on the Christian end of this spectrum. All these works probably need some degree of separation from others that might be included in this category that represent a more deist/humanist approach, especially in fleshing out the theological commitments connected to the nation itself: for the early expression of this view, see Sidney E. Mead's *The Nation with the Soul of a Church* (New York: Harper & Row, 1975) and *The Lively Experiment*; see also the later exposition of this position, informed by Mead's prior work but given a more explicit Christian interpretation by Franklin I. Gamwell in *Politics as a Christian Vocation: Faith and Democracy Today* (Cambridge: Cambridge University Press, 2005).

38. The most recent, and probably the most complete, argument in this regard is the one set forth by Philip Hamburger, *Separation of Church and State* (Cambridge, MA: Harvard University Press, 2002); see especially his chapter titled "Jefferson and the Baptists: Separation Proposed and Ignored as a Constitutional Principle" (144–89). Hamburger demonstrates the anti-Catholic connections to the historical development of the metaphor on 193f. See also Dreisbach's book-length treatment *Thomas Jefferson and the Wall of Separation between Church and State* (New York: New York University Press, 2002). Dreisbach and Hamburger are two of the more well-researched scholarly offerings challenging separationist viewpoints.

39. Other scholars have argued that the "wall of separation" metaphor did not accurately reflect the relationship between church and state in post-Bill of Rights America. See Sidney Mead, for example, "Neither Church nor State: Reflections on James Madison's 'Line of Separation,'" in Mead, *Nation with the Soul of a Church*, 78–94.

40. Sidney Mead argued "the religious ideal [of many of the Founders] was that of melding the many diverse sectarianisms into one cosmopolitan religion." Mead described this cosmopolitan religion as "the religion of the republic." Though it could degenerate into a civil religion that identifies the American way of life with God's way of doing things, when it did so, in Mead's view, it was heretical. Rather, he understood the "religion of the republic" as an essentially prophetic religion

that asserted the primacy of God over all human institutions and believed in "ideals and aspirations [that] stand in constant judgment over the passing shenanigans of the people, reminding them of the standards by which their current practices and those of their nation are ever being judged and found wanting." See "Nation with the Soul of a Church," in Mead, *Nation with the Soul of a Church*, 48–77.

41. See Dreisbach, "Religion and Legal Reforms in Revolutionary Virginia: A Reexamination of Jefferson's Views on Religious Freedom and Church-State Separation," in *Religion and Political Culture in Jefferson's Virginia,* ed. Garrett Ward Sheldon and Daniel L. Dreisbach (New York: Rowman & Littlefield, 2000), 189–218. Essentially, the same article was published as "In Pursuit of Religious Freedom: Thomas Jefferson's Church-State Views Revisited," in Lugo, *Religion, Public Life, and the American Polity*, 74–111.

42. See Esbeck, "A Typology of Church-State Relations," 15–23. The three listed by Esbeck are the "structural pluralists," the "nonpreferentialists," and the "restorationists." Each is discussed to some degree in the paragraphs that follow.

43. Abraham Kuyper, *Lectures on Calvinism* (Grand Rapids: Wm. B. Eerdmans Publishing Co., 1981).

44. Ronald F. Thiemann, *Religion in Public Life: A Dilemma For Democracy* (Washington, DC: Georgetown University Press, 1996), 60–64.

45. See *Wallace v. Jaffree*, 472 U.S. 38 (1985), at 106–7. See Miller and Flowers, eds., *Toward Benevolent Neutrality*, 559–66, where the body of the opinion is published.

46. Quoted in Levy, *Establishment Clause*, 92.

47. Ibid., 92–93.

48. Robert H. Bork, "What to Do about the First Amendment," *Commentary* 99 (February 1995): 23–29. Derek Davis has written a fine book exploring the notion of original intent as contained within the judicial philosophy of Chief Justice Rehnquist; see Davis, *Original Intent: Chief Justice Rehnquist and the Course of American Church/State Relations* (Buffalo: Prometheus Books, 1991).

49. The founders of the Rutherford Institute include John W. Whitehead and Franky Schaeffer, son of Francis Schaeffer. Rousas John (R. J.) Rushdoony and his son-in-law Gary North have both been prominent in this work. See John W. Whitehead, *The Separation Illusion: A Lawyer Examines the First Amendment* (Milford, MI: Mott Media, 1977), and Whitehead, *The Second American Revolution* (Elgin, IL: David C. Cook, 1982); see also Franky Schaeffer, *A Time for Anger* (Wheaton, IL: Good News Publications, 1982). David Barton, who raised a ruckus over a decade ago in the school district of a small town outside Fort Worth just a few miles from me, presented this kind of case in *The Myth of Separation: What Is the Constitutional Relationship between Church and State? A Revealing Look at What the Founders and Early Courts Really Said* (Aledo, TX: Wallbuilder Press, 1992); C. Gregg Singer also represents this Christian view of government in *A Theological Interpretation of American History*, rev. ed. (Phillipsburg, NJ: Presbyterian and Reformed Publishing Co., 1964). Carl Esbeck refers to those who hold this form of accommodationism as "the restorationists."

50. See John W. Whitehead and John Conlan, "The Establishment of the Religion of Secular Humanism and Its First Amendment Applications," *Texas Tech Law Review* 10 (Winter 1978). This argument has also been made with some degree of sophistication and without direct connections to the Religious Right by such scholars as Reichley (*Faith in Politics*).

51. Francis Schaeffer, *How Should We Then Live?* (Old Tappan, NJ: Fleming H. Revell, 1976); and *A Christian Manifesto* (Westchester, IL: Crossway Books, 1981).

52. See, for example, Robert L. Cord, *Separation of Church and State: Historical Fact and Current Fiction* (New York: Lambeth Press, 1982).

53. See Dreisbach, "Mr. Jefferson," 738–39.

54. On Madison's positions on these matters, see Leo Pffeffer, "Madison's 'Detached Memoranda': Then and Now," in *The Virginia Statute for Religious Freedom*, ed. Merrill D. Peterson and Robert C. Vaughan (Cambridge: Cambridge University Press, 1988), 282–312.

55. Douglas Laycock, "Original Intent and the Constitution Today," in Wood, ed., *First Freedom*, 87–112. Leonard W. Levy offers a more extensive analysis of the early legislative history and its relation to nonpreferential understandings in his chapter "The Nonpreferentialists," in Levy, *Establishment Clause*, 91–119.

56. Laycock ("Original Intent," 92–93, 103–6) makes this point about the position set forth by Steven Smith. See Steven D. Smith, "Separation and the 'Secular': Reconstructing the Disestablishment Doctrine," *Texas Law Review* 67 (1989).

57. See Laycock, "Original Intent," 103.

58. See John F. Wilson, "Original Intent and Comparable Consensus," in Wood, ed., *First Freedom*, particularly 128–31.

59. Generally, I think there is at least some truth to the claim that the Founders did not intend the kind of absolute separation that modern Court decisions have tended to represent, or that Jefferson represented with his "wall" metaphor in 1802. The most sophisticated recent argument in this regard is made by Philip Hamburger, the John P. Wilson Professor of Law at the University of Chicago. Though I disagree with many aspects of his argument, he makes a strong case for a distinction between the "separation of church and state" and the ideal of "religious liberty" that stands behind the establishment clause. See Hamburger, *Separation of Church and State*.

60. See Banning, *Sacred Fire*, 130, 207–8.

61. This paragraph draws from the statistics provided by Diana Eck, *A New Religious America: How a "Christian Country" Has Become the World's Most Religiously Diverse Nation* (San Francisco: HarperSanFrancisco, 2001), esp. 2–3.

62. "The New Colossus." These words were written by Emma Lazarus (1849–1887), a young Jewish woman from New York City, for an art exhibition hosted to raise money in America for the statue.

63. See, for example, the letter to the president, dated September 12, 2002, from a coalition of churches and religious leaders arguing against the notion of preventive war. The letter is found at http://www.cmep.org/letters/2002Sep12_Bush ReIraq.htm. The letter was signed by leadership associated with the National Council of Churches, the Quakers, the Roman Catholic Church, the Mennonites, the Christian Church (Disciples of Christ), the National Baptist Convention (USA), the Alliance of Baptists, the United Church of Christ, the Unitarian Universalist Association of Congregations, the Moravian Church, the United Methodist Church, the Church of the Brethren, the Evangelicals for Social Action, and the Evangelical Lutheran Church in America, among others.

Chapter 2: The Free Exercise Clause

1. This argument is made well by Carl H. Esbeck, "Differentiating the Free Exercise and Establishment Clauses," *Journal of Church and State* (Spring 2000): 313–34. Esbeck argues that "grammatically there is but one First Amendment clause (with two prepositional phrases) that explicitly concerns religion" (323, note 39). See 320–23 for his statement of the difference between the "structural clause" and the "rights clause."

2. *Engel v. Vitale*, 370 U.S. 421 (1962), at 431. Or see Robert T. Miller and Ronald

B. Flowers, eds., *Toward Benevolent Neutrality: Church, State, and the Supreme Court* (Waco, TX: Baylor University Press, 1992), 512, where this section of Black's argument is published. Esbeck quotes Black in note 18, 315–16.

3. See Esbeck, "Differentiating," 320, note 31.

4. Marvin E. Frankel, "Religion in Public Life—Reasons for Minimal Access," *George Washington Law Review* (March 1992): 643.

5. Leo Pfeffer, "The Unity of the First Amendment Religion Clauses," in *The First Freedom: Religion and the Bill of Rights*, ed. James E. Wood Jr., 134. Pfeffer here rehearses his argument found in various sources and the similar argument made by Philip B. Kurland. See Pfeffer, "Freedom and/or Separation: The Constitutional Dilemma of the First Amendment," *Minnesota Law Review* (1980); and Pfeffer, "The Case for Separation," in *Religion in America*, ed. John Cogley (New York: Meridian Books, 1958), 52–60. See also Philip B. Kurland, *Religion and the Law: Of Church and State and the Supreme Court* (Chicago: Aldine Publishing Co., 1962).

6. See Leonard W. Levy, *The Establishment Clause: Religion and the First Amendment* (New York: Macmillan Publishing Co., 1986); Leo Pfeffer, *Church, State, and Freedom* (Boston: Beacon Press, 1967); and Mary C. Segers and Ted G. Jelen, *A Wall of Separation? Debating the Public Role of Religion* (Lanham, MD: Rowman & Littlefield, 1998).

7. Ted G. Jelen, *To Serve God and Mammon: Church-State Relations in American Politics* (Boulder, CO: Westview Press, 2000), 12.

8. Richard John Neuhaus, "Contending for the Future: Overcoming the Pfefferian Inversion," in *Journal of Law and Religion* (1990): 115–29. The discussion described in this paragraph takes place primarily on 115–24. Esbeck also uses Neuhaus as an example of the conflation of nonestablishment into free exercise. Though he disagrees with him on this point, he agrees with Neuhaus that the establishment clause is only meant to protect religion from government, not government from religion. He does not cite this particular Neuhaus essay, but rather cites three others, the last of which is an earlier version of this essay: Richard John Neuhaus, "Proposing Democracy Anew—Part One," *First Things* (October 1999): 87–90; Neuhaus, "The Most New Thing in the Novus Ordo Seculorum," *First Things* 85 (August/September 1998): 75–90; and Neuhaus, "Establishment Is Not the Issue," *Religion and Society Report* (June 1987). These are cited in Esbeck, 323, note 39.

9. James Madison, "Memorial and Remonstrance," in *The First Liberty: America's Foundation in Religious Freedom*, ed. William Lee Miller (Washington, DC: Georgetown University Press, 2003), 259.

10. *Walz v. Tax Commission*, 397 U.S. 664 (1970), at 668–69; Miller and Flowers, eds., *Toward Benevolent Neutrality*, 317. On occasion, the Court has had to deal directly with something that could be described as tension between the two clauses. In its handling of *Walz*, the Court had to balance the claim that tax exemptions for churches constituted an establishment of religion (through subsidy) over against the understanding that taxing churches would create substantial free exercise problems. On the *Walz* case as an example of tension between the two clauses, see Derek Davis, *Original Intent: Chief Justice Rehnquist and the Course of American Church/State Relations* (Buffalo, NY: Prometheus Books, 1991), 117–19. This is a delicate balance, however, as illustrated in the Court's handling of *Texas Monthly v. Bullock*, 489 U.S. 1 (1989), where the Court decided that requiring buyers of religious periodicals to pay sales taxes does not constitute a burden on free exercise, and exempting religious publications from sales taxes does indeed violate the establishment clause.

11. Robert Handy, "Why It Took 150 Years for Supreme Court Church-State Cases to Escalate," in *An Unsettled Area: Religion and the Bill of Rights*, ed. Ronald C. White Jr. and Albright G. Zimmerman (Grand Rapids: Wm. B. Eerdmans Publishing Co., 1990), 55–56.

12. See Edwin Scott Gaustad and Philip L. Barlow, eds., *New Historical Atlas of Religion in America* (New York: Oxford University Press, 2001), 137 (Presbyterian), 98 (Congregationalists), and 100 (Episcopalians). The atlas also mentions the prediction made by Stiles, and explicitly indicates his prediction of 7 million Congregationalists; see 90.

13. Ibid., 79, 157–58, and 221.

14. See Handy, "Why It Took 150 Years," 55.

15. Edwin S. Gaustad and Leigh E. Schmidt, *The Religious History of America: The Heart of the American Story from Colonial Times to Today* (San Francisco: HarperSanFrancisco, 2002), 280.

16. *Reynolds v. United States*, 98 U.S. 145 (1879), at 164. Or see Miller and Flowers, eds., *Toward Benevolent Neutrality*, 51.

17. Miller and Flowers, eds., *Toward Benevolent Neutrality*, 49. The second Mormon case, *Davis v. Beason* (1890), used the belief-action doctrine to decide a second case associated with polygamy, but since that case, the doctrine has rarely been used as the sole justification for the Court's decision. The editors note that Professor Laurence H. Tribe has traced the Court's departure from this doctrine at considerable length in his book *The Constitutional Protection of Individual Rights: Limits on Government Authority* (Mineola, NY: Foundation Press, 1978). A particularly insightful treatment of this case is found in Catharine Cookson, *Regulating Religion: The Courts and the Free Exercise Clause* (New York: Oxford University Press, 2001), 7–12. Cookson clearly shows how the Court's decision was guided by a consideration of those things "proper for a Protestant country."

18. See *Cantwell v. Connecticut*, 310 U.S. 296 (1940), at 311; see Miller and Flowers, eds., *Toward Benevolent Neutrality*, 63. Miller and Flowers point out that the "clear and present danger" doctrine rested in the opinion of Justice Holmes in *Schenck v. United States* (1919); see 57. On the number of cases since 1938, see 55.

19. Miller and Flowers, eds., *Toward Benevolent Neutrality*, 57.

20. The case was *Minersville School District v. Gobitis*, 310 U.S. 586 (1940); see the discussion of the case by ibid., 57.

21. *Minersville School District v. Gobitis*, 310 U.S. 586 (1940), at 604.

22. *W. Virginia State Bd. of Education v. Barnette*, 319 U.S. 624 (1943), at 642; Miller and Flowers, eds., *Toward Benevolent Neutrality*, 91.

23. *Braunfeld v. Brown*, 366 U.S. 599 (1961), at 606; Miller and Flowers, eds., *Toward Benevolent Neutrality*, 381.

24. *Sherbert v. Verner*, 374 U.S. 398 (1963), at 406; Miller and Flowers, eds., *Toward Benevolent Neutrality*, 149.

25. Miller and Flowers, eds., *Toward Benevolent Neutrality*, 143.

26. The three prongs of the *Sherbert* test are clearly presented in Flowers, *That Godless Court? Supreme Court Decisions on Church-State Relationships* (Louisville, KY: Westminister John Knox Press, 1994), 30–32. *Wisconsin v. Yoder*, 406 U.S. 205 (1972), at 215; Miller and Flowers, eds., *Toward Benevolent Neutrality*, 236.

27. Flowers uses this case to make this point in *That Godless Court?* 33–34; for Burger's comments, also quoted in Flowers, see *Thomas v. Review Board of Indiana Employment Security Division*, 450 U.S. 707 (1981), at 716; Miller and Flowers, eds., *Toward Benevolent Neutrality*, 163.

28. Rehnquist speaks of the "tension" between the two clauses, and the causes for it,

at 721; Miller and Flowers, eds., *Toward Benevolent Neutrality*, 164. The extended quote here is found at 722–23. Davis raises the significance of the Rehnquist dissenting opinion in his book *Original Intent,* 120–23.

29. For the Scalia quotes, see *Employment Division v. Smith*, 494 U.S. 872 (1990), at 879 and 888; Miller and Flowers, eds., *Toward Benevolent Neutrality*, 172 and 174.

30. Scalia's hybrid argument is made at 881–82; the O'Connor quotes are found at 895 and 902–3; the Blackmun quote is at 908–9; see Miller and Flowers, eds., *Toward Benevolent Neutrality*, 173, 176, 178, and 180.

31. *City of Boerne v. Flores*, 521 U.S. 507 (1997); see Justice Kennedy's arguments at 519 and 536. This particular ruling, as argued by the majority, slapped the hand of Congress for reaching into state and local settings by reaching beyond the authority granted by the Fourteenth Amendment. For now, the Court left the RFRA intact where federal cases were concerned.

32. See O'Connor's arguments at 546–47 and this lengthy quote at 549; the historical argument made by O'Connor appears at 550–65.

33. *Cutter v. Wilkinson*, 544 U.S. (2005).

34. Flowers, *That Godless Court?* 130. A thoughtful argument on the side of *Smith*, the narrowing of interpretation of the free exercise clause, is Ellis West, "The Case Against a Right to Religion-Based Exemptions," *Notre Dame Journal of Law, Ethics & Public Policy* 3–4 (1990): 591–638.

35. A case in 1990, *Needham Pastoral Counseling Center v. Board of Appeals*, 557 N.E. 2d 43 (Mass. App. Ct. 1990), involved a pastoral counseling center attached to a seminary that used contemporary techniques in counseling, including secular techniques. A building permit to construct a center on church property was denied because the center's counseling could not be considered religious activity. See the interesting discussion of this case offered by Angela C. Carmella, "A Theological Critique of Free Exercise Jurisprudence," in *George Washington Law Review* (March 1992): 789–90. Carmella emphasizes the fact that most judges are not particularly savvy about theology and understand neither its tremendous variety nor its connections to secular discourse in the academy.

36. Flowers uses the example of the Hmong religion and its view of autopsies; see Flowers, *That Godless Court?* 168, note 14.

37. On the fact that Rehnquist's strategy is to call for a narrowing of both religion clauses, see Davis, *Original Intent,* 121–23.

38. Roberts favors dismantling the *Lemon* test, the three-pronged test used in establishment cases, in favor of the less restrictive "coercion test." The *Lemon* test requires government statutes to have a secular purpose, neither advance nor inhibit religion, and not engender "an excessive government entanglement with religion." See Flowers, *That Godless Court?* 66–67. The coercion test would allow government officials to endorse and engage in religious practices so long as listeners were not coerced to participate. O'Connor has regularly opposed this shift. See "Judge John G. Roberts Jr. Would Dismantle the Wall That Separates Church and State," on the Americans United Web site at http://www.au.org/site/Page Server?pagename=resources_talkingpoints_roberts. The reader will, of course, recognize that Americans United for Separation of Church and State represents a "strict separationist" perspective. However, their analysis of Roberts's work and that of other justices is generally accurate on Court cases. Though I would not describe myself a "strict separationist," I am a member of Americans United because the organization provides regular updates for members on all contemporary matters bearing on the relationship of church and state. I do believe broader interpretations of both the establishment clause and the free exercise

clause serve both religious groups and the state much better than narrower interpretations. My argument related to a greater accommodation of religious expression in public life appears in chapter 7.

39. Critics of Alito generally indicate he is a moderate on free exercise questions but
rather conservative on establishment questions, supporting a narrower interpretation of the establishment clause. For a summary of Alito's work on religion
clause cases, see "Report Opposing Confirmation of Samuel A. Alito Jr. as Associate Justice of the United States Supreme Court," at http://www.au.org/site/
DocServer/AU_Alito_Report.pdf?docID=401. The Baptist Joint Committee for
Religious Liberty evaluation of Alito is similar: http://www.bjcpa.org/resources/
articles/2006/060106_hollman_alito.htm. Melissa Rogers recently treated the
question of church-state as it pertains to Justice Alito in "Judging Alito," *Christian Century* (January 10, 2006): 9–11.

40. Sidney E. Mead has explored, in excellent fashion, the dynamics between rationalism and pietism and their impact on the establishment of religious liberty in
the United States in *The Lively Experiment: The Shaping of Christianity in America* (New York: Harper & Row, 1976), 38–71.

41. Stephen Carter, *The Culture of Disbelief* (New York: Basic Books, 1993).

42. I will have more to say about this point and the point at the end of the previous
paragraph in chap. 7.

43. On this point, see Franklin I. Gamwell, "Religion and the Public Purpose," *Journal of Religion* (1982): 272–88.

44. Richard John Neuhaus, *The Naked Public Square: Religion and Democracy in
America*, 2d ed. (Grand Rapids: Wm. B. Eerdmans Publishing Co., 1991).

45. Jeffrey Stout, *Democracy and Tradition* (Princeton, NJ: Princeton University
Press, 2004), 113.

46. On this point, for the "very particular religious content," what I call "priestly
faith," see chap. 4; for "cultural religious content," what I describe as "iconic
faith," see chap. 3.

47. See the discussion on these themes in Linnell E. Cady, *Religion, Theology, and
American Public Life* (New York: SUNY Press, 1993), 10f. As examples of descriptions treating the "cultural crisis" America faces in these areas, Cady mentions the
work of Daniel Bell and Christopher Lasch; see 17. Jeffrey Stout also points out
that Luther's convictions about the nature of the secular order and the work of
eighteenth-century deists and nineteenth-century atheists all contributed to the
secularization of public discourse. See Stout, *Ethics after Babel: The Languages of
Morals and Their Discontents* (Boston: Beacon Press, 1988), 80.

48. See Cady, *Religion*, 18.

49. Mary Ann Glendon, *Rights Talk: The Impoverishment of Political Discourse* (New
York: Free Press, 1991), 14. Alasdair C. MacIntyre, *After Virtue: A Study in Moral
Theory* (Notre Dame, IN: University of Notre Dame Press, 1981); Robert N. Bel-
lah, Richard Madsen, William M. Sullivan, Ann Swidler, and Steven M. Tipton,
Habits of the Heart: Individualism and Commitment in American Life (Berkeley:
University of California Press, 1985).

50. Stout, *Ethics after Babel*, 225.

51. Cady, *Religion*, 17.

52. See R. Laurence Moore, *Selling God: American Religion in the Marketplace of Culture* (New York: Oxford University Press, 1994), 6. Sociologists Roger Finke and
Rodney Stark have provided a theoretical analysis of American religion as a religious marketplace; see Finke and Stark, *The Churching of America, 1776–1990:
Winners and Losers in Our Religious Economy*, 2d ed. (New Brunswick, NJ: Rutgers University Press, 2005).

53. Marney once made this statement in my hearing when I was a seminary student in the fall of 1975.

54. Parker Palmer, *The Company of Strangers: Christians and the Renewal of America's Public Life* (New York: Crossroad, 1994), 23–24 (the longer quote is from 19).

55. Ibid., 22–23.

56. Martin Luther King Jr., *Strength to Love* (New York: Harper & Row, 1963), 31, 38.

57. Robert N. Bellah, Richard Madsen, William M. Sullivan, Ann Swidler, and Steven M. Tipton, *The Good Society* (New York: Alfred A. Knopf, 1991), 182.

58. See Cady, *Religion*, 23; Marty's quote, found there, comes from Martin E. Marty, *The Public Church* (New York: Crossroad, 1981), 16.

59. Alexis de Tocqueville, *Democracy in America,* translated, edited, and with an introduction by Harvey C. Mansfield and Delba Winthrop (Chicago: University of Chicago Press, 2000). For details on the routes he took across America, see the "Editors' Introduction," lv. For Tocqueville's comments on individualism, see 482f.; for his comments on the influence of religion on public virtue, see 280–81; also the sections dealing with religion and American culture in vol. 2.

60. Bellah et al., *Habits of the Heart*, 50.

61. Bellah et al., *Good Society*, 180, 184.

62. Marty, *Public Church,* 16–17 (the longer quote is found on 3).

63. Ibid., 136.

64. H. Richard Niebuhr, *The Responsible Self: An Essay in Christian Moral Philosophy* (Louisville, KY: Westminister John Knox Press, 1999), 45, 66–67; the longer quote is from 65 and 67. This book was originally published in 1963.

65. These points are made by James M. Gustafson in his introduction to *Responsible Self,* 32 and 35.

66. I have covered this debate between mainline Protestantism and Catholicism and its implications for the role of the public church in Toulouse, "Perspectives on Abortion in the Christian Community from the 1950s to the Early 1990s," *Encounter* (Autumn 2001): 327–403; on homosexuality and the public church, see Toulouse, "Muddling Through: The Church and Sexuality/Homosexuality," in *Homosexuality, Science, and the "Plain Sense" of Scripture*, ed. David Balch (Grand Rapids: Wm. B. Eerdmans Publishing Co., 2000), 6–41; or Toulouse, "The Muddled Middle: Protestantism's Encounter with Homosexuality since the 1960s," in *Sex, Religion, Media*, ed. Dane S. Claussen (Boulder, CO: Rowman & Littlefield, 2002), 43–63.

67. Bellah et al., *Good Society*, 181–82.

68. Michael Perry, *Love and Power: The Role of Religion and Morality in American Politics* (New York: Oxford University Press, 1991), 73.

69. Palmer, *Company of Strangers*, 29.

70. Carter, *Culture of Disbelief,* 36.

71. Palmer, *Company of Strangers*, 22.

Chapter 3: Iconic Faith

1. See http://www.m-w.com/cgi-bin/dictionary?book=Dictionary&va=icon.

2. Robert Wuthnow, *The Restructuring of American Religion: Society and Faith Since World War II* (Princeton, NJ: Princeton University Press, 1988), 10.

3. See Clifford Geertz, "Religion as a Cultural System," in *Anthropological Approaches to the Study of Religion*, ed. Michael Banton (London: Tavistock Publications, 1966), 1–46; esp. 3–4. The essay was first presented by Geertz at a Conference on "New Approaches in Social Anthropology," sponsored by the

Association of Social Anthropologists of the Commonwealth, held at Jesus College, Cambridge, 24–30 June 1963. Banton's book is a collection of those essays.

4. Ninian Smart, *The Religious Experience of Mankind*, 2d ed. (New York: Charles Scribner's Sons, 1976), esp. 6–12.

5. The motto is "Rebellion to Tyrants is Obedience to God." See Web site, "Religion and the Founding of the American Republic," especially where Lossing's version of the proposed seal is located: http://www.loc.gov/exhibits/religion/vc006418.jpg.

6. Cotton Mather and Timothy Dwight both made the comparisons. See as well, James H. Smylie, "The President as Republican Prophet and King: Clerical Reflections on the Death of Washington," *Journal of Church and State* 18 (Spring 1976): 233–53; and Robert P. Hay, "George Washington: American Moses," *American Quarterly* 21 (Winter 1969): 780–91.

7. See http://www.greatseal.com/ for information on how the "eye of God" became incorporated into the Great Seal.

8. *Sightings* is an Internet newsletter dealing with religion and public life, produced by the Marty Center of the University of Chicago Divinity School. See David Domke and Kevin Coe, "Petitioner or Prophet?" *Sightings* (May 26, 2005). The index for *Sightings* is found at http://marty-center.uchicago.edu/sightings/index.shtml.

9. Rob Boston, "No King But Jesus," *Church & State* (February 2001): 4.

10. Conrad Cherry, ed., *God's New Israel: Religious Interpretations of American Destiny*, rev. ed. (Chapel Hill: University of North Carolina Press, 1998), esp. 11.

11. The text of President George W. Bush's second inaugural is found at http://www.whitehouse.gov/news/releases/2005/01/20050120-1.html.

12. See Bennett, "Seizing this Teachable Moment," in *September 11: What Our Children Need to Know* (Thomas Fordham Foundation, September 2002), 16. This booklet is found on the Web at http://www.edexcellence.net/doc/September11.pdf.

13. Bruce Lincoln, "The Theology of George W. Bush," *Christian Century* (hereafter, *CC*) (October 5, 2004): 25.

14. Sidney E. Mead, *The Lively Experiment: The Shaping of Christianity in America* (New York: Harper & Row, 1976), 152. Conrad Cherry uses this illustration from Mead as well in his Introduction in *God's New Israel*. See 17.

15. Mead, *The Lively Experiment*, 66–68.

16. Cherry, *God's New Israel*, 13.

17. See Marty's essay "Scripturality: The Bible as Icon in the Republic," in *Religion & Republic: The American Circumstance* (Boston: Beacon Press, 1987), 140–65. The essay is also published as Marty, "America's Iconic Book," in *Humanizing America's Iconic Book*, ed. Gene M. Tucker and Douglas A. Knight (Chico, CA: Scholars Press, 1980). Originally, Marty delivered the address at the centennial meeting of the Society of Biblical Literature meeting in Dallas, at the Loews Anatole Hotel, in November 1980.

18. Ibid., 145.

19. This particular poll was conducted between November 7–10, 2004, and between December 5–8, 2004. See Josephine Mazzuca, "U.S. vs. Canada: Different Reads on the Good Book," the Gallup Organization at http://www.galluppoll.com/content/?ci=14512. Full content is available only to Gallup Poll on Demand subscribers.

20. See Albert L. Winseman, "Teens' Stance on the Word of God," the Gallup Organization at http://www.galluppoll.com/content/?ci=15313. This poll was conducted January 17–February 6, 2005. Full content is available only to Gallup Poll on Demand subscribers.

21. See Jennifer Harper, "Most Americans Take Bible Stories Literally," *The Washington Times* (February 17, 2004) at http://www.washtimes.com/national/20040216-113955-2061r.htm.

22. See Jennifer Robison, "In the Beginning Was the Word," the Gallup Organization at http://www.galluppoll.com/content/?ci=5671. This poll was taken during October 2000. Full content is available only to Gallup Poll on Demand subscribers.

23. Alec Gallup and Wendy W. Simmons, "Six in Ten Americans Read Bible at Least Occasionally: Percentage of Frequent Readers Has Decreased Over Last Decade," the Gallup Organization, http://www.galluppoll.com/content/?ci=2416. Full content is available only to Gallup Poll on Demand subscribers.

24. Quoted in Marty, *Religion & Republic*, 145. Elwell's comments originally appeared in "Belief and the Bible: A Crisis of Authority," *Christianity Today* (hereafter *CT*) (March 21, 1980): 19–23.

25. See Marty, *Religion & Republic*, 144–45.

26. George Gallup Jr. and D. Michael Lindsay, *Surveying the Religious Landscape: Trends in U.S. Beliefs* (Harrisburg, PA: Morehouse Publishing, 1999), 35, 49–50.

27. Marty makes this point. See *Religion & Republic*, 147.

28. John Wilson insightfully raises this point in *Public Religion in American Culture* (Philadelphia: Temple University Press, 1979), 77.

29. See "Court Orders 'God' Into Oath," *Washington Post*, June 30, 2004, A22; for the quote from Honeycutt, see http://www3.baylor.edu/Church_State/Notes2004Autumn.htm#United_States.

30. "President Reagan and the Bible: He Speaks Out Strongly for the Importance of Scripture," *CT* (March 4, 1983): 46–47, 50. Lengthy excerpts from the text of Reagan's address are presented here.

31. "President's Remarks to the Nation," Ellis Island, September 11, 2002, speech is found at http://www.whitehouse.gov/news/releases/2002/09/20020911–3.html. A student named Trent Williams brought this particular address to my attention in the fall of 2005 after a lecture in class dealing with the unique meanings presidents often give to Bible passages by the context within which they use them.

32. Reagan's address is quoted in Dean Peerman, "Presidential Proof-texting," *CC* (February 20, 1985): 176.

33. *Abington School District v. Schempp*, 374 U.S. 203 (1963), 269.

34. See ibid., 223–24 and 269–70.

35. See Marty, *Religion & Republic*, 150.

36. See Mark A. Noll, *One Nation Under God? Christian Faith & Political Action in America* (San Francisco: Harper & Row, 1988), 172.

37. See Kenneth Woodward, "Talking to God," *Newsweek,* January 6, 1992, 38–39.

38. All these statistics and these cases, in this paragraph and the preceding one, are discussed in Linda Lyons, "The Gallup Brain: Prayer in Public Schools," the Gallup Organization (December 10, 2002), found at http://www.galluppoll.com/content/?ci=7393. The poll data on offering nondenominational prayers at public school ceremonies is drawn from a poll taken between September 19–21, 2003. A summary of that particular poll is found in Frank Newport, "Americans Approve of Public Displays of Religious Symbols," the Gallup Organization (October 3, 2003), found at http://www.galluppoll.com/content/?ci=9391. Full content is available only to Gallup Poll on Demand subscribers.

39. See Terrence Stutz, "Time for Prayer in Schools Urged," *Dallas Morning News*, March 21, 1995, 11A.

40. David Barton, *America, To Pray or Not to Pray: A Statistical Look at What Has Happened Since 39 Million Students Were Ordered to Stop Praying in Public Schools* (Aledo, TX: Specialty Research Associates, 1988).

41. On the relationship between education and the demise of the traditional family, see Allan C. Carlson and Bryce J. Christensen, "Of Two Minds: The Educational and Cultural Effects of Family Dissolution," *The Family in America* 2, no. 8 (August 1988); and Ann M. Milne, "Family Structure and the Achievement of Children," in *Education and the American Family: A Research Synthesis*, ed. William J. Weston (New York: New York University Press, 1989).

42. *Wallace v. Jaffree*, 472 U.S. 38 (1985), at 67.

43. *Wallace v. Jaffree*, 472 U.S. 38 (1985).

44. These talking points, revised in July 2003, are found on the Americans United Web site at http://www.au.org/site/DocServer/Moment_Of_Silence_Legislation .pdf?docID=152.

45. *Stein v. Plainwell Community Schools*, 862 F.2ds 824 (6th Cir. 1987).

46. See the discussion of this case in Michael M. Maddigan, "The Establishment Clause, Civil Religion, and the Public Church," *California Law Review* 81, no. 293 (1993): 342–43.

47. Michael Kessler makes this point as well in a *Sightings* column that was also published in *Circa*. See Michael Kessler, "A Place for Prayer?" *Circa* (Spring 2005): 8–10.

48. See Elliott Wright, "Changing Cultural Habits: 'Particular' and 'Common' in the Struggle Over Religion in Public Education, 1944–1994," unpublished paper presented to the Church-State Study Group at the American Academy of Religion, November 20, 1993, p. 10. See also Charles L. Glenn and Joshua L. Glenn, "Making Room for Religious Conviction in Democracy's Schools," in *Schooling Christians: 'Holy Experiments' in American Education,* ed. Stanley Hauerwas and John H. Westerhoff (Grand Rapids: Wm. B. Eerdmans Publishing Co., 1992).

49. There is a good discussion of the way some school districts have begun to become more responsible in examining the role of religion in American life and history, especially in light of the Williamsburg Charter (1988). See Charles C. Haynes, "From Battleground to Common Ground," in *Religion in American Public Life: Living with Our Deepest Differences*, ed. Azizah Y. al-Hibri, Jean Bethke Elshtain, and Charles C. Haynes (New York: W. W. Norton, 2001), 98–115. A recent issue of *CC* also contained an article dealing with the topic of the Bible in public schools by reviewing the new book for public education edited by Cullen Schippe and Chuck Stetson, *The Bible and Its Influence* (Fairfax, VA: BLP Publishing, 2005); see Luke Timothy Johnson, "Textbook Case: A Bible Curriculum for Public Schools," *CC* (February 21, 2006): 34–37; for an alternative view, see Joseph L. Conn, "The Bible Literacy Project: Chuck Stetson's Trojan Horse," *Church & State* (January 2006): 19–21.

50. For those seeking a full history of the Pledge of Allegiance, one that connects it to five anxieties of the time (anxieties about immigration, radicals, communism, and the effects of capitalism and unrestricted individual liberties), see Richard J. Ellis, *To the Flag: The Unlikely History of the Pledge of Allegiance* (Lawrence: University Press of Kansas, 2005).

51. See Louis Harris, *The Flag Over the Schoolhouse*, in the C. A. Stephens Collection, Brown University, Providence, RI (1971), 69; this source is quoted in John W. Baer, "The Pledge of Allegiance: A Centennial History, 1892–1992," see http://history.vineyard.net/pdgech0.htm.

52. Quoted in Baer.

53. Quoted in Rob Martin's sermon titled "False Promises—The Real History of Our Pledge." Martin is pastor of First Presbyterian Church of Palo Alto, California. See the congregation's Web site: http://www.fprespa.org/falsepromises.htm. John

W. Baer discusses this point in chapter 4 of his "The Pledge of Allegiance: A Centennial History, 1892–1992," in the section titled "Liberty and Justice for All." Chapter 4 is found on the Internet at http://history.vineyard.net/pdgech4.htm.

54. The program is found in *The Youth's Companion* 65 (1892): 446–47. It is also reproduced at http://historymatters.gmu.edu/d/5762/ and in Baer, "The Pledge of Allegiance."

55. The first law passed in June of 1942 under H. J. Res. 303, 56 stat. 377, ch. 435—this quote is from section 7. This was originally codified in the U.S. Code Collection at 36 U.S.C. § 172 [now 4 USC 4]; see Web site http://caselaw.lp.findlaw.com/casecode/uscodes/4/chapters/1/sections/section_4_notes.html.

56. This point is made in the Supreme Court case *West Virginia State Board of Education v. Barnette*, 319 U.S. 624 (1943), at 627–28.

57. The change was made Dec. 22, 1942, ch. 806, § 7, 56 stat. 1077. See 36 USC chapter 10. History of the code is shown on the following Web site: http://resource.1800attorney.com/Content/Legal_Research/US_code/Title_36/title_36_10.htm. Evidently, in spite of the change in the code made in December 1942, the West Virginia State Board of Education still required the "stiff arm" salute with expulsion from school being dealt to those who, through "insubordination," failed to conform. The Supreme Court ruled in this case, involving a Jehovah's Witness child's refusal to participate, that school children could not be forced to say the Pledge of Allegiance. Justice Robert H. Jackson wrote the opinion, in which he said, "If there is any fixed star in our constitutional constellation, it is that no official, high or petty, can prescribe what shall be orthodox in politics, nationalism, religion or other matters of opinion or force citizens to confess by word or act their faith therein." *West Virginia State Board of Education v. Barnette*, 319 U.S. 624 (1943), at 642. Justice Jackson's opinion in this case built on Justice Harlon Stone's excellent dissenting opinion written in the case three years earlier, which had ruled that school districts could require students to salute the flag in spite of their religious objections to the practice. The *West Virginia Board of Education* case, in essence, reconsidered and reversed the earlier decision in *Minersville School District v. Gobitis* 310 U.S. 586 (1940).

58. June 14, 1954, ch. 297, 68 stat. 249.

59. "Out from Under God," *Newsweek*, August 19, 2002, 12.

60. See *Michael A. Newdow v. US Congress*, 9124. The full text of the case's opinion is found at http://www.ca9.uscourts.gov/ca9/newopinions.nsf/FE05EEE79C2A97B688256BE3007FEE32/$file/0016423.pdf?openelement.

61. Quoted in ibid., 9125–26.

62. Quoted in ibid., 9127.

63. As mentioned in an earlier footnote, the court case was *West Virginia State Board of Education v. Barnette*, 319 U.S. 624 (1943).

64. *West Virginia State Board of Education v. Barnette*, 319 U.S. 624 (1943), at 642; this is also quoted by the Ninth Circuit opinion in *Newdow v. U.S. Congress*, 9111, note 3.

65. *Newdow v. U.S. Congress*, 9122.

66. "Pledge of Allegiance ruling logical to a fault," Guest Editorial, *Pittsburgh Post-Gazette*, June 26, 2002; see http://www.naplesnews.com/02/06/perspective/d787977a.htm.

67. *Newdow v. U.S. Congress*, 9124.

68. Ibid., 9135–36.

69. This exchange is found on page 36 of the transcript of the hearing on March 24, 2004. The transcript is found online at http://www.supremecourtus.gov/oral_arguments/argument_transcripts/02-1624.pdf.

70. This exchange, discussing ceremonial deism, is found on pp. 39 and 40 of the transcript. For an examination of Justice David Souter's role in First Amendment cases, see John A. Fliter, "Keeping the Faith: Justice David Souter and the First Amendment Religion Clauses," *Journal of Church & State* (Spring 1998): 387–410.

71. See *Elk Grove Unified School District and David W. Gordon, Superintendent v. Michael A. Newdow, et.al.,* 542 U.S. 1 (2004). The opinion can be found online at http://caselaw.lp.findlaw.com/cgi-bin/getcase.pl?court=US&navby=case&vol =000&invol=02-1624. Newdow filed suit again, in early 2005, joining with other parents who have custodial rights to sue.

72. Olson's comments are found on pp. 16–17 of the transcript; the Cassidy exchange is found on p. 54 of the transcript, having taken place during his time for rebuttal following Newdow's presentation to the Court.

73. Martin E. Marty, *Second Chance for American Protestants* (New York: Harper & Row, 1963), 59f.

74. Ibid., ix, 3, and 8.

Chapter 4: Priestly Faith

1. These few paragraphs rely on Glenn F. Chestnut's excellent chapter, appearing for the first time in his "revised and enlarged edition" of *The First Christian Histories: Eusebius, Socrates, Sozomen, Theodoret, and Evagius* (Macon, GA: Mercer University Press, 1986), 111–40. The chapter is titled "Eusebius: From Youthful Defender of Religious Liberty to Spokesman for the Constantinian Imperial Church." See Eusebius, *Life of Constantine,* in *Nicene and Post-Nicene Fathers,* trans. E. C. Richardson (Grand Rapids: Wm. B. Eerdmans Publishing Co., 1961), 481–559. Eusebius was not alone in his understanding of the divine role of the empire. Others, including John Chrysostom in the East and Ambrose in the West, shared some of these sentiments. Johannes van Oort gives some particular attention to the work of Paulus Orosius, Augustine's "close assistant," who viewed the Roman Empire as "chosen" by God. For Orosius, "it was not coincidental that Christ came into the world a *Roman* citizen." See Johannes van Oort, *Jerusalem and Babylon: A Study into Augustine's* City of God *and the Sources of His Doctrine of the Two Cities* (Leiden: E. J. Brill, 1991), esp. 154–63.

2. Max Weber, *Sociology of Religion* (Boston: Beacon Press, 1963), 29.

3. Joachim Wach, *Sociology of Religion* (Chicago: University of Chicago Press, 1971), 365.

4. Quoted on http://www.geocities.com/capitolhill/7027/quotes.html.

5. Pat Oliphant, copyright 1980. Distributed by Universal Press Syndicate.

6. Pat Robertson, *The New World Order* (Dallas: Word Publishing, 1991), 218.

7. Randall Terry, founder of Operation Rescue, quoted in "Terry Preaches Theocratic Rule: 'No More Mr. Nice Christian' Is the Pro-Life Activist's Theme for the '90s," *The News-Sentinel* (Fort Wayne, Indiana), August 16, 1993, 1A.

8. See Dana Milbanks, "Religious Right Finds Its Center in Oval Office: Bush Emerges as Movement's Leader after Robertson Leaves Christian Coalition," *Washington Post,* December 24, 2001, A2.

9. Bill Keller, "God and George W. Bush," *New York Times,* May 17, 2003, A17.

10. Walter Capps, *The New Religious Right: Piety, Patriotism, and Politics* (Columbia: University of South Carolina Press, 1994), 19.

11. Conrad Cherry, ed., *God's New Israel: Religious Interpretations of American Destiny* (Chapel Hill: University of North Carolina Press, 1998), 20.

12. Ibid., p. 21.

13. Quoted in "Terry Preaches Theocratic Rule."

14. This story was published in various national news sources. See, for example, "Democrats Voted Out of Their Church Because of Their Politics," *USA Today*, May 7, 2005. The article is posted on the Web at http://www.usatoday.com/news/nation/2005-05-07-church-politics_x.htm.

15. Thomas G. Paterson, J. Garry Clifford, and Kenneth J. Hagan relate this anecdote in their *American Foreign Policy: A History/Since 1900*, 2d ed. (Lexington, MA: D. C. Heath and Co., 1983), 494. More detail on all the foreign policy events of these years may be found on 480–514.

16. On Sputnik, see "1957–1958," *Christian Century* (January 1, 1958): 6–7. This editorial referred to Sputnik as "a crisis in contemporary history. . . . It meant, if not an end for, at least a sharp shock to, some of their deepest preconceptions about themselves. . . . One preconception that is now inescapably tabbed a misconception is our unspoken assumption of a kind of general, built-in American superiority."

17. On education, see "Is Military Necessity a Basis for Education?" *Christian Century* (hereafter *CC*)(April 17, 1957): 477; "Are Technocrats Our Greatest Need?" *CC* (November 27, 1957): 1404; and "Education Act Shows Impressive Results," *CC* (September 16, 1957): 1045.

18. Richard W. Gray, "God, America and Sputnik," *Christianity Today* (hereafter *CT*) (December 9, 1957): 15–17. See also the article by Price Daniel, governor of Texas, "God and the American Vision," *CT* 2 (June 23, 1958): 13–14, where he assured readers Americans were "ahead of the Russian communists in that we have contact with God, and unless they are converted from their atheistic beliefs, they will never catch up with us."

19. Dulles, in many ways, represented priestly nationalism powerfully throughout his term as Secretary of State during the Eisenhower years. See Mark G. Toulouse, *The Transformation of John Foster Dulles: From Prophet of Realism to Priest of Nationalism* (Macon, GA: Mercer University Press, 1985).

20. Joseph M. Dawson, "The Christian View of the State," *CT* (June 24, 1957): 3–5.

21. In reviewing J. Paul Williams's book, *The New Education and Religion*, a 1963 editorial deemed the teaching of patriotism and democracy as "essential," but resisted exalting either "to the high level of religion. . . . These are 'other gods.'" See "Some Overtones," editorial, *CT* (October 11, 1963): 28.

22. "The Church and Public Relations," *CT* (April 14, 1958): 20–22; "Even the Devil Wears a Smile," *CT* (February 2, 1959): 22–23. All the editorials and articles addressing the topic during these years come from much the same perspective: for example, "Christian Responsibility and Communist Brutality," *CT* (November 26, 1956): 24; "Summit Talks—Useful or Communist Trap," *CT* (February 3, 1958): 21–22; "The Christian Citizen in the World Conflict," *CT* (October 27, 1958): 21; "The Christian's Duty in the Present Crisis," *CT* (January 5, 1959): 22; Frederick G. Schwarz, "Can We Meet the Red Challenge," *CT* (April 13, 1959): 12–14; Henry, "Christianity and Communism," *CT* 5 (April 24, 1961): 12–13; "Red Is Red After All," *CT* (December 4, 1964): 31; "Gamal Abdel Nasser," *CT* (October 23, 1970): 29; "The Demands of Detente," *CT* (August 29, 1975): 26. J. Edgar Hoover described communism as "Satanic." See, Hoover, "The Communist Menace: Red Goals and Christian Ideals," *CT* (October 10, 1960): 3–5.

23. "Marxism: A Missing Person Report," *CT* (May 23, 1975): 43–44; G. Aiken Taylor, "Why Communism Is Godless," *CT* (December 22, 1958): 13–14; "The Christian's Duty in the Present Crisis," *CT* (January 5, 1959): 22; David V. Benson, "Reflections on Communist Atheism," *CT* (April 13, 1959): 15–16; "NAE Reaffirms Strong Anti-Communist Stand," *CT* (May 9, 1960): 30; Harold John

Ockenga, "The Communist Issue Today," *CT* (May 22, 1961): 721–24; "The Evangelical Offensive in Contemporary Life," *CT* (January 5, 1962): 330–31; J. Edgar Hoover, "Spiritual Priorities: Guidelines for a Civilization in Peril," *CT* (June 22, 1962): 3–4; "On the Brink of a New Order," *CT* (December 21, 1962): 24–26 (this whole issue is subtitled "Confronting Communism"); Billy Graham, "Facing the Anti-God Colossus," *CT* (December 21, 1962), 6–8; A. Culver Gordon, "Theistic or Secular Government," *CT* (April 26, 1963): 12–13; "Communist Assault on Christian Faith," *CT* (August 27, 1965): 3–4. See E. L. H. Taylor, "Can a Christian Be a Communist?" *CT* (May 25, 1962): 39. Even the NCC agreed that "no truly committed Communist would favor or accept any kind of religion. . . . The Communist has no God and, therefore, no conscience . . . and no divine law as basic universal code of morality and human decency." Quoted in "Christianity and Communism," *CT* (March 16, 1962): 26–29.

24. Hoover, "The Challenge of the Future," *CT* (May 26, 1958): 3–4; Hoover, "Communism: The Bitter Enemy of Religion," *CT* (June 22, 1959): 3–5; Hoover, "Soviet Rule or Christian Renewal?" *CT* (November 7, 1960): 8–11; other articles written by Hoover include "The Communist Menace: Red Goals and Christian Ideals," *CT* (October 10, 1960): 3–5; "Communist Propaganda and the Christian Pulpit," *CT* (October 24, 1960): 5–7; "What Does the Future Hold?" *CT* (June 19, 1961): 10–12; "Spiritual Priorities: Guidelines for a Civilization in Peril," *CT* (June 22, 1962): 3–4; "Storming the Skies: Christianity Encounters Communism," *CT* (December 21, 1961): 3–5; "The Strength of a Nation," *CT* (November 23, 1962): 50; "The Faith of Our Fathers," *CT* (September 11, 1964): 6–7; "An Analysis of the New Left: A Gospel of Nihilism," *CT* (August 18, 1967): 3–6.

25. Member churches of the NCC found themselves continually charged with harboring members and ministers with communist affiliations. One Air Force Training Manual even went so far as to state that 30 of the 95 persons who worked on the Revised Standard Version (RSV) of the Bible "have been affiliated with pro-Communist fronts, projects, and publications." See "Air Force Training Manual Draws NCC Fire," news, *CT* (February 29, 1960): 29. The writer of the manual was Homer H. Hyde, who said "he had relied on information from Oklahoma evangelist Billy James Hargis of the Christian Crusade and M. G. Lowman of the Circuit Riders." See "A Crude Hassle," news, *CT* (March 14, 1960): 29. Not all such charges came from the government or from far-right organizations. Many of the essays in *CT* either implied a connection or explicitly stated a connection between "liberal" church leaders and the Communist Party. See, for example, Paul B. Denlinger, "The Bleak Harvest of the Liberal Protestant World Thrust," *CT* (March 14, 1960): 3–5; Harold John Ockenga, "The Communist Issue Today," *CT* (May 22, 1961): 721–24; J. Howard Pew, "The Church in Secular Affairs," *CT* (April 11, 1960): 8–11; "United Presbyterians and Angela Davis," editorial, *CT* (July 16, 1971): 21; "The Making of a Revolutionary," editorial, *CT* (January 5, 1973): 30.

26. See "Tribute in a Window," *CT* (July 22, 1966): 43. Strong support of these federal agencies and their leadership has been consistent in the journal: see "The CIA in the Spotlight," *CT* (February 14, 1975): 44; "In Strategy We Trust," *CT* (July 18, 1975): 21; and "High Honor," *CT* (May 23, 1975): 58.

27. "Red China and World Morality," *CT* (December 10, 1956): 20–22. This topic received a great deal of press, especially since the NCC recommended admission of China to the United Nations; for the "anti" position of *CT* see also William F. Knowland, Senate Majority Leader, "Admit Red China," *CT* (October 29, 1956): 10–11; "American Baptists Support U.S. Red China Policy," *CT* (June 22, 1959): 27; Frank Farrell, "Southern Presbyterians Challenge NCC Study," *CT*

(May 11, 1959): 23, 33; "The NCC General Board and Protestant Commitments," *CT* (March 2, 1959): 22–23; "Dulles Gone: World Peace Still an Elusive Hope," *CT* (June 8, 1959): 22; Emil Brunner, "A Fresh Appraisal: The Cleveland Report on Red China," *CT* (April 25, 1960): 3–6. The position began to change in 1971, when it became clear that China might "provide a balance of power to the Soviets, who share with China a very tense border." See "The Peking Gambit," *CT* (August 6, 1971): 24–25. Editors also came to hail the establishment of diplomatic relations with China as perhaps doing "more to bring an end to the war [Vietnam] than anything done in Paris so far." See "Viet Nam—Continuing Impasse," *CT* (August 6, 1971): 25.

28. "Exporting Democracy," *CT* (November 8, 1974): 29; see also "No More Bad Guys?" *CT* (May 12, 1989): 16.

29. See, for example, "Still the Evil Empire?" *CT* (July 15, 1988): 14–15. This editorial points out that "the Bible advocates neither modern democracy nor Marxism. Rather, it offers much more basic rules of thumb by which to measure the effectiveness of political systems . . . a good government does two things: it keeps the peace and promotes the common good."

30. Lyn Cryderman, "No More Bad Guys?" *CT* (May 12, 1989): 16; see also Anita and Peter Deyneka, "Russian Revolution?" *CT* (October 20, 1989): 22–25; and Kim A. Lawton, "Echoes of Glasnost," *CT* (October 20, 1989): 26–28.

31. Anticommunism in general is evident in "What Is Behind the War Scare?" and "That Unthinkable War Could Break Loose," editorials in *CC* (October 30, 1957): 1276; see also Reinhold Niebuhr, "Why Is Barth Silent on Hungary?" *CC* (January 23, 1957): 108–10; "When Containment Fails, What Next?" *CC* (December 18, 1957): 1499; "Russians Pull Ahead in the Space Race," *CC* (January 14, 1959): 37–38. The editorial "Confronting Communism" is found in *CC* (November 15, 1961): 1355–56.

32. For China, see "No Change in China Policy," *CC* (July 10, 1957): 835; on space, see "High Up Is Too Much," *CC* (May 24, 1961): 645; "Shall We Escape to the Moon?" *CC* (June 14, 1961): 732; "Claiming the Moon," *CC* (August 19, 1964): 1028.

33. "Defeat or Debacle?" *CC* (May 3, 1961): 547. The *CC* believed the government should have been more accepting of Castro's victory over Batista in early 1959. They published articles detailing the atrocities of the Batista regime shortly after Castro took power. Though they were not Castro supporters and became increasingly dismayed over his growing alignment with Moscow, they felt the U.S. had made several serious mistakes in its Cuban policy. See "Cuba Should Learn From Puerto Rico," *CC* (January 14, 1950): 36–37; Carleton Beals, "Cuba in Revolution," *CC* (February 4, 1959): 130–32; Beals, "Cost of Dictatorship in Cuba," *CC* (February 11, 1959): 165–67; "What Is Happening in Cuba?" *CC* (March 7, 1962): 286; "The Enemy Within," *CC* (November 7, 1962): 1343–44. On the recognition of East Germany, see "Time to Turn," *CC* (August 30, 1961): 1019–20.

34. "Universal Moral Myopia," *CC* (September 4, 1968): 1095–96.

35. Copies of various State of the Union addresses may be found at http://www .gpoaccess.gov/sou/.

36. "Give Us the Truth, Mr. President!" *CC* (April 25, 1962): 514.

37. See the following editorials: "Vietnam Regime Ends in Blood," *CC* (November 13, 1963): 1392; "Southeast Asia Next," *CC* (June 27, 1963): 799–800; "More War or Less in Vietnam?" *CC* (March 11, 1964): 326; "Getting Out of Vietnam," *CC* (December 23, 1964): 1582–83; "Urge Cease-Fire in South Vietnam," *CC* (January 13, 1965): 37. "Neutralization," *Commonweal* (February 14, 1964): 584–85; Reinhold Niebuhr, "President Johnson's Foreign Policy," *Christianity &*

Crisis (March 16, 1964): 31–32; the description of American involvement as a "defense of freedom" is found in Kenneth W. Thompson, "Deepening Crisis in Southeast Asia," *Christianity & Crisis* (June 22, 1964): 121–22; John C. Bennett defended the "justification of conducting a holding operation to prevent outright defeat, but too often," he wrote, "the American people are led to expect outright victory." See Bennett, "Questions About Vietnam," *Christianity & Crisis* (July 20, 1964): 141–42; "Fog Over Vietnam," *America* (March 7, 1964): 305–6; "McNamara's Mission," *America* (March 21, 1964): 355.

38. Fey, "Goldwater? No!" *CC* (July 1, 1964): 851. Haselden, "Johnson? Yes!" *CC* (September 9, 1964): 1099–1100; see also "A Time for Cool Heads and Steady Hands," *CC* (October 28, 1964): 1323–24. Self-righteousness about the necessity of support for Johnson over Goldwater is also evident in "The Churches' Mandate," *CC* (November 18, 1964): 1419–20.

39. John C. Bennett, "The Goldwater Nomination," *Christianity & Crisis* (August 3, 1964): 157–58; "We Oppose Goldwater," *Christianity & Crisis* (October 5, 1964): 181–83.

40. "Nothing Personal, Mr. President," *CC* (May 26, 1965): 667–68.

41. "Of Betrayal and Loyalty," *CC* (June 30, 1971): 792–93; James M. Wall, "Don't Say 'Nuts' to the IRS," *CC* (July 16–23, 1980): 723–24.

42. "An Echo, Not a Choice," *CC* (August 19, 1964): 1028–29. "Congress and the Undeclared War," *CC* (February 16, 1966): 195–96.

43. "Putting God on the Ballot," *CT* (November 6, 1964): 29; Paul Ramsey, writing for *Crisis,* leveled the charge of "idolatry" against the "Liberal Religious Establishment." See Ramsey, "Is God Mute in the Goldwater Candidacy?" *Christianity & Crisis* (September 21, 1964): 175–79.

44. "Halting Red Aggression in Viet Nam," *CT* (April 23, 1965): 32; see also "The Ground of Freedom," *CT* (July 3, 1964): 20–21; "The Last Battle in Asia," *CT* (June 19, 1964): 23; "Ignorance Often Has a Loud Voice," *CT* (February 12, 1965): 35; "A Time to Speak," *CT* (May 21, 1965): 26; "Religious Coalition in Washington," *CT* (May 21, 1965): 38; William K. Harrison, "Is the United States Right in Bombing North Viet Nam?" *CT* (January 7, 1966): 25–26; "Viet Nam: Where Do We Go from Here?" *CT* (January 7, 1966): 30–31; "The WCC and Viet Nam," *CT* (March 4, 1966): 31; "The Church and the Viet Nam Bound Soldier," *CT* (May 13, 1966): 30–31; "Dry Socks and Letters from Home," *CT* (December 23, 1966): 20–21; "Are Churchmen Failing Servicemen in Viet Nam?" *CT* (August 18, 1967): 30–31.

45. "Dodging the Draft," *CT* (November 5, 1965): 36; see also "The New Spirit of Defiance," *CT* (December 23, 1966): 19–20; "Ending Campus Chaos," *CT* 13 (February 28, 1969): 27. The NAE actually declared it treason at an April meeting in Denver in 1966. See "National University Proposed at NAE," *CT* 10 (May 13, 1966): 47–48.

46. "Viet Nam Profile," advertisement in *CT* (November 19, 1965): 16–17.

47. "Honesty in Government," *CT* (March 26, 1971): 25; see also "The Calley Verdict," *CT* (April 23, 1971): 27.

48. "Editor's Note . . . " *CT* (May 7, 1971): 3.

49. "The Right to Know," *CT* (July 16, 1971): 22–23.

50. "Shutting Down the Government," *CT* (May 21, 1971): 35.

51. "The Viet Nam Pact," *CT* (February 16, 1973): 34. Though the journal continued to support financial aid and military advisement in Vietnam, it maintained that America should never have become involved in the sending of military troops. See "The Indochina Fiasco," *CT* 19 (April 25, 1975): 27; and "What to Remember About Viet Nam," *CT* 19 (May 23, 1975): 45–46.

52. "Archbishop Rebukes Racists," *America* (October 29, 1955): 114; see also Reinhold Niebuhr, "The Race Problem in America," *Christianity & Crisis* (December 26, 1955): 169–70.

53. Gayraud S. Wilmore Jr., "The New Negro and the Church," *CC* (February 6, 1963): 169–71.

54. For Simon's article, see Paul Simon, "Montgomery Looks Forward," *CC* (January 22, 1958): 104–5.

55. For a record of Greeley's comments, see Greeley, "No More 'Radicals'?" *America* (March 19, 1960): 733–35. For the southern minister's diatribe, see Roy C. DeLamotte, "Southern Liberal: Prophet or Apostate?" *CC* (May 1, 1957): 555–56. On Niebuhr, see Niebuhr, "The Race Problem in America," *Christianity & Crisis* (December 26, 1955): 169. For Wilmore, see "The New Negro and the Church."

56. Most essays during this period in mainline Christian journals stressed the immorality of segregation. See "A Sense of the Essential," *CC* (September 18, 1957): 1092, where the editor stresses that "moral factors make the crucial difference in a world choosing up sides"; and Robert McAfee Brown, "Levittown and Little Rock," *Christianity & Crisis* (October 28, 1957): 138. Nonviolence will win out; see "Race Violence Will Defeat Itself," *CC* (September 17, 1958): 1046. For the quote of the minister, see "Money Talks on Race," *America* (June 17, 1961): 435; for another example of economic optimism, see "Race Tension Is Costly," *CC* (September 13, 1961): 1068.

57. The limits of congregational life for the Protestant are discussed in Reinhold Niebuhr, "School, Church, and the Ordeals of Integration," *Christianity & Crisis* (October 1, 1956): 121–22; and Waldo Beach, "The Southern Churches and the Race Question," *Christianity & Crisis* (March 3, 1958): 17–18.

58. Reinhold Niebuhr, "Bad Days at Little Rock," *Christianity & Crisis* (February 4, 1957): 131; Kyle Haselden, "Beneath the Mask of Prejudice," *CC* (November 13, 1957): 1345–46.

59. "Civil Rights and Christian Concern," editorial, *CT* (May 8, 1964): 28–29. Busing, "though never an ideal solution," might, "in at least some cases," be the "only effective way to start to improve the educational opportunities for black children." See "The Battle of Boston," editorial, *CT* 19 (January 31, 1975): 20.

60. The indented quote is from "The Unresolved Issue: Federal Versus State Powers," *CT* (October 26, 1962): 25–26; the quote just above it is from "Color Line in State University: A Wobbly Defense of Freedom," *CT* (October 12, 1962): 30. For yet another discussion of governmental power and the Supreme Court as a "policy-making" body, see "Race Tensions and Social Change," *CT* (January 19, 1959): 20–23.

61. The indented quote is from E. Earle Ellis, "Segregation and the Kingdom of God," *CT* (March 18, 1957): 6–9; for discussion of the evangelical moderate, see "Race Tensions and Social Change," *CT* (January 19, 1959): 20–23; for the implications of "forced integration," see, for example, "The Church and the Race Problem," *CT* (March 18, 1957): 20–22; and "Desegregation and Regeneration," *CT* (September 29, 1958): 20–21. For record of Faubus's use of this argument, see "Governor Faubus and Little Rock," *Commonweal* (June 12, 1959): 268.

62. See Henlee Barnette, "What Can Southern Baptists Do?" *CT* (June 24, 1957): 14–16; and Timothy L. Smith, "Christians and the Crisis of Race," *CT* (September 29, 1958): 6–8.

63. "The Church and the Race Problem," *CT* (March 18, 1957): 20–22; "Desegregation and Regeneration," *CT* (September 29, 1958): 20–21; Bell, "Christian Race Relations," *CT* (July 19, 1963): 23. At the heart of some of this feeling was

a fear of intermarriage among the races. See "What of Racial Intermarriage?" *CT* (October 11, 1963): 26–28; and "Evers' Murder Signals Eventual Burial of Segregation," *CT* (July 5, 1963): 27.

64. Carl F. H. Henry, "Perspectives for Social Action," part 2, *CT* (February 2, 1959): 13; quote on 14.

65. Ibid., p. 14.

66. See "Personalia," *CT* (January 17, 1964): 46; and "Personalia," *CT* (November 6, 1964): 54; "Lawlessness: A Bad Sign," *CT* (April 29, 1966): 29–30.

67. King, "Nonviolence and Racial Justice," *CC* (February 6, 1957): 165–167; King, "The Most Durable Peace," *CC* (June 5, 1957): 708–9; King, "The Church and the Race Crisis," *CC* (October 8, 1958): 1140–41; King, "Pilgrimage to Nonviolence," *CC* (April 13, 1960): 439–41. Fey, "An Announcement," *CC* (October 8, 1958): 1135. King, "Letter from Birmingham Jail," *CC* (June 12, 1963): 767–73.

68. Mary Douglas, *Purity and Danger* (Baltimore: Penguin, 1966), 165.

69. On Duke Divinity School, see "Duke Trustees Stand Alone," *CC* (June 25, 1958): 742; and "Duke Divinity School Denied Integration," *CC* (March 25, 1959): 349; "Negroes' Role Dominates Methodist Concerns," *CT* (May 23, 1960): 25, 30. On Vanderbilt's problems, see "Give Lawson a Fair Trial," *CC* (March 30, 1960): 371–72; Woodrow A. Geier, "Sit-Ins Prod a Community," *CC* (March 30, 1960): 379–82; "Vanderbilt Should Reinstate Lawson," *CC* (April 13, 1960): 436; "Vanderbilt Chancellor Replies," *CC* (April 13, 1960): 444, 454; "Vanderbilt Professors Resign in Protest," *CC* (June 8, 1960): 685–86; "Vanderbilt Crisis Deepens," *CC* (June 15, 1960): 716; "The Mood of Christian Protest," *CC* (June 15, 1960): 746–47; "Vanderbilt Offers Lawson Settlement," *CC* (June 29, 1960): 764; "Integration Resumes at Vanderbilt," *CC* (July 6, 1960): 798; "Lawson Rejects Proposal," *CC* (July 13, 1960): 821; J. Robert Nelson, "Vanderbilt's Time of Testing," *CC* (August 10, 1960): 921–25. Vanderbilt recently took a step to make amends to Lawson, inviting him to serve as a "distinguished professor" at Vanderbilt during 2006–2007.

70. The poll of Southern clergy conducted in 1958 by *Pulpit Digest* is referenced in "Episcopalians on Racial Peace," *Commonweal* (November 1, 1958): 123. Reinhold Niebuhr wrote in 1957 that "the white Protestant churches are not found wanting in regard to their leadership, but are found wanting in regard to their lay opinion"; see Niebuhr, "The Effect of the Supreme Court Decision," *Christianity & Crisis* (February 4, 1957): 3. For the results of the Maryland preferential poll, see ""Episcopal Leadership," *America* (September 12, 1968): 249. On the United Church of Christ, see "Who Won the Election? The Negro or White Bigotry?" *CC* (November 9, 1966): 1369. For a record of John Bennett's comments, see Benjamin L. Masse, "Fair Housing Splits Catholics in Milwaukee," *America* (October 7, 1967): 368.

71. King noticed the problem as well: "We see the new nations of Africa and Asia moving at jet speed toward independence and, on the other hand, we seem ourselves to be moving at horse-and-buggy speed just to get a cup of coffee at a lunch counter." Quoted in Stephen C. Rose, "Test for Nonviolence," *CC* (May 29, 1963): 714–16; a very similar quote appears in King's "Letter from Birmingham Jail"; see that famous essay in *CC* (June 12, 1963), esp. 768.

72. James O' Gara, "Muhammad Speaks," *Commonweal* (April 26, 1963): 130.

73. See William Stringfellow, "Race, Religion and Revenge," *CC* (February 14, 1962): 192–94. James Cone indicates that white America's introduction to Malcolm X and Black Muslims came with their appearance in a documentary presented on the *Mike Wallace Show* in late 1959. See Cone, *Martin & Malcolm &*

America: A Dream or a Nightmare (Maryknoll, NY: Orbis Books, 1991), 100. For some of the earliest references found in these journals, see "Nationalism, Not Separatism," *America* (August 20, 1960): 550–51; "Negroes in America," *Commonweal* (April 14, 1961): 67–68; "The Fight's Not Over," *Commonweal* (May 5, 1961): 141; "All, Here and Now," *CC* (June 28, 1961): 787–88.

74. The first comments, from the Emma Booker Elementary School, are found at http://www.whitehouse.gov/news/releases/2001/09/20010911.html; the Barksdale comments are found at http://www.whitehouse.gov/news/releases/2001/09/20010911–1.html; the evening address is found at http://www.white house.gov/news/releases/2001/09/20010911–16.html. Bruce Lincoln, in his essay, "The Theology of George W. Bush," described Bush's rhetoric by using the phrase "discourse of 'evil.'" It is online at http://marty-center.uchicago.edu/webforum/102004/commentary.shtml. For the published version, see Lincoln, "Bush's God Talk," *CC* (October 5, 2004): 22–29.

75. "International Campaign Against Terror Grows," September 26, 2001; see http://www.whitehouse.gov/news/releases/2001/09/20010925–1.html.

76. The September 20 address is found at http://www.whitehouse.gov/news/releases/2001/09/20010920–8.html; the address to the Warsaw Conference is found at http://www.whitehouse.gov/news/releases/2001/11/20011106–2.html.

77. See Lincoln, "The Theology of George W. Bush."

78. See Peter Ford, "Europe Cringes at Bush 'Crusade' Against Terrorists," *Christian Science Monitor* (September 19, 2001). See http://www.csmonitor.com/2001/0919/p12s2-woeu.html.

79. See http://www.whitehouse.gov/news/releases/2002/02/20020216–1.html.

80. James Carroll, "The Bush Crusade," *The Nation* (September 20, 2004); the article is posted at http://www.thenation.com/doc.mhtml?i=20040920&s=carroll.

81. See Peter Singer, *The President of Good and Evil* (New York: Dutton, 2004), 2. The word "evil" is used as a noun 914 times in Bush's addresses during this period and as an adjective only 182 times.

82. Emphasis is mine. "President Bush Calls for Action on Economy, Energy," October 26, 2001; see http://www.whitehouse.gov/news/releases/2001/10/20011026–9.html. See also "President Calls for Economic Stimulus," address to the National Association of Manufacturers, October 31, 2001, where he says "the evil ones thought they could affect the spirit of America"; see http://www.white house.gov/news/releases/2001/10/20011031–1.html. See also "German Leader Reiterates Solidarity with U.S.," October 9, 2001, when Bush said, "People ought to feel comfortable going about their lives, knowing that their government is doing everything humanly possible to disrupt any potential activity that the evil ones may try to inflict upon us"; see http://www.whitehouse.gov/news/releases/2001/10/20011009–13.html.

83. Emphasis is mine. "President Delivers State of the Union Address," January 29, 2002; see http://www.whitehouse.gov/news/releases/2002/01/20020129–11.html.

84. "President Condemns Attack in Bali," October 14, 2002, South Lawn of the White House, see http://www.whitehouse.gov/news/releases/2002/10/20021014–2.html.

85. "President Bush Calls for Renewing the USA Patriot Act," April 4, 2004, at the Hershey Lodge and Convention Center in Hershey, Pennsylvania. See http://www.whitehouse.gov/news/releases/2004/04/20040419–4.html.

86. The full Taguba Report, filed by Major General Antonio M. Taguba, is published on the Web at http://www.agonist.org/annex/taguba.htm.

87. Ron Suskind, "Without A Doubt," *New York Times Magazine* (October 17, 2004): 44–51, 64, 102, and 106.

88. Jim Wallis, "Dangerous Religion: George W. Bush's Theology of Empire," *Sojourners* (September-October 2003); see the online version at http://www.sojo.net/index.cfm?action=magazine.article&issue=soj0309&article=030910.

89. See "Beware Elvis Presley," *America* (June 23, 1956): 294–95. On Boone, see "Hollywood Seduces a Teen-Age Idol . . . and the Kids Love It," *CT* (May 11, 1962): 794.

90. "'Gays' Go Radical," *CT* (December 4, 1970): 40–41.

91. "The Justification of Rock Hudson," *CT* 29 (October 18, 1985): 16–17; see also Ben Patterson, "The Judgment Mentality," *CT* 31 (March 20, 1987): 16–17; this position is the official line: see Terry Muck, "AIDS in Your Church," *CT* 32 (February 5, 1988): 12–13.

92. Barbara Brown Zikmund, "Women and the Churches," in David Lotz, ed., *Altered Landscapes: Christianity in American, 1935–1985* (Grand Rapids: Wm. B. Eerdmans Publishing Co., 1989), 125–39.

93. "Breakthrough for the Woman Minister," *CC* (Jan. 23, 1957): 100; "Industry Turns to Womanpower," *CC* (April 3, 1957): 413; Cynthia C. Wedel, "Woman Power and the Churches," *CC* (July 10, 1957): 843–44; "Equal Pay for Equal Labor," *CC* (May 1, 1963): 572–73; and "'American Women'—The Federal Report," *CT* (November 22, 1963): 30–31.

94. See Mike Mount, "Air Force Probes Religious Bias Charges at Academy: Cadet Complaints Are Rising at Colorado School, Officials Say," *CNN Washington Bureau*; posted at http://www.cnn.com/2005/US/05/03/airforce.religion/. Amy Frykholm recently treated this topic in "Cadets for Christ: Evangelization at the Air Force Academy," *CC* (January 10, 2006): 22–25; Americans United for Separation and Church and State issued a statement titled "Air Force Issues Troubling Guidelines on Religion," February 9, 2006, which can be found at www.au.org.

95. For Michael Sheridan, see Laurie Goldstein, "Bishop Would Deny Rite for Defiant Catholic Voters," *New York Times*, May 14, 2004, posted at http://www.nytimes.com/2004/05/14/national/14bishop.html?ex=1085550377&ei=1&en=3d05a8ee441ec624; see also information pertaining to Archbishops Charles J. Chaput, of Colorado, and Raymond L. Burke, of St. Louis, on their statements about votes for Kerry, sin, and communion in David D. Kirkpatrick and Laurie Goldstein, "Group of Bishops Using Influence to Oppose Kerry," *New York Times*, October 12, 2004—the abstract is found at http://query.nytimes.com/gst/abstract.html?res=F4091EFB3A5F0C718DDDA90994DC404482&incamp=archive:search.

96. See Roy Moore, with John Perry, *So Help Me God: The Ten Commandments, Judicial Tyranny, and the Battle for Religious Freedom* (Nashville: Broadman & Holman, 2005), 235, 55. It is interesting to point out that not all religious conservatives agree with Moore's defense of his use of the Ten Commandments; see "Hang Ten? Thou Shalt Avoid Ten Commandments Tokenism," *CT* (March 16, 2000): 36–37; in that editorial, the editor stated, "Ripped from the context of sacred history, they provide very limited guidance. . . . They make little sense outside the context of the covenant [of] God's electing love."

97. See David D. Kirkpatrick and Sheryl Gay Stolberg, "How Family's Cause Reached the Halls of Congress," *New York Times*, March 22, 2005. A transcript of DeLay's comments can be found at http://www.au.org/site/PageServer?pagename=press_delayfristtranscript#delay.

98. An excellent book that analyzes and examines the "mythology" associated with the culture-war thesis is Rhys H. Williams, ed., *Cultural Wars in American Politics: Critical Reviews of a Popular Myth* (New York: Walter de Gruyter, 1997).

99. Contrast Bellah's *Beyond Belief: Essays on Religion in a Post-Traditional World* (New York: Harper & Row, 1970), which celebrated modern religion's freedom from traditional restraints, with his "Finding the Church: Post-Traditional Discipleship" (How My Mind Has Changed series, *CC* [November 14, 1990]: 1060–64), from which this quote was taken.

Chapter 5: Public Christian

1. H. Richard Niebuhr, *The Social Sources of Denominationalism* (New York: New American Library, 1929; repr. 1975).
2. Gerard O'Daly, *Augustine's City of God: A Reader's Guide* (New York: Oxford University Press, 1999), 54.
3. See Johannes van Oort, *Jerusalem and Babylon: A Study into Augustine's City of God and the Sources of His Doctrine of the Two Cities* (Leiden: E. J. Brill, 1991), 225–26. See especially his chapter dealing with potential sources for Augustine's work, 199–359.
4. Ibid.; see 154 for an elaboration of Augustine's thinking in this regard.
5. Ibid.; the first quote is from 256; the second, from 273.
6. Ibid., 273.
7. Augustine, *The City of God*, trans. Marcus Dods, Modern Library ed. (New York: Random House, 1993), Book xiv, 28, p. 477.
8. These following paragraphs are dependent on van Oort's extensive discussion in *Jerusalem and Babylon*, 276–301.
9. Ibid., 276–81.
10. Ibid., 294.
11. Ibid., 297–98.
12. Ibid., 299. The observation at the end is a quotation from W. H. C. Frend, *Martyrdom and Persecution in the Early Church: A Study of a Conflict from the Maccabees to Donatus* (Oxford: Basil Blackwell, 1965), 550.
13. Van Oort, *Jerusalem and Babylon*, 116.
14. Augustine, *The City of God*, Book v, 25, pp. 178–79.
15. See Peter Brown on this point, in *Religion and Society in the Age of Saint Augustine* (London: Faber & Faber, 1972), 44; further, see his essay on Augustine and religious coercion, 260–78.
16. Augustine, *The City of God*, Book xxii, 6, pp. 816–18.
17. Ibid., Book xix, 17, p. 697.
18. This point is made by Robert L. Wilken in his essay "Augustine's *City of God* Today," in *The Two Cities of God: The Church's Responsibility for the Earthly City*, ed. Carl E. Bratten and Robert W. Jenson (Grand Rapids: Wm. B. Eerdmans Publishing Co., 1997), 28–42.
19. Augustine, *City of God*, Book i, 35, p. 38.
20. Ibid., Book xix, 17, p. 696.
21. Ibid., Book xix, 20, p. 698.
22. The distinction between the "city of God within history" and the "city of God" should not be lost on the reader. The city of God is the broader concept, which includes not only the church but also the angelic beings as well. Further, Augustine knows there are some in the church on earth who are not really Christian, and who will not be persons who actually will see the eschatological city of God. See van Oort, *Jerusalem and Babylon*, 128.
23. See ibid., 141.
24. Actually, H. Richard Niebuhr uses Augustine to illustrate Christ as "transformer of culture." I see Augustine's understanding of the irreconcilable nature of the

relationship between the city of God and the city of man ultimately causing many Christians who followed him to develop an inability to relate meaningfully the work of the church to the transformation of the public life they shared. Niebuhr, *Christ & Culture*, 206f.

25. Augustine, *City of God*, Book 15, sec. 22, p. 510.

26. Ibid., Book 19, sec. 17, p. 696.

27. Martin Luther, "Temporal Authority: To What Extent It Should be Obeyed," in *Martin Luther's Basic Theological Writings*, ed. Timothy F. Lull (Minneapolis: Fortress Press, 1989), 663. Luther's treatise is found on 655–703. The point of this paragraph is made well in Bernhard Lohse, *Martin Luther's Theology: Its Historical and Systematic Development* (Minneapolis: Fortress Press, 1999); see esp. 151–59. Lohse has emphasized how Luther's treatment of the distinction between the two kingdoms and governments is related to Luther's historical situation. In his view, one cannot systematize it too concretely as part of some concrete, highly organized "two-kingdoms doctrine."

28. Luther, "Temporal Authority," 669.

29. For more on this point, see Paul Althaus, *The Theology of Martin Luther* (Philadelphia: Fortress Press, 1966), 143–44.

30. Luther, "Temporal Authority," 665–66.

31. Van Oort, *Jerusalem and Babylon*, 154–63.

32. The term *neoevangelicalism* is more accurate, actually, than *evangelicalism*. This evangelicalism should not be confused with the evangelicalism of the nineteenth century, for it grows out of a reform of fundamentalism during the 1940s. This point is covered later in the chapter.

33. See, for example, Donald Dayton, ed., *The Variety of American Evangelicalism* (Knoxville: University of Tennessee Press, 1991). See also the definition offered by James Davison Hunter in *American Evangelicalism: Conservative Religion and the Quandary of Modernity* (New Brunswick, NJ: Rutgers University Press, 1983), 7: "At the doctrinal core contemporary Evangelicals can be identified by their adherence to (1) the belief that the Bible is the inerrant Word of God, (2) the belief in the divinity of Christ, and (3) the belief in the efficacy of Christ's life, death, and physical resurrection for the salvation of the human soul. Behaviorally, Evangelicals are typically characterized by an individuated and experiential orientation toward spiritual salvation and religiosity in general and by the conviction of the necessity of actively attempting to proselytize all nonbelievers to the tenets of the Evangelical belief system."

34. See Richard G. Hutcheson Jr., *Mainline Churches and the Evangelicals* (Atlanta: John Knox Press), 39.

35. This kind of grouping of evangelicals is presented in Hunter, *American Evangelicalism*, 7–9. The Presbyterian Church in America (PCA) is a remnant of the Presbyterian Church in the United States (Southern), the PCUS, from the split in 1973 over the liberal trends operating in the PCUS. Other Presbyterian groups merged with the PCA a bit later, including the Reformed Presbyterian Church, Evangelical Synod.

36. David Wells, *No Place for Truth: Or Whatever Happened to Evangelical Theology?* (Grand Rapids: Wm. B. Eerdmans Publishing Co., 1993), 132

37. Christ's reference to the camel and the eye of the needle is relevant here (Mark 10:25), as are the beatitudes (Luke 6:20) and James's judgments on the rich (Jas. 5:1–3). On this point, see John G. Gager, *Kingdom and Community: The Social World of Early Christianity* (Englewood Cliffs, NJ: Prentice-Hall, 1975), 24.

38. Gager makes these points; see ibid., 32–33. He references Victor Turner's work on liminality. See Victor Turner, *The Ritual Process: Structure and Anti-Structure* (London: Routledge & Kegan Paul, 1969).

39. See Arthur W. Wainwright, *Mysterious Apocalypse: Interpreting the Book of Revelation* (Nashville: Abingdon Press, 1993), esp. 33–34 and 12. These last couple of paragraphs also depend on Wainwright's discussion of millennialism in the early church. He points out that not all these Christians were chiliasts; some doubted whether Revelation was an inspired book that belonged in the church's canon. His book is an excellent accounting of the history of millennialism in all its complex forms.

40. I will have more to say about this in the next chapter.

41. Ernest R. Sandeen, *The Roots of Fundamentalism* (Chicago: University of Chicago Press, 1970), xix.

42. For an interesting bit of cultural kitsch associated with dispensational premillennialism, take a look at the "Rapture Ready" Web site, which sells t-shirts, coffee cups, etc., and provides a "Rapture index" scale that keeps track of how much closer we are to the Rapture based on current events. For those left behind, the site also provides a "post-rapture survival guide." See http://www.raptureready.com/. For those readers who would like to understand some of the diversity associated with neoevangelical and fundamentalist views of the millennium, see Darrell L. Bock, ed., *Three Views on the Millennium and Beyond: Premillennialism, Postmillennialism, and Amillennialism* (Grand Rapids: Zondervan, 1999). A new book by Timothy P. Weber tracks the development of dispensationalism in America; see *On The Road to Armageddon: How Evangelicals Became Israel's Best Friend* (Grand Rapids: Baker Academic, 2004). Weber briefly traces the different kinds of millennialism noted here; see 9–11.

43. See M. Eugene Boring's *Revelation* (Louisville, KY: Westminster/John Knox Press, 1989), itself a representative of a preterist view, wherein Boring discusses various types of interpretation related to millennialism (47–51).

44. There are exceptions today, particularly due to the influence of postliberalism, narrative theology, and the work of Stanley Hauerwas (chapter 7 of this book addresses these influences).

45. Mark A. Noll, *The Scandal of the Evangelical Mind* (Grand Rapids: Wm. B. Eerdmans Publishing Co., 1994): 212–14, 221.

46. See Carl F. H. Henry, "Perspective for Social Action: Part I," *Christianity Today* (hereafter *CT*) (January 19, 1959): 11.

47. Stanley J. Grenz and Roger E. Olson, *20th-Century Theology: God & the World in a Transitional Age* (Downers Grove, IL: InterVarsity Press, 1992), 287.

48. Carl F. H. Henry, *The Uneasy Conscience of Modern Fundamentalism* (Grand Rapids: Wm. B. Eerdmans Publishing Co., 1947), 19; see also the discussion on 7 about personal sins.

49. Ibid., 19.

50. See Henry's chapter on "The Apprehension Over Kingdom Preaching," in *The Uneasy Conscience*, 41–54.

51. George Marsden, *Reforming Fundamentalism: Fuller Seminary and the New Evangelicals* (Grand Rapids: Wm. B. Eerdmans Publishing Co., 1987), 81–82. Marsden's book provides a detailed look at the development of this reforming movement among fundamentalists.

52. Carl F. H. Henry, *Aspects of Christian Ethics* (Grand Rapids: Wm. B. Eerdmans Publishing Co., 1964), 10.

53. Ibid., 30, 76, 122–23.

54. Ibid., 124.

55. Carl F. H. Henry, *The Christian Mindset in a Secular Society* (Portland, OR: Multnomah Press, 1984), 114.

56. Henry, *Aspects of Christian Ethics*, 135.

57. For Paul Henry's views on politics and faith, see Paul B. Henry, *Politics for Evangelicals* (Valley Forge, PA: Judson Press, 1974).

58. Henry, *Aspects of Christian Ethics*, 129.

59. Carl F. H. Henry, "Perspective for Social Action: Part II," *CT* (February 2, 1959): 13–16.

60. See "Summer of Racial Discontent," *CT* (July 21, 1967): 27. The National Association of Evangelicalism viewed things similarly: see "NAE and Civil Rights," *CT* (May 8, 1964): 50. *CT* continued to affirm the need to address racism one individual at a time: see Lyn Cryderman's editorial in response to the Howard Beach incident, "Lingering Racism," *CT* (March 6, 1987): 15.

61. Waldo Beach, "Piety and Racial Poverty," *Christianity & Crisis* (January 20, 1964): 257. For a later criticism of the approach of *CT* with respect to civil rights, see John Oliver, "A Failure of Evangelical Conscience," *Post-American* (May 1975): 26–30.

62. See, respectively, "Land of the Free," *CT* (June 21, 1963): 24–25; "What Is the Way to a New Society?" *CT* (November 26, 1956): 23–24; Thomas B. McDormand, "Church and Government," *CT* (April 23, 1965): 14–15; "Good News and Good Works," *CT* (June 23, 1967): 21; and "The Art of Soul Winning: Let the Church be the Church," *CT* (July 4, 1960): 22–23. This last editorial recognizes that the phrase in its title originally came from John A. Mackay of Princeton Theological Seminary. See also "Christian Social Action," *CT* (March 14, 1969): 24–25.

63. "Evangelicals and Public Affairs," *CT* (January 17, 1964): 24–25.

64. Henry has identified these in various locations. Here he speaks of "proclamation of the state divinely willed but limited in power, of man's inalienable freedom and duty under God, of private property as a divine stewardship, of free enterprise under God, and much else that speaks relevantly to our social crisis." See Henry, "Perspective for Social Action: Part II," 16.

65. The evangelical theology of politics described in the previous five paragraphs is found in Henry, "Perspective for Social Action: Part II." Henry argued that the problem with the liberal social gospel was the belief it could "transform the social order by grafting assertedly Christian ideals upon unregenerate human nature." For Henry's criticism of the social gospel, see also Henry, "Perspective for Social Action: Part I."

66. Alister McGrath, "Calvin and the Christian Calling," in *The Second One Thousand Years: Ten People Who Defined a Millennium,* ed. Richard John Neuhaus (Grand Rapids: Wm. B. Eerdmans Publishing Co., 2001), 74.

67. For a more detailed analysis of how *CT* has applied faith to public life, see Mark G. Toulouse, "*Christianity Today* and American Public Life: A Case Study," *Journal of Church and State* 35 (Spring 1993): 241–84.

68. http://en.wikipedia.org/wiki/Chicago_Declaration_of_Evangelical_Social_Concern; see also http://www.esa-online.org/conferences/chicago/chicago.html—a site maintained by Evangelicals for Social Action. Both sites contain the full text of the Chicago Declaration.

69. Joel Carpenter, "Compassionate Evangelicalism," *CT* (December 2003): 40–42.

70. More will be said about the work and perspectives of Jim Wallis in the last section of this chapter.

71. George M. Marsden, *Understanding Fundamentalism and Evangelicalism* (Grand Rapids: Wm. B. Eerdmans Publishing Co., 1991), 63. Henry is quoted on that page as well.

72. This is consistent with Henry's emphasis on persuasion in all matters, both in evangelism and in applying Christianity to the social order. He often used the word "voluntary," as in the responsibility of the Christian "to stir the masses to an awakened voluntary interest in those vitalities essential to the soundness and

stability of the political arena." See Henry, *Christian Mindset*, 127. See, for example, John Warwick Montgomery, "The Limits of Christian Influence," *CT* (January 23, 1981): 60, 63, where Montgomery indicates his belief that "gospel preachment comes first, and if we must choose—as occasionally we must in a fallen world—between moral betterment and non-Christians willing to listen to the gospel from those who offer it freely, without compulsion, we will need to choose the latter. Our goal in secular society is not to force the society, come what may, into the framework of God's kingdom, but rather to bring it as close as we can to divine standards consistent with effective gospel preachment to those for whom Christ died."

73. "The Church and Political Pronouncements," *CT* (August 28, 1964): 29–30; "The Church, Politics, and the NCC," *CT* (October 14, 1966): 35–36; Malcolm Nygren, "The Church and Political Action," *CT* (March 14, 1969): 9–12; "The WCC: The Same Colors at Half-Mast," *CT* (September 7, 1979): 14–15. *CT* offered similar criticisms of any recommendations based on neoorthodox theology or found in the pages of *Christian Century*. See "Theological Journalism and the Contemporary Social Crisis," *CT* (February 2, 1962): 430; and Frank Farrell, "Liberal Social Ethics: Confronting the Four Horsemen: Part I," *CT* (November 9, 1962): 3–7; and "Part II" in *CT* (November 23, 1962): 14–18. On the NAE, see, for example, "NAE Reaffirms Strong Anti-Communist Stand," *CT* (May 9, 1960): 30. Yet *CT* itself never urged the church to engage in political activities nor did it specifically endorse NAE resolutions. For more recent expression of disapproval of the methods of the Religious Right see "Lost Momentum: Carl F. H. Henry Looks at the Future of the Religious Right," *CT* (September 4, 1987): 30–32; and Lyn Cryderman, "Exit Right," *CT* (August 18, 1989): 14–15.

74. http://www.nae.net/index.cfm?FUSEACTION=nae.statement_of_faith.

75. See the link "Membership" from the Web site's main page found at http://www.nae.net/index.cfm. The site provides the history of the NAE, from which these paragraphs have drawn liberally, at http://www.nae.net/index.cfm?FUSEACTION=nae.history.

76. Henry, *Aspects of Christian Ethics*, 128.

77. Ibid. The first sentence of the indented quote is found on 106; the remainder of the quote is on 138. Henry made this kind of criticism of the NCC in a number of places; see, for example, "Evangelicals in the Social Struggle," *CT* (October 8, 1965): 3–11.

78. Richard J. Mouw, "This World Is Not My Home," *CT* (April 24, 2000): 87.

79. Wells, *No Place for Truth*, 208–11.

80. See Richard Cizik, "The Real Christian Coalition: Evangelical Politics Is Bigger Than the Religious Right," *CT* (June 12, 2000): 82–83. Charles Colson also stresses the "cultural commission" in his "Reclaiming Occupied Territory," *CT* (August 2004): 64: " 'Of course we're called to fulfill the Great Commission,' I replied. 'But we're also called to fulfill the *cultural* commission.' Christians are agents of God's *saving grace*—bringing others to Christ, I explained—but we are also agents of his *common grace*: sustaining and renewing his creation, defending the created institutions of family and society, critiquing false worldviews." There is now a Web site called "The Cultural Commission," established by evangelical Christians who want to extend the influence of "the Christian worldview in an effort to educate and encourage the body of Christ to reform the prevailing American culture through intercessory prayer, evangelism, apologetics, sound reason, speech and debate to guarantee our biblical liberties and to share the Good News of salvation through Jesus Christ our Lord. As a product of this process we

glorify God and lead the lost to Christ. It is vital to understand that our agenda is not fundamentally political or cultural, but evangelistic, with profound political and cultural implications." See the "vision and mission statement" of http://theculturalcommission.org/.

81. See the Web site for the Center for Public Justice, which contains a strong statement of theological rationale under the link titled "About the Center"—http://www.cpjustice.org/.

82. Skillern is named by Esbeck as the chief advocate for the "structural pluralist" version of accommodationism described by him in "A Typology of Church-State Relations in Current American Thought," 30, note 33. See the discussion of "structural pluralism" in chapter 1.

83. This thoughtful document relating evangelical faith to civic responsibility can be found at http://www.nae.net/images/civic_responsibility2.pdf .

84. This work includes a wide variety of theological perspectives and endeavors; see the section on political reflection found in Noll, *Scandal of the Evangelical Mind*, 211f.

85. "Post-American Christianity," *Post-American* (Fall 1971): 2.

86. James Wallis, "Sojourners," *Post-American* (October–November, 1975): 3.

87. See, for example, Larry Rasmussen, "In the Face of War," *Sojourners* (January 2005): 12–17; and James Wallis, "High Stakes for Church and State," *Sojourners* (November 2004): 12–19, 46. Jim Wallis and Duane Shank, "Stop . . . In the Name of Abused Humanity," http://www.sojo.net/index.cfm?action=sojomail .display&issue=040519#3.

88. For a bit more extended treatment of the history of *Sojourners*, see Mark G. Toulouse, "*Sojourners*," in *Popular Religious Magazines of the United States*, ed. Mark Fackler and Charles H. Lippy (Westport, CT: Greenwood Publishing Group, 1995), 444–51.

89. The group's Web site is http://www.calltorenewal.org.

90. Jim Wallis, *God's Politics: Why the Right Gets It Wrong and the Left Doesn't Get It* (New York: HarperCollins, 2005), 76.

Chapter 6: Public Church

1. Paul Tillich, *The Protestant Era*, abridg. ed. (Chicago: University of Chicago Press, 1957), 230, 163.

2. In chapter 7, I make the argument that our current context actually offers Christianity a renewed opportunity to speak publicly without struggling to translate language born in faith into some other form before speaking in public.

3. Leo Perdue, *Wisdom and Creation* (Nashville: Abingdon Press, 1994), 35, 326.

4. Leo Perdue, *Proverbs* (Louisville, KY: John Knox Press, 2000), 48.

5. Terrence E. Fretheim, *God and the World in the Old Testament: A Relational Theology of Creation* (Nashville: Abingdon Press, 2005), xi.

6. Ibid., esp. 5–9. The lengthy quote is on 8.

7. This definition alters slightly one offered by Clark M. Williamson. See *Way of Blessing, Way of Life* (St. Louis: Chalice Press, 1999), 81–82. I have added the emphasis on creation.

8. See H. Richard Niebuhr, *The Kingdom of God in America* (New York: Harper & Row, 1937), 38–39.

9. These quotations come from John Calvin, *Institutes of the Christian Religion*, book 4, chap. 20, dealing with "civil government." These sections of the *Institutes* are contained in *John Calvin: Selections from His Writings*, ed. John Dillenberger (New York: Anchor Books, 1971), 472–77.

10. For a quick rehearsal of the story of some of these struggles, see William G.

Naphy, "Calvin and Geneva," in *The Reformation World*, ed. Andrew Pettegree (London: Routledge, 2000), 309–22.

11. Niebuhr, *Kingdom of God in America*, 39–40.

12. Ibid., 26.

13. See, for example, Matt. 5:3, 10; 11:11–12 (par. Luke 16:16); Matt. 12:28; 13:24f., 38f.; 21:31; 23:13; Mark 10:14; Luke 17:21. These passages are all listed by C. J. Cadoux as examples of a "present" kingdom. See Cadoux, *The Early Church and the World* (Edinburgh: T. & T. Clark, 1925), 12, note 1.

14. These understandings of the prophets and of Jesus are analyzed in Norman Perrin, *The Kingdom of God in the Teaching of Jesus* (Philadelphia: Westminster Press, 1963), 160–85; quotation on 178.

15. Ibid.; see 13–36, where Perrin discusses the work of Weiss and Schweitzer. Perrin also discusses these questions in *Jesus and the Language of the Kingdom* (Philadelphia: Fortress Press, 1976), 32–56. See also Johannes Weiss, *Jesus' Proclamation of the Kingdom of God*, ed., trans., and intro. Richard H. Hiers and D. Larrimore Holland (Philadelphia: Fortress Press, 1971; first published in 1892); and Albert Schweitzer, *The Mystery of the Kingdom of God* (New York: Schocken, 1914; first published in 1901). Wendell Willis has written a brief essay clearly examining these topics as well: see Willis, "The Discovery of the Eschatological Kingdom: Johannes Weiss and Albert Schweitzer," in Willis, ed., *The Kingdom of God in 20th-Century Interpretation* (Peabody, MA: Hendrickson Publishers, 1987), 1–14.

16. The first quote comes from Perrin, *Jesus and the Language of the Kingdom*, 38. Perrin discusses, in this context, the work of C. H. Dodd, particularly his book, originally published in 1935, titled *Parables of the Kingdom* (New York: Charles Scribner's Sons, 1938). The second quote comes from the work of John Bright, who also stressed the presence of the kingdom in his *The Kingdom of God* (Nashville: Abingdon Press, 1953), see esp. 187–214; the quote is from 218.

17. J. N. D. Kelly makes this argument in his classic *Early Christian Doctrines* (New York: Harper & Row, 1959), 459–62.

18. Perrin, *Kingdom of God*, 185–201. Perrin turns to ethical questions in 201–6.

19. Brian K. Blount, *Then the Whisper Put on Flesh: New Testament Ethics in an African-American Context* (Nashville: Abingdon Press, 2001), 47–51.

20. Ibid., 92.

21. Ibid., 43. Perrin was influenced by Amos Wilder's work on the gospel, *Early Christian Rhetoric: The Language of the Gospel* (Cambridge, MA: Harvard University Press, 1971).

22. See W. Emory Elmore, "Linguistic Approaches to the Kingdom: Amos Wilder and Norman Perrin," in Willis, *Kingdom of God in 20th-Century Interpretation*, 65.

23. See Bright, *The Kingdom of God*, 222, on this point.

24. Franklin I. Gamwell, *Politics as a Christian Vocation* (New York: Cambridge University Press, 2005).

25. Gamwell depends on Wayne Meeks for some of this argument, see 10–11. Wayne Meeks, *The Moral World of the First Christians* (Philadelphia: Westminster Press, 1986). Gamwell briefly discusses Augustine's views and how they represented Christianity's response to the fact that the end had not come. See 12–15.

26. H. Richard Niebuhr, Daniel Day Williams, and James Gustafson, *The Purpose of the Church and Its Ministry: Reflections on the Aims of Theological Education* (New York: Harper & Brothers, 1956), chap. 1.

27. Gamwell, *Politics*, 20.

28. See the wonderful little volume edited by Nonna Verna Harrison, *St. Basil the*

Great: On the Human Condition (Crestwood, NY: St. Vladimir's Seminary Press, 2005). This paragraph on Basil the Great depends heavily on Harrison's introduction, where she emphasizes Basil's concern for social justice; see 22–29. This book, part of the Popular Patristics Series, contains excerpts from Basil. For Basil's emphasis on love of God and neighbor, see *Long Rules* in *St. Basil the Great*, 117–118, 120.

29. See *The Epistle to Diognetus* in Colman J. Barry, ed., *Readings in Church History: From Pentecost to the Protestant Revolt*, vol. 1(Westminster, MD: Newman Press, 1960), 37–43.

30. Cadoux argued in the 1920s that, from the very beginning of Christianity, there was a tension between separation from the world and association with it, and between condemnation of the state and approval of it; Cadoux, *The Early Church*, particularly 97f., and 161f.

31. See Gamwell, *Politics*, 15–21.

32. Ibid., 21–24.

33. Ibid., 24–27.

34. See Ernest Lee Tuveson, *Redeemer Nation: The Idea of America's Millennial Role* (Chicago: University of Chicago Press, 1968). Tuveson discusses the millennialism of Edwards on 26–31.

35. Stephen J. Stein, ed., *Apocalyptic Writings* (New Haven, CT: Yale University Press, 1977), 53–54.

36. Niebuhr, *Kingdom of God in America*, 137.

37. Stephen J. Stein, "Jonathan Edwards," in *Makers of Christian Theology in America*, ed. Mark G. Toulouse and James O. Duke (Nashville: Abingdon Press, 1997), 61.

38. Timothy Dwight, "A Valedictory Address . . . at Yale College, July 25, 1776," in *Nationalism and Religion in America: Concepts of American Identity and Mission*, ed. Winthrop S. Hudson (Gloucester, MA: Peter Smith, 1978), 59–62.

39. Patricia Bonomi, *Under the Cope of Heaven: Religion, Society, and Politics in Colonial America* (New York: Oxford University Press, 1986), 216. The influence of Christianity during these years is also chronicled in Nathan O. Hatch, *The Sacred Cause of Liberty: Republican Thought and the Millennium in Revolutionary New England* (New Haven, CT: Yale University Press, 1977) and Mark A. Noll, *Christians in the American Revolution* (Grand Rapids: Wm. B. Eerdmans Publishing Co., 1977).

40. Mark A. Noll, *One Nation Under God? Christian Faith & Political Action in America* (San Francisco: Harper & Row, 1988), 46–47.

41. Robert T. Handy, *A Christian America: Protestant Hopes and Historical Realities* (New York: Oxford University Press, 1984), 28.

42. "Prospectus," *Millennial Harbinger* (January 1830): 1. See Mark G. Toulouse, *Joined in Discipleship: The Shaping of Contemporary Disciples Identity*, rev. ed. (St. Louis: Chalice Press, 1997), esp. 101–35, which examines Alexander Campbell's postmillennial views in detail. The emphasis is Campbell's own.

43. Handy, *A Christian America*, 33.

44. Ibid., 31.

45. Timothy L. Smith, *Revivalism and Social Reform: American Protestantism on the Eve of the Civil War* (Nashville: Abingdon Press, 1957), 149. Smith's book remains an excellent resource for understanding the social activities of Protestants during these years.

46. Handy discusses the failure of persuasion and the turn by some Christians to coercion (*A Christian America*, 47–56).

47. Smith covers Christian activities opposing slavery in two major chapters of his book (*Revivalism and Social Reform*, 178–224).

48. See Noll on this point (*One Nation Under God*, 126–27).

49. These types of social endeavors are covered well in Henry F. May, *Protestant Churches and Industrial America* (New York: Harper & Brothers, 1949), 39–50. On Christianity's relationship to the cities, see Josiah Strong's well-known book *Our Country: Its Possible Future and Its Present Crisis* (New York: Baker & Taylor, for the American Home Missionary Society, 1885). Mark A. Noll tells the story of the temperance crusade in *One Nation Under God*, 128–41.

50. Lyman Abbott, *The Christian Ministry* (Boston: Houghton, Mifflin & Co., 1905),138, 136.

51. Lyman Abbott, "An Agnostic's Creed," *Christian Union* 44 (October 24, 1891): 782.

52. Charles Howard Hopkins, *The Rise of the Social Gospel in American Protestantism* (New Haven, CT: Yale University Press, 1940), 19; the quotes of Edward Beecher, from an essay written in 1865, are found on 19–20.

53. For an excellent treatment of this particular point, see the doctoral dissertation completed by John E. Smylie, *Protestant Clergymen and America's World Role, 1865–1900: A Study of Christianity, Nationality, and International Relations* (Princeton Theological Seminary, 1959).

54. Niebuhr, *Kingdom of God in America*, 164–98, esp. 179–81 and 193.

55. The best biography available of Rauschenbusch is the one recently written by Christopher Evans, *The Kingdom Is Always But Coming: A Life of Walter Rauschenbusch* (Grand Rapids: Wm. B. Eerdmans Publishing Co., 2004). Evans discusses Rauschenbusch's understanding of Jesus and the prophets on 177–78. The quote used here is found on 186.

56. Rauschenbusch, *Christianity and the Social Crisis* (New York: Harper & Row, 1964, first published by Macmillan in 1907), 420–21.

57. Walter Rauschenbusch, *Christianizing the Social Order* (New York: Macmillan Co., 1912).

58. Evans (*The Kingdom Is Always But Coming*) analyzes this book briefly on 231–36. The quote is found on 232.

59. Walter Rauschenbusch, *A Theology for the Social Gospel* (New York: Macmillan Co., 1917).

60. Ibid., 95.

61. Ibid., 145.

62. Ibid., 141.

63. Evans, *The Kingdom Is Always But Coming*, 253–55.

64. On this point, see Warren L. Vinz, *Pulpit Politics: Faces of American Protestant Nationalism in the Twentieth Century* (Albany, NY: SUNY Press, 1997), particularly chap. 2 on Walter Rauschenbusch, titled "Bifurcated Nationalism."

65. Rauschenbusch, *Theology for the Social Gospel*, 168.

66. The NCC story relating to these points is told in James F. Findlay Jr., *Church People in the Struggle: The National Council of Churches and the Black Freedom Movement, 1950–1970* (New York: Oxford University Press, 1993), 15–17. I have covered the story of white Christian involvement in a somewhat different way by examining white independent Christian journals in Mark G. Toulouse, "Liberty and Equality: Christian Faith and the Civil Rights Movement," in *The Papers of the Henry Luce III Fellows in Theology*, vol. 4, ed. Matthew Zyniewicz (Pittsburgh: Association of Theological Schools, 2000), 135–73.

67. The National Conference of Catholic Bishops published two major documents testifying to the work of the Catholic Church in America as Catholic Church: see *The Challenge of Peace: God's Promise and Our Response* (Washington, DC: National Conference of Catholic Bishops and United States Catholic Conference,

1983); and *Economic Justice for All: Pastoral Letter on Catholic Social Teaching and the U.S. Economy* (Washington, DC: National Conference of Catholic Bishops and United States Catholic Conference, 1996). On Catholics and the abortion question, see Toulouse, "Perspectives on Abortion in the Christian Community from the 1950s to the Early 1990s," *Encounter* (Autumn 2001): 327–403. A recent book edited by Corwin E. Smidt examines sociological data bearing on denominational involvements in politics, as well as those of pastors; see *Pulpit and Politics: Clergy in American Politics at the Advent of the Millennium* (Waco, TX: Baylor University Press, 2004). The story of Riverside Church is told in Peter Paris, John W. Cook, James Hudnut-Beumler, Lawrence H. Mamiya, Leonora Tubbs Tisdale, and Judith Weisenfeld, *The History of the Riverside Church in the City of New York* (New York: New York University Press, 2004).

68. Branch covers these events in *Parting the Waters: America in the King Years, 1954–1963* (New York: Simon and Schuster, 1988), 73–74, 95.

69. "Pilgrimage to Nonviolence," originally published in the *Christian Century* (April 13, 1960): 439–41. It is republished in Mark G. Toulouse and James O. Duke, *Sources of Christian Theology in America* (Nashville: Abingdon Press, 1999), 485–91. The reference to Niebuhr is found on 486; this longer quote is found on 488.

70. This story is told in Branch, *Parting the Waters*, 128ff.

71. Luther D. Ivory, *Toward a Theology of Radical Involvement: The Theological Legacy of Martin Luther King* (Nashville: Abingdon Press, 1997), 99–103.

72. Martin Luther King Jr., "Peace on Earth," in King, *The Trumpet of Conscience* (New York: Harper & Row, 1967), 67–78; the quote is on 69. The sermon was preached at Ebenezer Baptist Church in Atlanta on Christmas Eve in 1967, less than four months before King died.

73. See, for example, Jo Ann Gibson Robinson, *The Montgomery Bus Boycott and the Women Who Started It* (Knoxville: University of Tennessee Press, 1987); and Rosetta E. Ross, *Witnessing and Testifying: Black Women, Religion, and Civil Rights* (Minneapolis: Augsburg Fortress, 2003).

74. James H. Cone, *Martin & Malcolm & America: A Dream or a Nightmare* (Maryknoll, NY: Orbis Books, 1991), 143–45. Cone does note, of course, that not all black ministers supported the movement. The most prominent example he noted was J. H. Jackson, leader of the National Baptist Convention.

75. These two types are discussed in Robert M. Franklin, *Another Day's Journey: Black Churches Confronting the American Crisis* (Minneapolis: Augsburg Fortress, 1997), 44–45. In discussions with my colleague Dr. Stacey Floyd-Thomas, a womanist and social ethicist on Brite's faculty, I expressed my belief that "God as Creator" did not seem to fit this type well. She expressed her belief that the stress placed on the notion of the sovereignty of God by accommodationists enabled this perspective theologically. That theological emphasis behind this type of approach makes greater sense to me.

76. Cone, *Martin & Malcolm*, 7.

77. See C. Eric Lincoln and Lawrence H. Mamiya, *The Black Church in the African American Experience* (Durham, NC: Duke University Press, 1990), 202 and 58, where these two points are discussed.

78. See Henry M. Turner, "God is a Negro," in Toulouse and Duke, eds., *Sources of Christian Theology*, 328–29. On Turner's influence, see Gayraud S. Wilmore, *Black Religion and Black Radicalism: An Interpretation of the Religious History of Afro-American People,* 2d ed. (Maryknoll, NY: Orbis Books, 1983), 122–34. On analysis of black theology's developments from Turner to the mid-1990s as they pertain to theological claims about God and Jesus, including womanist thought

about the "Black Christ," see the book by Kelly Brown Douglas, *The Black Christ* (Maryknoll, NY: Orbis Books, 1994).

79. See Franklin, *Another Day's Journey*, 47–49.

80. See Wilmore, *Black Religion and Black Radicalism*, 135–91.

81. Frederick C. Harris, *Something Within: Religion in African-American Political Activism* (New York: Oxford University Press, 1999); see particularly 3–11 as an introduction to the traditional counterarguments presented by scholars representing both the "opiate theory" and the "inspiration theory." Lincoln and Mamiya also address the nature of this debate; see *The Black Church*, 221f. On Gary Marx, see *Protest and Prejudice* (New York: Harper & Row, 1967). For "inspiration" arguments, see John Brown Childs, *The Political Black Minister: A Study in Afro-American Politics and Religion* (Boston: G. K. Hall, 1980); Charles V. Hamilton, *The Black Preacher in America* (New York: Morrow, 1972); and Hart M. Nelson and Anne K. Nelson, *The Black Church in the Sixties* (Lexington: University of Kentucky Press, 1975). Technically, Lincoln and Mamiya could also be placed in the "inspiration" category of this debate.

82. Here the word *priestly* does not refer to the sociological connotation connected to my description of priestly faith (chap. 4). Rather, *priestly* in this context refers to the way this community functions in its congregational life to form Christian identity. Generally, this dialectic has emphasized how black congregations have given attention to, in their priestly life, "those activities concerned with worship and maintaining the spiritual life of members." This role in their life provides a haven from the discrimination of the world external to congregational life and nurtures the spiritual strength to cope with it on a daily basis. Through their prophetic life, congregations have been involved "in political concerns and activities in the wider community" and act in ways that represent liberation from the social problems associated with poverty and other social ills that plague the black community. But Lincoln and Mamiya have presented a much broader notion of how dialectic works in the black church, by raising six different forms of dialectic tension. One of them, the dialectic between resistance and accommodation, obviously connects with Harris's work in this area. See Lincoln and Mamiya, *Black Church*, 10–19.

83. Ibid., chaps. 2–6.

84. Ibid., 125.

85. Franklin, *Another Day's Journey*, 49–50.

86. Anthony P. Pinn, *The Black Church in the Post-Civil Rights Era* (Maryknoll, NY: Orbis Books, 2002), 136–39.

87. Franklin, *Another Day's Journey*, 50–52.

88. Pinn, *Black Church in the Post-Civil Rights Era*, 27–36.

89. See Lincoln and Mamiya, *Black Church*, 212–15.

90. Ibid., 2–7.

91. James H. Cone, *A Black Theology of Liberation: Twentieth Anniversary Edition* (Maryknoll, NY: Orbis Books, 1990; originally published in 1970), 63.

92. Ibid., 64–66.

93. Peter J. Paris, *The Social Teaching of the Black Churches* (Philadelphia: Fortress Press, 1985), 15, 17.

94. Ibid., 134.

95. See the "Preface to the 1994 Edition," in the latest publication of J. Deotis Roberts, *Liberation and Reconciliation: A Black Theology* (Louisville, KY: Westminster John Knox Press, 2005), xiv.

96. Diana L. Hayes, *And Still We Rise: An Introduction to Black Liberation Theology* (New York: Paulist Press, 1996), 189–90. Pinn also stresses that it has been

difficult in the past few decades to connect black theology to congregational activity; see Pinn, *Black Church in the Post-Civil Rights Era*, 25.

97. See, for example, Katie Geneva Cannon, *Black Womanist Ethics* (Atlanta: Scholars Press, 1988); Cannon, *Katie's Canon: Womanism and the Soul of the Black Community* (New York: Continuum, 2003); and Delores S. Williams, *Sisters in the Wilderness* (Maryknoll, NY: Orbis Books, 1993).

98. My colleague Stacey Floyd-Thomas and her husband, Juan Floyd-Thomas, were instrumental in founding this organization. Stacey currently serves as the Executive Director for the BRSG.

99. Cornel West, *Democracy Matters* (New York: Penguin Press, 2004), 157–59.

Chapter 7: Faith and Public Life in a Postmodern Context

1. Jeffrey Stout, *Democracy and Tradition* (Princeton, NJ: Princeton University Press, 2004), 63.

2. Richard Rorty, "Religion as Conversation-Stopper," *Philosophy and Social Hope* (London: Penguin Books, 1999), 170–71. Originally, the essay appeared in *Common Knowledge* (Spring 1994): 1–6.

3. Rorty briefly treats the "Jeffersonian compromise" in his essay noted in note 2. A longer treatment is accorded the topic's relationship to democracy in Richard Rorty, "The Priority of Democracy to Philosophy," in *The Virginia Statute for Religious Freedom,* ed. Merrill D. Peterson and Robert C. Vaughan (New York: Cambridge University Press, 1988), 257–82. Franklin Gamwell has argued, for example, that the Founders intended for religion to be taken very seriously in the public debate. In fact, "the very character of the public debate makes certain religious demands upon all participants." He describes these demands as, first, "that all public purposes are finally to be assessed in light of some religious purpose, some all-inclusive requirement or ideal"; and second, that "all participants are required to affirm that the religious demands upon public policy are to be discerned by reason and persuasion." See Gamwell, "Religion and the Public Purpose," *Journal of Religion* (July 1982): 272–88.

4. Nicholas Wolterstorff, "Why We Should Reject What Liberalism Tells Us about Speaking and Acting for Religious Reasons," in *Religion and Contemporary Liberalism*, ed. Paul J. Weithman (Notre Dame, IN: University of Notre Dame Press, 1997), 162–81; see also Wolterstorff, "An Engagement with Rorty," *Journal of Religious Ethics* (Spring 2003): 129–39.

5. Stout, *Democracy and Tradition,* 85–91.

6. Richard Rorty, "Religion in the Public Square: A Reconsideration," *Journal of Religious Ethics* (Spring 2003): 141–49.

7. Reinhold Niebuhr, *The Irony of American History* (New York: Charles Scribner's Sons, 1952), viii.

8. See Linell E. Cady, "Resisting the Postmodern Turn: Theology and Contextualization," in *Theology at the End of Modernity,* ed. Sheila Greeve Davaney (Philadelphia: Trinity Press International, 1991): 81–98.

9. For the quote, see Richard Rorty, *Consequences of Pragmatism* (Minneapolis: University of Minnesota Press, 1982), xix. Rorty takes up the topic of truth in his books *Contingency, Irony, and Solidarity* (Cambridge: Cambridge University Press, 1989) and *Objectivity, Relativism, and Truth: Philosophical Papers I* (Cambridge: Cambridge University Press, 1991). Sheila Greeve Davaney offers an excellent, and accessible, analysis of Rorty's "historicist" perspective of truth and other matters in *Pragmatic Historicism: A Theology for the Twenty-First Century* (Albany, NY: SUNY Press, 2000), esp. 119–29.

10. See Jeffrey Stout, *Ethics after Babel: The Languages of Morals and Their Discontents* (Boston: Beacon Press, 1988), 22–32, 82–103.

11. Ibid., 23–24.

12. Ibid., 181–82.

13. Roger E. Olson has developed the discussion of these two "loose coalitions" in "The Future of Evangelical Theology," *Christianity Today* (hereafter *CT*) (February 9, 1998): 40–48. He offers Edward Veith's *Postmodern Times: A Christian Guide to Contemporary Thought and Culture* (Wheaton, IL: Crossway Books, 1994) as the example of traditionalist rejection of postmodernism. As examples of the reformists, Olson offers Stanley Grenz, *A Primer on Postmodernism* (Grand Rapids: Wm. B. Eerdmans Publishing Co., 1996); Nancey Murphy, *Beyond Liberalism and Fundamentalism: How Modern and Postmodern Philosophy Set the Theological Agenda* (Harrisburg, PA: Trinity Press International, 1996); and J. Richard Middleton and Brian Walsh, *Truth Is Stranger Than It Used to Be: Biblical Faith in a Postmodern Age* (Downers Grove, IL: InterVarsity Press, 1995).

14. Roger Olson argues that evangelicals ought to pay attention to the postliberals in "Back to the Bible (Almost): Why Yale's Postliberal Theologians Deserve an Evangelical Hearing," *CT* (May 20, 1996): 31–34. A solid treatment of evangelicalism's response to postliberalism and the postmodern context is offered by Stanley J. Grenz and John R. Franke, *Beyond Foundationalism: Shaping Theology in a Postmodern Context* (Louisville, KY: Westminster John Knox Press, 2001).

15. Sheila Greeve Davaney has provided an examination of the "historicist turn" in her book *Pragmatic Historicism*; this discussion occurs on 24–26.

16. Alasdair C. MacIntyre, *After Virtue: A Study in Moral Theory* (Notre Dame, IN: University of Notre Dame Press, 1981), 6.

17. Ibid., 263.

18. William C. Placher, *Unapologetic Theology: A Christian Voice in a Pluralistic Conversation* (Louisville, KY: Westminster/John Knox Press, 1989), 163–64.

19. George Lindbeck, *The Nature of Doctrine: Religion and Theology in a Postliberal Age* (Philadelphia: Westminster Press, 1984), esp. 31–41.

20. Ibid., 135.

21. Linell Cady, *Religion, Theology and American Public Life* (Albany, NY: SUNY Press, 1993), 134.

22. Cady, "Resisting the Postmodern Turn: Theology and Contextualization," in Davaney, *Theology at the End of Modernity*, 89–90.

23. Hauerwas does not necessarily endorse the term "postliberal." Dorrien discusses this point in Gary Dorrien, "The Future of Postliberal Theology," *Christian Century* (hereafter *CC*) (July 18–25, 2001): 2222–29.

24. Stanley Hauerwas and William Willimon, *Resident Aliens: Life in the Christian Colony* (Nashville: Abingdon Press, 1989), 38.

25. Ibid., 80–83.

26. Ibid., 92.

27. There now exists an Ekklesia Project, begun in 1999, with the purpose of bringing together those drawn to Hauerwas in order to connect his academic arguments to the life of actual communities of faith. See Jason Byassee, "Becoming Church," *CC* (September 7, 2004): 32–41.

28. Stanley Hauerwas, *A Better Hope: Resources for a Church Confronting Capitalism, Democracy, and Postmodernity* (Grand Rapids: Brazos Press, 2000), 24.

29. Stout, *Democracy and Tradition*, 140, 153.

30. Stanley Hauerwas, *Performing the Faith: Bonhoeffer and the Practice of Nonviolence* (Grand Rapids: Brazos Press, 2004), 231. For Henry's use of the term, see "Land of the Free," *CT* 7 (June 21, 1963): 24–25; "What Is the Way to a New Society?"

CT 1 (November 26, 1956): 23–24; Thomas B. McDormand, "Church and Government," *CT* 9 (April 23, 1965): 14–15; "Good News and Good Works," *CT* 11 (June 23, 1967): 21; "The Art of Soul Winning: Let the Church be the Church," *CT* 4 (July 4, 1960): 22–23. This last editorial recognizes that the phrase in its title originally came from John A. Mackay of Princeton Theological Seminary. See also "Christian Social Action," *CT* 13 (March 14, 1969): 24–25.

31. Hauerwas, *A Better Hope*, 26.

32. In particular, as they spoke about abortion, *Commonweal* argued that Catholic Christians arrived at their positions through the use of common moral reasoning. See, for example, "Untidiness Revisited," *Commonweal* (February 8, 1985): 69; and by David R. Carlin Jr., a Democratic Senator in the Rhode Island state legislature, "Rules For Liberals," *Commonweal* (September 21, 1984): 486–87.

33. *Commonweal* recognized the first of these two sentences, but not the second. See "Abortion, Religion and Political Life," *Commonweal* (February 2, 1979): 35–38.

34. Wall, "Scrambling for a Moral Vocabulary," *CC* (December 5, 1990): 1123–24; Martin E. Marty broached the topic of including religious communities in public discourse in "When My Virtue Doesn't Match Your Virtue," *CC* (November 30, 1988): 1094–96.

35. Hauerwas, *A Better Hope*, 33. It is on this point that Hauerwas takes American religious historians to task for connecting too easily the Christian story in America to the American story. "For all his sophistication," writes Hauerwas, "Marty, like Christian ethicists, still stays wedded to the project of writing church history to show what kind of Christianity will be good for America." He discusses these points in a lengthy footnote, note 8, on 219–20.

36. Stout, *Democracy and Tradition*, 154.

37. This quote and the quote in the preceding paragraph are found in Stout, *Democracy and Tradition*, 10; the indented quote is on 97; see also 296–97.

38. This insight comes from Linell Cady's lengthy, thoughtful, and analytical review of Stout's book: Cady, "Secularism, Secularizing, and Secularization: Reflections on Stout's *Democracy and Tradition*," *Journal of the American Academy of Religion* (September 2005): 871–85. Cady believes in the "both/and" here; there is a both a tradition of secular activists, who sought privatization of religion, and a tradition of pluralism that affirms the role that religious beliefs can play positively within the culture. On the power of secular activists in accomplishing the process of secularization, see Christian Smith, ed., *The Secular Revolution: Power, Interests, and Conflict in the Secularization of American Public Life* (Berkeley: University of California Press, 2003).

39. Stout, *Democracy and Tradition*, 156.

40. Ibid., 296.

41. Hauerwas and Willimon, *Resident Aliens*, 38; Hauerwas, in response to Stout, drew Stout's attention to this passage; see Hauerwas, *Performing the Faith*, 229, note 28. Pages 215–41, titled "Postscript: A Response to Jeff Stout's *Democracy and Tradition*," are found at the end of this book.

42. An unofficial Web site on Hauerwas, complete with links to online resources and interviews, helps illustrate the point: http://www.bigbrother.net/~mugwump/ Hauerwas/.

43. Dan Rhoades, "An Interview with Stanley Hauerwas," *TheOtherJournal.com: An Intersection of Theology and Culture* (Fall 2005), at http://www.theotherjournal .com/article.php?id=25.

44. Jean Bethge Elshtain, "Christian Contrarian," *Time* (September 17, 2001), found at http://www.cnn.com/SPECIALS/2001/americasbest/TIME/society .culture/pro.shauerwas.html.

45. Hauerwas, *Performing the Faith*, 239, note 51.
46. Ibid., 15.
47. Carl F. H. Henry was critical of the development of narrative and postliberal theology when it originally appeared in the work of Hans Frei. As Gary Dorrien describes it,

> Carl F. H. Henry summarized the problem: Narrative theology drives a wedge between biblical narrative (which it plays up) and historical factuality (which it plays down). Moreover, by failing to ground their assertions about scripture in a logically prior doctrine of biblical inerrancy, the narrative theologians undermine their purported desire to uphold the unity and authority of scripture. Narrative theology has no substantive doctrine of biblical inspiration, no objective theory of biblical authority, no objective criterion for establishing religious truth, and only a partial account of scriptural unity. Furthermore, Henry noted, much of scripture consists of nonnarrative material, which makes the narrative category insufficient by itself to account for the canonical unity of scripture. As for the postliberal claim to eschew the experiential subjectivism of liberal theology, Henry charged that in elevating narrative over factuality, narrative theology becomes unable to distinguish truth from error or fact from fiction.

Gary Dorrien, "The Origins of Postliberalism," *CC* (July 4–11, 2001): 16–21.
48. Hauerwas prefers the "churchly" tradition found among Catholicism to the emphasis on the New Testament found among evangelicals. See Dorrien, "The Future of Postliberal Theology," on this point.
49. Cornel West, *Democracy Matters* (New York: Penguin Press, 2004): 162.
50. James Gustafson, "The Sectarian Temptation: Reflections on Theology, the Church, and the University," *Proceedings of the Catholic Theological Society of America* 40 (1985): 93–94; a more productive and theological conversation appears between Gustafson and William Placher, a representative of postliberalism, in a series of articles in the *CC* in the spring of 1999. See Gustafson, "Just What is 'Postliberal' Theology?" *CC* (March 24–31, 1999): 353–55; William C. Placher, "Being Postliberal: A Response to James Gustafson," *CC* (April 7, 1999): 390–92; Gustafson, "Liberal Questions: A Response to William Placher," *CC* (April 14, 1999): 422–25.
51. Dorrien, "The Future of Postliberal Theology."
52. See David Tracy, *Blessed Rage for Order: The New Pluralism in Theology* (New York: Seabury Press, 1975). Tracy introduces the terms of a revisionist theology on 32–34. "More exactly," he writes, "the revisionist model for Christian theology ordinarily bears some such formulation as the following: contemporary Christian theology is best understood as philosophical reflection upon the meanings present in common human experience and the meanings present in the Christian tradition."
53. David Tracy, *The Analogical Imagination: Christian Theology and the Culture of Pluralism* (New York: Crossroad, 1981), 54f.
54. David Tracy, "The Role of Theology in Public Life," *Word & World* (Summer 1984): 232.
55. See the discussion on classics in Tracy, *Analogical Imagination*, 107–15.
56. Ibid., 430.
57. Ibid., 55.
58. David Tracy, *Plurality and Ambiguity: Hermeneutics, Religion, Hope* (San Francisco: HarperSanFrancisco, 1987), 48; other quotes in this paragraph are found on 16.

59. Ibid., 18–19; the earlier quote in the paragraph is on 23.

60. Tracy, "Role of Theology," 234–35, 238–39; the earlier quote in the paragraph is on 234.

61. Tracy, *Dialogue with the Other: The Inter-Religious Dialogue* (Grand Rapids: Wm. B. Eerdmans Publishing Co., 1990).

62. David Tracy, *On Naming the Present: God, Hermeneutics, and Church* (New York: Orbis Books, 1994), 139.

63. Tracy, *Plurality And Ambiguity,* esp. 31 and 36.

64. Ibid., 104.

65. See Davaney, *Pragmatic Historicism,* 45.

66. This is quoted in E. Harold Breitenberg Jr., "To Tell the Truth: Will the Real Public Theology Please Stand Up?" *Journal of the Society of Christian Ethics* (2003), see 96, note 138. The original citation is from James Gustafson, "The Bishops' Pastoral Letter: A Theological Ethical Analysis," *Criterion* (Spring 1984): 10.

67. James Gustafson, *Ethics from a Theocentric Perspective: Theology and Ethics,* vol. 1 (Chicago: University of Chicago Press, 1981), 15–16. Tracy's definition of "fundamental theologies" is found in *Analogical Imagination,* 57.

68. Gustafson, *Ethics,* vol. 1, 134.

69. Ibid., 112–13.

70. Ibid., 181–82.

71. Ibid., 314.

72. Ibid., 339.

73. Ibid., 97–99; 251–72.

74. All these descriptions are found in Gustafson, *Ethics from a Theocentric Perspective: Ethics and Theology,* vol. 2 (Chicago: University of Chicago Press, 1984): 143–44.

75. Gustafson, *Ethics,* vol. 2, 22. The biblical quotation is Phil. 2:4.

76. Gustafson, *Ethics,* vol. 1, 327–28; chapter 7 offers an extended treatment of the "moral life in theocentric perspective," 327–342.

77. For the discussion related to these past few paragraphs, see Linell E. Cady, *Religion, Theology, and American Public Life* (Albany, NY: State University of New York Press, 1993), 34–39.

78. Ibid., 48; Cady has renamed the category Dworkin had named "naturalist."

79. Ibid., 52–53.

80. Ibid., 73.

81. Ibid., 78–80.

82. Ibid., 80–83.

83. Ibid., 112–18.

84. The quote in the sentence before the block quotation is found in ibid., 152. The block quotation is on 115.

85. Ibid., 23–26.

86. Ibid., 27.

87. Ibid., 33.

88. Ibid., 64.

89. Sheila Grave Davaney offers an extensive treatment of theology from the historicist perspective by examining the work of Gordon Kaufman, Sallie McFague, William Dean, and Linell Cady. Along the way, and in a concluding chapter, she offers her own methodological and theological reflections about what she defines as "pragmatic historicism." Davaney, *Pragmatic Historicism,* esp. 81–118 and 147–91. It is worth noting that Davaney is hesitant to affirm Cady's sense of the importance of the "whole." Davaney rightly questions whether concern for the "whole" might actually discount the reality that the Christian community,

through time, is actually composed of a "multiplicity of traditions." She would rather make judgments based on those parts of the tradition that are most relevant to situations we face today (103) than try to define and apply some sense of the whole.

90. See James M. Wall, "Bring Back the Conscience Vote," *CC* (December 17, 1980): 1235–36; "Untidiness Revisited," *Commonweal* (February 8, 1985): 69. David R. Carlin Jr., a Democratic Senator in the Rhode Island state legislature, wrote "Rules For Liberals," *Commonweal* (September 21, 1984): 486–87. Also see "Abortion, Religion and Political Life," *Commonweal* (February 2, 1979): 35–38.

91. See Martin E. Marty, "When My Virtue Doesn't Match Your Virtue," *CC* (November 30, 1988): 1094–96.

92. Robin Lovin, "Faith Seeking Articulation: Doing Theology in Politics," Hoover Lecture, Disciples Divinity House, April 25, 1989; see p. 2 of typed and non-published manuscript.

93. Cady, *Religion, Theology, and American Public Life,* 20.

94. Niebuhr, *Irony of American History,* viii.

95. Davaney, *Pragmatic Historicism,* 191.

96. Stout, *Democracy and Tradition,* 298.

97. Ibid., 293.

98. Ibid. These quotes are found on 298 (for sentences before the second ellipsis) and 300.

Index of Persons

Index of Subjects